Literature and Psychoanalysis

Related titles from the same publishers

C. G. Jung and Literary Theory   Susan Rowland
Deconstructions   Nicholas Royle
Psychoanalysis and Woman   Shelley Saguaro (editor)
*The Destructive Element: British Psychoanalysis and
   Modernism*   Lyndsey Stonebridge

Literature and Psychoanalysis

Intertextual Readings

Ruth Parkin-Gounelas

palgrave

First published 2001 by
PALGRAVE
Houndmills, Basingstoke, Hampshire RG21 6XS and
175 Fifth Avenue, New York, N.Y. 10010
Companies and representatives throughout the world

PALGRAVE is the new global academic imprint of St. Martin's Press LLC
Scholarly and Reference Division and Palgrave Publishers Ltd (formerly
Macmillan Press Ltd).

ISBN 0–333–69211–X hardback
ISBN 0–333–69212–8 paperback

This book is printed on paper suitable for recycling and
made from fully managed and sustained forest sources.

A catalogue record for this book is available
from the British Library.

Library of Congress Cataloging-In-Publication Data
Parkin-Gounelas, Ruth, 1950–
    Literature and analysis: intertextual readings/Ruth Parkin-Gounelas.
        p. cm.
    Includes bibliographical references (p.) and index.
    ISBN 0–333–69211–X
        1. Psychoanalysis and literature. 2. Literature–History and criticism–
Theory, etc. 3. Criticism I. Title.

    PN56.P92 P375 2000
    801′.92–dc21
                                                                00-033343

10   9   8   7   6   5   4   3   2   1
10   09   08   07   06   05   04   03   02   01

Printed in China

FOR DIMITRI, ANGELIKA AND FRANK

Contents

Acknowledgements   ix

Preface   x

1 Representing the Unconscious
The Text of Our Experience; The Mirror Stage and the Image
Repertoire; 'In Unity Defective': Milton's *Paradise Lost*; The
Apple Tree and the Sardine Can; The Dream-Work; Dream
Representation: The Surrealist Project; W. H. Auden:
Surrealism and the Conscious Mind   1

2 The (Lost) Object
The Kleinian Object; Fairy Tales; The Dictates of the Super-
Ego: Ishiguro's *The Remains of the Day*; Loss and Mourning
in Derek Walcott's *Omeros*; Castration and the Signifier; The
Disseminar on Poe   30

3 Abjection and the Melancholic Imaginary
Mourning, the Mobilizing Affliction; Beckett: Warding off
the Unnamable; The Archaic Dyad; Mourning the Maternal
Object; Abjection and the Sacred; I or Not-I; The Container
and the Uncontained (Beckett with Bion); Devouring
Mothers and Words; Beckett and the Anal Imaginary; Food
and Flows; Ending in Limbo   54

4 The Tragedy of Desire
Oedipal Textuality: *Hamlet*; The Feminine Oedipal; Phallic
Desire: Lacan Reads *Hamlet*; The Proper Place of Desire:
Sophocles' *Antigone*; The Imaginary and the Symbolic;
Fathers: Primal, Imaginary and Symbolic; *Othello* and
The Real of Desire   82

5   The Uncanny Text
Freud Reads the Gothic (Hoffmann's 'The Sandman'); To
Double or Die: 'Christabel'; Hauntologies: Derrida, Abraham
and Torok, and Gaskell's 'Old Nurse's Story'; The Phantom
Within: LeFanu's 'Strange Disturbances'; Extimacy   103

6   The Subject of Hysteria
Hysteria: Construction and Deconstruction; Suffering From
Reminiscences; Telling a Clear Story: The Dora Case;
Transference and the Dora Case; Literature as Case Study:
George Eliot's *The Lifted Veil*; Performing Hysteria: Terry
Johnson's *Hysteria*   131

7   Femininities and Other Masquerades
Freud Defines the Terms; Women Reply; Femininity as
Masquerade; Representation and the 'Other Side': Can Alice
Go Through the Looking-Glass?; *Orlando*; Performing
Sexualities: Angela Carter's 'Reflections'   163

8   The Phantasy of Death
Dracula and the Death Drive; Civilization and its Sacrifices;
Symbolic Murder: Lacan and the Death Drive; Mortal
Meanings: Kyd's *The Spanish Tragedy*; The Fetish: From
Persons to Things (Sylvia Plath)   196

Notes   223

Works Cited   241

Index   254

Acknowledgements

Completion of this book would have been impossible without the generous leave of absence granted by Aristotle University, Thessaloniki, and the extra work load taken over by colleagues in my absence. I am particularly grateful to Karin Boklund-Lagopoulou and Katie Douka-Kabitoglou for their friendship and support. The students in my graduate seminar on 'Literature and Psychoanalysis' have, through their intelligence and enquiry, contributed greatly to the shaping of the material in this book. The staff of the libraries of the English Department, Aristotle University, and the Bodleian Library, Oxford, have been very helpful in the location of material. Many thanks, also, to Margaret Bartley of Palgrave for her encouragement and support of this project from its inception. To my immediate family, Dimitri, Angelika and Frank, and my mother Betty, I owe a debt which only they will understand.

Earlier versions of small parts of this book have appeared in the following journals and volumes: 'The Other Side of the Looking Glass: Women's Fantasy Writing and Woolf's *Orlando*', *Gramma/ Γράμμα: Journal of Theory and Criticism*, I (1993): 137–53; 'Aphonia and the Talking Cure: Language and Silence in Psychoanalysis', *Anatomies of Silence*, ed. Ann R. Cacoullos and Maria Sifianou, Athens: Parousia, 1998, 163–71; 'Antigone and the Tragedy of Desire', *(Dis)Placing Classical Greek Theatre*, ed. Savas Patsalidids and Elizabeth Sakellaridou, Thessaloniki: University Studio Press, 1999, 308–16; 'Anachrony and Anatopia: Spectres of Marx, Derrida and Gothic Fiction', *Ghosts: Deconstruction, Psychoanalysis, History*, ed. Peter Buse and Andrew Stott, Basingstoke: Macmillan, 1999, 127–43.

Grateful acknowledgement is made to Faber for permission to reproduce copyright material from Derek Walcott's *Omeros* and to John Calder for extracts from Samuel Beckett's *Works*. Every effort has been made to contact all the copyright-holders, but if any have been inadvertently omitted the publishers will be pleased to make the necessary arrangement at the earliest opportunity.

Preface

Literature and psychoanalysis. The conjunction of these two disciplines has allured and worried literary criticism since Freud's first inspired but often clumsy literary analyses a hundred years ago. Recent decades have seen a further acceleration in the convergence of the two, now evident in the way the vocabulary of each permeates the other at every level. On the one hand, psychoanalytic ('scientific') writings, most famously Freud's case studies of Dora or the Wolf Man, have become the object of 'literary' scrutiny, with focus on features such as narrative strategy, symbolic patterns or repressed subtexts. At the same time, certain styles of psychoanalytic writing, Lacan's in particular, have drawn attention to their own signifying operations in ways reminiscent of the most 'literary' of practices. On the other hand 'literature', now attracting the obligatory scare-quotes, has become increasingly loath to separate itself off from other disciplines which impinge upon it, whether these be 'science' or the law, the visual arts or popular culture, and has proved itself resistant to containment within purely aesthetic boundaries. At the beginning of this long process of convergence, Freud himself worried that his work read like fiction and lacked the 'serious stamp of science' (PF 3: 231).[1] For their part, in the early years, literary writers and critics such as Virginia Woolf held the new science at arm's length and insisted that its findings, though 'interesting' to 'the scientific side of the brain', were dull and irrelevant to 'the artistic side' ('Freudian Fiction' 153). Nowadays, however, with a postmodern discourse more likely to celebrate a blurring of boundaries between disciplines and the interlocution of all 'texts', there seems little justification for worrying about the differences between the two fields when they clearly have so much in common.

Fundamental to this shift has been the linguistic revolution of the twentieth century as mediated, in particular, by structuralism and deconstruction. Freud's intuitions about the implication of words in psychic processes, investigated in Chapter 1 here, were to prove enormously suggestive to his successors in different fields of cultural analysis, generating an array of insights that have become like cultural sign-posts for our age: '*the unconscious is structured like a language*' (Lacan, *Four Fundamental Concepts* 20), 'textual pleasure' (Barthes, *The Pleasure of the Text*), the unconscious as made up of 'memory traces' which constitute a form of 'psychic writing' (Derrida, *Writing and Difference* 213). Psychoanalysis, as Nicolas Abraham points out, has brought a 'radical semantic change' to signifying practice ('The Shell and the Kernel' 83), to which he gives the name 'anasemia', a reconceptualization of the unconscious sources of signification. Between the 'I' and the 'me', he writes, the subject of self-conscious reflexivity and the object of reflection or representation, lies a 'founding silence' which is the mark of the unconscious (84). This book will attempt to argue that the role of a psychoanalytic literary criticism is to explore the ways in which the silences and gaps in texts, the unconscious in all its inaccessibility, can be approached through a range of different psychoanalytic concepts or structures which the Freudian revolution has engendered: desire, the object, abjection, the uncanny, the death drive, and so on. These structures offer ways of describing the effects of or the processes that intersect with the unconscious. They should not, however, be confused with its definition, which has had the tendency to elude the various attempts to fix it – from Coleridge's theory of the unconscious as a vital, creative faculty, to Jung's Collective or Impersonal Unconscious, to (most influentially of all) the Freudian and post-Freudian unconscious as a set of phantasies and desires which have undergone repression and which must always be different from their conscious or cultural manifestations.

Like Melanie Klein after him, Freud described the workings of the unconscious in figurative, even mythic terms, usually as a battle for supremacy between instinctual forces, to which he gave different names at different times – such as the ego and the id, or the life and death drives. For exemplification, as everyone knows, he turned to literature, and found there corresponding conflicts – the Oedipus complex in Sophocles' *Oedipus Rex,* the uncanny in E. T. A. Hoffmann's 'The Sandman'. And then these in turn he formulated into myth-like structures to found a whole psychoanalytic system. From the start, the exchange between the two disciplines was direct.

When it came to the 'application' of psychoanalytic theory to the reading of literary texts, however, it was discovered that the process involved was very different from that which takes place in the clinical situation. Clearly, automatic symbol hunting ('a phallus at every lamppost') was not going to take things very far. And Ernest Jones, who was one of the first to undertake a sustained Freudian literary analysis with his *Hamlet and Oedipus* (1949), came up immediately against the problem that the literary character has no life before the first page (Jones 17). Given that psychoanalysis knows no present divorced from the past, that 'fresh experiences, however novel, are always assimilated by the unconscious mind to older ones' (18), the process of analysing textual rather than real-life human characters must always be partial and speculative. The work of art, as André Green puts it, 'can say nothing more than is incorporated in it', and 'remains obstinately mute, closed in upon itself' (Green, *Tragic Effect* 18–19). This is not to say, however, that it cannot, like the analysand, put up a set of defences against its interpretation. As we shall see in the following chapters, defences such as repression, reversal, splitting and denial may act as significant nodes of revelation. Nor is it to say that the processes of free association and transference, crucial to the analytic reaction, cannot occur in written texts, as recent psychoanalytic criticism in the reader-response tradition has shown. If it can in a strict sense 'say nothing more' than itself, the literary text can certainly be 're-said' in the process of dynamic exchange between text and reader, meaning and desire.

With everything that has been said in recent years about 'textual desire', a shift of critical attention has been effected from the analysis of author or character (or their conflation) in the text to that of the text itself as signifying structure.[2] According to a Lacanian reading, to write or to read is to enter a Symbolic order where meaning and desire are mediated through trans-individual structures of otherness which both possess and dispossess us at the same time. Language, as we shall see, institutes a relation of being to loss, loss of meaning (the non-coincidence of the signifier with the signified), which symbolizes a loss of primary unity with the first 'other', the mother, in the Oedipus complex. Desire follows the direction of signification – ever onwards towards that which escapes it.

In what follows I will attempt to test out ways in which different configurations of post-Freudian psychoanalytic theory, from sources as diverse as Lacan, Klein, Riviere, Kristeva, Abraham and Torok, and Bion, provide structures through which to read literary texts. The high profile of psychoanalysis and of Freud himself in literary studies at the turn of the twentieth century owes much to the discovery that it is not a question of the 'application' of psychoanalytic insights to a body of literary texts, a practice which leaves each ultimately separate, but rather, as Shoshana Felman has pointed out, their 'implication' one in the other (*Literature and Psychoanalysis* 5–10). Each can be seen to have developed in relation to the other and can now be described as intersecting in ways that change the dimensions of both. Many studies now exist which provide summaries and assessments of psychoanalytic theory. The purpose of this study is to explore the practice as much as the theory of reading psychoanalysis with literature. Paradigmatic intertextual readings will be offered: Freud with Ishiguro, Lacan with Milton or with Derek Walcott, Joan Riviere with Woolf, and so on. Some texts are treated comprehensively and in depth – examples here are the 'abjectal' reading of Beckett's trilogy, which occupies the whole of Chapter 3, or the analysis of *Dracula* through the death drive in Chapter 8. Others, such as *Othello*, or Plath's 'Daddy', are referred to briefly to illustrate a specific psychoanalytic phenomenon.

Perhaps inevitably, my choice of literary texts has sometimes followed the contours of Freud's own experience, whether that be his choice of literary texts for analysis or the cultural events that shaped his thought. *Oedipus Rex*, *Hamlet* and Hoffmann's 'The Sandman' are re-examined within the Freudian canon and reassessed in the light of more recent developments. Freud's contemporaries – such as Wilde, Bram Stoker, Strindberg, Woolf, and later contemporaries such as Beckett and Auden – provide a rich source for intertextual analysis, for all their often open hostility to his findings. The same is true, to a lesser extent, with Lacan, whose theoretical insights, however, tend to dominate this study. The theoretical shift that occurred between the style of literary analysis available to Freud in the first decades of the twentieth century and that in which Lacan participated in the 1950s– 70s is a fundamental one, assuming a radical change in reading strategies which will be examined in the pages that follow. While Freud put it, for example, that Shakespeare was a 'great psychologist' (qtd. in Meisel and Kendrick 333), for the Lacanian critic Slavoj Žižek, it seems more appropriate (let alone playfully paradoxical, in true Lacanian style) to say that it is 'beyond any doubt that Shakespeare had read Lacan' (*Looking Awry* 9). These two positions act as the poles between which this book will operate and into which must also be inserted a whole series of alternative psychoanalytic and literary discourses, from Klein's to Kristeva's, and from Barthes' to Derrida's.

A final word, however, about the charge of ahistoricism, the eliding of historically specific determinants, that Žižek's deliberately outrageous statement seems to invite, and which has certainly often been levelled against psychoanalytic literary criticism itself on many occasions. A powerful reply to this charge has been given by Julia Kristeva, who like many others recently has paid close attention to Freud's speculative analysis of the origins of social behaviour, in *Totem and Taboo* (1913; PF13: 43–224). At the beginning of human history, Freud argues, primitive people sought to master their mental conflicts by projecting them on to the environment and enshrining them in taboos or laws (against parricide and incest, in particular). Now, in a later stage of human development, it is our task to 'translate' these laws back into psychology in order to understand how we have constructed our world in different ways at different cultural and historical moments.

The social/ Symbolic order, Kristeva argues, 'corresponds' to the structuration of the human psyche as speaking subject, a word she favours for its avoidance of any cause–effect relationship between the psychic and the social. In the challenge that lies before us in a postmodern age, defined by her as the 'great demystification of Power (religious, moral, political, and verbal') (*Powers of Horror* 210), psychoanalysis has a crucial role to play as translator of cultural (and literary) practices into their psychic correspondents in order to understand how change may be effected. If in a sense the two (the psychic and the cultural) can be seen as different languages, which when transposed the one into the other must incur the loss involved in all translation, the gain from their conjunction must be not merely a change in the status of each individually, the way each discipline is prepared to re-define itself in relation to the other, but the production of a new discourse which I have called, following Kristeva again, intertextual. Texts, she wrote in 1969, are constructed as 'a mosaic of quotations', so that 'any text is the absorption and transformation of another' ('Word, Dialogue and Novel' 37). 'Literature *in* Psychoanalysis' (in the sense that a patient is 'in analysis'), or 'The Psychoanalysis of Literature' , might have been better titles for this study, were they not so awkward as phrases. The test, however, must ultimately be in the practice, not in the theorization of their conjunction.

R. P.-G.

1
Representing the Unconscious

When Samuel Beckett re-wrote the founding statement of Genesis with the famous words 'In the beginning was the pun', he was being less iconoclastic and more Freudian than he would have cared to admit. A generation on from Freud, Beckett shared with many writers of his time an anxious defensiveness about the encroachments of the Viennese sage's insights that intersected with his own in many ways. Beckett's character Murphy, to whom this statement is ascribed via the narrator, would probably have wanted to follow it by the question: 'the beginning of what?' But origins are not Murphy's strong point. He is more interested in (*non*) *sequiturs*, in what follows – 'on, on!', as Beckett's characters keep goading themselves. The famous quip is itself followed by a punning *non sequitur*: 'In the beginning was the pun. And so on' (*Murphy* 41).

Myths of origin and their implications in language, however, lie at the heart of the Freudian project. This chapter will concern itself with both beginnings and puns, though not with Samuel Beckett, who will return in a later chapter. Freud was of the generation that still believed in the possibility of discovering origins. Darwin's *Origin of Species*, published three years after his birth in 1856, was an important lifetime model for Freud in the radical possibilities of grand new systems which change the way we think. Darwin's 'origins' (of life) may have seemed to go much further back than Freud's. In fact, Freud was to find that his investigations into the origins of individual mental disorders, and consequently of the human psyche as a whole, would lead him on his own journey into human 'prehistory', into the origins of human social organization.

But his starting point, like Darwin's, was with specific empirical evidence, with an attempt to define human psychology in neurological

1

terms. At the same time he was beginning to experiment on a very different level, in listening to hysterical patients talk, surmising in the process that language may be the key to the understanding of the psyche. This was in 1895. Thirty-five years later, in the early 1930s, Jacques Lacan was embarking on his own case studies in Paris. He was to classify his patients, women convicted of attempted or actual murder, as paranoiacs, and from this would develop a theory of paranoid modes of cognition and discourse which would introduce an indispensable linguistic element into the psychoanalytic project.

Lacan's impact on contemporary cultural and critical theory, and in particular on the concept of the human subject as the effect of language, has been so profound that it is impossible to imagine its development without him. In turn, Freud's impact on Lacan was so far-reaching that it has become impossible to disentangle them – or, at least, to read Freud today entirely free of Lacan's mediation. In postulating the subject as the effect of language rather than its cause, Lacan claimed to be doing no more than reformulating the major elements of the Freudian corpus, distilling its essence. A 'return to Freud' was a conveniently authoritative shield for the young medical intern anxious to carve out his own space against the reactionary forces of Parisian psychiatry. This presumption was boosted by an unusually eclectic range of reading at the time, enabling him to translate Freudian theory into cultural terms. In philosophy he was reading and studying Spinoza, Jaspers, Nietzsche, Husserl, Bergson, Hegel and Heidegger.[1] Ferdinand de Saussure, whom Lacan and others generally consider the founder of modern linguistics, was to be of crucial importance in the definition of subjectivity and significa- tion.[2] And the surrealist movement from the beginning provided an important model for the encounter between the aesthetic and analytic processes, as I shall show later. These three disciplines, fuelled by a re- reading of Freud, were to produce in Lacan's writing a series of radical formulations of the subject and the signifier which have had a crucial influence on literary criticism over the past twenty-five years.

THE TEXT OF OUR EXPERIENCE

Freud regarded a study of languages and institutions, of the resonances, whether attested or not in memory, of literature and of the significations involved in works of art as necessary to an understanding of the text of our experience. (Lacan, *Écrits* 144)

In the late 1920s, a heated debate took place in psychoanalytic circles over the most appropriate training for psychoanalytic practice. Freud came down on the liberal side of the acceptance of 'lay analysts', those with no medical training, stating his case as follows:

> analytic instruction [should] include branches of knowledge which are remote from medicine and which the doctor does not come across in his practice: the history of civilization, mythology, the psychology of religion and the science of literature. Unless he is well at home in these subjects, an analyst can make nothing of a large amount of his material. ('The Question of Lay Analysis' [1926]. PF 15: 349).[3]

Being able to 'make something' of the speech of patients involved hermeneutic skills whose sophistication it was left to Lacan to define. The move from a general prerequisite of literary sensitivity (to nuance, the reading of symbol and allegory, and so on) to that of the ability to read 'the text of our experience' took him, at the outset, back to the origins of the modern concept of subjectivity in Descartes' *cogito ergo sum* (I think, therefore I am). In challenging the Cartesian *cogito* on the first page of his first major psychoanalytic work, 'The Mirror Stage',[4] Lacan set about reversing the Enlightenment practice of regarding the ego as centred on the perception–consciousness system, as present to itself through self-reflection. 'Our experience shows', he said, 'that we should start instead from the *function of méconnaissance* [misrecognition] that characterizes the ego in all its structures' (*Écrits* 6).

In listening to his hysterical patients in the 1890s, Freud had been confronted by the reality of a speech divided against itself, and on the basis of this 'radical heteronomy that Freud's discovery shows gaping within man', as Lacan put it (*Écrits* 172), had postulated the theory of the unconscious. Chapter 6 will examine in detail the way the construction of the condition of hysteria at this time laid the foundations of the psychoanalytic definition of subjectivity as not only divided against itself but also a matter of 'make believe', an assumption of fabricated personalities or masks. Literature was working towards similar ends. That consummate self-fashioner Oscar Wilde, a slightly older contemporary of Freud's famous hysterical patient Dora and like her a victim of conflicted personalities and sexualities, propounded an aesthetic of masks and appearances that refused the commonplace assumption that they are a mere cover for a truth or reality beneath. A charismatic performer in his own life, Wilde wrote plays that put forward 'character' as a matter of performance or style.

For Lacan, the challenge to Western concepts of subjectivity as self-conscious rationality leads to the very grammar of our being. His writings often playfully draw the Cartesian *cogito* into grammatical traps to show up the split between the subject that speaks (of him/herself) and the subject that becomes the 'object' of the grammatical sentence. 'It is not a question', he wrote, 'of knowing whether I speak of myself in a way that conforms to what I am, but rather of knowing whether I am the same as that of which I speak.' (*Écrits* 165) Hence the deliberate sliding into near-nonsense, which is the hallmark of so much of Lacan's writing:

> I think where I am not, therefore I am where I do not think. Words that render sensible to an ear properly attuned with what elusive ambiguity the ring of meaning flees from our grasp along the verbal thread.
>
> What one ought to say is: I am not wherever I am the plaything of my thought; I think of what I am where I do not think to think. (*Écrits* 166)

But it is not so much a matter of whether we read such passages *either* as serious philosophical discourse *or* as nonsense. A training in Carrollian nonsense (which Lacan greatly admired) is in fact helpful in reading Lacan in that it teaches us the art of receptivity to the polyvalence of signifiers without demanding that we come to rest on one fixed signified. Lacan calls up new reading strategies, ones dependent on a vast knowledge of philosophy, linguistics and Freud but at the same time relaxed about the way words speak 'the truth'. At the beginning of a television presentation, Lacan once said:

> I always speak the truth. Not the whole truth, because there's no way, to say it all. Saying it all is literally impossible: words fail. Yet it's through this very impossibility that the truth holds on to the real. (*Television* 3)

In taking the two worn-out words 'truth' and ' real' as the site of radical destabilization (and I shall be returning to 'the Real' later), Lacan intended to challenge the most cherished bases of Western rationality. 'In a spoken or written sentence something stumbles' (*Four Fundamental Concepts* 25). If Freud's contribution had been to draw attention to the significance of this elusive 'something', the sign of the unconscious, Lacan's was to construct an entire psychoanalytic method upon its inscription.

At the same time that Lacan was formulating his theories of the divided subject in the 'Mirror Stage' paper of 1936, Melanie Klein, across the Channel in England (where she had established herself, from Budapest and Berlin, in 1926), was developing Freudian theory in the direction of the object. The subject, for Klein, cannot be thought of as an entirely separable unit in that it is colonized by a set of 'introjects', mental structures made up of internalized images ('imagoes') of parental figures. As Mikkel Borch-Jacobsen argues, Freud's theories had contained, in embryo, a whole 'nonsubjectival' theory of the subject, one based on the subject in its relatedness to both primary (individual) objects such as the mother and social 'others' ('The Freudian Subject' 68). As leader of the new 'object relations' school of psychoanalysis in London, Klein was to dedicate a lifetime to the analysis of very young children in order to explore ways in which the subject develops in relatedness to external objects (the maternal breast, in particular). Lacan, on the other hand, though influenced by Klein in his early formulation of the maternal imago, was to take a more 'sociological' approach in his focus on the 'other' as inhabitant of the subject in culture and discourse.[5]

Instead of focusing, as the practitioners of British object-relations theory would do, on the impact of intersubjective relationships in early development, Lacan argued that the subject's history is constructed in the 'intersubjective continuity of [his/her] discourse' (*Écrits* 49). In the psychoanalytic situation, the model and testing ground of all human relationships, the analyst and patient engage in an 'allocution' involving a 'locutor' (*un locuteur*) and an 'allocutor' (*un allocutaire*). The 'otherness' (from the Greek *allos*, the other) is thus present in speech from the very beginning. As Juliet Mitchell puts it, the subject can only conceptualize itself when it is mirrored back to itself from the position of another's desire ('Introduction I' 5). Desire emerges at the moment of its incarnation in speech, at that moment, as we shall see in Chapter 4, when the child learns to replace its longed-for, absent mother by a word. The subject, therefore, can in a very special sense be said to *be* (structured by) the other, which in turn *is* (structured by) the discourse of the 'big Other' (culture) that we all inhabit. Julia Kristeva, adapting to psychoanalysis the cultural theory of Mikhail Bakhtin, was to call this the 'dialogic' model of all human experience.

THE MIRROR STAGE AND THE IMAGE REPERTOIRE

Lacan's 'Mirror Stage' essay, short as it is, has proved one of the most suggestive and influential of all the works of contemporary culture for the way it brings together crucial questions relating to the subject and the image, the formation of the 'I' via its transformation in the mirror. The image of itself seen in the mirror by the infant of 6–18 months can be regarded as a form of object which acts in dialectic relation to the viewing subject throughout its life. It is no accident that the word 'dialectic' occurs repeatedly throughout the essay. Lacan had attended the famous lectures by Alexandre Kojève on Hegel's *Phenomenology of Spirit* in the mid 1930s, and like many others of his generation was deeply influenced by them.[6] In particular, Kojève had drawn attention to Hegel's formulation of human desire as that which is always a 'desire for another desire' (qtd in Nobus 111), a dialectic of desiring which results in a deadly struggle for supremacy. The other, in Lacan's reading of Hegel, is that which by its very nature 'frustrates' the human being (*Seminar 1*: 177). In gazing in the mirror, the infant experiences two contradictory responses, not necessarily simultaneously. On the one hand, it fulfils that perpetual human desire for identification and fusion when it 'recognizes' itself with a 'flutter of jubilant activity' (*Écrits* 1). Yet on the other, it learns that this image, which offers a promise of wholeness and (self-) identity, is in fact a mirage, a mere reflecting surface which disguises the fragmentation of the infant's felt experience. This realization that the image is a fake, that its representation does not fit, is the founding experience of alienation on which all human subjectivity is based. Lacan liked to repeat the words of the witty poet, who once remarked that the mirror would have done well to reflect a little before returning our image to us (*Écrits* 138). For the child, like Narcissus, 'loses' itself at the very point of self-recognition, which is in fact a misrecognition. We can't both 'see' as subjective experience and 'be seen' as object. There is a fundamental gap or disjunction between these two operations. Hence Lacan's view of the inaugurally 'paranoiac' nature of human knowledge (3).

Human knowledge is thus defined by its 'mediatization' through the image, which becomes our perpetual other (5). This intra-personal dialectic interacts with and becomes the foundation for the subsequent 'social dialectic' of the individual in relation to culture and language: the 'specular *I*', as Lacan puts it, becomes the 'social *I*' (5). This occurs at the moment of entry into the Symbolic, around the age of two, when the Oedipus complex introduces an externally embodied Other (dignified with a capital) which represents the Father, the law, castration and language. One of the central themes of contemporary psychoanalytic theory, to which I shall return frequently in the following chapters, is the way language functions to disinherit the subject from a primary, would-be identification with itself, its image/ double, and with meaning.

And yet the longing for unity and identification with its own image remains a passion which dogs the ego (*le moi*) throughout life. Lacan sees this dependence on the image as a trap, luring the ego into attempts at self-replication and sameness which are perpetually frustrated. Future identifications will always be haunted by this Imaginary wholeness, projected onto others. The role of psychoanalysis as conceived by Lacan is to bring the subject to an awareness of these projections. His critique of the 'ego psychology' practised mainly in the United States was that it encourages the patient to dwell on these Imaginary images rather than assisting in an accommodation to the Symbolic. As Jane Gallop notes, Lacan believed that the role of the analyst was to be 'une surface sans accidents' (a neutral reflecting surface). She writes: 'In the ethical imperative to be in the symbolic, the charge is to look into the mirror and see not the image but the mirror itself' (*Reading Lacan* 62). Through exposure to the death-bearing losses of the Symbolic, via language, the subject is led in the direction of renouncing its own idealized specularization.

To understand the ways in which Lacan's theory of the Imaginary and the Symbolic has been transposed into contemporary cultural practice, I want now to look briefly at a work which has high representative (if not actual) status in cultural theory, *Roland Barthes by Roland Barthes* (1975, translated 1977). Of all literary theorists, Barthes has played the most prominent role in the examination of the image as psychic and cultural determinant, of the way subjectivity can be conceived only in terms of the images or codes that constitute it. Through structuralism, discourse analysis and semiology from the 1950s through to 1980, Barthes' work recorded a sustained testing-out of the post-Freudian problematic of the subject and its representation, the transposition of the subject into the discourse about it. The self-consciously reflexive title of Barthes' postmodern autobiography, *Roland Barthes by Roland Barthes,* foregrounds the question of the relation between writer and text, speaker and spoken. Barthes' conclusion, like Lacan's, is that it is a relationship of disjunction.

Barthes' text presents a series of 'images' of its subject, both photographic and linguistic, in order to demonstrate their elusive non-coincidence with any referent ('Roland Barthes' as a real person). These images, he writes, 'no longer [have] anything to do with the reflection, however oneiric, of an identity'. Something about them arouses a sense of 'disturbing familiarity', causes an uncanny (mis)-recognition: 'I see the fissure in the subject' (3). Opposite two photos of himself in 1942 and 1970 he puts the following caption:

> *'But I never looked like that!' – How do you know? What is the 'you' you might or might not look like? Where do you find it – by which morphological or expressive calibration? Where is your authentic body? You are the only one who can never see yourself except as an image; you never see your eyes unless they are dulled by the gaze they rest upon the mirror or the lens (I am interested in seeing my eyes only when they look at you), even and especially for your own body, you are condemned to the repertoire of its images. (36)*

Barthes' 'repertoire of images', like Lacan's Imaginary on which it is based, offers a perpetual lure to identification, sameness, analogy (this is 'like' that), which it is the writer's task to resist:

> The bull sees red when his lure falls under his nose; the two reds coincide, that of rage and that of the cape: the bull is caught in analogy, i.e., in the imaginary. When I resist analogy, it is actually the imaginary I am resisting: which is to say: the coalescence of the sign, the similitude of signifier and signified, the homeomorphism of images, the Mirror, the captivating bait. All scientific explanations which resort to analogy – and they are legion – participate in the lure, they form the image-repertory of Science. (44)

Like Brecht, who seems to have 'written especially for him [Barthes]' (52), Barthes sets himself the task of breaking such illusions, of demystifying the tendency to treat the 'natural' as a source of truth. The 'I' that writes is a mere plurality of others' texts, communal signifiers. The act of writing is thus an act of dispossession. Identity is simply a role. *Roland Barthes by Roland Barthes*, therefore, 'must all be considered as if spoken by a character in a novel' (1). All the writer has is language, a textual subjectivity, which is no more than a point of disappearance in the image repertoire of signs and codes in which we all participate.

When I pretend to write on what I have written in the past, there occurs in the same way a movement of abolition, not of truth. I do not strive to put my present expression in the service of my previous truth (in the classical system, such an effort would have been sanctified under the name of *authenticity*). I abandon the exhausting pursuit of an old piece of myself. I do not try to *restore* myself (as we say of a monument). I do not say: 'I am going to describe myself' but: 'I am writing a text, and I call it R.B.' I shift from imitation (from description) and entrust myself to nomination. Do I not know that, *in the field of the subject, there is no referent*? The fact (whether biographical or textual) is abolished in the signifier, because it immediately *coincides* with it . . . I myself am my own symbol, I am the story which happens to me: freewheeling in language, I have nothing to compare myself to; and in this movement, the pronoun of the imaginary, 'I,' is *im-pertinent;* the symbolic becomes literally *immediate:* essential danger for the life of the subject: to write on oneself may seem a pretentious idea; but it is also a simple idea: simple as the idea of suicide. (56)

For Lacan, the role of the analyst is to bring the patient to terms with Symbolic structures and ultimately with death. Barthes' adaptation of this Lacanian injunction was to assert the inescapability of the 'doxa' (the set of inherited opinions, the law of the Other), but also to stress the importance of its disruption by the 'para-dox'. Barthes' method of argument by paradox allows the 'concretions' of discourse and meaning (71) to be kept perpetually on the move, thus according the writer the superior status of a 'freewheeler' in (rather than a slave to) language.

Barthes also shares with Lacan a fascination with the signifier. Having absorbed the Saussurean doctrine of the arbitrary relation of signifier and signified, they decide (unlike writers of the earlier Modern period such as Beckett) that this should be a matter for celebration. Polysemy and arbitrariness are built into the very structure of Barthes' text. Fragmentary observations are arranged according to that most arbitrary of codes, the alphabet, although care is taken to disrupt even this 'doxa'. The last page of Barthes' book poses the question of 'What to write now?' – after the doodlings of the previous page ('the signifier without the signified' [187]) and the end of the alphabet. The answer is one word – 'desire' : 'One writes with one's desire, and I am not through desiring' (188). Much of Barthes' late work was taken up with the idea of the 'pleasure' of the text, 'value shifted to the sumptuous rank of the signifier' (*Pleasure of the Text* 65), although he made little attempt to reproduce Lacan's complex theories of the inextricability of desire and the (metonymic) chain of signification. (This latter is a subject which will be treated in Chapter 4.) Barthes' model of playful polysemy, of the lure of the spectacle and the image, and of a life as a fictional construct, however, is paradigmatic of a great deal of contemporary fiction – from Thomas Pynchon to Salman Rushdie. I shall return to the image in fiction in Chapter 8, in particular as the embodiment of the death drive in language.

'IN UNITY DEFECTIVE': MILTON'S *PARADISE LOST*

Lacan drew a distinction between the ego (*le moi*) and the subject (*le sujet*), which helps us understand the way he envisaged the necessary passage from the Imaginary, the world of illusory identifications, and the Symbolic, the world of the signifier divorced from a signified. The ego he treated as that which is seen in the mirror stage, a 'mirage, a sum of identifications' (*Seminar 2*: 209) – with an other, whether that be one's own image or that of the m/other. The subject, on the other hand, is that which *disappears* (Lacan borrowed the Greek word *aphanisis*, disappearance, from Ernest Jones [*Écrits* 283]). For that reason it is written in the Lacanian system of mathemes as $, that which is crossed through or out in its inscription. It can be conceived only in terms of signification, as what Bruce Fink calls a '*breach in discourse*':

> The subject of the unconscious manifests itself in daily life as a fleeting irruption of something foreign or extraneous. Temporally speaking, the subject appears only as pulsation, an occasional impulse or interruption that immediately dies away or is extinguished, 'expressing itself,' as it does, by means of the signifier. (Fink 41)

Hence Lacan's seemingly paradoxical definition of the signifier not in terms of itself, but as 'that which represents the subject for another signifier' (*Écrits* 316). Unlike the ego psychologist, however, Lacan believed that mental health is promoted not through the shoring up of the ego but through the exposure of its fictionality and acceptance of its erasure, as subject, in language.

Book IX of Milton's *Paradise Lost*, which depicts the myth of the Fall of our First Parents from a state of idealized unity, can be read in Lacanian terms as the painful but necessary progress from the Imaginary to the Symbolic, from ego-hood, let us say, to subject-hood. As Jina Politi has argued,[7] Milton's poem, Book IX in particular, can be read as a 'Grand Narrative of Man's Fall and Entry into the Symbolic Order', as 'humanity's tragic fall into language and representation' (Politi, ' "Is This the Love" ' 152 and 137). This Fall is specifically depicted in terms of the lure of the visual, in which through a complex play of eyes and gazes, looking and being looked at, the subject is propelled into a world of illusion and division. The climax of Milton's poem, I shall argue, traces the doubleness of response at the founding moment of human experience – when the ego, through its own mirror identification, is transformed into the subject. To trace this shift, I shall concentrate on the two central relationships depicted in Book IX: first that of Adam and Eve, both before and after the Fall, and then that of Eve and the Serpent (Satan), who acts as agent of this shift.

In a traditional reading of the poem, Eve is regarded as embodying the flaw in human nature, the un-reason and vanity which prevents it from achieving its celestial potential. According to a Lacanian reading, however, she can be seen to represent not that which hereafter enslaves humanity but rather that which frees it from Imaginary illusions and initiates a necessary transition to psychic maturity.

Eve's relationship to seeing and being seen, perception and appearance, is crucial. She is what 'shows', while Adam is 'her Head' (Milton VIII, 574–75) in an economy which valorizes mind over body. Much earlier in the poem, in Book IV, she has described the day of her creation, before the meeting with Adam, and being drawn to peer at her reflection in the mirroring lake:

> I thither went
> With unexperienc't thought, and laid me down
> On the green bank, to look into the clear
> Smooth Lake, that to me seem'd another Sky.
> As I bent down to look, just opposite,
> A Shape within the wat'ry gleam appear'd
> Bending to look on me, I started back,

It started back, but pleas'd I soon return'd,
Pleas'd it return'd as soon with answering looks
Of sympathy and love; there I had fixt
Mine eyes till now, and pin'd with vain desire,
Had not a voice thus warn'd me, What thou seest,
What there thou seest fair Creature is thyself,
With thee it came and goes; but follow me,
And I will bring thee where no shadow stays
Thy coming, and thy soft imbraces, hee
Whose image thou art, him thou shalt enjoy
Inseparably thine, to him shalt bear
Multitudes like thyself, and thence be call'd
Mother of human Race. (IV, 456–75)

While still unconscious of 'what [she] was' ('With unexperienc't
thought') Eve is drawn to the lake to repeat the game of Ovid's
Narcissus, a game of reflexive interaction between self and double: 'I
started back,/It started back, but pleas'd I soon return'd,/Pleas'd it
return'd as soon with answering looks'. The dominant sensation is one
of pleasure; the human animal, unlike other primates, Lacan notes,
initially performs an act of 'homeomorphic identification'(*Écrits* 3)
with its mirror image, whereas the monkey soon loses interest when it
discovers its image's emptiness. In recognizing their image as their
own, humans are brought to an awareness of the distinction between
acting and being acted upon, active and passive. Ovid's Narcissus says:
'I am on fire with love for my own self. It is I who kindle the flames
which I must endure. What should I do? Woo or be wooed?' (Ovid
86).[8] The acts of reflexive play, Lacan states, set up a relationship
'between the movements assumed in the image and the reflected
environment, and between this virtual complex and the reality it
reduplicates' (1), a relationship which founds a lifetime of 'irreducible'
relatedness to the other (3).

   Led by the warning voice of God, Eve is brought to her first sight of
Adam, whom she finds

            fair indeed and tall,
Under a Platan, yet methought less fair,
Less winning soft, less amiably mild,
Than that smooth wat'ry image; back I turn'd,
Thou [Adam] following cri'd'st aloud, Return fair *Eve*,
Whom fli'st thou? (Milton IV, 477–82)

No image will ever be as fair as her own; nothing can compensate for the loss of that illusion. And yet Eve accepts her fate, which is to reconcile herself to the first step towards self-alienation and to accept to be not her own image, but that of the other (Adam).

Book IX takes up where this scene left off, and traces the progress of this advancing alienation, with Eve, again, as the index of change. The Book, like the poem as a whole, is flooded with references to light in order to foreground the significance of the act of perception in the development of the human psyche. In creating the world, we remember, Milton's God repeats Genesis in commanding 'Let there be Light'; 'Light/Eternal' is 'first of things' in the process of creation (VII, 243–44). 'Holy Light' is 'offspring of Heav'n first born' (III, 1), prominently preceding 'the Word' which represents another, later beginning. Now, for a time, it is Adam's perception which is highlighted. Eve functions for him as the lake has done for her, as that which reflects back his own image:

> I now see
> Bone of my Bone, Flesh of my Flesh, my Self
> Before me; Woman is her Name, of Man
> Extracted. (VIII, 494–97)

But he does not recoil at the other's difference, as Eve did on first seeing him. For him, in proprietorial arrogance, she *is* his image – 'Best Image of myself' (V, 95). Unlike her, most importantly, he is content to remain in a permanent state of illusory 'union' with her – 'Union without end', as God has falsely predicted (VII, 161), a perpetual Heaven on Earth. In response to the paired animals around him, Adam has pleaded with God to end his solitude: 'In solitude/ What happiness . . . ?' (VIII, 364–65). God is solitary,

> But Man by number is to manifest
> His single imperfection, and beget
> Like of his like, his Image multipli'd. (VIII, 422–24)

From the ego's drive to correct this 'imperfection', he has constructed an ideal of 'unfeign'd/Union of Mind, or in us both one Soul;/ Harmony to behold in wedded pair' (VIII, 603–5).

In the famous debate between the couple before the Fall, Adam defends the ideal of 'Conjugal Love' (IX, 263) by arguing that only 'harm' can 'Befall thee sever'd from me' (IX, 251–52). But Eve (and this is a phrase Milton uses, 'But Eve . . .', to introduce division into the harmony, to set up the dialectic of the relationship)[9] seems to want to repeat the creative process performed by God Himself when He inaugurated a series of 'dividing' acts described in Book VII: light from darkness, the Earth from the Waters, and so on. She demands from Adam that they should 'divide [their] labors' (IX, 214), finding his engulfing vision oppressive: 'so near/Looks intervene', she argues, to interrupt their work (IX, 221–22). Just as the unified *Gestalt* of the idealized ego-image is an illusion, masking division and fragmentation, so, Eve asks in her famous question,

> . . . what is Faith, Love, Virtue unassay'd
> Alone, without exterior help sustain'd? (IX, 335–36)

Unity means fixity, rigidity, neurosis, psychosis. Division into parts or recognition of our necessary fragmentation by 'exterior help' is a step towards health. And so, reluctantly, Adam consents to recognize division or difference as an inevitable effect of his union with his 'Image'. Having been repeatedly depicted 'hand in hand' with Adam until now, Eve takes the crucial step and 'from her Husband's hand her hand/Soft she withdrew' (IX, 385–86). Now, at this moment of entry into the Symbolic Order, what Lacan calls 'this junction of nature and culture', the ego must, in his words, sever 'this knot of imaginary servitude' (identification) in which love, in its naivety, would have us bound (*Écrits* 7). It is upon such a severance that are based the tensions and divisions of necessary growth, bringing about the awakening of desire, the perpetually elusive 'desire for the object of the other's desire' (19).

THE APPLE TREE AND THE SARDINE CAN

Book IX had begun with the announcement of new themes of 'breach' and 'alienat[ion]' (Milton IX, 6 and 9) to be introduced at the Fall. 'Knowledge' is to be gained at the cost of harmony. As we have seen, Adam's prelapsarian wish had been for 'unfeign'd/Union of Mind' with Eve; with the entrance of Satan, the element of 'feigning' takes on a new and prominent role. Satan has been described earlier in the poem as 'Self-lost' (VIII, 154), the embodiment of that second discovery of the mirror stage, that of losing the image we think we have gained. If the relationship between Adam and Eve has been that of the ego and the image, that between Eve and Satan could be described in Imaginary terms as that between the ego and the mirror itself. For Satan functions not so much as the object of Eve's gaze, but rather as that which gives back to her her own inverted, alienated subjectivity.[10]

Before insinuating himself into her presence, Satan has reared up in self-display like not one but a set of glittering, multiply reflecting mirrors:

> on his rear,
> Circular base of rising folds, that tow'r'd
> Fold above fold a surging Maze, his Head
> Crested aloft, and Carbuncle his Eyes;
> With burnisht Neck of verdant Gold, erect
> Amidst his circling Spires. (IX, 497–502)

His 'circling Spires' (from the Greek *spira*, coil, winding) travel not ever upwards but back upon themselves, down again, making him at once mirror and its inverted image. This is a trope which has been prepared for in Book IV, just before his famous soliloquy when he is described as 'back recoil[ing]/Upon himself' (17–18) like a 'devilish Engine' in his tormented quest. His role is to 'pervert' or 'invert', as his famous words in the soliloquy suggest: 'Evil be thou my Good' (IV, 110). Similarly, the 'rising folds', 'Fold above fold', echo the dazzling 'Gold' in a later line, as if to foreground his function as a specularizing duplicator of what confronts him. He is 'lovely . . . lovelier' (404–5) in replication of Eve herself, and when he does finally capture her eye and begin his compliments, his very words function as repetitive projections of her response: 'Wonder not, sovran Mistress, if per-haps/Thou canst, who are sole Wonder' (532–33). His task has been that of the 'smooth Lake' in Book IV, to 'lure her Eye' (IX, 518), and having captured it he sets about initiating her, as several critics have pointed out, into the economy of the gaze (Politi 147;[11] Schwartz 147).

In his later work, Lacan developed his 'Mirror Stage' theory towards a theory of the gaze, in particular in the second of the *Four Fundamental Concepts of Psychoanalysis*: 'Of the Gaze as *Objet Petit a*', which was delivered as part of the seminars of 1964. Here the emphasis was again on the dialectic of seer and seen, now formulated as 'The Split between the Eye and the Gaze' (*Four Fundamental Concepts* 67). When we gaze at ourselves in the mirror, not only do we confront our own alienation, but we are also forced to face up to the fact that something is 'lost' in the gaze. As Mladen Dolar explains, we are never able to see ourselves close our eyes or blink in the mirror ('At First Sight' 139). In other words, while we can see our eyes there, we can never see our own gaze, and in this discrepancy something is lost, which Lacan calls the *objet a* (to which I shall return in a later chapter). The field of the 'scopic drive', which Lacan regarded as one of the several fundamental human drives, is dominated by 'the illusion of the consciousness of *seeing oneself see oneself*, in which the gaze is elided' (*Four Fundamental Concepts* 83):

> In our relation to things, in so far as this relation is constituted by the way of vision, and ordered in the figures of representation, something slips, passes, is transmitted, from stage to stage, and is always to some degree eluded in it – that is what we call the gaze. (73)

And

> From the outset, we see, in the dialectic of the eye and the gaze, that there is no coincidence, but, on the contrary, a lure. When, in love, I solicit a look, what is profoundly unsatisfying and always missing is that – *You never look at me from the place from which I see you.*
>
> Conversely, *what I look at is never what I wish to see*. And the relation that I mentioned earlier, between the painter and the spectator, is a play, a play of *trompe-l'oeil*. (102–3)

'Generally speaking', he concludes, 'the relation between the gaze and what one wishes to see involves a lure' (104).

Lacan illustrates his theory of the split between the eye and the gaze by the well-known anecdote of the sardine can. One day, when in his early twenties, he went out in a boat with a family of Brittany fishermen. Suddenly, a young boy on board pointed out to him something floating on the waves:

> It was a small can, a sardine can . . . It glittered in the sun. And Petit-Jean said to me – *You see that can? Do you see it? Well, it doesn't see you!*

He found this incident highly amusing . . . Why did I find it less
amusing than he? . . .

To begin with, if what Petit-Jean said to me, namely, that the can
did not see me, had any meaning, it was because in a sense, it was
looking at me, all the same. It was looking at me at the level of the
point of light, the point at which everything that looks at me is
situated. (95)

The viewer, in other words, not only constructs images of objects, but
is illuminated by them, by the light emitted from them.The point
brought home by this strange little boating incident is that objects
outside us may disrupt with uncanny effect the everyday assumption
of a subject(ive) seer and an object(ive) seen.[12] As described by Slavoj
Žižek, this is how the Hitchcock effect works. An ordinary object,
such as an empty house, is rendered uncanny to the viewer through the
sensation that it is the house that is looking at us, rather than *vice
versa* (*Looking Awry* 126).

In the confrontation between Eve and Satan, it is the 'lure' (a
Lacanian term used, as we have seen, by Milton himself) which is at
issue. The uncanniness of Satan's presence before Eve has to do with
the fact that while it is 'the Eye of Eve' which is the focus of attention
(IX, 528), this Eye is met not by the confirmation of its own self-
presence but rather by the gaze of the other (Satan, the mirror), which
displaces it. It is significant that at his first approach, just before Eve
catches sight of him, he stands before her '*as* in gaze admiring' (524,
emphasis added). 'As if' is Satan's most appropriate epithet (if we can
use it in adjectival form). He is the 'fraudulent Impostor', the 'false
dissembler' (III, 692 and 681), the master of disguises whose role as
mirror is to call up 'resemblances' in the other which always deceive.
Hence his first words to Eve refer to her as 'Fairest resemblance of thy
Maker fair' (538),[13] a comparison which she is soon to disprove, with
such momentous consequences. Through Satan, we could say, 'resemblance' (to Eve) rapidly switches to 'dissemblance'.

Having initiated Eve into the lure of the gaze, Satan now leads her
to the object of ultimate deception, the Tree of Knowledge, where she
will complete her epistemological quest. The Tree and its 'Ruddy and
Gold' Fruit have already been intensely visualized through his descriptions (IX, 576–78). Satan's ultimate task is to persuade Eve that
the Tree's function is 'To open Eyes' (866); his own are now 'opener'
(875) since he has tasted, he lies to her. 'Your eyes', he says, 'that seem

so clear,/Yet are but dim' (706–7). But paradoxically, his falsehoods constitute him as purveyor of truth in the Lacanian scheme whereby initiation into 'knowledge' (of evil) means a confrontation with the split or 'slip' between the eye and the gaze. Eve's eyes were indeed 'dim' in their prelapsarian state of illusion (of oneness). Right up until the moment she tastes the apple, which she sees as 'Fair' (in resemblance to herself), Eve suffers the illusion of its immediate access to her vision. Having been tasted, however, the apple, like the sardine can for Lacan, sets off a chain of reactions in her which bring her to a crucial awareness of the meaning of deception, loss and death.

So at the level of the scopic drive, Adam and Eve do indeed become, as Satan predicted, 'as Gods,/Knowing both Good and Evil as they know' (708–9). Such knowledge, in Lacan's terms, is a 'paranoiac knowledge' (*Écrits* 2), bringing with it an immediate awareness on Eve's part of being *looked at* by all around her: 'what if God have seen,/And Death ensue?' (IX, 826–27)[14] As Lacan writes: 'The world is all-seeing, but it is not exhibitionistic – it does not provoke our gaze. When it begins to provoke it, the feeling of strangeness begins too.' (*Four Fundamental Concepts* 75) In this new uncanny world,[15] the subject (now a subject and not an ego) experiences what Joan Copjec, glossing Lacan, calls a ' "televisual" fear' (*Read My Desire* 15), a fear of being completely visible on all sides by the ever-encroaching gaze of the other. In this new state, themselves with 'opener . . . Eyes' (875), the First Parents now seek to 'hide' or 'obscure' themselves, both from God, and from each other by covering their nakedness. They have entered, in other words, the world of desire, which (as we shall see in Chapter 4) is a world of loss, language and death. The 'Fall' of humanity in the Miltonic schema, like the entry into the Symbolic in the Lacanian, will ultimately transform these terms of negation into something positive. To gain knowledge of 'evil' (splitting and self-loss) is to 'attain . . . the sum/Of wisdom' (XII, 575–76), as the Angel Michael tells the fallen couple. We thus leave them at the end in a state of healthy human division – Adam says:

> full of doubt I stand,
> Whether I should repent me now of sin
> By mee done and occasion'd, or rejoice
> Much more, that much more good thereof shall spring.
>   (XII, 473–76)

THE DREAM-WORK

So far we have been dealing with literary representations of the drive towards self-identification, via the visual image, which Lacan regarded as fundamental to the ontological structure of the human world. If identity, as we have seen with *Paradise Lost* and *Roland Barthes by Roland Barthes*, is a matter of misrecognition, the next question to be asked is: how does this discordance with our own reality affect the way the ego constitutes its objects – or, in other words, the way a writer gives form to the world around him/her?

Another way of putting this question would be to ask how literature (and art in general) is produced. By what mechanisms, psychic or otherwise, does human phantasy come to expression? Freud's answer to this fundamental question was to compare creative writing to day-dreaming or 'phantasying', and to relate this, in turn, to dreams and the unconscious. Writing, like the dream, is an attempt of 'His Majesty the Ego' to fulfil its deepest wishes (PF 14: 132 and 138), which are usually sexual, or at least related to the ego's drive to power and mastery. Both dreams and creative writing attempt to disguise the nakedness of these aims, or divert them into something more accep-table to the social conscience. Art is a form of 'sublimation', defined by Cornelius Castoriadis as

> the process by means of which the psyche is forced to replace its own or private objects of cathexis, including its own image of itself, with objects that exist and have value in and through their social institution, and to make them for itself 'causes', 'means' or 'supports' of pleasure. (29)

It was his detailed descriptions of the processes of disguise, which Freud called the 'dream-work', which formed the core of his theory of dreams. The influence of these descriptions on recent cultural theory has been particularly important because of Freud's preoccupation with conditions of representation, how what he called a 'thing-presentation', the image or imago in the unconscious, is converted into a 'word-presentation', the verbal form given to it by the conscious mechanisms (PF 11: 206–7). The Freudian unconscious is a very different affair from that of the Romantics a hundred or so years earlier, which had its natural successor, in Lacan's opinion, in Jung

(*Four Fundamental Concepts* 24). It was not the 'locus of the divinities of the night' (24), or the source of imaginative creation which, according to Coleridge, produced organic wholes out of an assemblage of disparate parts. In fact it was not a 'locus' or even a 'content' at all,[16] but rather a system or set of processes or primal phantasies which are driven to find expression in images and words. One of its main characteristics, however, was its intractability, its inaccessibility to conscious penetration or scrutiny. It had to be got at indirectly, just as it revealed itself – in slips of the tongue, parapraxes, symptoms and dreams. It was to be found, first and foremost, in the defences erected against it, the gaps that open up when the conscious mind tries to censor its most protected secrets. To access the unconscious, the analyst must adopt the famous attitude of 'evenly-suspended attention' (SE 12: 111),[17] an attitude which brings into relief the 'nodal points' in the patient's speech – 'points of intensity, of absence of intensity, lacunae, hollows' (Laplanche and Leclaire 125).

In *The Interpretation of Dreams* (1900), Freud described the 'dream-work', which he regarded as the essence of the dream process, in terms that have provided a fascinating model for literary reading, especially within a post-structuralist context. The dream-work's function, to distort and thus censor the dream-thoughts, rendering them more acceptable to the conscious mind, involves a process of 'secondary revision', giving coherence to otherwise unintelligible material. This secondary revision has to be deconstructed if the dream-work, which is 'more careless, more irrational, more forgetful and more incomplete than waking thought' (PF 4: 650) is to be exposed. There is no 'hidden meaning' waiting to be prized out of a dream. Its essence can be got at only by 'look[ing] firmly at the letters [the words as signifiers], pay[ing] no attention to their ostensible arrangement' (643) in the manner of a deconstructive reading of a literary text. A whole series of 'translations' takes place for the original dream-thoughts to take the form of a dream. First they have to be reproduced as images, as 'the material of visual and acoustic memory-traces', and then these, in turn, have to be translated into words, by the process of free association in the analytic situation. These '*considerations of representability*' (650–51), central to the Freudian system, formed the basis of Lacan's 'return' to Freud.

Two short examples of Freudian dream analysis may help to explain these processes. In the first one, 'C. dreamt of *seeing a girl on the – Road, who was bathed in white light and was wearing a white blouse*'. A crude 'symbolic' reading of this dream might have attempted to interpret the concept of whiteness in terms of purity or innocence, or perhaps blankness, or as a counter to death (blackness).[18] The free associations of the dreamer, however, revealed that he had 'had intimate relations with a Miss White for the first time on this road' (538). The 'meaning' of the dream, therefore, was contained in the pun on white rather than in its symbolic significance; the word acts as a substitute for some inaccessible piece of knowledge in the dreamer's unconscious. The dream-work, Freud explains elsewhere, translates into 'another script or language' in the attempt 'to condense two different thoughts by seeking out (like a joke) an ambiguous word in which the two thoughts may come together' (PF 1: 207). A dream, he said, is like a 'rebus', a picture-puzzle in which the pictorial elements stand for a word or syllable in a very literal sense. This is illustrated in another well-known example of a dream which interested Freud, that of Alexander the Great as reported with slight variations by both Plutarch and Artemidorus of Daldis:

> When the king was laying siege to the obstinately defended city of Tyre (322 B.C.), he once dreamt that he saw a dancing satyr. Aristander, the dream-interpreter, who was present with the army, interpreted the dream by dividing the word '*Satyros*' into σὰ Τύρος [sa Turos] (thine is Tyre), and therefore promised that he would triumph over the city. Alexander was led by this interpretation to continue the siege and eventually captured Tyre. The interpretation, which has a sufficiently artificial appearance, was undoubtedly the right one. (PF 1: 274–75)

Successful dream interpretation depends on learning to concentrate on the 'artificial appearance' or literal meaning of a dream, avoiding the lure of its organic totality.

DREAM REPRESENTATION: THE SURREALIST PROJECT

For Lacan, the dream provides us with the ultimate paradigm of the nonreferential nature of discourse, a discourse whose 'grammar' it had been Freud's genius to detect (*Écrits* 264). Lacan's essay on 'The Agency of the Letter in the Unconscious or Reason since Freud' (1957) elaborates in detail on the links between the unconscious and language, at one point comparing dreams to the game of charades –

'the parlour-game in which one is supposed to get the spectators to guess some well known saying or variant of it solely by dumb-show'. He explains:

> It is precisely the fact that both the game and the dream run up against a lack of taxematic material for the representation of such logical articulations as causality, contradiction, hypothesis, etc., that proves they are a form of writing rather than of mime. (*Écrits* 161)

On the basis of Freud's analysis of the distortions of the dream-work and of Saussure's analysis of the linguistic sign, Lacan outlines a difficult theory of the parallels between the mechanisms of the unconscious and the laws of operation of language. In attempting to represent *connection* between two ideas or images, the dream-work uses the process Freud called 'displacement' (of one mental image onto another) and which, in poetry, we call metonymy – that is, when an attribute or cause or effect of a thing signifies the thing.[19] In attempting to represent the *substitution* (or replacement) of one idea or image for another, the dream-work uses the process of 'condensation' (PF 4: 650–51), which in poetry is called metaphor. The dream, in other words, 'follows the laws of the signifier' in all its operations (*Écrits* 161), proving the famous dictum that '*the unconscious is structured like a language*' (*Four Fundamental Concepts* 20).

With this interest in the connections between the unconscious and language (and thus of poetic diction), it is not surprising that Lacan followed very closely the experiments of the surrealist movement in representing the unconscious in poetry. At the time when the surrealist project was at its height, in the early 1930s, Lacan was an enthusiastic supporter of its aims: radical politics, influenced by Hegel and Marx, an interest in dreams, madness and the unconscious, and above all the experiments with what André Breton in 1934 called '*the problem of human expression in all its forms*' (Breton 131). Summarizing in 1957 the achievements of surrealism in relation to his own analysis of displacement and condensation, metonymy and metaphor, Lacan wrote:

> It should be said that modern poetry and especially the Surrealist school have taken us a long way in this direction by showing that any conjunction of two signifiers would be equally sufficient to constitute a metaphor, except for the additional requirement of the

greatest possible disparity of the images signified, needed for the production of the poetic spark, or in other words for metaphoric creation to take place. (*Écrits* 156)

The 'conjunction of two signifiers' was Lacan's way of describing what the surrealists, following Freud, had called the 'free association' of mental images and thoughts, Freud's 'fundamental rule' which structures the analytic situation. The rule had to be applied by both analysand and analyst, the former in saying whatever comes to mind, without conscious interference, the latter in attending 'freely' to the patient's associations without directing attention to anything in particular (SE 12: 111–12). Breton described the surrealist project as an attempt to shake off the 'logical mechanism[s] of the sentence' in order to explore the gap between what we think we know and what our words reveal us to know at the unconscious level (132–33).[20] Throughout their work, but especially in the early period between 1919 and the mid 20s, the surrealists experimented with automatic writing as a way of tapping the riches of the unconscious – or, at least, of seeing how far they could go in doing away with conscious control. The results, predictably, were usually tedious and often nonsensical. They were to show that out of a mass of seemingly random material, it is the meaningful or determined connections that are interesting, and that these require conscious recognition and selection.

From the psychoanalytic point of view, these experiments were to show that automatic writing, like free association in the clinical situation, does not provide direct access to the primary processes of the unconscious in their pure form. It is through the detection of the operations working *against* the revelation of this material that the most immediate access to the unconscious is to be gained. These, as we have seen, are the processes of 'secondary revision', the attempt to give coherence to the material, and of resistance against it – the gaps, the distortions, the unsaid. Lacan argued that the experiments in automatic writing are based on a false assumption, for the reason that

The creative spark of the metaphor does not spring from the presentation of two images, that is, of two signifiers equally actualized. It flashes between two signifiers one of which has taken the place of the other in the signifying chain, the occulted signifier remaining present through its (metonymic) connexion with the rest of the chain. (*Écrits* 157)

The 'meaning', in other words, is to be found not in the conjunction but in the gap between the two images, what is lost or occluded in the replacement of the one by the other. In its immediate effect, the 'creative spark' comes from what slips away between the two images, causing the 'emotive shock' which the surrealists hoped would revolutionize our ways of feeling (Breton 132). In its more profound effect, this slippage bespeaks the constant presence of absence, which for Lacan, as we shall see in Chapter 4, points ultimately to the paternal function, to castration, and to death. It is for this reason that the experiments of later surrealists, especially of Salvador Dali, who joined the movement in 1929, could be described as more Lacanian than Freudian. Or perhaps it would be more accurate to say that the early experiments of Lacan were as much Daliesque as they were Freudian. Dali had formulated his theory of 'the paranoiac-critical method' of artistic production in the years immediately preceding Lacan's medical thesis on *Paranoid Psychosis and its Relation to Personality* (1932); it was this, undoubtedly, which was responsible for shaping Lacan's clinical experiments with paranoia into a theory (Roudinesco 31–32).

W. H. AUDEN: SURREALISM AND
THE CONSCIOUS MIND

Auden's work is not normally associated with the surrealist movement, even though he followed its developments closely at a time when his own poetry was taking shape. In 1937 he wrote an essay on 'Psychology and Art To-Day', in which he put forward the arguments for and against surrealism's adoption of 'a technique resembling the procedure in the analyst's consulting room' (61). One of Freud's contributions to literature, he writes, has been to encourage emphasis on 'the use of words in associational rather than logical sequence' – although this method, he adds, probably with surrealists in mind, has been 'misappropriated by irrationalists eager to escape their conscience' (71). Throughout the history of poetry, 'There have always been two views of the poetic process, as an inspiration and as a craft, of the poet as the Possessed and as the Maker' (65). Auden himself comes down on the side of craft, of poetry as a 'making'. Even in a short lyric poem, let alone a sustained work, he argues, 'the material immediately "given" to consciousness, the automatic element, is very small'. Psychology's concentration on symbols ignores the significance of *words* – 'the management of consonants and vowels':

> Psycho-analysis, he [the writer, and Auden himself] would agree, has increased the artist's interest in dreams, mnemonic fragments, child art and graffiti, etc., but that the interest is a *conscious* one. Even the most surrealistic writing or Mr. James Joyce's latest prose shows every sign of being non-automatic and extremely carefully worked over. (66)

Auden's arguments for the significance of 'conscious' operations in the making of poetry should not distract us from the importance in his own poetry of the attempt to represent the unconscious – an importance which, like his contemporary Samuel Beckett, he preferred to under-play. In a well-known poem written the same year (1937) as his essay on psychology and art, 'As I Walked Out One Evening', Auden put to the test the possibility of presenting an array of unconscious material – dream images, hallucinations, paranoia – at the same time examining the ways in which this material needed to be handled by the conscious processes.

At first sight, this poem strikes us as the antithesis of anything by Breton or English surrealists such as David Gascoyne. Its form is that of the ballad, with its strict alternation of iambic tetrameter and trimeter and its abcb rhyme seeming to offer every obstacle to the unchecked outpourings of automatic association:

> As I walked out one evening,
> Walking down Bristol Street,
> The crowds upon the pavement
> Were fields of harvest wheat. (*Collected Poems* 114)

The quatrain, however, is clearly making use of a certain 'dialectical' method in the Lacanian sense referred to earlier in this chapter. On the general level, there is the contrast between on the one hand the romantic rural effect of the ballad form itself ('As I walked out one evening . . .') as well as the 'fields of harvest wheat', and on the other hand the stark rural image of the crowds on the prosaic 'Bristol Street'. More specifically, the shock conjunction of two disparate images characteristic of the surrealist method, the replacement of the 'crowds' by the 'fields of harvest wheat',[21] illustrates the dialectic of paranoia whereby objects in the outside world are radically split off from the consciousness that perceives them. Herbert Read, a member of the Surrealist Group in London working under the influence of Dali, described the process in this way in 1936:

> In dialectical terms we claim that there is a continual state of opposition and interaction between the world of objective fact – the sensational and social world of active and economic existence – and the world of subjective fantasy. This opposition creates a state of disquietude, a lack of spiritual equilibrium, which it is the business of the artist to resolve. He resolves the contradiction by creating a synthesis, a work of art which combines elements from both these worlds, eliminates others, but which for the moment gives us a qualitatively new experience. (Read 40–41)

In attempting to conflate two unrelated terms, the surrealist poets were practising what Freud had described the dream-work to be doing in the process of condensation. The 'manifest' part of the dream, the part remembered and repeated by the dreamer, is a condensation of several associative chains leading back, through interpretation, to its 'latent' content. Dreams often attempt to combine different visual elements into one composite form – Freud uses mythical figures such as the centaur as an example here (PF 4: 436). Although the surrealist poets claimed to be doing something similar in attempting a 'synthesis' of the different elements, they were to learn the difficulty if not impossibility of achieving this on a lexical level, as a pun, because of the inevitable privacy of verbal associations. (James Joyce, however, was to attempt to put into practice the Freudian process of condensation with his portmanteau words in *Finnegans Wake*, published in 1939.) Visually, however, as if they were paintings, two images (such as Auden's crowds and harvest wheat) *can* be held together (Dali's double-images) so that their opposition may effect what Read calls a 'state of disquietude'. A later stanza in Auden's poem, intensifying the atmosphere of panic and nightmare, uses a surrealist conjunction of threatening natural forces (the glacier, the desert, death) and mundane household objects:

> The glacier knocks in the cupboard,
> The desert sighs in the bed,
> And the crack in the tea-cup opens
> A lane to the land of the dead. (115)

Auden's poem is presented in the form of two juxtaposed monologues – of a lover's apostrophe to eternal love, and of the 'clocks in
the city' which represent the devastating incursions of time. The
poem's preoccupation with time is also reflected in its use in both
monologues of a range of images from a lost childhood past, especially
from nursery rhymes. The lover proclaims

> I'll love you, dear, I'll love you
> Till China and Africa meet,
> And the river jumps over the mountain
> And the salmon sing in the street. (114)

The clocks, in response, call up 'the burrows of the Nightmare/Where
Justice naked is':

> Where the beggars raffle the banknotes
> And the Giant is enchanting to Jack,
> And the Lily-white Boy is a Roarer,
> And Jill goes down on her back. (115)

The childhood experience, recalled into adulthood, can only take a
perverted form; its images, long repressed, return as monstrosities. In
an analysis of surrealist painting in terms of Freud's definition of the
uncanny, Elizabeth Wright has argued that the surreal effect derives
from the shock of the 'where have I seen this before?' reaction – the
heimlich or homely suddenly rendered shockingly unfamiliar (*unheimlich*). The affinity of surrealism and psychoanalysis, she argues,
following Adorno, depends 'on the way that they both focus on the
attempts of the unconscious to evoke and reveal in sudden bursts of
shock the images of our childhood past still crystalized within us'.

> The giant egg [in a surrealist painting], for instance, from which a
> monster threatens to emerge at any moment, is big because we were
> so very small when we first gazed at an egg in extreme trepidation.
> The uncanny effect is brought about because we are confronted with
> a subjectivity now alien to us, because we have had to move on.
> ('The Uncanny and Surrealism' 268)

In Lacanian terms, here, it is important to recognize that it is not the
'synthesis' of the two images or of the perceiver and perceived which is

at issue, as Herbert Read argued, but rather their disparity or discontinuity. 'In the dream, in parapraxis, in the flash of wit – what is it that strikes one first? It is the sense of impediment to be found in all of them', Lacan writes. 'Discontinuity, then, is the essential form in which the unconscious first appears to us as a phenomenon' (*Four Fundamental Concepts* 25), for the reason that the object out there, onto which we have projected our own mirror image, is always irrevocably other to our perception. In yoking together these incommensurables, then, the surreal image offers a reminder of our own self-alienation.

It is not a matter, therefore, of reading the link between the two images (say wheat and crowds, or glacier and cupboard) *metaphorically*, the one as a replacement of the other, but rather of reading them *literally*, as Freud suggested we read dream images. Auden has placed them side by side as an invitation to participate in the experience of their discontinuity, letting them float loose in our own daydreams. Freud believed that the unconscious of one person can react upon that of another, without the mediation of the conscious of either (PF 11: 198). For all his emphasis on his controlling craftsmanship, Auden's poem depends upon this belief.

*   *   *   *

If Lacan's post-1930s work was to move him ever deeper into definitions of divided subjectivity, surrealism never gave up its attempt to bring about a unification of subjective experience and the world of objects. In his 1934 manifesto, Breton stated that recent developments in the movement had seen it take 'a decisive step towards the unification of the personality', which it found threatened by the encroaching forces of fascism in Europe. Today, he said, surrealism is attempting to '*bring about the state where the distinction between the subjective and the objective loses its necessity and its value*':

> its most recent advance is producing a *fundamental crisis of the object*. It is essentially on the *object* that surrealism has thrown most light in recent years. Only the very close examination of the many recent speculations to which the object has publicly given rise (the oneiric object, the object functioning symbolically, the real and virtual object, the moving but silent object, the phantom object, the found object, etc.) can give one a proper grasp of the experiments that surrealism is engaged in now. (138)

At this very time, among London psychoanalytic circles, heated debates were taking place between Kleinians and Freudians over the status and role of the object in the development of subjective experience. The Kleinians, in particular, were defining the object in more immediate terms than Breton's, terms relating to the symbolic presence of the maternal body. On one thing they were to agree: the object was never 'found', as Breton claimed, but an object perpetually lost.

2

The (Lost) Object

So far, I have been referring to the subject as if s/he were an autonomous monad, albeit embedded in and produced by a complex of cultural and linguistic forces, but with separate boundaries nonetheless. But psychoanalysis has seldom been willing to accept the monadic model of subjectivity. From birth, it argues, the infant is reared through relatedness, the first object, usually the mother, being simultaneously identified with and internalized.

It is these two processes of identification and internalization, which form the basis of object choice in later life, that I want to focus on in this chapter. The main areas of debate on the topic have come from the different schools of object relations theory in Britain and the United States. Until recently, these have attracted little attention in literary criticism, which has from the time of Freud's first attempts in the field, kept mainly to the Freudian and then the Lacanian model, with a separate if less influential tradition in Jungian criticism. But in the last decade or so, object relations theories have come to occupy a dominant place in Anglo-American criticism, especially feminist criticism, with the work of Nancy Chodorow (in the 1980s) and Melanie Klein (in the '90s) at the forefront.

When Freud wrote about objects and identification in the developing infant, which he did less directly than his followers, it was always in terms of a primary narcissism. For Lacan, as we have seen in the previous chapter, to 'find' the self in the mirror is simultaneously to 'lose' it as object of desire. Freud's primary narcissism was previous to any possibility of identification with an object. But if the object, in Freud's view, is fundamentally a creation of the subject, it could also be said that for him the subject is little else than that object with which it identifies or which it chooses. As Mikkel Borch-Jacobsen puts it, in the Freudian schema Narcissus 'never loses himself in objects other than to find himself in them' ('The Freudian Subject' 67).

Put another way, this is a distinction between 'being' the object and 'having' it, a distinction often ignored but which was crucial for Freud, as it was to be for Lacan. Identification ('being') comes first, as Freud puts it in his chapter on 'Identification' in *Group Psychology and the Analysis of the Ego* (1921); it is 'the original form of emotional tie with an object' (PF 12: 137). It is only later that object cathexes ('having') develop, and these, always precarious, may sometimes regress to primitive identifications at a later stage. Freud's thinking on primary fusion with the mother in the pre-Oedipal period was of a fairly elementary nature; development of this rich area was to be left to his followers. It is interesting to recall, however, a little-known passage scribbled in his notes at the end of his life (in July 1938: he was to die in September 1939) in which can be detected the degree of his familiarity with and interest in many of the major arguments among object-relations theorists that had been raging throughout the 1920s and '30s:

> 'Having' and 'being' in children. Children like expressing an object-relation by an identification. 'I am the breast.' 'Having' is the later of the two; after loss of the object it relapses into 'being'. Example: the breast. 'The breast is part of me, I am the breast.' Only later: 'I have it' – that is, 'I am not it' . . . (*SE* 23: 299)

The mutual implication of gender and object relation suggested here is fundamental. The phrase 'I am the breast' , which could stand as a summary of the work of Melanie Klein and subsequent theories of the centrality of the pre-Oedipal, maternal relation, comes as something of a surprise from Freud, in view of his notoriously patricentric views of primary identification with a paternal figure (elaborated, as we shall see in Chapter 4, in *Totem and Taboo*). The father in late Freud is both the object of (individual) Oedipal identification and, more primarily, the Father of individual prehistory, an innate and primitive identification preceding socialization but ultimately determining all its basic contours. (He was, at the time of writing the above note, engaged in seeing through the press his controversial last work, *Moses and Monotheism*, which treats Moses as founding patriarch of monotheism.)

So what is Freud's position on the perplexed question of whether primary identification for each sex is masculine or feminine? That the answer to this question is far from clear is indication of Freud's lifelong sensitivity to the difficulty of separating innate and experienced factors affecting development. One of his first major works treating object relations, one that gives full play to this complexity, is his speculative analysis in 1910 of the psycho-sexual characteristics of Leonardo da Vinci. Although known chiefly as an account of the genesis of homosexuality (or, alternatively, as a naïve 'pathography'),[1] Freud's study of Leonardo is particularly interesting for the way it broaches the question of the complex relation between narcissism and object relation. Here is a passage from Chapter 3 of the study:

> The child's love for his mother cannot continue to develop consciously any further; it succumbs to repression. The boy represses his love for his mother: he puts himself in her place, identifies himself with her, and takes his own person as a model in whose likeness he chooses the new objects of his love. In this way he has become a homosexual. What he has in fact done is to slip back to auto-erotism: for the boys whom he now loves as he grows up are after all only substitutive figures and revivals of himself in childhood – boys whom he loves in the way in which his mother loved *him* when he was a child. He finds the objects of his love along the path of *narcissism* . . . (PF 14: 191)[2]

Narcissism and object choice, therefore, are like two mirrors reflecting each other back and forth. The boy, having as an infant first 'been' and then 'taken' the mother as an object, on repression of this love again 'becomes' her in order to take his own person as object, on the basis of which he then chooses new objects which 'are' himself. Here, in this dizzying play of reflections and counter-reflections are the seeds of Lacan's famous dictum that our desire 'is the desire of the Other' (*Écrits* 264) – that is, the desire for ourselves on the part of the other. Here, too, are the seeds of the concepts of *introjection*[3] (the process whereby an object is internalized as a mental representation) and of *projection* (attributing to objects impulses of one's own split feelings and experiences), both of which have been crucial in Kleinian and post-Kleinian theory and practice. The concept of the 'internal object' was about to be born.

THE KLEINIAN OBJECT

One of the main distinctions that has been drawn between the classic Freudian and the Kleinian views is that for Klein, ego development is less a matter of a progress of the self through a series of (intra-psychic) stages than a process of *inter*-psychic reactions resulting from the introjection and projection of objects. And yet this opposition between the Freudian intra-psychic and the Kleinian inter-psychic model makes too clear-cut a distinction between inner and outer, a distinction notoriously difficult to establish in the work of both writers. For Klein, the object has as much to do with phantasy (spelt with a 'ph' to indicate the unconscious component) as it does with reality. When the baby introjects the primary objects or rather part objects (the mother's breast, the father's penis), s/he does so in response to an already-existing, innate 'knowledge' of these objects. The objects, having been established as 'images' within the ego, form the basis of what is then projected out onto 'real' objects actually encountered.[4] This simultaneous process of introjection and projection means that objects both construct and are constructed by the subject. As Juliet Mitchell puts it, 'In Klein's concept, phantasy emanates from within and imagines what is without' ('Introduction' 23).[5] Whereas for Donald Winnicott, one of Klein's most influential (if often sceptical) followers, the object, particularly the mother, pre-exists the subject and responds in 'real' terms to its introjections and projections, for Klein it was more a matter of the constitutive role of phantasy in the early developmental period.

Although uneasy about Klein's assumption of the biological ('essentialist') nature of gender identity, feminist critics have been attracted to Klein's work for its reconceptualization of the very early relation between mother and infant. (Freud had called this the pre-Oedipal period; Klein saw it as the Oedipal commencing much earlier.) It is a misconception, however, to assume that Klein was interested either in the mother as subject or active agent, or to idealize her as source of all good; when Klein talked about the 'good' and the 'bad' breast, this had little to do with the mother's treatment of the child – contrary to Winnicott, again, for whom the 'good enough' mother was one capable of sustaining the child's needs.[6] Rather, it defines the *child's* innate capacity to oppose good (that which satisfies) and bad (that which deprives), and its subsequent internalization and reformulation of this opposition. True, the child's libidinal phantasies of a good or bad breast are reinforced by positive or negative experiences. But, as Hanna Segal (one of Klein's most influential interpreters) notes, 'phantasy may override reality and the infant under the sway of persecutory anxieties may turn away angrily and in fear from the approaching breast' (100).

In speaking in terms of 'positions' rather than 'stages', Klein brought a new concept of time to the analysis of the psychic apparatus. For Freud, the ego regresses in psychosis to the very early disturbances or traumas of infancy. For Klein, however, psychotic elements are present in everyone at all times and function, perhaps more spatially than temporally, as positions to which we may return over and over throughout our lives. Mental health, in other words, is a relative state that may be lost or regained at any time.

The only sense in which development could be said to come into Klein's model of the psyche is in the sequence of the two crucial positions she described. The first few months of life are dominated by part-objects (the breast in particular), which are perceived as split into ideal and persecutory aspects. This splitting causes a paranoid anxiety; hence the term '*paranoid–schizoid*' *position* which she settled on in the early 1940s. The description she gives of this position in 'Notes on Some Schizoid Mechanisms' (1946) is one of the neonate besieged by a terrifying array of persecutory forces from both without and within:

> I hold that anxiety arises from the operation of the death instinct within the organism, is felt as fear of annihilation (death) and takes the form of fear of persecution. The fear of the destructive impulse seems to attach itself at once to an object – or rather it is experienced as the fear of an uncontrollable overpowering object. Other important sources of primary anxiety are the trauma of birth (separation anxiety) and frustration of bodily needs; and these experiences too are from the beginning felt as being caused by objects. Even if these objects are felt to be external, they become through introjection internal persecutors and thus reinforce the fear of the destructive impulse within. (*Selected Melanie Klein* 179–80)

It is perhaps understandable that other analysts of the period, looking in some alarm at this new view of the inner world of the infant, should have regarded it, as Edward Glover did, as ' a matriarchal variant of the doctrine of Original Sin' (qtd in Phillips 42).

With these anxieties to overcome, the infant resorts to a series of defences which result in the next position, occurring around the second quarter of the first year (and often coinciding with weaning), the *depressive position*. It is here that the infant attempts reparation by rebuilding the good objects that it has destroyed with its own hatred and sadism. Here, too, it learns to construct a whole object comprising both the good and the dangerous features that it has previously split out. Hence the crucial new experience of ambivalence, and the beginning of the testing of inner reality against outer reality (the 'real' mother). The position is 'depressive' because

> only when the ego has introjected the object as a whole and has established a better relationship to the external world and to real people is it able fully to realize the disaster created through its sadism and especially through its cannibalism and to feel distressed about it. ('A Contribution to the Psychogenesis of Manic-Depressive States', *Selected Melanie Klein* 124)

For Klein, the normal development of the child and its capacity for love rests largely on how the ego is able to work through 'this nodal position' (145).

FAIRY TALES

What is at stake in Klein's view of normal development is the learning to transform an identity based on primitive phantasies into one based on reality. And yet the transformation is never complete, even in the most favourable of circumstances. Such a view of the perpetual recurrence, throughout life, of conflicts like these can help explain the universal appeal of narratives of archetypal conflict, particularly myths, folk tales and fairy tales.

Many fairy tales start from the situation of the splitting of the mother into the good (often missing or dead) and the evil (step-mother), as in *Cinderella*, *Snow White* or *Hansel and Gretel*. Many feature motifs of oral sadism, incorporation or engulfment. In being eaten (or nearly eaten) by the dangerous object (the wolf in *Little Red Riding Hood* or in *The Three Little Pigs*, or the giant in *Jack and the Beanstalk*), the ego is rehearsing the defence of projection as well as the persecutory anxiety of the paranoid–schizoid position. Reparation (of the depressive position) may be rehearsed in a figure like the fairy godmother in *Cinderella*, who has the power to annul the acts of the sadistic step-mother.

For Bruno Bettelheim in his well-known Freudian reading of fairy tales, *The Uses of Enchantment* (1976), these narratives play out the fundamental conflicts and resolutions of the family romance and the various stages of the Oedipus complex. Bettelheim reads *Little Red Riding Hood*, for example, as a depiction of 'the daughter's unconscious wish to be seduced by her father (the wolf)' (175).

Klein, on the other hand, asks a more fundamental question: 'How does it come about that the child creates such a phantastic image of its parents – an image that is so far removed from reality?' The answer, she says, can only be found through investigation of the psychic mechanisms of the (pre-)Oedipal child and in tracing the way aggression is a projection of innate, repressed impulses:

> In penetrating to the deepest layers of the child's mind and discovering those enormous quantities of anxiety – those fears of imaginary objects and those terrors of being attacked in all sorts of ways – we . . . lay bare a corresponding amount of repressed impulses of aggression and can observe the causal connection which exists between the child's fears and its aggressive tendencies. ('The Early Development of Conscience in the Child', *Love, Guilt and Reparation* 249).

Julia Segal has argued that the Cinderella story illustrates the way Klein's theory emphasizes the difficulty of separating real-life ill-treatment by a (step-)mother from the daughter's own feelings of resentment towards her, above all in relation to jealousy of the relationship with the father (Julia Segal 30). Phantasies of attack on the mother or on parts of her body are figured in the tale in an elaborate tri-partite maternal configuration. The good mother is dead, as she so often is in literature. (Charlotte Brontë's novels are a typical example here.) The live mother is ugly and ferocious, and has produced two replicas of herself for emphasis. And the fairy godmother, as Segal notes, must pay a price for her goodness by existing only for Cinderella and having no sexual life of her own. Segal writes:

> At the end of the story Cinderella openly gets her revenge on her sisters and her mother either by punishing them or by being magnanimous and better than them: the story itself has satisfied, perhaps, an ordinary little girl's desires for revenge on a sexual mother preferred by her father, with a life and daughters of her own. (32)

THE DICTATES OF THE SUPER-EGO:
ISHIGURO'S *THE REMAINS OF THE DAY*

Initially, in her early work, Klein had referred to all introjected objects as 'the superego' (later, she wrote more frequently of 'internal objects') (Hanna Segal 103). Freud's super-ego, however, was a much more restricted concept. He first used the term when formulating his second theory of the psychical apparatus in *The Ego and the Id* (1923), where it is defined as an agency of censorship operating at the unconscious level. As Laplanche and Pontalis define it, 'one part of the ego [is] set against the other, so to speak, which comes for the subject to have the value of a model and the function of a judge.' (436) For Freud, it involved a form of identification with and internalization of the super-ego of the parents, in particular the prohibitions of incest with the parents associated with the Oedipus complex. With the decline of the Oedipus and the successful setting up of this prohibition within the unconscious, the child is set to negotiate the regulatory mechanisms of our culture: education, morality, the law.

One of the most influential of Freud's ideas on the super-ego is that no primary object is ever given up; instead of being renounced, it is introjected. As he put it: 'It may be that this identification [that is, introjection of the object] is the sole condition under which the id can give up its objects.' (*The Ego and the Id*, PF 11: 368) For Freud, for whom, as I have said, the pre-Oedipal relation with the mother was of secondary importance, the father was the primary object of desire and, on introjection, stood as prototype of all subsequent authority figures. Hence his preoccupation, from the 1920s in particular, with forms of religious and political behaviour which demonstrate reactions to paternalistic authority.

The super-ego exacts a harsh, punitive toll in Freudian terms: it 'rages . . . cruelly' against the ego (PF 12: 139); the child has to learn to renounce aggression, but 'every piece of aggression whose satisfaction the subject gives up is taken over by the super-ego and increases the latter's aggressiveness (against the ego)' (PF 12: 321). The severity of the super-ego may not necessarily be in direct relation to that of the parents. Some Freudian theorists have even argued that it may be in inverse proportion to theirs (Laplanche and Pontalis 438). Whichever way, there seems little doubt that, as Lacan put it, glossing Freud in *Civilization and its Discontents*, the super-ego 'operates according to an economy such that the more one sacrifices to it, the more it demands' (*Seminar* 7: 302).

A harsh, crippling force of authority was often explored in the Victorian novel, sometimes in the form of literal fathers, as in Dickens' *Dombey and Son*, Edmund Gosse's *Father and Son* or Samuel Butler's *The Way of All Flesh*. Alternatively, the inhibiting force was a more abstract institution, like the Puritan morality that left Maggie Tulliver no option but renunciation and death in George Eliot's *The Mill on the Floss*, or that which led Angel Clare to give up Tess in Hardy's *Tess of the d'Urbervilles*. In the modern period, with the decline of both Victorian morality and organized religion, authority tends to be still further internalized. An interesting recent exploration of a stunting super-ego can be found in Kazuo Ishiguro's *The Remains of the Day* (1989). Here, in the character of Stevens, butler at Darlington Hall before and after World War II, Ishiguro explores the way the imperatives of deference and duty may rage with savage cruelty against the ego, with devastating consequences.

Stevens' extreme obsequiousness is placed within a specific socio-historical context involving generations of initiation into concepts of servility. His every gesture and above all his language apes that of what he calls 'the most distinguished gentlemen of the land' (227), whom he and his kind serve. When talking to his father, which, through 'mutual embarrassment' (64), he does very little in spite of the fact that the two work together at the end of the old man's career, Stevens addresses him in a strait-laced third person:

> His lordship [Lord Darlington] is of the view, as indeed I am myself, that while Father is allowed to continue with his present round of duties, he represents an ever-present threat to the smooth running of this household (Ishiguro 65).

(For himself, Stevens usually uses the self-evasive, class-arrogant 'one' rather than the first person.) Stevens Senior, for all the 'embarrassment', is the immediate model for his son's emotional and linguistic sterility. As the latter records it, proudly, his father succeeded so completely in subordinating his personal feelings to the duty of professionalism that he was able to serve, with special commendation, a Colonel who had wantonly caused the death of his eldest son. Stevens Senior betrays 'no emotion whatsoever' (65) when told of his removal from the position of service to which he has dedicated a lifetime; he proceeds, like an automaton, to perform the lesser duties until he drops. His final hours are given in a characteristic Ishiguro cameo:

> my father's figure could be seen frozen in a posture that suggested he was taking part in some ceremonial ritual. He had dropped down on to one knee and with head bowed seemed to be pushing at the trolley before him, which for some reason had taken on an obstinate immobility. Two chambermaids were standing at a respectful distance, watching his efforts in some awe. (93)

For Freud, it is not so much the parents' advice or example but rather *their super-ego* which is introjected. As he puts it in one of the *New Introductory Lectures on Psychoanalysis*:

> a child's super-ego is in fact constructed on the model not of its parents but of its parents' super-ego; the contents which fill it are the same and it becomes the vehicle of tradition and of all the time-resisting judgements of value which have propagated themselves in this manner from generation to generation. (PF 2: 99)

The 'tradition' of Stevens' dedication to service is given in Ishiguro's novel in ever-deepening layers, reaching down to the most basic of historical and cultural forces. Behind the model of his father, Stevens looks to the standards of the 'Hayes Society' for butlers, which admitted those of 'only the very first rank' (Ishiguro 31). The society stipulated that its members, who were very few in number, must be 'attached to a distinguished household' (32), and Stevens spends much of the book speculating on the meaning of 'distinction', 'dignity' and 'calibre' as a guide to demeanour. Significantly, his definitions have to do not so much with moral criteria as with 'a professional being he inhabits' (42). That is, it involves the literal internalization (what he 'inhabits') of the imperative of submission to the hierarchy of class, obliterating not only personal emotion or need (what he elsewhere calls 'not removing one's clothing in public' [210]) but also all moral judgement of the employer's ethos.

Lord Darlington represents the risks of submission to another kind of super-ego. Stevens' narrative is played out against a background of rising fascism in Europe in the 1920s–30s in which Lord Darlington, for all his gentlemanly 'dignity', plays a prominent role. The insidiousness of Darlington's quiet attempts to further the German cause in Britain, which include the dismissal of two of his Jewish maids, washes over Stevens' head as he bristles with inflated pride at being 'at the very fulcrum of great affairs' (139), in contact with 'those great gentlemen who further the cause of humanity' (138). As a fascist sympathizer, Darlington displays a phenomenon of group psychology whereby individuals, as Freud puts it, have 'introduced the same person', a strong leader, 'into their super-ego and, on the basis of this common element, have identified themselves with one another in their ego' (PF 2: 99). The 'same person' in this case, Hitler, forms the bond of identification for Darlington and his cronies as they sit over port and cigars debating the evils of democracy, with the willing Stevens the butt of their jokes. As with Jean Brodie in Muriel Spark's *The Prime of Miss Jean Brodie* (1961), Darlington's fascist super-ego rages so savagely that it leaves behind only the wreck of a ruined ego.

In resorting to an over-harsh super-ego, each in their different ways, both Stevens and his employer are attempting, as Freud would put it, to 'render [their] desire for aggression innocuous'. Turned in upon them, the aggression is 'sent back to where it came from – that is, it is directed towards [their] own ego' (PF 12: 315). Freud explains that with the identification with the father, a form of 'desexualization' takes place, after which

> the erotic component no longer has the power to bind the whole of the destructiveness that was combined with it, and this is released in the form of an inclination to aggression and destruction. This defusion would be the source of the general character of harshness and cruelty exhibited by the ideal – its dictatorial 'Thou shalt'. (PF 11: 396)

Both Stevens and Darlington have dedicated themselves to the 'renunciation of instinct' (PF 12: 286); sexuality and women are noticeably left out of account in the novel. Who was and what became of Stevens' mother, for example? Why did Lord Darlington never marry? Here, we could say, is a classic example of the way masculinity can be seen to be inhabited by repressed femininity, a phenomenon which has received attention in recent feminist criticism. There are a couple of arresting moments when the 'feminine' breaks through this arid, masculine setting. One is when Miss Kenton, the housekeeper whose love Stevens is pitilessly incapable of acknowledging, brings flowers into his cell-like room (a replica, incidentally, of his father's [52 and 64]). The other occurs when (at his father's death, or after meeting Miss Kenton again many years later) emotion breaks eerily through his facial mask to be noticed by others. His *own* narrative at these moments, however, continues blank and inscrutable to the last. One of the greatest illusions of the novel is Miss Kenton's, that Stevens is always 'pretend[ing]' (154). There is no deception in Stevens' act. The dictates of the super-ego do not *repress* Stevens' emotions; they have *replaced* them. Appallingly, there is nothing there when the clothing is finally removed in public.

LOSS AND MOURNING IN DEREK WALCOTT'S *OMEROS*

The ability to love, so lacking in Stevens, is relative to the successful negotiation of early object relations; the ego has to balance the dictates of the super-ego against those of the id. Or, put in Kleinian terms, it involves the ability to set up a 'good breast' without excessive idealization. Idealization, she stresses, is a defence established against the threat of persecution.[7] (The term 'ego-ideal', it is worth remembering, was sometimes used by Freud synonymously with 'super-ego'.)[8]

For Freud himself, however, objects were not so much good or bad as forever lost. His description in 'Beyond the Pleasure Principle' of the infant's attempts at reparation of early object loss has become a founding moment in contemporary cultural theory. He happened, one day, to notice his eighteen-month-old grandson at play throwing a wooden reel into his curtained cot, out of sight, and then drawing it out again by an attached string. Each time it was thrown in, the child uttered a sound that was identified as 'fort' (gone); each time it was retrieved, he gave a joyful 'da' (here it is). This game of disappearance and return, Freud recognized, was a representation of the child's anxiety at separation from the mother and its attempt, through repetition, to 'master' the loss. He also noticed that it was the first, painful part of the game, the loss, that was performed more frequently. It was from evidence like this that he was to formulate his theory that there is an instinct working 'beyond' the pleasure principle, against the life drive and towards death. This idea, fundamental to all of Freud's late work, will be examined more closely in a later chapter.

Freud's preoccupation with lost objects received its most detailed elaboration in his paper on 'Mourning and Melancholia' published in

1917 (three years before 'Beyond the Pleasure Principle'). Both conditions of mourning and the similar but more serious melancholia, what would today be called depression, have to do with reactions to an early object loss. The difference between the two is that mourning is a reaction to a real object loss, usually the death of someone close, whereas the melancholic 'knows *whom* he has lost but not *what* he has lost in him' (PF 11: 254). His loss, in other words, has become unconscious. The melancholic's erotic cathexis in regard to the object undergoes a 'double vicissitude'. Part of it has regressed from object choice to *identification* with the object. And the other part, through ambivalence, has regressed to the stage of sadism (PF 11: 261). The object, that is, may have been got rid of, but 'has nevertheless proved more powerful than the ego itself' (261). The 'shadow of the object', as Freud puts it, has fallen upon the ego (258).

Mourning, Freud states at the beginning of his essay, may be a reaction not only to the loss of a loved person but also 'to the loss of some abstraction which has taken the place of one, such as one's country, liberty, an ideal, and so on' (252). I want now to look at an example of a literary text which explores the implications of the loss of an abstraction like this, one in which the narrative is predicated on the perpetual non-presence of the object, its failure to come into being – or, in Freudian terms, its 'shadow' presence within the text.

Derek Walcott's recent book-length poem *Omeros* is a narrative of nation, Walcott's own native St Lucia in the Caribbean. Like many other contemporary works concerned with the post-colonial experience, *Omeros* presents nationhood as a pastiche of fragmentary representations: the colonial British rulers (in the presence of Major Dennis Plunkett), the ex-colonizing French, present mainly in linguistic vestiges, the black African origin of the St Lucian people (present in an extended fantasy of a return to roots), or their own Creole culture which contains but is not contained by its variegated history. Walcott highlights the effect of this cultural disjunction by setting the narrative against a backdrop of Homeric references to paternity, homeland, conquest and empire, borrowing names and incidents at random from the *Iliad* and the *Odyssey*, more often than not in order to disavow rather than reinforce the analogy.

But if the Odyssean structure fails, ultimately, to represent contemporary St Lucian culture, what the two narratives, Walcott's and Homer's, have in common is the representation of the way the object

sought, the mother/fatherland, is always already lost. *Omeros* depicts
the search for original objects as a masculine quest for both the mother
and the father. The maternal object is contained in images of the island
of St Lucia itself, which is compared in turn to nature and to the
female protagonist, Helen. Like her Homeric analogue, Helen is the
focus of all masculine desire. Her supple ('ebony' [Walcott 29]) body
flits alluringly before the gaze of her two rivalrous lovers, the fisher-
man Achille and the driver Hector, as well as before that of her
(ex-)employer Plunkett. And yet like her island, the victim of colonial
domination, she eludes the grasp of all of them. Her beauty, the
narrator suggests, 'is what no man can claim/any more than this bay'
(288). The following passage near the beginning of the poem gives an
indication of the way the many strands of mythological, historical and
desiring narratives are interwoven by free association, in a manner
similar to Joyce's *Ulysses*, an obvious parallel. Plunkett's gaze is
following Helen as she saunters across the beach wearing his wife's
cast-off yellow dress, and he muses on his research project, the history
of the British–French conflict over St Lucia from the seventeenth
century onwards. I quote at some length to give an idea of the scope of
the references as they float out and are drawn in under Plunkett's gaze:

> . . . Plunkett, following the butterfly's
> yellow-panelled wings that once belonged to his wife,
> the black V of the velvet back, near the shallows.

> Her head was lowered; she seemed to drift like a waif,
> not like the arrogant servant that ruled their house.
> It was at that moment that he felt a duty

> towards her hopelessness, something to redress
> (he punned relentlessly) that desolate beauty
> so like her island's. He drained the foaming Guinness.

> Seychelles. Seashells. One more. In the olive saucer,
> the dry stones were piling up, their green pith sucked dry.
> Got what we took from them, yes sir! Quick, because the

> Empire was ebbing . . .

> . . . . . .

> . . . Helen needed a history,
> . . . Not theirs, but Helen's war.

> The name, with its historic hallucination,
> brightened the beach . . .

> . . . Her village was Troy,
> its smoke obscuring soldiers fallen in battle.
> Then her unclouding face, her breasts were its Pitons,

> . . . for her Gaul and Briton
> had mounted fort and redoubt, the ruined barracks

> with its bushy tunnel and its penile cannon;
> for her cedars fell in green sunrise to the axe.
> His mind drifted with the smoke of his reverie

> . . . . . .

> He smiled at the mythical hallucination
> that went with the name's shadow; the island was once
> named Helen; its Homeric association

> rose like smoke from a siege . . .
> . . . after thirteen treaties

> while she changed prayers often as knees at an altar . . .
>   (29–31)

Characteristically, it is the 'historic hallucination' of Helen's name that haunts Plunkett, the way the analogy falls apart rather than holds; or, we could say, the analogy is overtaken by his lazy desire, distorted through the smoky haze of militarized sexuality ('bushy tunnel and its penile cannon'). But with not only the 'historic' but also the 'mythical hallucination/that went with the name's shadow', what 'story' can Helen have? As fabrication of the narrator's, Achille's, Hector's and Plunkett's desire, she is inseparable from their (and their cultures') myths of desirability with which she is encrusted. Like the 'perniciously elegiac' (311) photos taken by the tourists, which determine the island's image of itself (the village 'had become a souvenir/of itself' [310]), Helen 'and her shadow were the same' (97). As Homi Bhabha writes, in connection with the situation of colonial domination in Algeria:

> The ultimate referent – the Country, Nation, Honour – is never present to itself within the narrative 'in person'. The space of narration is asymptotic, which shows that the 'original' reference or Ideal is itself touched by fiction and constructed in a deferred narrative, as a form of repetition. ('A Question of Survival' 101)

*   *   *   *

If the place always sought (to have) is the enclosing maternal source, the 'motherland', it is with its would-be paternal occupant that the traveller seeks to identify (to be). In the Odyssean (Homeric) model, the traveller effects a perpetual *nostos*, an imaginary return, to the homeland. This 'nostalgia', the condition of mourning or melancholia, propels him to return always to occupy the maternal space, even if that space, as the *Odyssey* shows, is both misremembered and (on return) misrecognized. As Jina Politi argues in relation to the island as the place of ultimate return in the Greek imaginary,

> the Island, that breast in the midst of a liquid abyss, at once memory and anticipation, becomes a trope of desire signifying the gaping void in the life of the mourning subject. ('The Lover of his M[other]land' 161)

Robinson Crusoe renounces his source and denies that he is anybody's son (Politi 161); Odysseus' son, Telemachus, observes that 'It's a wise child that knows its own father' (*Odyssey* 30). Achille, in the central section of Walcott's *Omeros*, attempts in a dream sequence to return to Africa in search of his paternal inheritance, of 'who he was' (*Omeros* 130). The colonial slave suffers a double dispossession, of both home and name:

> our only inheritance that elemental noise,
> of the windward, unbroken breakers, Ithaca's
> or Africa's, all joining the ocean's voice (130).

As slaves, shipped to different parts of the world,

> . . . each man was a nation
> in himself, without mother, father, brother.

. . . . . .

> . . . each carried
> the nameless freight of himself to the other world. (150)

And yet to recover the father as both name and presence, as Achille does, is paradoxically the ultimate loss. As we shall see in the next section, recovering the lost signifier (Name-of-the-Father), in Lacanian terms, means renouncing for ever an imaginary oneness with the primal object. To enter the fatherland of naming is to learn estrangement, shadows or reflections rather than substance, as Achille discovers in his dream of arrival at his father's river village in Africa:

> Achille, among those voluble leaves, his people,
> *estranged* from their chattering, *withdrew in discontent.*
> He brooded on the river. The canoe at its pole,
>
> doubled by its stillness, looked no different
> from its reflection, nor the pier stakes, nor the thick
> trees inverted at their river line, but the shadow face
>
> swayed by the ochre ripples seemed homesick
> for the history ahead, as if its proper place
> lay in unsettlement . . .
>
> Even night was not the same. *Some surrounding sorrow*
> with other stars that had no noise of waves
> thickened in silence. At dawn he heard a cock crow
>
> in his head, and woke, not knowing where he was.
> *The sadness sank into him slowly that he was home –*
> that dawn-sadness which ghosts have for their graves,
>
> because the future reversed itself in him.
> He was his own memory, the shadow under the pier.
> His nausea increased, he walked down to the cold river
>
> with the other shadows, saying, 'Make me happier,
> make me forget the future.' (140–41, emphasis added)

The beginning of this passage, dominated as it is by the inverted reflections of Africa (the canoes, the pier stakes, the trees) rather than Africa itself (which has been gained only to be lost) is a stark illustration of Freud's 'shadow of the object' on the ego. And then, via the images of inversion in the river, the concern widens to questions of the ego in time, reflecting back to the past in order to project forward to the future. In Africa, Achille later muses, 'he had been his own father and his own son' (275), his own past and future, named to be lost. And as with time, so with space. It is now St Lucia, with its 'noise of waves' and its cock crow, which is the lost homeland, replacing the previously lost African village, suggesting an endless series of replacements of lost objects, signifiers seeking the lost signified. The 'proper place' of all mourning subjects, the poem shows, 'l[ies] in unsettlement' (140).

CASTRATION AND THE SIGNIFIER

In recent years, interesting work has been done by feminist critics on the gender implications of nostalgia. Freud's theory, exemplified (in his essay on the 'Uncanny') in the common saying that 'Love is home-sickness' (PF 14: 368), is predicated upon a masculine desire for the recovery of the maternal body. But what happens if the desiring subject is feminine? The problem with this question is immediately obvious in my necessary choice of the adjectives 'masculine' and 'feminine' rather than 'male' and 'female', to allow for the fact, insisted on by Freud himself and referred to earlier in this chapter, of the multiple and shifting possibilities of sexual identification and object choice by both sexes.

This is not to say that for Freud the sexual divide was perpetually dissoluble. For him there is an originary moment of division which comes about through a visual experience: the sight of the female genitalia, which produces in the boy the fear of losing his and in the girl the shame at the inferiority of hers (or envy of his).[9] (That this happens by 'deferred effect' [PF 1: 359], a construction after the event, makes it no less potent.) Lacan endorsed the concept of castration as instituting this primary moment of division between the sexes, but for him, as Jane Gallop observes, the distinction is less between the threat of loss and an awareness of deprivation than between threat and 'nostalgia'. As Gallop puts it,

Man's desire will henceforth be linked by law to a menace; but woman's desire will legally cohabit with nostalgia: she will not be able to give up her desire for what she can never have (again). (*Reading Lacan* 146)

The implications of this new construction of the gender distinction are suggestive for feminist criticism, as Mary Jacobus shows in her application of Gallop on Lacan to a reading of Adrienne Rich's 'Transcendental Etude' (*First Things* 20–21).

Castration and its corollary, penis envy, is the one subject guaranteed to draw an angry divide between feminist and non-feminist readings of Freud and Lacan. Freud's tendency towards biological reductionism, characteristic of his time, led, especially in the first wave of feminism in the late 1960s and early '70s, to the misconception that he was prescribing female sexuality rather than simply offering a description of what he saw in bourgeois Vienna of the 1890s. In her seminal essay 'Women's Time' (1979), Julia Kristeva makes the important point that castration for Freud was not a physical phenomenon but rather an *imaginary* formation, a matter of anguish, fear, or envy. A careful reading of Freud, she argues, shows that castration for him is a mere hypothesis, a postulation set up as 'origin' in order to explain the otherwise inexplicable castration phantasies so prevalent in neurotic discourse. As a hypothesis, she continues, it can be compared to the 'big bang' theory of astrophysics:

the reality of castration is no more real than the hypothesis of an explosion which, according to modern astrophysics, is at the origin of the universe: nothing proves it, in a sense it is an article of faith. (*The Kristeva Reader* 197)

For Lacan, the castration complex was not merely an 'article of faith' but the bedrock of subjectivity itself. It stood, on the symbolic level, for the moment of division not only between the sexes but within each human subject. If the sexual divide is posited on either having or being the phallus, as Freud argued, the subject has to learn, in Jacqueline Rose's words, that ' "having" only functions at the price of a loss and "being" as an effect of division' (Mitchell and Rose 40). Lacan's notorious privileging of the phallus must be seen not in physiological terms, but on the level of its symbolic constitution, as a 'specular image' of the penis (*Écrits* 319). What counts for him, as

Rose puts it (42), is not so much the perception of the presence or absence of the phallus; something can only be seen to be missing according to an already established system of meaning and value. What matters, rather, is what the phallus is held to stand for: prohibition (of incest), division, loss. It is this which constitutes the law, what Lacan called the Symbolic.

The process of symbolization is instituted upon a system of substitutions for loss; we make a symbol to stand in for the (missing) object (as we saw with the Africa as constructed in the dream of Walcott's Achille). Language, as a system of symbols, typifies for Lacan this process of endless substitution – for the missing signified. The phallus, as the 'privileged signifier' (*Écrits* 287), is the mark of desire, posited on the perpetual threat of loss or nostalgia for what has been lost (289). As Lacan put it elsewhere:

> This is our starting point: through his relationship to the signifier, the subject is deprived of something of himself, of his very life, which has assumed the value of that which binds him to the signifier. The phallus is our term for the signifier of his alienation in signification. When the subject is deprived of this signifier, a particular object becomes for him an object of desire. ('Desire and the Interpretation of Desire in *Hamlet*' 28).

One of Lacan's most well-known excursions into literary criticism, his seminar on Poe's 'The Purloined Letter', focuses on the conjunction and interdependence of these concepts of castration, the phallus, sexual difference, signification and the Symbolic. As a classic piece of Lacanian criticism, it has attracted much interest. I refer the reader particularly to Muller and Richardson's *The Purloined Poe* (1988), which reprints the major debates over the story and Lacan's reading of it – by Marie Bonaparte, Shoshana Felman, Jacques Derrida, Barbara Johnson and others. For our purposes here, I want to focus briefly on Lacan's reading of the story as an illustration of loss in its coincidence with the process of signification.

The 'letter' of the title of Poe's story has been stolen from the Queen by a duplicitous Minister who, hoping to use it to gain advantage, hides it in his room. Anxious for its return, the Queen employs the Prefect of Police, who is however, in spite of the minutest investigations of the room in the Minister's absence, unable to find it. The Prefect calls on Dupin, the brilliant detective of several of Poe's stories, who finds the letter straight away and has it returned, after substantial payment, to the Queen.

For Lacan, the story illustrates the endless circularity of the signifier/letter, its failure to coincide with any unequivocal, determinate meaning (the sender and contents of the letter are never disclosed to us), its 'preeminence . . . over the subject' (Lacan, 'Seminar on "The Purloined Letter" ' 51). 'Falling in possession of the letter – admirable ambiguity of language – its meaning possesses them [the characters]' (44). It belongs, as Lacan puts it, 'to the dimension of language' (35), the order of the Symbolic by which we are all constructed. Being 'by nature symbol only of an absence' (39), the signifier functions to 'displace' each of the characters who have to do with it.

How did Dupin guess the hiding place straight away? According, he tells us, to the assumption that the clever Minister would be sure to avoid all the most obscure places of concealment (which were bound to be searched by the conscientious police), and would place the letter in a prominent, open position. The average intellect, Dupin argues, 'suffers to pass unnoticed those considerations which are too obtrusively and too palpably self-evident' (Poe, 'The Purloined Letter' 20). By Lacanian extension, the 'proper place' of the letter, obvious only to Dupin (who stands in for the analyst), is the place of castration represented by the woman's body. Lacan describes the 'spot' in these terms:

> the name most likely to foil a beginner [in a game of map reading] will be one which, in large letters spaced out widely across the map, discloses, often without an eye pausing to notice it, the name of an entire country . . .
>
> Just so does the purloined letter, like an immense female body, stretch out across the Minister's office when Dupin enters. But just so does he already expect to find it, and has only, with his eyes veiled by green lenses, to undress that huge body.
>
> And that is why without needing any more than being able to listen in at the door of Professor Freud,[10] he will go straight to the spot in which lies and lives what that body is designed to hide . . . Look! Between the cheeks of the fireplace, there's the object already in reach of a hand the ravisher has but to extend . . . (48)

What is so obvious it cannot be seen must also not be named. The phallus, unspecified, is thus reinserted on the woman's body through the seductive play of phallocratic signification. What is lost, the phallus/letter, is returned to circulation, back to the Queen/the woman's body, from which it has been castrated. As empty signifier, the phallus, like the letter, is something to which meaning is ascribed by everyone but from which it is always missing.

THE DISSEMINAR ON POE

One of the most important challenges to Lacan's reading of literature has come from Jacques Derrida, whose own debt to psychoanalysis is profound. In a 1975 essay on Lacan's Poe seminar, 'Le facteur de la Vérité' (The Postman/Factor of Truth),[11] Derrida outlined his reservations about Lacan's postulation of castration as a factor of ultimate 'truth'. His objection is not to castration itself, but rather to its promotion to 'transcendental' signifier. Both men share the view of the signifier as empty, sustaining itself only by displacement. Thus Derrida pays tribute to Lacan's playful, punning style, 'constructed so as to check almost permanently any access to an isolatable content' according to a logic of signification which 'disrupts naive semanticism' (*The Post Card* 420).

For Lacan, as analysed by Derrida, castration is the sign of the simultaneous presence and absence of the phallus: the object of desire is always a substitute for something that was never present (the mother's phallus). This is expressed in Lacanian terms as a phallus always both 'veiled' and 'unveiled'. Derrida cites from a well-known passage in Lacan's 'The Signification of the Phallus', which writes that the phallus

> can play its role only when veiled, that is to say, as itself a sign of the latency with which any signifiable is struck, when it is raised (*aufgehoben*) to the function of signifier.
>
> The phallus is the signifier of this *Aufhebung* [lifting] itself, which it inaugurates (initiates) by its disappearance. That is why the demon of Αἰδώς (*Scham*, shame) arises at the very moment when, in the ancient mysteries, the phallus is unveiled . . . (*Écrits* 288; cf. *The Post Card* 480)

And yet, Derrida complains, this veiling–unveiling is set up as '*the* structure of the lack' (*The Post Card* 463, emphasis added). In this way it restores to the phallus, as well as to castration, 'a fixed, central place, freed from all substitution' (441), thus undermining the attack on the metaphysics of presence to which Derrida's deconstructive enterprise is dedicated.

Interestingly, three years before his essay on Lacan's Poe seminar, Derrida had written about Freud's view of castration as comparable and convergent with his own theory of dissemination. In *Dissemination* (1972) he commends Freud's essay on the 'Uncanny' for its demonstration 'without contradict[ion]' of *both* castration anxiety ('behind which no deeper secret') *and* 'the process of interminable substitution' in language (268n67). Dissemination deploys this same (non-) contradiction; it could be described, in Robert Young's apt phrase, as 'castration's rhetorical, its conceptually ungovernable linguistic effect' ('Psychoanalytic Criticism' 105).[12] As the affirmation of what Derrida calls 'the remarkable empty locus of a hundred blanks no meaning can be ascribed to' (*Dissemination* 268n67), dissemination is a theory of the convergence of language and psychoanalysis far closer to Lacan's than the trumpeted differences between the two thinkers would allow us to believe. In fact, Derrida's 'Disseminar' on 'The Purloined Letter'. as Barbara Johnson punningly calls it (Muller and Richardson 226), would perhaps in his estimation be underpinned by a more faithful 'return to Freud' than that of his older rival. Whether Lacan would have accepted this claim, however, is another matter. Each, clearly, had his own Freud.

*   *   *   *

From the time of what Derrida appropriately calls Freud's 'legend' of the wooden reel ('Coming into One's Own' 115), it has been objects as much as subjects which constitute the field of debate in psychoanalysis. We could summarize the course of this debate as a series of postulations of substitutes for lack – whether these be inanimate objects (a reel) or the words for them (fort, da), whole objects (the mother), or part objects (the breast, the phallus). Lacan's view on this debate, as we might expect, is that all objects are part objects,[13] not in the sense of being part of a whole, 'but because they represent only partially the function that produces them' (*Écrits* 315). As a function of separation and lack, they found the signifying relationship. These, as we have seen, Lacan called '*objets petit a*' (the 'a' standing for *autre* [other]).[14]

In her *Tales of Love* (1983), Julia Kristeva quotes from this section of Lacan's work in an attempt to position her own view of object love – what she calls 'an objectality in the process of being established rather than in the absolute of the reference to the Phallus as such' (30). In the next chapter I shall be examining Kristeva's radical re-reading of Freud and Klein, as well as of Lacan. Curiously, in her theory of the maternal imaginary it was again to be an 'a' which would make the difference: in the formulation not of an 'object', but of an 'abject'.

3

Abjection and the Melancholic Imaginary

Julia Kristeva is a writer for our time. Through linguistics and (post-)structuralism, psychoanalysis and fiction, her writing has directed many of the most significant developments in recent cultural theory. One of the attractions of her work, for our purposes here, lies in its subtle synthesis and development of the psychoanalytic work of both Klein and Lacan, no mean feat given the variance usually emphasized between these two most influential of Freud's followers. Where this conjunction becomes most fruitful is in the area of object relations.

This is particularly the case in Kristeva's more recent theoretical work: *Powers of Horror* (first published in French in 1980), *Tales of Love* (1983) and *Black Sun* (1987). In the first of these, she signalled her departure from the outward-looking political radicalism of earlier work by focusing on the narrower psychological question of the process of the constitution of subjectivity. Her description of this process is at one point significantly reminiscent of the work of Klein and other British object-relations theorists: 'the subject's constitution . . . is nothing other than a slow, laborious production of object relation' (*Powers of Horror* 47–48). Its difference from the British school, however, lies in the *manner* in which the subject is 'produced' by objects – or rather, in the very nature of these objects themselves. Jacqueline Rose has put it that Kristeva's is an object relations theory without the idea of adequacy (*Sexuality* 155), without, that is, Winnicott's insistence on the fundamental importance of 'good enough' mothering for healthy psychic development. Like Klein (and indeed Freud) before her, Kristeva regards objects as constituting an inextricable combination of circumstances ('reality'), memory and phantasy. She summed up this whole range ('gradation') of objects with which the subject has to deal as follows:

> do we not find a whole gradation within modalities of separation: a real *deprivation* of the breast, an imaginary *frustration* of the gift as maternal relation, and, to conclude, a symbolic *castration* inscribed in the Oedipus complex; a gradation constituting, in Lacan's brilliant formulation, the object relation insofar as it is always 'a means of masking, of parrying the fundamental fund of anguish' .
> (*Powers* 32–33)

In case this sounds like a vaguely compromising accommodation of all camps, Kristeva is quick to draw a distinction to clarify her position in relation to her debt to both Klein and Lacan. The *object*, she says, needs to be distinguished from the *other*, the former being that which the subject attempts throughout life to exclude or expel, the latter being that which has succeeded in differentiating itself, in setting itself up as 'outside'. (Kristeva's interest in these distinctions between outside and inside, expelled and unexpelled, forms the basis of her theory of abjection, as we shall see shortly.) For healthy development, the object, associated by Kristeva with the maternal figure or function, needs to be replaced by 'the paternal function', what Lacanians have come to call 'the big Other' comprising language, the law, paternal prohibition. As she puts it: 'A representative of the paternal function takes the place of the good maternal object that is wanting. There is language instead of the good breast.' (*Powers* 45) Speaking beings, Kristeva writes, are 'always already haunted by the Other' (12); language, once entered, enters us to coincide with our archaic phantasies and direct our primal drives. This is what Kristeva seems to mean when she writes, in clarification of Lacan's famous dictum, that 'the unconscious is not structured like a language but like all the imprints of the Other' (*Black Sun* 204).

MOURNING, THE MOBILIZING AFFLICTION[1]

The move from 'the good breast' to 'language', which is Kristeva's re-formulation of entry into the Oedipus complex, has a particular significance for her in relation to the theory of writing. From the time

of her early book *Revolution in Poetic Language* (1974), Kristeva has
been interested in the writer's psychic investment in language, how it is
that language enables or disables primary psychic processes. As is well
known she described these as emanating from the semiotic *chora*,
corresponding to the experience with the mother, and defined as the
totality of pulsating drives present in and potentially disruptive of all
representation. In more recent work she has, like many psychoanalysts
in the last decade, returned to Freud's theory of mourning, in her case
to examine the ways in which loss, both actual and symbolic, can in
fact be seen as a 'mobilizing' affliction, propelling the mourning
subject towards signification. *Black Sun* is about this process. Signs,
she writes here,

> are arbitrary because language starts with a *negation* (*Verneinung*) of
> loss, along with the depression occasioned by mourning. 'I have lost
> an essential object that happens to be, in the final analysis, my
> mother,' is what the speaking being seems to be saying. 'But no, I
> have found her again in signs, or rather since I consent to lose her I
> have not lost her (that is the negation), I can recover her in
> language.' (43)

Mourning is 'endemic with all speaking beings' (152), but in some the
trauma of loss can be converted into finding through the creative
process. Freud had called this sublimation. Klein, too, had referred to
the tendency by the subject to engage in the creative activities in order
to repair the good object destroyed by the destructive instinct.
Symbolism, she wrote,

> is the foundation of all sublimation and of every talent, since it is by
> way of symbolic equation that things, activities and interests
> become the subject of libidinal phantasies. ('The Importance of
> Symbol Formation in the Development of the Ego', *Selected
> Melanie Klein* 97)

Where Kristeva's view of sublimation differs from those before her
is in its probing *beyond* language or symbolization as libidinal conversion in order to confront what she saw as some more archaic
authority behind it. Naming the object is thus not the ultimate goal.
Something deeper, which she calls variously 'an unnameable domain'
or 'that *Thing*' (*Black Sun* 145), haunts all writing, 'hollowing it out',
bringing it up short against – nothing:

The mature writer . . . never stops harking back to symbolization mechanisms, within language itself, in order to find in a *process* of eternal return, and not in the *object* that it names or produces, the hollowing out of anguish in the face of nothing. (*Powers* 43)

So it is not the naming itself but the '*process* of eternal return' attempted through it which drives or mobilizes the writer. This is a crucial idea in all of Kristeva's work. Freud had argued that the child's fort/da enunciations *stood in for* loss (the lost mother). Kristeva extended this by treating language as a means rather than an end, a means whereby the 'impossible' or 'unnamable' is gestured at. And like Lacan's Real, which will be discussed in the next chapter, the unnamable is finally that which escapes representation, whose essence is always both sought and missed. Everything, Kristeva writes, 'points to the elusive nature of that *Thing* – necessarily lost so that this "subject," separated from the "object," might become a speaking being.' (*Black Sun* 145)

BECKETT: WARDING OFF THE UNNAMABLE

When Kristeva uses phrases like 'the unnamable' and 'Not I' in her work in the 1980s, as she does in a pivotal way, readers of Samuel Beckett's work are put immediately on the alert. Given her close interest in avant-garde writing, evident from her analysis of the writing of Mallarmé, Lautréamont, Bataille, Joyce and others in *Revolution in Poetic Language* and leading up to the studies of writers like Gérard de Nerval and Marguerite Duras in *Black Sun*, it can hardly have been an accident that she used these titles from Beckett's works as a focus for a discussion of various psychic phenomena. (She does in fact refer directly to Beckett in introducing the concept of the 'Not I' in both *Desire in Language* [148–58] and *Tales of Love* [41].) Beckett may at first seem an unlikely ally for Kristeva in her psychoanalytic explorations. He is known for his comic send-ups of psychoanalytic terminology and practice – the 'dog vomit jargon' (qtd in Baker xi) used in sifting through 'time's forgotten cowpats' (*Collected Shorter Prose* 10), and this in spite (or perhaps because) of his own two-year analysis with the influential Wilfred Bion at the Tavistock Clinic in London in the 1930s.[2] Freudian readings of Beckett's work have been tested since this time, often rather nervously in the face of Beckett's own ridicule of the process.[3] He was particularly cynical about the abuses of heavy-handed Oedipal readings. His postmodern characterization pointedly refuses antecedence of any kind, familial or cultural. In *Molloy*, the first novel in the trilogy, which I want to focus on in this chapter, Moran 'pride[s] [him]self on being . . . free from spurious depth' (*Trilogy* 113). '[I]f you don't mind', Molloy snaps, 'we'll leave my mother out of all this' (*Trilogy* 56).

Kristeva's particular focus on the concept of the unnamable, however, offers opportunities for a fruitful intertextual reading of questions of the role of representation, meaning and desire which clearly dominate most of Beckett's writing. In calling the third volume of the trilogy *The Unnamable*, Beckett was choosing to highlight what critics have recognized as the central preoccupation and paradox underlying all his work: the endless expression of the certainty that there is nothing to express.[4] The opening and closing passages of the novel run as follows:

> Where now? Who now? When now? Unquestioning. I say I. Unbelieving. Questions, hypotheses, call them that. Keep going, going on, call that going, call that on . . . (*Trilogy* 293)

and

> . . . I don't know, I'll never know, in the silence you don't know, you must go on, I can't go on, I'll go on. (418)

In between these, the text is played out along a metonymic chain of signifiers that refuse to signify, 'nameless images . . . [and] imageless names' (411), expressing what the Unnamable calls 'the compulsion I am under to speak' (303–4), 'to unravel my tangle' (317), 'any old process will do, provided one sees through it' (345), 'the terror-stricken babble of the condemned to silence' (357).

The effect of all this is of something beyond language's reach, a residue suggested ominously in Kristeva's blank term 'that *Thing*'. *Powers of Horror* describes the writer as a 'phobic' who uses narrative to ward off the unnamable – 'who succeeds in metaphorizing in order to keep from being frightened to death' (*Powers* 38). 'Narrative', she writes further on, is 'the recounting of suffering: fear, disgust, and abjection crying out, they quiet down, concatenated into a story' (145). This description, even down to the use of that favourite Beckett term 'concatenation',[5] reads like a metatextual commentary on the desperate trilogy narratives of Molloy, Moran, Malone and the Unnamable.

THE ARCHAIC DYAD

For Kristeva, object relations reach down to a level beneath anything envisaged by Freud or perhaps even by Klein. Her aim is at what she calls 'a deep psycho-symbolic economy' (*Powers* 68), a convergence of cultural anthropology, religion and the psychoanalysis of neurosis which she labelled 'the sacred'. It was here, beneath both historical and structural explanations,[6] that she came up against the relation of the subject to the mother, an 'archaic dyad' (58) both desired and feared, unspeakable, unnamable. Every sacred structure, based ostensibly on the worship of the Father and the Son, has this maternal function as its 'lining' (58). On one level, societies pay obsessive tribute to the dead father, seeking atonement for his desired (symbolic) murder. On another, secret and invisible level, they seek to return to that fusion with the mother which every aspect of culture has worked to render threatening and repulsive. Parricide and incest, Freud's description of the Oedipal, reinforced by Lévi-Strauss, is given a new twist here by Kristeva's depiction of the maternal. She elaborates further:

> What we designate as 'feminine,' far from being a primeval essence, will be seen as an 'other' without a name, which subjective experience confronts when it does not stop at the appearance of its identity. Assuming that any Other is appended to the triangulating function of the paternal prohibition, what will be dealt with here, beyond and through the paternal function, is a coming face to face with an unnamable otherness–the solid rock of jouissance and writing as well. (*Powers* 58–59)

The subject, threatened by a non-differentiation from the maternal body, which could 'swamp' it at any time,

> risk[s] the loss not of a part (castration) but of the totality of his living being. The function of . . . religious rituals is to ward off the subject's fear of his very own identity sinking irretrievably into the mother. (64)

Beckett's writing, for all its refusal of subjectivity, seems to call for inclusion within this context. First, critics have noticed the 'sacred' quality of his writing, the way its spare, symbolic structures, whether these be dramatic or fictional, invoke primal quests for salvation in face of loss, abandonment and fear. When Christian imagery is used in Beckett's work, as it is constantly, its effect is somewhere between the plaintive and the blasphemous, a voice repeating the terms in defiance of their inability to signify. Beckett's interest in the sacred, bordering as it does on obsessional neurosis, lends it a distinctive Kristevan quality.

The sacred is most literally treated in Beckett's work in his depiction of the dominant stages in Christ's life: the Nativity, the Passion and the Resurrection. It is these very stages, Kristeva argues, which attempt to provide image and narrative of primary psychic processes – of 'birth, weaning, separation, frustration, castration' (*Black Sun* 132). Christianity, she argues, set rupture at the very heart of subjectivity. Above all, the death of Christ 'offers imaginary support to the nonrepresentable catastrophic anguish' distinctive of melancholia (133).

This nexus of figures is used over and over again throughout Beckett's work. The most well known is probably the setting of *Waiting for Godot*, with the tree clearly suggesting a cross and the figures outlined against it a pattern of waiting-salvation-damnation-waiting in hopeless rotation. In the trilogy, the Christian calendar, condensing the key events in the life of the psyche, acts both implicitly and explicitly as a touchstone for the fading lives of the four main characters. That this is treated ironically makes it no less pointed – as the opening of *Malone Dies* shows:

> I shall soon be quite dead at last in spite of all. Perhaps next month. Then it will be the month of April or of May . . . Perhaps I am wrong, perhaps I shall survive Saint John the Baptist's day . . . I would not put it past me to pant on to the Transfiguration, not to speak of the Assumption. But I do not think so, I do not think I am wrong in saying that these rejoicings will take place in my absence, this year. (*Trilogy* 179)

In the final hopelessness of *The Unnamable*, the subject's aim is simply to 'go on' from beginning to end, to fill in time without gap or residue. The '*panting* on' of this earlier debatably more hopeful version in *Malone Dies* conveys the tormenting ambivalence of desire. To 'pant' is both a propulsion forward (expectation of something to come) and a dragging back (with exhaustion); all Beckett's prose follows this to-and-fro rhythm as his characters repeat the sacred names against a background of increasing unnamability.

Secondly, moving still further into a Kristevan ambiance, there is much evidence in Beckett's work of an obsessional association between unnamability and the maternal function. Maternity is, as Mary Bryden puts it in *Women in Samuel Beckett's Prose and Drama*, a 'dreaded life-inflicting potentiality' (134) in Beckett's work. When Molloy snapped at his imagined auditor to 'leave my mother out of all this', he was doing neither more nor less than what Beckett's texts themselves do in their defensive, often violent ejection of maternity.

And yet of all Beckett's narratives, Molloy's itself comes closest to a search for (the meaning of) that mother. It begins, in characteristic Beckett fashion, with the end of the cycle, which is the finally achieved return, Molloy having arrived 'in my mother's room' (*Trilogy* 7). The stated aim throughout the ensuing narrative is to find and return to his *mother* rather than her room. The replacement is significant. Once he has got there, the mother herself, as distinguished from her son's need for her, is deleted; her room is an adequate replacement for her body. This pattern of naming in order to unname (the mother) recurs repeatedly in the narrative and syntactic structure – as for example in the following denial (which, as every reader of Freud knows, is a form of admission) of the maternal bond:

> with this deaf, blind, impotent, mad old woman, who called me Dan and whom I called Mag, and with her alone, I – no, I can't say it. That is to say, I could say it, but I won't say it, yes, I could say it easily, because it wouldn't be true. (19)

A couple of pages earlier, he has explained why he calls her Mag: 'because for me, without my knowing why, the letter g abolished the syllable Ma, and as it were spat on it, better than any other letter would have done' (17). Although every 5–10 pages of Molloy's narrative are punctuated by the 'frenzy' (34) of the need to get to her, by his being 'harrow[ed]' (75) by the 'painful and thorny' (86) question of his relations with his mother, the matter is always deferred: 'And when I was with her . . . I left her without having done anything. And when I was no longer with her I was again on my way to her' (87). He never succeeds, he concludes, in '*liquidating* this matter of my mother' (87, emphasis added), although his purported failure is well compensated for by the relished violence of the verb.

MOURNING THE MATERNAL OBJECT

The ruthless nature of such resentment makes it necessary to go much further than a straightforward Oedipal reading of the maternal fixation in Beckett's work. These affects, I would argue, have more to do with mourning and melancholia, endemic to a greater or lesser extent with all speaking beings, than with the Oedipal. Theories of mourning, we must remember (those of Karl Abraham, Freud and Klein) have traditionally pointed to the way the affliction conceals aggression towards the lost object – as Kristeva notes (*Black Sun* 11).[7] Melancholia as described by Freud involves coming to terms with the introjected object, against which the ego levels repeated reproaches but with which it finally identifies. Sometimes, however, this object represents such a threat that it must be violently jettisoned in an attempt to maintain the clarity of psychic and bodily boundaries. This results when the lure of merging with the mother is so strong that it threatens individuation. 'I imagine a child', Kristeva graphically explains, 'who has swallowed up his parents too soon, who frightens himself on that account, "all by himself," and, to save himself rejects and throws up everything that is given to him – all gifts, all objects.' (*Powers* 5–6)

It was to these expelled objects that Kristeva gave the name 'abjects'. We experience abjection, she writes, 'only if an Other has settled in place and stead of what will be "me"' (10), only if there has been, as it were, an unlawful takeover of the ego. In this case, the stakes are so high that only the most violent of battles will enable the ego to survive 'separately'. For the body 'must be what the French call *propre'* – both clean and one's own. It must bear no trace of its debt to nature' (102) if it is not to be 'defiled'. Horror arises when the borders between subject and object collapse, when the edges break down and the body's contents flow out, threatening repulsive engulfment. Kristeva writes:

> It is as if the skin, a fragile container, no longer guaranteed the integrity of one's 'own and clean self' but, scraped or transparent, invisible or taut, gave way before the dejection of its contents. Urine, blood, sperm, excrement then show up in order to reassure a subject that is lacking its 'own and clean self.' The abjection of those flows from within suddenly become [*sic*] the sole 'object' of sexual

desire – a true 'ab-ject' where man, frightened, crosses over the horrors of maternal bowels and, in an immersion that enables him to avoid coming face to face with an other, spares himself the risk of castration. But at the same time that immersion gives him the full power of possessing, if not being, the bad object that inhabits the maternal body. Abjection then takes the place of the other, to the extent of affording him jouissance. (53–54)

ABJECTION AND THE SACRED

Religions, Kristeva argues, have always recognized the horror and threat of maternal defilement and have set up elaborate systems for its containment. Rites of purification accompany all religious structures, from pagan polytheism through to Judeo-Christianity. Following Georges Bataille, who had argued that collective existence is 'founded on' the act of excluding abject things (*Powers* 56), Kristeva traced in detail in *Powers of Horror* the way symbolic institutions of ritual have throughout human history been dependent on the 'scription' (73) of such exclusion of the maternal.

As anthropologists have noted since at least the nineteenth century, the opposition between purity and impurity governs the hierarchic order of most societies. Significantly, rituals against pollution are strongest in those societies where patrilineal power is weakest, where the maternal threat, in other words, is seen to be greatest. Most of these rituals have to do with dietary taboos, for food is, as Kristeva puts it, 'the oral object (the abject) that sets up archaic relationships between the human being and the other, its mother' (75–76). Setting up patterns of exclusion of certain foods is a means of holding separate those elements (blood, milk, urine, excrement) which designate the mother and which seek to penetrate the culturally-achieved 'proper' body. In what she calls a 'semiotics of Biblical Abomination' (90), Kristeva cites Leviticus 12 in order to analyse the way Judaic law is predicated on the importance of rituals of separation. In childbirth, the impurity, defilement, blood of the mother requires a sacrifice in order to establish her separation from the child – either a burnt offering and a sin offering if a girl, or circumcision if a boy. A 'being who speaks to his God' must be kept apart from the phantasmatic power of the mother, that archaic Mother Goddess who actually haunted the imagination of a [Judaic] nation at war with the surrounding polytheism. A phantasmatic mother who also constitutes, in the specific history of each person, the abyss that must be established as an autonomous (and not encroaching) *place* and *distinct* object, meaning a *signifiable* one, so that such a person might learn to speak. At any rate, that evocation of defiled maternality, in Leviticus 12, inscribes the logic of dietary abominations within that of a limit, a boundary, a border between the sexes, a separation between feminine and masculine as foundation for the organization that is 'clean and proper,' 'individual,' and, one thing leading to another, signifiable, legislatable, subject to law and morality. (100)

In abolishing dietary taboos, Christianity is distinguished from Judaism in its interiorization of abjection. The New Testament attempts to rehabilitate the oral. Jesus says: ' "Not that which goeth into the mouth defileth a man; but that which cometh out of the mouth, this defileth a man" (Matthew 15: 11)' (*Powers* 114). Henceforth, Kristeva argues, the emphasis will be placed on the inside/ outside boundary, with Christ's admonition being to 'cleanse first that which is within' (114), within our own thoughts and speech. And yet there is a division within Christianity, whereby this tendency towards the interiorization and spiritualization of the abject is undercut by that archaic instinct, the 'lust for swallowing up the [m]other' (118), a 'deathly drive' to devour, of which the Eucharist is the catharsis. Through the phantasy of devouring, Christianity effects its own division: communion sanctifies me at the same time that it reminds me of my defilement.

I OR NOT-I

Simply to list the titles of Beckett's works is to place his writing within a context of abjection: *First Love, The Expelled, Six Residua, Disjecta,* and above all *Not I.* His writing is riddled with images of expulsion (-pulsion and -jection are favourite suffixes), of things, mainly body parts or contents, that have to be got rid of. What clearly dictates this is an abject need to expel the primary object which threatens engulfment, to keep shouting 'Not I', as so many of his characters do.[8]

The range of grammatical and psychoanalytic meanings that can be attributed to the phrase 'not I' makes it an ambivalent nodal point of Beckett's work. Let us begin by tracing its polysemantic progress in the third novel of the trilogy, *The Unnamable*. Here, clearly, saying 'not I' involves at one level an investigation of narrative practices, in particular what it means for a narrator to say 'I'. Beckett was not alone in the 1950s in his challenge to conventional concepts of narrative voice and identity. As the novel moved out of the Modernist period, which had culminated in the work of Woolf, Lawrence and Joyce, among others, concepts of stable identity began to erode into a scepticism about the possibility of representing identity at all. Beckett has sometimes been referred to as the writer of anti-novels, for the reason that his novels seem to be preoccupied with *un*telling stories rather than telling them, with revealing the arbitrariness and absurdity of the conventions of truth telling, reliability, coherence and meaning on which the novel as a genre has traditionally depended.

So when the Unnamable says 'I say I, knowing it's not I' (*Trilogy* 408), we are clearly being asked to participate in a tragi-comic uncertainty about semantic boundaries. If narrators adopt a first-person mode, what is their relation to their characters? Where the nineteenth-century novelist generally replied 'omniscient and proprie-torial' to this question, Beckett clearly replies that the relationship is one of ignorance and impotence. I, the Unnamable, has unlike Malone given up all attempt at creating 'characters'. His problem is that this 'I' may also 'be' one of several names or characters lurking in the wings – Basil, Mahood or Worm in particular. Let us trace the progress of this doubt throughout the novel:

> But now, is it I now, I on me?[9] Sometimes I think it is. And then I realize it is not. (*Trilogy* 312)

> But it's time I gave this solitary a name, nothing doing without proper names. I therefore baptise him Worm. It was high time. Worm. I don't like it, but I haven't much choice. It will be my name too, when the time comes, when I needn't be called Mahood any more, if that happy time ever comes . . . But let me complete my views, before I shit on them. For if I am Mahood, I am Worm too, plop. Or if I am not yet Worm, I shall be when I cease to be Mahood, plop. On now to serious matters. (340)

(I shall return shortly to the excremental side of this.)

But enough of this cursed first person, it is really too red a herring. I'll get out of my depth if I'm not careful. But what then is the subject? Mahood? No, not yet. Worm? Even less. Bah, any old pronoun will do, provided one sees through it. (345)

I don't know where I end . . . These stories of Mahood are ended. He has realised they could not be about me . . . Worm . . . To think I saw in him, if not me, a step towards me! To get me to be he, the anti-Mahood. (348–49)

In the meantime no sense in bickering about pronouns and other parts of blather. The subject doesn't matter, there is none. (363)

This 'blather' about pronouns, touching sardonically on but never really engaging with fundamental ontological questions, begins about half way through *The Unnamable* to turn into the more postmodern question of the role of language in signification. From a linguistic convention, a signifier which misses its mark, the 'I' becomes that which is held in thrall by others – 'they', who dictate the terms of its use and rob it of its individual ownership. 'Is there a single word of mine in all I say?' (350), the Unnamable wonders, anticipating by nearly two decades the arguments that were to be put forward in the late sixties by Roland Barthes for the 'death of the author'. What Barthes would come to call the 'tissue of quotations' ('Death of the Author' 146) which makes up the storehouse of a writer's repertoire Beckett calls 'the voices and thoughts of the devils who beset me' (350). These voices, mimicking conventions of pronoun consistency, have the Unnamable say that 'since I couldn't be Mahood, as I might have been, I must be Worm, as I cannot be.' (350)

However, traces of nostalgia for authenticity remain:

I imagine I hear myself saying, myself at last, to myself at last, that it can't be they, speaking thus, that it can only be I speaking thus. Ah if I could only find a voice of my own, in all this babble. (351)

Trouble arises when he is silent, for silence reveals the yawning chasm ('these gulfs' [351]) of unsignifiability beneath the babble. Neither he nor 'they' dare be silent for long, as 'the whole fabrication might collapse' (351). And yet as soon as he starts talking, guilt about his complicity with 'their' manipulations returns:

Did they ever get Mahood to speak? It seems to me not. I think Murphy spoke now and then, the others too perhaps, I don't remember, but it was clumsily done, you could see the ventriloquist. (351)

What distinguishes Beckett's view of ventriloquism from Barthes', what perhaps makes him late modernist rather than postmodern, is both this guilt and a psychic anxiety about the 'gulfs' beneath words. Immediately after exposing language (in this next instance, the fashionable jargon of existentialist philosophy) as a set of arbitrary signifiers, all surface, he 'falls' into a terrifying but desirable phantasy of a pre-Oedipal space beyond or beneath language, where he is safe and protected, where Worm might 'be':

> all their balls about being and existing. Yes, now that I've forgotten who Worm is, where he is, what he's like, I'll begin to be he. Anything rather than these college quips. *Quick, a place. With no way in, no way out, a safe place. Not like Eden. And Worm inside. Feeling nothing, knowing nothing, capable of nothing, wanting nothing.* Until the instant he hears the sound that will never stop. Then it's the end. Worm no longer is. We know it, but we don't say it, we say it's the awakening, the beginning of Worm, for now we must speak, and speak of Worm. It's no longer he, but let us proceed as if it were still he. (351, emphasis added)

The italicized passage in the middle here, embedded within the enclosing narrative, represents an anxious, guilty snatch at a 'not-Eden' (the denial is again telling). The moment of safe enclosure in a womb-like space with 'no way in, no way out' , beyond verbal or physical incursion, remains an evanescent and precarious utopia at the centre of Beckett's nightmare, in-between landscapes – before language takes up again to continue on its stupefying yet reassuring way.

Saying 'not I' in Beckett's work is always underpinned by this dark abject lining. It is as if the failure of the signifier (this 'I' that language uses to refer to me alienates me) collapses into something more psychologically disturbing, a disruption of the clarity of 'I *versus* not-I' which every infant has to learn to negotiate. Instead of facing up to accepting a relationship of separation from the object, whereby the not-I becomes an autonomous 'she', the Beckett character harks back constantly to the trauma of that break and refuses to give due recognition to the 'she'.

Kristeva, as we have seen, argues that the archaic dyad of mother and child, a threatening fusion, is based on 'the non-separation of subject/object, on which language has no hold' (*Powers* 58). From this point of view we could say that the 'I' is an achievement of language and the Symbolic order, representing success in breaking with the archaic dyad of the 'I am her' or rather 'she is me' of primary narcissism. The Symbolic, however, has only a tenuous hold on the Unnamable, whose 'I' keeps slipping out of place into the irresistible Mahoods or Worms or any other object that refuses to separate itself from him cleanly and properly. Primary loss involves facing up to the fact that the mother is not-I – as Kristeva puts it: 'Abandonment represents the insuperable trauma inflicted by the discovery – doubtless a precarious one and for that very reason impossible to work out – of the existence of a *not-I*.' (*Black Sun* 241) When the Unnamable says 'I shall not say I again, ever again . . . I shall put in its place . . . the third person' (358), foreshadowing the vehement refusal of Mouth in *Not-I* to relinquish the third person, he might seem to be resigning himself to the inevitability of regression back to pre-Symbolic modes. The last words of the novel, already quoted ('I can't go on, I'll go on' [418]), however, show him ploughing on in numb compliance with the necessity of using the bold vertical, the Symbolic's marker of identity.

Driving this point home, the text has the I's regression in *The Unnamable* taking place on a literal/corporeal level as well. It has often been noted that Beckett's characters are frequently depicted in infantile states ranging from supine inertia to foetal helplessness. They lie in ditches, cower in shelters or caves, stay in bed all day, are buried up to the waist or neck in mounds – or, as in the case of the Unnamable, are 'stuck like a sheaf of flowers in a deep jar' (329). Their physical state is trimmed to match. Many of them have trouble walking and some, like Molloy and the Unnamable, have lost a leg, reducing mobility to crawling. (Just before Molloy is rescued in the forest, he is depicted 'crawling on his belly, like a reptile' [90], in an act of double regression: adult to infant, human to reptilian.)

The Unnamable, one stage further on in his regression than the crawling Molloy and the bed-ridden Malone, will never move again ('unless it be under the impulsion of a third party' [329]). '[O]nly the trunk remains (in sorry trim)' (329), although there is some doubt about this, as he is at times described as having one leg and at others as being egg-shaped. His mouth is one organ that stands out – literally, as it is flush with the neck/mouth of the jar and is the only part of him visible from the outside.[10] In some ways, the Unnamable *is* his jar, the opening of each to what is outside it being conterminous. His life is literally 'insupportable' without it; food is fed into the top and waste removed from the bottom, by the proprietress of the chop-house. Sometimes he confuses himself with his jar, 'And sometimes I don't' (343), he says, in characteristic vacillation between attempted and failed separation.

THE CONTAINER AND THE UNCONTAINED (BECKETT WITH BION)

Beckett's obsession with jars (or any enclosing form) is strikingly reminiscent of a metaphor used byWilfred Bion, with whom Beckett was in analysis from 1934–35.[11] In his work with psychotic and schizophrenic patients in the decades after his treatment of Beckett (who was one of his first patients), Bion was a dominant figure in British object-relations circles, making significant additions to Klein's theory of the paranoid–schizoid and depressive positions, as well as that of projective identification. In the paranoid–schizoid position, the infant projects into the mother its fear and aggression, and then identifies with that part of itself in her, relying on her ability to tolerate these affects and transmit them back in manageable form. This process was called 'holding' by Winnicott, who interpreted it in terms of the physical relationship between mother and child. For Bion, the container (ultimately the mother's breast) was related to the contained (child) in a range of symbolic ways, reaching out, eventually, to symbolization/language itself, and could be regarded as one of the fundamental tropes of psychological operation.[12] One way in which this relationship can be detrimental to the child is if the container is 'damaged or porous' (Symington 55) and not able to contain the child, so that the frustration, guilt and anxiety of the child leaks out, and emotional experience is emptied of meaning. Whereas for Winnicott the 'holding environment' is positive and growth-producing, for Bion the relationship between container and contained may be parasitic or mutually crushing. The same applies to the relationship between analyst and patient, as well as that between language and meaning. When a patient told Bion that he couldn't 'take something in', Bion realized that this was no mere figure of speech. The container-contained configuration, he believed, 'may appear in a verbal formulation or in a realization, in a visual image or an emotional experience in one language but not in another' (*Second Thoughts* 141). Its implications, in other words, cross the literal and figurative boundaries repeatedly, and back again.

When Beckett put the Unnamable in a deep jar (or the three characters in *Play* in urns, or Nagg and Nell in *Endgame* in ashbins) which both stifles and protects him, which sometimes *is* him and sometimes isn't, it was as if his characters, too, had to test out the ambivalently holding or crushing potential of the enclosing form. Even if we leave aside the question of Beckett's own refusal to break with his mother, which most biographers treat as the source of his psychosomatic ailments,[13] we can say that the theme of containment has a breadth and depth of significance in his writing, acting as a fundamental locus of meaning, from its preoccupation with uterine containment or expulsion[14] to a concern with language and its ability or otherwise to contain meaning. As regards the latter, his biographer Deirdre Bair records a significant conversation Beckett had with Tom Driver in 1961 in which Beckett, characteristically describing the confusion of existence as 'mess', said that whereas in the past art had considered it its task to impose 'form' upon the mess, the situation had now changed and the mess could no longer be kept out – 'because we have come into a time when "it invades our experience at every moment. It is there and it must be allowed in"' (Bair 555). From aesthetic principle to dramatic image, Bion's tropes of containment and ejection, separation and merging, appear in Beckett's writing with insistent urgency.

DEVOURING MOTHERS AND WORDS

It is a short step from this Bion-oriented context to the Kristevan, which is hardly surprising given the debt to Klein which both liberally acknowledge.[15] When Bion wrote in his *Second Thoughts* (1967) about the way the object, 'angered at being engulfed, swells up, so to speak, and suffuses and controls the piece of personality that engulfs it' (40), he was using a vocabulary that Kristeva was to make her own in *Powers of Horror* thirteen years later. Engulfment is a dominant trope in her description of abjection, and its connection with orality, anality and flows makes it more than relevant for an analysis of Beckett's work.

The most obvious basis of this figurative nexus is the oral phase as described by Klein. From Freud and Karl Abraham, Klein had learnt that in the early pre-genital stages of libidinal organization, sadistic impulses of the child are paramount. The oral-sucking is followed by the oral-sadistic stage, and with this are associated aggressive, cannibalistic phantasies. Psychotic anxieties, she discovered, can frequently be traced back to an oral-sadistic relation to the maternal figure and the internalization of a devoured and therefore devouring breast. She writes:

> The anxieties derived from phantasied attacks on the mother's body and on the father she is supposed to contain, proved in both sexes to underlie claustrophobia (which includes the fear of being imprisoned or entombed in the mother's body). (*Selected Melanie Klein* 50)

Soon, urethral and anal sadistic phantasies are added to the oral ones. Klein stressed throughout her writing that the significance of this phase cannot be over-estimated.

> The sadistic phantasies directed against the inside of her body constitute the first and basic relation to the outside world and to reality. Upon the degree of success with which the subject passes through this phase will depend the extent to which he can subsequently acquire an external world corresponding to reality. (*Selected Melanie Klein* 98)

In one of the many definitions she gives of it, Kristeva describes the abject as 'the vacillating, fascinating, threatening, and dangerous object . . . into which the speaking being is permanently engulfed' (*Powers* 67). Further on, she calls it 'that non-introjected mother [that is, the mother not 'taken over' or *assimilated* as mental representation] who is incorporated [*ingested whole*, in phantasy] as devouring, and intolerable' (102). And in a move characteristic of both Bion and Beckett, she equates devouring the mother with 'devouring language' (40):

> Through the mouth that I fill with words instead of my mother whom I miss from now on more than ever, I elaborate that want, and the aggressivity that accompanies it, by *saying*. It turns out that, under the circumstances, oral activity, which produces the linguistic signifier, coincides with the theme of devouring . . .

and

> verbalization has always been confronted with the 'ab-ject' that the
> phobic object is. Language learning takes place as an attempt to
> appropriate an oral 'object' that slips away and whose hallucina-
> tion, necessarily deformed, threatens us from the outside.
> (*Powers* 41)

Many of Beckett's characters are orally fixated to such a degree that
their bodies have been whittled away to little more than a mouth,
whether that be the ambiguously memberless Unnamable with his
mouth flush with that of the jar, or Mouth in *Not I*. 'Here', the
Unnamable announces cheerfully, 'all is killing and eating' (*Trilogy*
343). Beckett downplays the psychic transparency of this statement by
setting the Unnamable in his jar between the shambles and the chop-
house ('the spot is well chosen, from my point of view' [330]). Molloy
vacillates between phantasies of cannibalism and a desire for engulfment himself: 'The daily longing for the earth to swallow me up'
(80–81). Threatened by abjection, the non-differentiation from the
maternal body, Molloy finally (that is, at the beginning, where all
stories end) succumbs to an engulfment by/merging with the maternal
body disguised as a defensive takeover on his part: 'I have her room. I
sleep in her bed. I piss and shit in her pot. I have taken her place. I
must resemble her more and more. All I need now is a son' (8).
Savage flashes of cannibalism and murder in relation to the
maternal object punctuate Beckett's writing in a near-subliminal
manner, affording his characters the only *jouissance* they ever know
– as with the following phrase, which I italicize, embedded in *The
Unnamable*:

> Ah! Where was I, in my lessons? That is what has had a fatal effect
> on my development, my lack of memory, no doubt about it. Pupil
> Mahood, repeat after me, Man is a higher mammal. I couldn't.
> Always talking about mammals, in this menagerie. Frankly,
> between ourselves, what the hell could it matter to pupil Mahood,
> that man was this rather than that? Presumably nothing has been
> lost in any case, since here it all comes slobbering out again, let loose
> by the nightmare. I'll have my bellyful of mammals, I can see that
> from here, before I wake. *Quick, give me a mother and let me suck
> her white, pinching my tits.* But it's time I gave this solitary a name,
> nothing doing without proper names. I therefore baptise him
> Worm. (340)

It doesn't surprise us when he finally faces up, at the end of his narrative, to the object of his quest: 'I'm looking for my mother to kill her, I should have thought of that a bit earlier, before being born' (395). The same repressed matricidal drive can be seen in *From An Abandoned Work*, a short piece of 1958, which I quote again at length to give the context of the seeming irrelevance of the sudden flash of savagery:

> Yes I believe all their blather about the life to come, it cheers me up, and unhappiness like mine, there's no annihilating that. I was mad of course and still am, but harmless, I passed for harmless, that's a good one. Not of course that I was really mad, just strange, a little strange, and with every passing year a little stranger, there can be few stranger creatures going about than me at the present day. *My father, did I kill him too as well as my mother*, perhaps in a way I did, but I can't go into that now, much too old and weak. The questions float up as I go along and leave me very confused, breaking up I am. (*Collected Shorter Prose* 133)

Phil Baker, a sensible Freudian analyst of Beckett's work, describes this murder reference as 'puzzling' (12), which it certainly is on the level of plot (the mother, until this point, has been not only alive but unusually present). In terms of the text's underlying matricidal (and to a secondary extent parricidal) drive, however, it is utterly consistent.[16] Matricide, as Kristeva puts it, 'is our vital necessity, the sine-qua-non condition of our individuation' (*Black Sun* 27–28).

BECKETT AND THE ANAL IMAGINARY

Beckett's texts display what could be called a massive genital anxiety, which they attempt to control by idealizing or unleashing partial drives such as orality, sado-masochism, or anality (see *Powers* 162). The anal, as every Beckett reader knows, is an obsessive point of return in his writing, which contains enough scatological puns and jokes to fill a separate book. Shit, as his characters like to pun, is 'serious matter' (*Trilogy* 340). In many ways this was a preoccupation he shared with Joyce, whose *Ulysses* has sometimes been described as an odyssey, throughout the day, through the digestive tract. Play with the materiality of language, such as the proliferating puns evident in both writers' work, is often regarded as being of an anal nature

(Baker 49). Swift, another Irishman, notorious for his 'scatological poems'[17] or his depiction of Gulliver being 'almost stifled' by the filth of Yahoos excreting on him from trees (Swift 238–39), was author of 'A Modest Defence of Punning'. Swift is, according to David Nokes, 'a fairly classic case-study' of 'obsessive [anal] retentiveness' (Nokes 372). He also seems to have shared Beckett's loathing for anything mammalian, as his description of the nauseously gross breast of the nurse in the Brobdingnag section of *Gulliver's Travels* shows (95).

This comes close to the spirit of Beckett's work. But where Beckett's seems to go one step further than Joyce's and perhaps even Swift's is in its abject lining, its phobic anxiety about the perviousness of borders which refuse to maintain the discreteness between inside and out, and about the possibility, ultimately, of sinking irretrievably into the maternal Thing. Leopold Bloom's digestive tract may be focused on as the organ linking the mouth and the anus. But Joyce's low comic celebration of eating and excreting has nothing to do with the kind of phobic *confusion* (or conflation) of the processes that goes on in Beckett's texts. As readers we become used to how a Beckett character description goes: the hat, the stick, the boots – the familiar Charlie Chaplin details, rounded off with a ferocious jab at the oral or anal aspect – or their conjunction, as in the description of the man whom Moran murders, who had 'a thin red mouth that looked as if it was raw from trying to shit its tongue' (*Trilogy* 151).

Part of the point of Worm, whose name is so different from the others in the trilogy that start with Ma-, is that the top is easily confused with the rear end. The Unnamable gets his mileage of grim humour out of this: 'look, here's the face, no no, the other end' (381). Or,

> I apologize for having to revert to this lewd orifice, 'tis my muse will have it so . . . We underestimate this little hole, it seems to me, we call it the arse-hole and affect to despise it. But is it not rather the true portal of our being and the celebrated mouth no more than the kitchen-door. Nothing goes in, or so little, that is not rejected on the spot, or very nearly. (79–80)

The real point behind the mock heroic here is surely less a Swiftian desire to degrade humanity (though there is of course an element of that) than a more serious obsession with the role of and links between these two 'portals' between inside and out. Most of Beckett's characters have difficulty distinguishing between poles, on a variety of levels: Molloy 'confuse[s] east and west, the poles too' (20), Moran makes a joke to his son about 'which mouth' to put the thermometer in (118), and Malone muddles (eating) dish and (excreting) pot until they become blurred. As the Unnamable puts it, 'I don't know where I end' (348) – meaning everything from his relation to his characters and theirs to him, to where his body starts and ends in relation to its jar, to, at base, the 'I' as opposed to the 'not I'.

Discussing body waste and 'waste-body', Kristeva explains:

> Contrary to what enters the mouth and nourishes, what goes out of the body, out of its pores and openings, points to the infinitude of the body proper and gives rise to abjection. Fecal matter signifies, as it were, what never ceases to separate from a body in a state of permanent loss in order to become *autonomous*, *distinct* from the mixtures, alterations, and decay that run through it. That is the price the body must pay if it is to become *clean and proper*. (*Powers* 108)

She then goes on to analyse the excremental abjection alluded to by the Prophets and the emphasis on the importance of the separation of food and dung: 'A mouth attributed to the anus: is that not the ensign of a body to be fought against . . . ?' (109). It is within this psychic context, then, that the abjection-driven Unnamable pays such lavish tribute to 'this little hole' (as opposed to the voracious, gaping mouth). Its virtue is that 'Nothing goes in, or so little, that is not rejected on the spot' (80). If the outside or Other can be kept neither entirely out nor entirely in, its incursions can at least be kept under rigid control. Like Bakhtin, whose work was an enormous influence on Kristeva, Beckett depicts a grotesque body (and psyche) under siege, the battle taking place at the borders between the body and the outer world, in particular the skin and orifices.[18]

FOOD AND FLOWS

Food in Beckett's writing is often an 'abomination' in the Kristevan sense of that which borders on defilement. It penetrates the subject's clean and proper body from the outside, occupying that borderland where order shades into chaos, the clean becomes filth. It is either an oral object that sets up the archaic relation to the maternal, like milk, which is all that Watt drinks, or 'me pap' that Nagg mews for from his ashbin (*Complete Dramatic Works* 96). Or it is 'mess', that 'compound between same and other that all nourishment signifies' (*Powers* 76). 'Remainders', Kristeva writes, 'are residues of something but especially of someone. They pollute on account of incompleteness.' (76) Picking over the leavings takes on ritualistic solemnity in Beckett's writing, where rummaging in rubbish dumps is more than the aimless activity of society's rejects that it at first appears. Molloy first meets Edith/Ruth in a rubbish dump, where he 'was bent double over a heap of muck in the hope of finding something to disgust me for ever with eating' (*Trilogy* 57). Eating is all about self-pollution or else being polluted by others. Molloy accuses the nurturing Lousse of trying to 'insinuate' substances 'into my various systems' (54). When one of Beckett's characters is placed in the position of receiving clean food and drink on a regular basis, his/her attitude is, like Molloy's, one of complete terror:

> My appetite! What a subject. For conversation. I had hardly any. I ate like a thrush. But the little I did eat I devoured with a voracity usually attributed to heavy eaters . . . I flung myself at the mess, gulped down the half or the quarter of it in two mouthfuls without chewing . . . then pushed it from me with loathing. One would have thought I ate to live! Similarly I would engulf five or six mugs of beer with one swig, then drink nothing for a week . . . I felt more or less the same as usual, that is to say, if I may give myself away, so terror-stricken that I was virtually bereft of feeling. (53–54)

As being human means being constantly threatened by engulfment, the only option is to attempt to master it before it masters you, to fling yourself at it, gulp it down voraciously, or, still better, to 'engulf' the mess before it engulfs you.

The logical sequence to the dish and pot, eat and excrete continuum is the sewer, which represents a further pouring out and away from the cosmic body, in a permanent state of loss. About half way through *Malone Dies*, Malone's character Saposcat, whose name suggests both rotting (from the Greek σαπρός meaning rotten or putrid) and things scatological, has his narrative terminated in 'favour of Macmann's, although the moment, like Malone's arse 'can hardly be accused of being the end of anything' (235) for it is accompanied by gurgles and flows of excretory continuity. The writing takes on sudden energy as

sewage, metonymically connected to both the river and the workers
spewed out from factories, gushes out to be devoured by the cannibalistic gulls:

> His [Macmann's] back is turned to the river, but perhaps it appears
> to him in the dreadful cries of the gulls that evening assembles, in
> paroxysms of hunger, round the outflow of the sewers, opposite the
> Bellevue Hotel. Yes, they too, in a last frenzy before night and its
> high crags, swoop ravening about the offal. But his face is towards
> the people that throng the streets at this hour, their long day ended
> and the whole long evening before them. The doors open and spew
> them out, each door its contingent. (230)

This, if the pun can be excused, is a foretaste of things to come. The
ending of *Malone Dies* picks up these flowing, oral-scatological images
and carries them to the ultimate point of abjection. Dominated by
intestinal release, it invests expulsion with a *jouissance* bordering, like
all abject literature, on perversion. It is at moments like these that
Beckett's writing joins with that of others like Céline, which Kristeva
describes as 'twentieth-century "abject" literature . . . that takes up
where apocalypse and carnival left off' (140–41). Discharge comes to
represent the site of mingling – of the clean and the defiled, inside and
out, life and death, begetting and dying, as Malone gives birth to
himself through an ambivalent 'cunt'/anus, unto death:

> And I? Indubitably going, that's all that matters. Whence this
> assurance? Try and think. I can't. Grandiose suffering. I am
> swelling. What if I should burst? The ceiling rises and falls, rises and
> falls, rhythmically, as when I was a foetus. Also to be mentioned a
> noise of rushing water . . . Leaden light again, thick, eddying,
> riddled with little tunnels through to brightness, perhaps I should
> say air, sucking air. All is ready. Except me. I am being given, if I
> may venture the expression, birth to into death, such is my
> impression. The feet are clear already, of the great cunt of existence.
> Favorable presentation I trust. My head will be the last to die.
> Haul in your hands. I can't. The render rent. My story ended I'll be
> living yet. Promising lag. That is the end of me. I shall say I no
> more. (285)

Giving birth to oneself, into death, is perhaps the closest the human
phantasy can come to the figuration of turning oneself inside out, of

attempting to expel something which one has incorporated and subsequently become.

Appropriately, the short scene that follows this near-end of self-parturition is dominated by a phantasmatic mingling of watery out-flows and unexplained violence. Abjection, Kristeva writes, 'is edged with murder, [just as] murder is checked by abjection' (150). Lemuel, the final murderer in charge of the *Malone Dies* narrative, propels his grotesque band of characters towards their end, plunging downhill in the waggonette towards the sea in birthing spasms. One of the grotesques is the 'huge, big, tall, fat woman', Lady Pedal, her 'bust flung back' with the violent motion (286). The narrative, as Kristeva puts it about Céline's writing, 'is always umbilicated to the Lady' (*Powers* 146). At the end woman, 'The brink' (144), is left (probably murdered) on the shore along with the corpses of her two 'sailors', as Lemuel and the asylum inmates drift out into the bay to the 'Gurgles of outflow' (289).

To the very end language, in its attempt to represent fear and horror, has been 'the only way out, the ultimate sublimation of the unsignifiable' (*Powers* 23). But as it yields progressively to the cry of horror, coinciding with the boundary subjectivity of abjection, it too must disintegrate, and the novel ends like this:

> Lemuel is in charge, he raises his hatchet on which the blood will never dry, but not to hit anyone, he will not hit anyone, he will not hit anyone any more, he will not touch anyone any more, either with it or with it or with it or with or
> or with it or with his hammer or with his stick or with his fist or in thought in dream I mean never he will never
> or with his pencil or with his stick or
> or light light I mean
> never there he will never
> never anything
> there
> any more (*Trilogy* 289)

Kristeva:

> If one wished to proceed further still along the approaches to abjection, one would find neither narrative nor theme but a recasting of syntax and vocabulary – the violence of poetry and silence. (*Powers* 141)

ENDING IN LIMBO

It is only in this way, through such 'recasting[s] of syntax', the 'violence of poetry and silence', that Beckett's works can ever be said to 'end'. Each end is always a 'going on'; to conclude is to mark where one text/body ends and another begins, to draw a clean line of demarcation. For the abject phantasy, the impossibility of marking boundaries takes the form of a perpetually frustrated attempt to do so. Beckett's trilogy, as I have tried to show, never moves far from the problem of where one person or narrative ends and another starts, what could be called an anxiety of nomination or pronomination. If *The Unnamable* is a narrative of quest for the right (pro)noun, the conclusion is, as the Unnamable puts it at the end, that 'there is no name for me, no pronoun for me' (408). All is overtaken by continuity or flows (or sometimes dribbles), whether these be the flowings on of language, endless verbiage, or the vast array of bodily fluids that gush, ooze or leak out of decrepit bodies. According to the logic of separation, as Kristeva puts it, 'it is flow that is impure. Any secretion or discharge, anything that leaks out of the feminine or masculine body defiles.' (*Powers* 102) The messy 'going on' from one text, body or pronoun to the next is the only *jouissance*.

After *The Unnamable*, published in the early 1950s, Beckett's fiction did the inevitable but seemingly impossible and 'went on', in spite of ever-decreasing momentum. By the end of the decade he was saying that he had given up all thought of writing for theatre and radio for the time being and was 'struggling to struggle on from where the Unnamable left me off, that is with the next next to nothing' (qtd in Knowlson 461), that is, with the text that would become *How it Is*. Maud Ellmann has called Eliot's *The Waste Land* 'one of the most abject texts in English literature' ('Eliot's Abjection' 181) for its preoccupation with waste and the in-between and its 'inability to close its boundaries or to void itself of other texts' (190). *How it Is* must surely deserve at least equal claim to this (dubious) distinction, plunging us as it does still further into an abject space, beyond the minimal props of the shambles, asylums and marine drifts of the trilogy, into an exclusively digestive terrain where the narrator's progress, in struggle and involuntary spasm, is through the human gut. Eaten but unable to be spewed, 'no going back up there' (*How it Is* 8), he wallows like a worm in an intestinal morass of 'mud' which is both the source of nourishment and its end product.

Here, as in *Krapp's Last Tape*, the digestive 'tract' is repeatedly conflated with the narrated one.[19] This is the climax of Beckett's phantasmagoria of anal creation, an idea that underpins his work from the beginning. Speaking of 'her who brought me into the world' at the beginning of the trilogy, Molloy describes the moment of begetting as occurring 'through the hole in her arse if my memory is correct. First taste of the shit' (*Trilogy* 16) Nearly four hundred pages later, the Unnamable is still harping on the same theme, but with a shift from babies to literary begetting:

> I'll let down my trousers and shit stories on them, stories, photographs, records, sites, lights, gods and fellow-creatures, the daily round and common task, observing the while, Be born, dear friends, be born, *enter my arse*, you'll just love my colic pains, it won't take long, I've the bloody flux. (383–84, emphasis added)

The vindictive glee of these passages bespeaks a significance well beyond the mockery of Modernist aesthetics, the high valuation of writing, that it might at first seem to be.

Pollution rites, as we have seen, can be discovered to be mainly about fear of the generative power of women. 'Fear of the uncontrollable generative mother repels me from the body' (*Powers* 78–79), Kristeva writes. 'But by means of what turn-about is the mother's interior associated with decay?' (101). Kristeva's answer is, once again, a remarkably accurate description of the otherwise inexplicable, phobic qualities of Beckett's writing. If birth is perceived as violent expulsion, a tearing away from maternal matter, this matter, persecuting and threatening, leaves an indelible trace on the psyche.

> One additional step, and one refuses even more drastically a mother with whom pre-Oedipal identification is intolerable. *The subject then gives birth to himself by fantasizing his own bowels as the precious fetus of which he is to be delivered*; and yet it is an abject fetus, for even if he calls them his own he has no other idea of the bowels than one of abomination, which links him to the ab-ject, to that non-introjected mother who is incorporated as devouring, and intolerable . . . Phantasmatically, he is the solidary obverse of a cult of the Great Mother. (101–2, emphasis added)

This, I think, is a very different matter from the envy of women's generative capacity sometimes attributed to male artists. Neither is this a question of simple misogyny (though perhaps misogyny is never simple). The Ma- prefix of so many of Beckett's characters, male and female,[20] is enough to signal that what is at issue here is as much identification (or, more accurately, 'incorporation') as expulsion. It is sometimes said that there is a 'relenting' towards women in Beckett's later woman-centred plays like *Not I*, *Footfalls* and *Rockaby*. This point seems to me less important than that made by Mary Bryden, that there is a 'sexual mutuality' (160) in Beckett's later work, where characters are 'randomly gendered bodies' (136) – according, I would argue, to a logic of abjection whereby what is being evoked is the maternal function rather than 'the feminine'. Like Jacques Lacan, with whose definition of desire, discussed in the next chapter, she was to concur, Kristeva argued that the category 'woman' can not in fact be said to exist.[21] The same could be said about Beckett's texts.

As Beckett's own life was about rejection – of his country, his (conscious) memories, his 'mother' tongue – so too his texts jettison as much as possible to clear away for an eerie spatial and temporal borderland, between inside and out, beginning and end, life and death. One can understand his liking for the word 'limbo', which he suggested as a subtitle for his story 'The End'.[22] Limbus, in Latin, means a border or edge, and by extension the edge of nowhere, oblivion. 'The End' is about (a memory of) 'a story [told] in the likeness of my life', a story 'without the courage to end' (*Collected Shorter Prose* 70). For ending means separating, which is the one thing Beckett's texts never stop representing their inability to do.

4

The Tragedy of Desire

If language, as we have seen, is constitutive of reality and meaning, it is desire which is its permanent condition. Desire emerges, as Lacan says, at the moment of its incarnation into speech.[1] And yet its fate is never to be incarnate in speech; it always passes beyond. 'Desire, a function central to all human experience, is the desire for nothing namable.' Flowing through the signifying chain, it flows beneath it as well, in the unconscious, and always either exceeds or falls short of its (linguistic) mark. It is, as Lacan's most famous definition puts it, 'a relation of being to lack' (*Seminar* 2: 223), the fundamental condition of human existence.

Although Lacan liked to argue that in this as in other respects he was following Freud, that '*Desidero* is the Freudian *cogito*' (*Four Fundamental Concepts* 154), it is hard to believe that Freud would have agreed with him. Desire was not a term Freud used in any central way. For him, it was a matter of libido, or of the 'instinct' or 'drive' (as the German *Trieb* is variously translated),[2] that semi-psychical, semi-bodily force which appears in his work as either (in the early phase) measurable biological energy or (later) a more figurative concept of relationships among forces.[3] But Freud prepared the ground for Lacan's definition of desire by his insistence that the object of the drive/instinct, what it aims at, is ultimately contingent or arbitrary. As he put it in 'Instincts and their Vicissitudes': 'It [the object] is what is most variable about an instinct and is not originally connected with it, but becomes assigned to it only in consequence of being peculiarly fitted to make satisfaction possible' (PF 11: 119). This original disparity between the drive/instinct and its object forms the basis of the Lacanian definition of desire.

Freud was more comfortable with the concept of 'pleasure' (*Lust* or *Wunsch*) than with that of desire (*Begierde*, as used by Hegel before him). The pleasure principle, as opposed to the reality principle, was for him (at least initially) a quantifiable ('economic') force, related to the increase or decrease of instinctual tension. 'Unpleasure' was caused by an increase in tension which the subject early learns to discharge by hallucinating satisfaction. Reality only takes over with ego development, and yet the subject is incessantly drawn to pleasure – or, rather, to the avoidance of unpleasure.

As a Victorian, Freud had regarded the harnessing of pleasure by reality as proper and necessary, if costly. For Lacan, two generations later, pleasure or enjoyment (*jouissance*) was a libidinal imperative, whose frustration, however, lies at the heart of human suffering. The subject, he wrote, 'does not simply satisfy a desire, he enjoys [*jouit*] desiring' (qtd in Evans 5). In lacking the satisfying object, desire endlessly pursues a phantom satisfaction, deriving *jouissance* only from the pursuit.[4] In his development of Freud's analysis of pleasure, Lacan chose to follow the direction mapped out by Freud's 'Beyond the Pleasure Principle', which led towards a 'beyond' or surplus that had more to do with death than with pleasure. Desire, propelled towards a *jouissance* that it can not have, is synonymous with lack. In *jouissance*, Kristeva writes, 'the object of desire, known as object *a* [in Lacan's terminology] bursts with the shattered mirror where the ego gives up its image in order to contemplate itself in the Other' (*Powers* 9).

By the time Roland Barthes came to use the word *jouissance* in the 1970s, libidinal pleasure is redefined to suggest an orgasmic abandonment as a positive good. In his seminar for 1972–3, Lacan had argued that it is the signifier which is the cause of *jouissance* (*Seminar 20*: 24). In *The Pleasure of the Text*, also of 1973, Barthes set about experimenting with ways in which desire can be written, in what he called 'the science of the various blisses of language' (6). 'How can the signifier cause bliss? Barthes' answer reveals his indebtedness to both Freud (on fetishism) and Lacan (on desire):

> The text is a fetish object, and *this fetish desires me*. The text chooses me, by a whole disposition of invisible screens, selective baffles: vocabulary references, readability, etc.: and, lost in the midst of a text (not *behind* it, like a *deus ex machina*) there is always the other, the author.

> As institution, the author is dead: his civil status, his biographical
> person have disappeared . . . but in the text, in a way, *I desire* the
> author: I need his figure (which is neither his representation nor his
> projection), as he needs mine . . . (27)

Having banished the author from the front door in 'The Death of the
Author' a few years earlier, Barthes here brings him in through the
back door in the form of the other. Just as for Lacan what we desire is
'*le désirant dans l'autre*', the desire both of and for the other, the desire
for ourselves by the other, so for Barthes, an erotics of reading
involves an experience of the ways in which the texts we construct
'choose' us, that is, reflect and give back to us our own desiring
impulses. Uncomplicated by Lacanian death and lack, Barthes' *jouissance* of language was an experiment of its time, when it almost
seemed possible to remove repression. A stricter psychoanalytic
agenda, however, would quickly reintroduce prohibition as the controlling force behind both language and desire.

OEDIPAL TEXTUALITY:[5] *HAMLET*

Arbitrary and undirected as it may seem, desire, for all its shifting
definitions, is far from untethered. Its bedrock, most contemporary
schools of psychoanalysis would agree, is the Oedipus complex,[6] even
though you are just as likely nowadays to meet the term with a
qualifying prefix (the pre-Oedipal, Anti-Oedipus, 'Beyond Oedipus').
It is not always remembered that while Lacan's most well-known
definition of desire is that it is 'the desire of the Other' (*Écrits* 264), the
necessary complement to this postulate is that the Other, 'strictly
speaking, is the Oedipus complex' (*Four Fundamental Concepts* 204).
In making this claim, Lacan was simply taking Freud's theory of the
Oedipal to its logical (Lacanian) conclusion.

Analysis of the origins of the Oedipus complex must inevitably
begin with that famous letter, a hundred years ago (in October 1897),
in which Freud wrote to Wilhelm Fliess about what he had discovered
during his experimental self-analysis: 'I have found love of the mother
and jealousy of the father in my own case too, and now believe it to be
a general phenomenon of early childhood' (Freud, *The Origins of
Psycho-Analysis* 223). In a characteristic move, Freud then transposed
this observation from the autobiographical to the mythical level,
drawing on his knowledge of literature both ancient and modern:

If that is the case, the gripping power of *Oedipus Rex*, in spite of all the rational objections to the inexorable fate that the story presupposes, becomes intelligible . . . Every member of the audience was once a budding Oedipus in phantasy, and this dream-fulfilment played out in reality causes everyone to recoil in horror, with the full measure of repression which separates his infantile from his present state.

The idea has passed through my head that the same thing may lie at the root of *Hamlet* . . . How better [to explain Hamlet's hesitation to avenge his father's murder] than by the torment roused in him by the obscure memory that he himself had meditated the same deed against his father because of passion for his mother . . . ? (223–24)

It was a move (from the personal to the mythical/literary) which was to characterize his theoretical work throughout the next forty years.

For Freud, the dramatic dilemma of tragedy, with its underlying history and its inevitable consequences, was a model of the clinical situation. Like the analyst, we as spectators are confronted with a mysterious crisis in both *Oedipus Rex* (the plague in Thebes) and in *Hamlet* (Hamlet's inability to act), and are called on to wonder about its causes as well as participate in the anguish of its development. The action of Sophocles' tragedy, Freud wrote in *The Interpretation of Dreams*, 'consists in nothing other than the process of revealing, with cunning delays and ever-mounting excitement – a process that can be likened to the work of a psycho-analysis.' (PF 4: 363) Oedipus, like the analysand, is made to suffer in ignorance of his responsibility. His every effort has been to avoid the oracle's prediction that he will murder his father and marry his mother. Having committed these crimes unwittingly, he can only stand back and watch in horror the appalling but inevitable outcome of his unrepressed desire.

With *Hamlet*, we are presented with a different, modern version of the trauma that was exposed and realized in Oedipus. In Freud's view, 'the changed treatment of the same material reveals the whole difference in the mental life of these two widely separated epochs of civilization: the secular advance of repression in the emotional life of mankind.' (PF 4: 366) The repression of basic drives, in Freud's opinion, is the hallmark of our modern age. It is what makes of Hamlet an hysteric, so that the source of his 'madness', feigned and unfeigned, becomes the dominant interest in the play. The necessary repression of the Oedipal, culture's refusal of our basic drives, incestuous and parricidal, could be (and has been) called the elementary alienating structure of the modern personality.

Freud's view of the Oedipal was to deepen as well as diversify in the decades that followed. By mid-late career (as in 'The Dissolution of the Oedipus Complex' in 1924), he was talking about it as if it were a universal in the unconscious itself, a phylogenetic phenomenon laid down by heredity, which crucially affects our social as well as our individual psychic structures. As we shall see shortly, in the discussion of *Totem and Taboo*, Freud's later excursions into psychoanalytic anthropology were dominated by this conviction that the Oedipus complex in the individual is of such a fundamental nature that it cannot help but overtake all forms of social behaviour and organization as well.

When he spoke of the 'dissolution' of the Oedipal, Freud meant what he saw as its necessary dispersal after its peak during the 'phallic' phase of childhood (ages 3–5). Failure to dissolve the Oedipal results in its repression, a repression, as Hamlet demonstrates, which has serious psychic consequences. In the traditional Freudian reading of Shakespeare's play, outlined at length by Freud's English disciple Ernest Jones in his *Hamlet and Oedipus* (1949), Hamlet's Oedipus complex has not only not dissolved, but has been given a violent boost first by the death of his father, which he had unconsciously desired all along, and second by his replacement by his uncle in his mother's bed. The intense misogyny of Hamlet's treatment of his mother and, by extension, of Ophelia, is part of his ambivalent and necessarily thwarted passion for her. The expression of love for Ophelia at her graveside has seemed to some commentators far in excess of his response to her earlier in the play: 'Forty thousand brothers/Could not with all their quantity of love/Make up my sum' (V, i). But this hyperbole has a logic of its own. Similarly, as Jones points out, Hamlet's aggression towards his mother Gertrude takes surprising precedence over that towards his uncle Claudius, who may seem to have done him a far greater wrong. From the start, his overwhelming grievance is his mother's misdirected sexuality.

THE FEMININE OEDIPAL

The classical Freudian reading of the play has been challenged from two different quarters within psychoanalytic criticism, each stemming from modifications to the Oedipal suggested by Freud himself in his later writings. The first can be broadly classified as the feminist reaction. For a long time Freud assumed that his model of the Oedipal, based on the little boy, could be applied with a simple sexual reversal to the little girl. Finally, however, under the pressure of persuasive evidence for a *pre*-Oedipal bond between mother and child demonstrated in particular by Klein in the 1920s and '30s, Freud came to admit that the maternal influence had been under-rated in his work and that for girls in particular, there is an 'original exclusive attachment' to the mother (PF 7: 389). As Jacqueline Rose argues, it is at this point, the point where the girl's desire for the father can no longer be taken for granted, that 'psychoanalysis can become of interest to feminism' (*Sexuality in the Field of Vision* 135). The full extent of feminism's challenge to Freud will be examined in Chapter 7.

For Oedipus to enter Thebes, as the Sophoclean version of the myth has it, he had to solve the riddle of then kill the sphinx, that powerful feminine principle barring access to desire. For feminist criticism, the traditional Freudian version of the Oedipus complex involves a crucial suppression or bypassing of femininity. Matricide, as Jean-Jacques Goux argues in *Oedipus, Philosopher*, is 'the great unthought element of Freudian doctrine' (Goux 27). In his influential study of *Hamlet* of 1919, T. S. Eliot argued that Hamlet's revulsion against his mother's behaviour exceeds its ostensible object. His disgust, he writes, does not have an 'adequate equivalent' in his mother, whose 'character is so negative and insignificant that she arouses in Hamlet the feeling which she is incapable of representing'. Being 'a feeling which he cannot understand', it thus 'remains to poison life and obstruct action' ('Hamlet' 145–46). The feeling not understood here, we could say, is Eliot's own refusal to recognize not only the primacy of Hamlet's maternal orientation, but also the complexity (that terrifying 'excess') of the implications of femininity within masculinity itself.

Freud's patients were to prove to him increasingly over the years that the Oedipal myth in its simple triangular form needed to be revised to accommodate a varied complex of multiple identifications. The little girl is emphatically mother- as well as father-directed; the boy's rivalry with his father is complicated by a ('feminine') identification with him as well. As Freud put it in 'The Ego and the Id' (1923):

> a boy has not merely an ambivalent attitude towards his father and an affectionate object-choice towards his mother, but at the same

time he also behaves like a girl and displays an affectionate feminine attitude to his father and a corresponding jealousy and hostility towards his mother. (PF 11: 372)

Freud's 'Wolf Man' case gives a striking example of the variety and multiplicity of a young boy's sexual identifications and object choices. Freud's patient, a Russian in his twenties, had as a young boy been terrified by a dream of wolves in a tree, which Freud interpreted as a fear of castration in association with a fixation on his father. The perversions of his adult sexuality took the form of a complex of rebirth and womb phantasies which Freud separated out into an incestuous desire for the mother (to be 'in' the womb again) combined with that for the father (the desire to be in the womb in order to replace the mother during intercourse with the father) (PF 9: 342–43). An unresolved conflict between the two incestuous wishes can result in neurosis. Most of us achieve some precarious resolution, but in all of us femininity and masculinity, homo- and heterosexuality, take shape then dissolve in an endless sequence of realignments.

Both the masculine and the feminine Oedipus complexes, then, are not a matter of separate, symmetrical triangles but rather the intersection of the masculine by the feminine and the feminine by the masculine, a lifelong reassertion of primary bisexuality and a recognition of the fluidity of gender identity. Freud's writing on the masculine and the feminine Oedipal, at its most intricate (especially in the famous case studies), provides a crucial model for the early challenge to stable sexual identity. Perhaps, in this light, it is not too far-fetched to restore at least metaphorical validity to the notorious suspicion among some Shakespeare scholars that, all along, 'Hamlet was a woman'![7]

PHALLIC DESIRE: LACAN READS *HAMLET*

If feminism, in particular, has excavated beneath the Oedipal to discover its pre-Oedipal strata, others, feminist or otherwise, have attempted to move 'beyond' Oedipus, via Lacan.[8] To move beyond is not to lose sight of. The Oedipal in Lacanian terms looms large but in a different form: that of the hugely inflated phallus.

Freud had initiated this development, too, with his argument in the 1923 essay on 'The Infantile Genital Organization' that for both sexes in the Oedipal stage there is only one organ, the phallus. Until a relatively late stage, the antithesis between maleness and femaleness does not exist in children. Gender antithesis for both sexes, as we have seen, is established on the basis of whether one has male genitalia or has lost them (has been castrated) (PF 7: 312). This *'phallic primacy'* (310), still highly controversial in psychoanalytic theory today,[9] became the cornerstone of Lacan's view not only of the Oedipal but of all psychic organization.

Lacan's reading of *Hamlet* is, as we might expect, a highly provocative one. It has particularly irritated feminist readers such as Elaine Showalter, who complains that when Lacan promises to speak about Ophelia he does nothing of the sort, except to refer to her as 'O-phallus', bait/object of Hamlet's desire (Showalter, 'Representing Ophelia' 77 and 92). For Lacan, above all in his work in the late 1950s when the *Hamlet* essay was written, the primacy of the phallus had to do with its signifying rather than its biological function. The phallic signifier is the mark of desire, that which is lacking or threatened. The tragedy of human love, he writes in 'The Signification of the Phallus' (1958), is that

> The demand for love can only suffer from a desire whose signifier is alien to it. If the desire of the mother *is* the phallus, the child wishes to be the phallus in order to satisfy that desire. (*Écrits* 289)

Thus,

> man [people?] cannot aim at being whole (the 'total personality' is another of the deviant premises of modern psychotherapy), while ever the play of displacement and condensation to which he is doomed in the exercise of his functions marks his relation as a subject to the signifier.
>
> The phallus is the privileged signifier of that mark in which the role of the logos is joined with the advent of desire. (287)

In some ways, Lacan's reading of *Hamlet* is consonant with the tradition of object-relations theory discussed in Chapter 2. Indeed, in 'The Signification of the Phallus' he refers to Klein as his source in investigating 'the fact that the child apprehends from the outset that the mother "contains" the phallus' (288–89). More specifically, he focuses on mourning as the central preoccupation of the play, asking the question 'What is the connection between mourning and the constitution of the object in desire?' ('Desire and the Interpretation of Desire in *Hamlet*' 36). The answer he gives is that 'only insofar as the object of Hamlet's desire has become an impossible object can it become once more the object of his desire' (36). It is the gap or hole that results from this loss which 'calls forth' mourning on the part of the subject.

With the decline of the Oedipal the phallus, the original lost object, is set up for lifelong mourning. In Lacanian terms, Hamlet's problem is that he is unable to give up 'being' the phallus for the mother in order to mourn, as he should for normal development, its symbolic castration. He suffers, in other words, from 'insufficient mourning' (39). His inability to avenge his father's death results from his reluctance to strike at himself in the form of the phallus, represented by Claudius, both his own replacement and the ultimate signifier of power (like Hitler, Lacan notes, another phallic leader whom no one could bring themselves to assassinate).

> The very source of what makes Hamlet's arm waver at every moment, is the narcissistic connection that Freud tells us about in his text on the decline of the Oedipus complex: one cannot strike the phallus, because the phallus, even the real phallus, is a *ghost*. (50)

But the ghost, we must remember, is the form taken by Hamlet's father, the original possessor of the phallus, Name-of-the-Father and representative of the law (the Symbolic). It is his refusal to stay dead which is the cause of 'something rotten' in Hamlet's relation to the world. In the rest of this chapter I shall be examining the implications, for the individual psyche and for tragedy as a genre, of desire's necessary investment in the Symbolic, as well as its relation to the Imaginary and the Real.

THE PROPER PLACE OF DESIRE: SOPHOCLES' *ANTIGONE*

For Lacan, as Malcolm Bowie puts it, desire is 'the mental fact *par excellence*' (*Lacan* 163). Its centrality derives, as we have seen in Chapter 2, from its implication in speech and the signifying chain, of which the Other is an inseparable part. Instituted upon lack (castration), desire is that 'impossibility' whose fulfilment is, never-

theless, constantly sought. In a notorious definition in 'The Signification of the Phallus', Lacan calls desire

> neither the appetite for satisfaction ['need'], nor the demand for
> love, but the difference that results from the subtraction of the first
> from the second, the phenomenon of their splitting (*Spaltung*).
> (*Écrits* 287)

Desire is not need; it is crucial to distinguish, he writes, 'the paradoxical, deviant, erratic, eccentric, even scandalous character by which
it is distinguished from need' (286). Nor is it the demand (for
unconditional love, for presence), the request for satisfaction via
language. It makes itself felt in the residue after the subtraction of
need from demand. It is 'the power of pure loss' (287).

Tragedy, long recognized as the genre which lays bare the conflict
('splitting', what's left over) in human desire, lends itself naturally to a
Lacanian reading. Lacan himself dedicated several of his seminars to
tragedy, returning in particular to that founding moment in psychoanalysis, Freud's recognition via Sophocles of the Oedipus complex.
Through his reassessment of not only *Oedipus Rex* but also the other
two 'Theban' plays, *Oedipus at Colonus* and *Antigone*, Lacan mapped
out in detail his triadic structure of intersubjectivity: the Imaginary,
the Symbolic and the Real. These difficult, polysemic concepts take us
a long way from Freud. (More often than not, it has been argued,
Lacan's supposedly filial gesture, the much-vaunted 'return to Freud',
turns out to be what André Green wryly calls 'a one-way ticket to
Lacan' [Caldwell 18].)

In his series of seminars on 'The Essence of Tragedy: A Commentary on Sophocles's *Antigone*',[10] however, Lacan begins traditionally
enough with a detailed reference to the Aristotelian terms that have
dominated definitions of tragedy since classical times: catharsis, pity
and fear, *hamartia*, *tyche*. The terms, however, are called up more to
be challenged than endorsed; in reading the play, he urges his students
with characteristic arrogance, we must 'attempt to wash our brains
clean of all we have heard about *Antigone* and look in detail at what
goes on there' (*Seminar 7*: 250). The first concept he examines is that
of *hamartia*, traditionally defined as the flaw or error of judgement
which brings about the downfall of the tragic hero(ine). For Lacan,
hamartia could be defined as a mere 'mistake' or 'blunder', and is
appropriate to describe the actions of Creon – his 'obstinacy and his

insane orders' (277). But for Antigone, the true heroine of the play (as
well as – according to Lacan – for all true tragic hero[ine]s), it is a
question not of *hamartia* but of *Atè*, and this is what gives her
situation its distinctive interest as well as its seminal position in the
Lacanian definition of desire.

Atè can be variously defined as perdition or devastation (Žižek,
Looking Awry 25), a zone of the 'second death' (*Seminar* 7: 251), that
which is 'between-life-and-death' (272), a life lived in relation to death
(later described in terms of the Freudian death drive [281]). For
Antigone is from the start associated with death, emphasizing her
own commitment to the place where both her parents and her two
brothers dwell. From her point of view, Lacan writes, 'life can only be
approached, can only be lived or thought about, from the place of that
limit where her life is already lost, where she is already on the other
side' (280). However it is only at the moment when she enters,
physically, into what will be her tomb that her association with *Atè*
is 'consecrated' (280).

> It is because she goes toward *Atè* here, because it is even a question
> of going ἐκτὸς ἄτας, of going beyond the limit of *Atè*, that Antigone
> interests the Chorus. It says that she's the one who violates the limits
> of *Atè* through her desire. (277)

Antigone's 'beauty', a Kantian term used repeatedly to describe her
in Lacan's text, has to do with this limit, the crossing over into a zone
explored ruthlessly by Sade. Through his obsession with transgression,
Lacan writes, Sade was able to 'pursue nature to the very principle of
its creative power, which regulates the alternation of corruption and
generation'; through crime, 'man is given the power to liberate nature
from its own laws'. Both Antigone and Sade's heroes, in their
disparate ways, have passed this 'limit of the second death' (260),
and '[i]t is around this image of the limit that the whole play turns'
(268).

In the matter of Polynices' burial, as Kowsar observes (Kowsar
103), neither civic nor divine law holds power over Antigone, driven as
she is by her commitment to the other order of *Atè*. And it is here that
Lacan takes the next step in his explanation of the cause of Antigone's
difference. What alone motivates her to oppose Creon's edict is the
fact that her brother is her brother, carrying with him 'the memory of
the intolerable drama of the one whose descendence has just been

destroyed in the figures of her two brothers' (263). Oedipus, now dead and seldom mentioned in the play, is its dominating presence in the Lacanian schema. And his children function primarily in relation to his fate, bearing the mark of *his* desire, the impossible desire for incest and parricide. *Atè*, for Antigone, is strictly a matter of 'the family *Atè*' (283) in which the whole house of Labdacus is implicated. After her secret burial of Polynices, Antigone reiterates her implication in the curse of incest by insisting on the primacy of blood relations over those of the law (marriage):

> O but I would not have done the forbidden thing
> For any husband or for any son.
> For why? I could have had another husband
> And by him other sons, if one were lost;
> But, father and mother lost, where would I get
> Another brother? (Sophocles 150)

The 'forbidden thing', in other words, is a matter within the blood family, and we remember here, of course (although Lacan does so only by implication), that Polynices is 'another brother' to her *after* Oedipus, who is to her both father *and* brother, both being children of Jocasta. Like her father, whose tragic flaw she shares, she dares to go 'beyond the limit' (305), to attempt to 'know the last word on desire' (309), refusing to recognize that which has been written in advance, in the oracle, in the law. For André Green, 'the art of the theatre is the art of the *malentendu*, the misheard and the misunderstood', what Hegel saw as the tension between 'knowing and not-knowing' ('Prologue' 41 and 39), and this is certainly true of Oedipus, who is, of course, someone other than what he knows himself to be (the son of King Polybus of Corinth). For Lacan, Oedipus' drama depends on the veiling of the discourse of the unconscious. The world of symbols, into which we are so cruelly thrust, causes the subject 'always [to] realise himself elsewhere', 'causes his truth [the truth of the unconscious] to be always in some part veiled from him.' (*Seminar* 2: 210).

In his quest for an explanation of the workings of desire Lacan next introduces another Aristotelian element in order, again, to redefine it radically. Catharsis, the purgation (discharge/purification) of pity and fear, needs to be seen, he argues, in relation to what he calls 'the proper place of desire in the economy of the Freudian Thing' (*Seminar* 7: 247). The Freudian Thing, a phrase used as the title of one of

Lacan's well-known earlier essays,[11] has a characteristic Lacanian resonance combining the defiantly banal with erudite reminiscences of Kant, Heidegger, and others. It suggests, throughout Lacan's work, a drawing together of the three central concepts from which all else derives: language, the unconscious, desire.

The 'proper place of desire' in this economy, as Lacan's sense-defying, 'excessive' prose attempts to demonstrate throughout the seminar,[12] is in the gaps opened up by the unconscious in language. It is here that Lacan makes his most radical move. Catharsis in tragedy, he states, takes its significance from the relationship of pity and fear to the *image* of the central tragic figure. In *Antigone*, he continues, it is 'the fascinating image of Antigone herself' which reveals to us the meaning of the tragedy of desire. And the reason for this is that 'through the intervention of pity and fear . . . we are purged, purified of everything of . . . the order of the Imaginary' (*Seminar* 7: 247–48).

THE IMAGINARY AND THE SYMBOLIC

In calling up at this point his theory of the Imaginary, Lacan was returning to one of his earliest and most influential concepts to give it a further twist. As expounded in the 'Mirror Stage' article, as we have seen in Chapter 1, the Imaginary has to do with the mechanisms of identification that the subject sets up, identifications with objects outside ourselves, whether these be material objects, other people, or our own image in the mirror. During the mirror stage the infant experiences the full impact of the ambivalence of identification: jubilation at the recognition of its own whole image, marred by a sense of alienation at the fictionality or fraudulence of this wholeness. In an attempt to escape the necessary breaking of the dyadic relation with the mother, the subject 'fixes upon himself an image that alienates him from himself' (*Écrits* 19). The 'ego', in Lacan's terms, is an imaginary illusion, a false impression of wholeness. It is through entry into the Symbolic order of language that the infant learns to face up to the inevitability of its incompleteness. Thus to be 'purged or purified' of the order of the Imaginary, as Lacan claims happens in *Antigone*, would in his terms be a positive, cathartic experience – equivalent to the revised clinical agenda to which he dedicated a lifetime of polemical energy.

What, then, does this 'image' of Antigone represent to us as audience? 'That', quips Lacan, in tragic mood, 'is the question' (252), and his answer is characteristically elliptical. The play is usually interpreted as a conflict between different types of moral order, that of Creon, ruler of Thebes after his brother-in-law Oedipus, and that of Antigone, Oedipus' daughter (as well as his sister). After Oedipus' death, the curse that hung over him lingers on in the form of the division among his four children. The two brothers, Polynices and Eteocles, die at each other's hand when Polynices attacks his own city with an army of Argive allies. Creon, determined to make an example of the treachery of the invader, orders that while Eteocles, defender of Thebes, should be buried with honour, Polynices must be left on the plain where he fell, unburied and dishonoured.

Antigone's resistance to this edict, outlined in the opening scene of the play in her debate with her sister Ismene, stems from her adherence to a concept of family allegiance which runs counter to the laws of public duty (the Law, the Symbolic order). Ismene, refusing to 'act/ Against the state' (Sophocles 128), declines to help her sister defy Creon and perform the burial rites over Polynices. For Antigone, the issue is very different: 'I shall be content/To lie beside a brother whom I love' (128). For all Antigone's claim to be serving the gods,[13] the play, as Lacan puts it, is 'something other than a lesson in morality' (*Seminar 7*: 249).

Must we relinquish, then, the question of human responsibility? Does the tragic flaw (*hamartia*) present in Oedipus and Antigone have nothing to do with hubris (over-weening pride, which Aristotle singled out as the cause of tragedy) and everything to do with their complicity in parricide and incest? Readings based on Freud argue that what is at stake here is a flaw inherent in the whole human condition. Oedipus can hardly be blamed, after all, for having killed a stranger in a chance quarrel on the road while attempting to flee Corinth and the dreaded consequences of the oracle.

Lacan takes Freud one step further. For him, Oedipus' (and Antigone's) flaw is the 'tragic liberty' of having 'to deal with the consequence of that desire that led him to go beyond the limit, namely, the desire to know. He has learned and still wants to learn something more.' (*Seminar 7*: 305) Both Jocasta and the Shepherd beg Oedipus to let well alone, not probe further into the cause of the plague. But having solved the riddle of the sphinx, Lacan argues, Oedipus has to learn what others cannot or will not face. 'Oedipus's desire is the desire

to know the last word on desire' (309), and it is this 'flaw' that is
transmitted to his daughter. In this, too, he is like Shakespeare's Lear,
who also attempted to 'cross . . . over' the boundary of knowledge
(305), if in a 'reverse and derisory' form (310). 'Poor Lear', Lacan
jeers,

> doesn't understand a thing and . . . makes the ocean and the earth
> echo because he tried to enter the same region ['the desire to know
> the last word on desire'] in a salutary way with everyone agreeing.
> He appears in the end as still not having understood a thing and
> holding dead in his arms the object of his love [the 'reverse' of the
> Oedipus–Antigone relationship], who is, of course, misrecognized
> by him. (310)

'Misrecognition' is the key concept here, returning us to the
Freudian Thing. In *Oedipus Rex*, this is made starkly apparent in
Oedipus's refusal to recognize his desire as expressed in the oracle.
Written in advance, outside his agency, the oracle emphasizes the way
Oedipus is not what he thinks he is (someone else's son and wife), does
not in other words, recognize his desire as the desire of the other.

FATHERS: PRIMAL, IMAGINARY AND SYMBOLIC

Contemporary ego psychology, prevalent in the United States, as well
as much object relations theory have, in Lacan's contemptuous
opinion, made the error of focusing exclusively on imaginary relationships in the analytic situation, at the expense of the necessary coming
to terms with the Symbolic. As a result, patients are often coerced into
adopting the imaginary constructions projected on to them by the
desiring analyst, becoming victims of the analyst's own counter-
transference. In like manner Antigone, too, refuses initially to face
up to the incomplete, gap-filled Symbolic order in her blind quest for
the fraudulent wholeness of the Imaginary.

In her play, Antigone calls up our pity and fear for what Lacan
calls, with full irony, the process of 'mourning for the imaginary father
. . . that is a mourning for someone who would really be someone'
(*Seminar* 7: 308). This refusal to let go of the imaginary relationship
can perhaps be better understood by looking at one of the final
moments in the play set chronologically between *Oedipus Rex* and

Antigone, Oedipus at Colonus, the play in which we witness Antigone's relationship to her father both before and after his death. Immediately after Oedipus' death she laments:

> I never knew how great the loss could be
> Even of sadness; there was a sort of joy
> In sorrow, when he was at my side.
> Father, my love, in your shroud of earth
> We two [herself and Ismene] shall love you for ever and ever
> . . . . . .
> Take me to the place and let me die there too.
>   (Sophocles 122–23)

After years of faithful attendance on her father in his wanderings in exile from Thebes, Antigone realizes only at the moment of his death that she 'never knew' his meaning to her (as imaginary, that is). If the imaginary father known during his lifetime is the lost father (a loss of imagined oneness – 'joy/In sorrow'), the loss of this loss which she here mourns represents for her a coming to terms with its implication in the Symbolic. She yearns to be taken to 'the place' where his absence is symbolized. And yet the 'shroud of earth' is known only to the representative of the law, the ruler of Athens (and Colonus), The-seus;[14] it is forbidden to Antigone and Ismene. Just as the symbol, the name of the object, represents its irrevocable replacement and death, so the burial of the body represents its commitment to an order of naming, the Symbolic, which incorporates prohibition and lack, a lack we seek perpetually to fill. Small wonder, therefore, that Antigone subsequently develops an immovable obsession with shrouds of earth, with the all-importance of the symbolic rites to be performed over the body of Oedipus' rightful successor, his eldest son Polynices.

The father in the Lacanian scheme is ultimately always the symbolic father, as *Oedipus Rex* shows only too clearly. As several commenta-tors have noted, Oedipus is ironically the only man in the world who *doesn't* suffer from an Oedipus complex. He has, as Cynthia Chase notes, 'murdered his father and married his mother in an appreciation of expediency rather than in satisfaction of a desire' (Chase 62). Lacan puts it like this: 'If Oedipus is a whole man [and we need to feel the full force of Lacan's negation of the illusory condition of wholeness], if Oedipus doesn't have an Oedipus complex, it is because in his case there is no father at all' (*Seminar* 7: 309). He only knew an adoptive father. 'As far as the father that Oedipus knew is concerned, he only becomes the father, as Freud's myth indicates, once he is dead.' Lacan continues:

> It is thus here, as I've said a hundred times, that one finds the paternal function. In our theory the sole function of the father is to be a myth, to be always only the Name-of-the-Father, or in other words nothing more than the dead father, as Freud explains in *Totem and Taboo*. (309)

In *Totem and Taboo* (1913), Freud extended his views on individual psychology to speculate on their origins in the social arrangements of the earliest prehistoric times. Darwin had talked about the primal patriarchal horde as the earliest form of human community. The father of this horde, Freud speculated, would eventually have had to be killed by his sons if they were to overcome his tyrannical domination and possession of the women. But remorse would quickly have replaced triumph at his death. In compensation, he would soon have been elevated into a symbol of power – just as the totem animal, a substitute for the primal father, is still today simultaneously killed and mourned in so-called primitive communities. In effect, therefore, 'The dead father became stronger than the living one had been' (PF 13: 204). And in order to avoid sharing their father's fate, the sons would then have instituted laws prohibiting the killing of the father/totem as well as forbidding access to the women they all desired but could not possess alone. Freud concludes that

> They thus created out of their filial sense of guilt the two fundamental taboos of totemism, which for that very reason inevitably corresponded to the two repressed wishes of the Oedipus complex. (205)

Hence, therefore, the 'longing for the father' at the root of every form of religion (210), as well as the ambivalent guilt and rebelliousness towards the father to be found behind every psychoneurosis.

The dead father, then, gathers into himself all these fields of mythical, symbolic and imaginary force, resulting in what Lacan punningly calls a '*père-version*': a perverse 'turning towards' the father. The father acts not only as symbolic restraint but also, most 'perversely' of all, as imaginary decoy, luring us away from a healthy acceptance of the Symbolic. For Lacan, imaginary illusion is as powerful and inevitable an ingredient of human subjectivity as is symbolic delusion. The true condition of being-as-lack, he writes, can only be apprehended 'in moving along the joint between the imaginary and the symbolic in which we seek out the relationship of man to the signifier and the "splitting" it gives rise to in him' (*Seminar 7*: 274). (As we shall see in Chapter 7, this patricentric model, at the heart of Freudian–Lacanian psychoanalysis, has proved to be its most radical point of challenge, from Horney, Deutsch and Klein in the 1920s through to Kristeva, Irigaray and beyond in our day.)

OTHELLO AND THE REAL OF DESIRE

The Real, the third point of Lacan's triadic structure of intersubjectivity, is the most ambiguous and elusive of the three. Lacan's refusal of a stable definition has here its justification in what he sees as the essential unrepresentability of the Real. What he means by it has nothing to do with the reality of the external, empirical world. Rather, it is a matter of psychic experience. It is that which escapes representation, the first and 'missed encounter' with the primordial object that lies behind phantasy (*Four Fundamental Concepts* 54–55). As *objet petit a*, it represents the imaginary position of the mother, or the lost/ missing phallus. The primordial object (the 'Thing') is always missed and missing. Put another way, it is that which constitutes loss or trauma, both at the bodily level (primary separation from an original phantasized oneness) and at the level of speech (the 'missed encounter' between signifier and signified).

Although unrepresentable, it is that which never 'stops not being written' (*cesse de ne pas s'écrire*) (*Seminar 20*: 94), that is, that which makes its presence felt in the gaps or holes in the Symbolic, the ' "hard kernel" around which every symbolization fails'. Desire is for Lacan 'the real thing' (the Freudian Thing plus the Real), the central impossibility around which every signifying network is structured (Žižek, *Looking Awry* 36 and 143). New to psychoanalysis, Lacan's concept of the Real became, particularly in his later work of the 1960s–70s, the resounding echo at the centre of his view of subjectivity.

Tragedy, I have suggested, can be viewed as the genre where this 'missed encounter' is most prominently exposed. Lacan said that tragedy 'is a question of the relationship between action and desire,

and of the former's fundamental failure to catch up with the latter'
(*Seminar* 7: 313). The tragedy of desire, in other words, is that it is
marked by the Real – as a brief reference to Shakespeare's *Othello* or
King Lear may indicate. The dominant image of *Othello*, the one
which every cover illustration of the printed text picks up on, is that of
Othello's agonized expression as he holds the murdered Desdemona in
his arms. (The equivalent in *Lear* is that mentioned by Lacan, of Lear
holding dead in his arms the misrecognized object of his love.) What is
at issue here is the human confrontation with the inevitability of loss,
the loss of what was most desired but ultimately impossible, due to our
own inability to encounter it, which is our fate.

The Greek word for fate or chance, *tyche*, which played an
important part in Aristotle's definition of tragedy, is focused on by
Lacan in his definition of the Real. For him, *tyche* is '*the encounter
with the real*' (*Four Fundamental Concepts* 53). To explain this, Lacan
goes back to Freud's fort/da paradigm which was discussed in
Chapter 2. The origin of the analytic experience is the trauma of loss,
a trauma, Lacan says, that 'determin[es] all that follows, and impos[es]
on it an apparently accidental origin' (*Four Fundamental Concepts* 55).
The subject seeks to repair loss through the process of repetition, just
as the theatre-goer returns repeatedly to the theatre to participate in
the process of catharsis. He continues:

> it is necessary to ground this repetition first of all in the very split
> that occurs in the subject in relation to the encounter. This split
> constitutes the characteristic dimension of analytic discovery and
> experience; it enables us to apprehend the real . . . (*Four
> Fundamental Concepts* 69)

Repetition, as we have seen, is inherently connected with death.
Desire began, with the child, with a repeated cry or demand intended
to bring back a prior satisfaction. Soon, repetitions became an end in
themselves, a comforting suggestion of the (only) possibility of fulfilment. And yet, as Ellie Ragland points out,

> because the 'object' being sought to satisfy desire does not displace
> something that was actually possessed in the first place, no
> substitute can ever be the 'real thing.' Thus, repetitions bear the
> structure of obsession, pointing to the death in desire, i.e., the
> impossible task of finding Oneness. (*Essays* 167)

In death and only in death, therefore, can the tragic hero(ine) find a satisfying resolution. Death touches everything, as the corpse-strewn endings of tragedy from Sophocles through Seneca and Shakespeare testify. For it is our own death *in the Other* that is sought. The original lost object (the *objet petit a*) is as close as it will ever be to attainment at the moment of death at the tragic climax. As Lacan puts it, chillingly: '*I love you, but, because inexplicably I love in you something more than you* – the objet petit a – *I mutilate you*' (*Four Fundamental Concepts* 263); this is perhaps as apt an explanation as we could get for the 'cause' of Othello's tragedy.

Some interesting observations have been made about the names Shakespeare gave his central protagonists in *Othello*. The name Desdemona, which derives from the Greek δυσδαίμον (*dusdaimon*, the unfortunate), marks its bearer as fitting object of Othello's ill fortune (*tyche*). The name Othello, it seems, is one Shakespeare chose himself; his source, Cinthio's *Hecatomithi* (III,7) refers to its hero as simply 'the Moor'. Shakespeare's 'small Latine and less Greeke' notwithstanding,[15] we may trace the name back to the Greek ἐθέλω (*ethelo*, to will, wish or desire), thereby locating at the centre of the play the exploration of desire in its relation to *tyche*. Othello's notoriously enigmatic words as he enters Desdemona's chamber before the murder: 'It is the cause, it is the cause, my soul./Let me not name it to you, you chaste stars./It is the cause' (V, ii, 1–3) relate the terrifying causelessness of his jealousy, his over-readiness to be gulled by Iago, to a deeper 'cause' of human misfortune, the missed encounter.

As Joel Fineman points out, Othello can be seen to move, as the play progresses, ever further from the identification with his own name – until he reaches the point of saying, at the very end, 'That's he that was Othello? Here I am' (V, ii, 280; Fineman 38). The loss of a name (and in this case the name of desire), the failure to coincide with one's own signifier, constitutes in the play the mark of the Real. As Lacan puts it in 'The Subversion of the Subject': 'This cut in the signifying chain alone verifies the structure of the subject as discontinuity in the real' (*Écrits* 299).

*   *   *   *

All theory, as our investigation of the Oedipus complex via Freud and Lacan has shown, is myth, intertwined with memory and desire. Freud's myth of the Oedipal, several people have argued, was based on his memory of his relation to his recently lost father. 'In recreating himself as an Oedipal subject', Madelon Sprengnether writes, 'Freud clearly found relief from his personal crisis [of mourning for his father]' ('Mourning Freud' 155). Lacan's post-Freudian Oedipal, in turn, was based on his nostalgia for an early psychoanalysis dominated by a paternal Freud (Jacobus, *First Things* 19). Feminism has presented its own counter-myths – for example that of Kore and Demeter – to displace the patricentric emphasis of much Freudian and post-Freudian psychoanalysis. One of the attractions of Lacan's reading of literary texts, however, is its foregrounding of the way all relationships are mediated, retroactively, by desire – its refusal, in other words, to endorse imaginary relationships.

At its most self-conscious, then, psychoanalysis is careful to remember the mythic component of not only the Oedipal but of all its so-called founding theories, including, of course, those feminist attempts to counter the Oedipal by emphasizing the mother–child bond as source and origin of human desire. Desire, as the Oedipus complex itself illustrates, has no origin; it can only work retroactively – by what Freud called 'deferred action' (Nachträglichkeit), that is, 'loss . . . inferred on the basis of a retrospective view that sees the past as fuller than the present' (Gallop, *Reading Lacan* 143).[16] Loss and trauma have always already occurred. Founding theories suggesting origins, therefore, need to keep reminding themselves of their mythic status, of desire's tendency to reify imaginary presence, at the expense of symbolic loss.

5

The Uncanny Text

The last three chapters have focused on what could be called the fundamental psychic drives: narcissism, projection and introjection, the Oedipal, castration, mourning, abjection, desire. I want now to move in these next chapters to investigate specific psychological phenomena which emerge from these drives, phenomena such as the uncanny, transgenerational haunting, hysteria and the masquerade. The death drive, perhaps the most 'fundamental' or archaic of all drives, I save till the end, where it logically belongs.

A great number of psychoanalytic 'objects' have been discussed in the preceding chapters. But of all the objects that have interested literary analysts, it is the 'frightening object', which constitutes the nucleus of *das Unheimliche* (the uncanny),[1] which has interested them most. We all love to be frightened, at one remove (on screen or in books) in particular, but are less inclined to delve into the causes of this seeming masochism, no doubt out of a sense of displaced anxiety about the disturbance of such murky depths. When Freud set out to look into the question of horror in his essay on the uncanny in 1919,[2] he seems to have been initially unaware of the enormity of the undertaking. This essay, one of his most frequently quoted, contains more in the way of speculative theorizing than its modest dimensions can hold.

One of the attractions (or difficulties) of the essay, as critics have noticed, is its own implication in the processes of uncanniness that it attempts to describe (Young, 'Psychoanalytic Criticism' 93). In pointing out the variety and complexity of elements involved in the production of the uncanny effect, Freud is drawn into ever more ambivalent zones. This has to do, first of all, with the ambivalence of the word *das Unheimliche* itself, which Freud famously spent pages trying to define. *Das Heimliche* (the homely/familiar) ultimately shades into its opposite, *Das Unheimliche* (the unhomely/unfamiliar), he noted. It is this implication of familiarity, of something known but long since forgotten (repressed), which makes its emergence so eerie:

> this uncanny is in reality nothing new or alien, but something which is familiar and old-established in the mind and which has become alienated from it only through the process of repression . . . the uncanny . . . [is] something which ought to have remained hidden but has come to light. (PF 14: 363–64)

Derrida, who reads Freud's essay in relation to the effects of what he calls the 'dissemination' of meaning through the infinitely displaced *différance* of signifiers, describes its effect like this:

> In *The Uncanny*, Freud – here more than ever attentive to undecidable ambivalence, to the play of the double, to the endless exchange between the fantastic and the real, the 'symbolized' and the 'symbolizer,' to the process of interminable substitution – can without contradicting this play, have recourse both to castration anxiety, behind which no deeper secret . . . and to the substitutive relation . . . for example between the eye and the male member. Castration is that nonsecret of seminal division that breaks into substitution. (*Dissemination* 268n67)

Through these elements of castration and doubling, which I shall come on to shortly, substitutions lead us further and further from what we know, ever deeper into undecidability. It is these deconstructive elements that have made the uncanny one of the most popular concepts in critical analysis today.

Hélène Cixous, who refers to Derrida's reading in her essay 'Fiction and its Phantoms', focuses on the way in reading 'The "Uncanny"' we are faced with nothing but uncertainty, with what she calls 'a text and its hesitating shadow' (525). Far from being a stable, definable concept, *das Unheimliche* is for her 'a composite that infiltrates the interstices of the narrative and points to gaps we need to explain' (536). It is, in other words, a 'relational signifier' (536), disturbing meaning and security wherever it occurs. Instead of signifying, in fact, it draws attention to the 'No meaning' lying behind castration, which Cixous (like Derrida, following Lacan), saw as the ultimate of ultimates. The uncanny arouses 'the elusive moment of fear [which] returns and eclipses itself again . . . dodging from fear to fear' at every threat of castration (536). For castration, as we have seen, resembles all primal phantasies in coming to significance *after* its imagined occurrence. It has, as the phrase goes, 'always already' taken place. It is like a mirage (a threatening one) in that it is always appearing but never there – as Lacan puts it: 'Everyone knows that castration is there on the horizon and that it never, of course, occurs' (*Seminar 7*: 308). It is in this omnipresent but elusive form, as we shall see, that castration haunts and terrifies through the gaps of Gothic writing.

When Derrida says (in the above-quoted passage) that 'Castration is that nonsecret of seminal division that breaks into substitution', he is being more faithful to the dominant spirit of Freud's essay than his deconstructive emphasis may suggest. Because for Freud, castration and repetition are inextricably linked, and form the bedrock of the uncanny. Repetition is, in many ways, Freud's main subject, for all the diversions into an array of related areas. The year 1919, in which 'The "Uncanny"' was written, was a time of great theoretical development in Freud's work, and would result in his seminal paper 'Beyond the Pleasure Principle' in the following year. Although he had written in earlier work about 'the compulsion to repeat' as a clinical phenomenon, it was not until this period that he began to regard it as an instinct or drive (PF 11: 272). In 'Beyond the Pleasure Principle' repetition was to be linked, crucially, with the death drive. In the slightly earlier 'Uncanny' essay, however, it's as if death is waiting in the wings, shaping repetition but staying out of the limelight. (We shall return to this in the final chapter on the death drive.)

The link between castration and repetition had been noticed by Freud as early as the *Dreams* book, where he drew attention to the way a doubling or multiplying of a phallic symbol in dreams 'is to be regarded as a warding-off of castration' (PF 4: 474) – as an act, in other words, of narcissistic self-preservation. Giving this a Lacanian formulation, we could say that when something is lost, in phantasy, a repetition of the loss can be used as a form of substitution or compensation (like the child's repeated cry). Repetition becomes an end in itself, edging us closer each time to the ultimate loss, death, yet at the same time always deferring it. Ellie Ragland writes:

> In psychoanalysis, the meaning of repetition concerns pain repressed in the body that catches us in the very *cause* we seek to avoid. But we encounter our displeasures over and over anyway, because they define our limits in the real of splits, cuts, and enigmas that constitute the formal envelope of the symptom. (*Essays* 167)

Freud's own particular focus in the 'Uncanny' essay is to attempt to explain why repetition should cause uncanny sensations. Acknowledging that the reason is far from obvious, he sets about invoking dreams, neurosis and the transference situation, drawing attention to the way the 'helplessness' we feel in face of repetition is similar to that which immobilizes us in dreams. It has to do with something involuntary, 'unintended', which we find ourselves doing in spite of all efforts to the contrary. What in some circumstances we would describe as 'chance' – say the meeting of the same person several times in one day – takes on the feeling of 'something fateful and inescapable' (PF 14: 359–60). As Neil Hertz points out, one of the many odd things about Freud's repetition theory is that it is the becoming aware of the *process* of repetition, rather than the particular item in the unconscious that is repeated, that constitutes the eerie for Freud. It is, in other words, the compulsion factor which scares us, investing it with what he calls, in 'Beyond the Pleasure Principle', a 'daemonic' force (PF 11: 292 and 307). Gothic fiction, long before Freud, had learnt to make effective use of this power.

FREUD READS THE GOTHIC
(HOFFMANN'S 'THE SANDMAN')

E. T. A. Hoffmann 's story 'The Sandman' (1816) was a perfect choice of Gothic text for Freud to analyse in 'The "Uncanny"'', as it combines not only conspicuous elements of castration, repetition and doubling, but also a central ambivalence about whether or not the events are to be read literally (as actually occurring) or as the product of a disturbed mind. This ambivalence has been picked up by readers as a central feature of the Gothic genre ever since – notably by Tzvetan Todorov, whose book *The Fantastic* (1973) provides a classic structuralist analysis of the different categories of fantasy writing. He isolates three main groups: the marvelous (what is purely supernatural), the uncanny (where the seemingly supernatural is explained away as the distortions of a neurotic consciousness) and the pure 'fantastic', where both the character and reader hesitate between these two and ambivalence is unresolved.

Freud did not choose to foreground these distinctions, though he did appear to waver between interpretations with apparent unconcern. The hero of Hoffmann's tale, Nathaniel, is besieged by anxieties relating to a dreaded figure Coppelius, the family lawyer, whom he has associated in his childhood with the Sandman who tears out children's eyes. His father dies in mysterious circumstances connected with Coppelius. Later in life, a travelling vendor of optical instruments named Coppola returns to revive old fears related to the eyes. For Freud, the interest in the story centres on the doubling of the father figures, good and bad, and its implications in the castration complex. Successful negotiation of the Oedipal, as we have seen, involves coming to terms with the prohibiting father threatening castration; the source of the law, the father forbids access to the mother on pain of castration. (Freud's fullest exploration of castration and paternal prohibition appears in the 'Little Hans' case [PF 8: 165–205] in 1909.)

This thread of the story, concerned with castration, would seem to connect it to what we could call a 'psychic' rather than a realistic reading (Todorov's 'uncanny' category). Nathaniel's terror, which leads to his end when he throws himself off a tower, results from his inability to lay to rest the childhood threat (the Sandman will blind/castrate you). Coppelius/Coppola is simply the composite figure onto whom these fears are (phantasmatically) projected. Or so it would seem. And yet Freud blurs the issue by insisting on the 'reality' of these figures after all. Any uncertainty we may have had at the beginning as to whether the world of Hoffmann's tale is real or fantastic, he writes, 'disappears' as it develops,

> and we perceive that he intends to make us, too, look through the demon optician's spectacles or spy-glass . . . For the conclusion of the story makes it quite clear that Coppola the optician really *is* the lawyer Coppelius and also, therefore, the Sand-Man. (PF 14: 351–52)

Freud is attempting here to refute the thesis of fellow psychologist Ernst Jentsch, who a few years earlier had argued that the uncanny effect of the story derives from its creation of uncertainty over the automaton/woman Olympia, with whom Nathaniel falls in love. Freud's refutation, however, has an element of over-kill about it.[3] In clearing away Jentsch's point about the importance of Olympia in the story in order to make room for himself, Freud removes rather too much, including many of his own more subtle observations about the 'reality' or otherwise of the primal castration phantasies.

As many recent critics have noted,[4] Freud's neglect of the role of the narrator and the narrative complexity of the tale leads to some serious omissions. When Freud cites from the story, he cites only from the dialogues; the words of the narrator are ignored. This, as Hertz puts it, gives 'the illusion of watching Nathanael's actions through a medium considerably more transparent than Hoffmann's text' (Hertz 304), and omits the significant emphasis, sustained by the narrator, on another, related kind of compulsion, the compulsion he was under to tell the tale. (I shall be returning to this question of narrative compulsion later in the chapter.)

Another charge, however, that Freud neglects the role of the women in Hoffmann's tale,[5] raises a more ambivalent set of issues. Neither Clara (Nathaniel's *fiancée*) nor Olympia (the automaton) are regarded in any way by Freud as agents in the narrative or as true objects of desire. Instead, he writes (in the famous long footnote, to which much of his argument about 'The Sandman' is relegated), that Olympia is, 'as it were, a dissociated complex' of Nathaniel's own narcissism, that she 'can be nothing else than a materialization of Nathaniel's feminine attitude towards his [castrating] father in his infancy' (354n1). Once again, objects Cixous, woman is 'effaced' by what she represents for man; this is yet another example of what Irigaray calls 'hom(m)osexuality', the reduction of everything to the same/masculine. But if we stay within the context of Freud's 'uncanny' reading, the next point in the long footnote gives Freud his rationale. He writes:

> The psychological truth of the situation in which the young man, fixated upon his father by his castration complex, becomes incapable of loving a woman, is amply proved by numerous analyses of patients whose story, though less fantastic, is hardly less tragic than that of the student Nathaniel. (345n1)

Coppelius/Coppola appears in Nathaniel's adult life at the precise moment when his relationship first with Clara and then with Olympia is about to be consummated. The invisibility of the women in Nathaniel's story, therefore, stems not from Freud's lack of interest in them but from Nathaniel's own incapacity to see them. The pocket-telescope supplied by Coppola, that he uses to gaze at Olympia in the house across the street, can be read as an emblem of a necessary but ultimately ineffectual aid to this blindness. Cixous complains that Freud is throwing sand in our eyes ('Fiction and its Phantoms' 532), which to a certain extent he is, with his blinkered reading of Hoffmann's tale. But the real point surely has more to do with the sand thrown in *Nathaniel's* eyes, in childhood, which has 'blinded' him irrevocably. When the eye-penis has 'gone', no amount of reality in the form of a flesh-and-blood woman (or even a doll) can restore it.

TO DOUBLE OR DIE:
'CHRISTABEL'

The appearance of the Sandman as a response to erotic anxiety in Nathaniel makes him what Freud, following Otto Rank, calls a 'double', a projection outward, onto a related figure, of aspects of one's own mental conflict. Such duplication, Rank writes, 'brings about an inner liberation, an unburdening' (Rank 76), a release, through repetition, of one's guilt or anxiety. A feared self, within the psyche, may sometimes appear to obstruct erotic attachments. Its externalization, as other, gives at least a temporary appearance of relief from disunity.

One of the chapters of Rank's study traces the folkloric and anthropological manifestations of doubling, from shadows and reflections to brothers and twins. Primitive communities have traditionally had a variety of superstitions about shadows, most of them demonstrating an association between the shadow and the soul. In the Solomon Islands, for example, anyone who steps on the King's shadow is put to death; in many communities throughout the world it is dangerous to let your shadow fall on a corpse; whoever has no shadow will soon die or become impotent, and so on (Rank 52–53). Superstitions relating to our image in water, mirrors or portraits/ photographs are similar. The soul of the dead is said to reside in mirrors, hence the custom, still apparent today in many European countries, of veiling mirrors in the house of the deceased so that the soul may not remain there (Rank 63). The shadow or mirror image as double here acts as a safeguard against division and loss.

But the double as shadow or image is also a threat, a prediction of death. To gaze at your reflection/soul for long is to lose it, as the Narcissus myth shows. As we shall see in the chapter on specularity, doubling in the Lacanian schema originates in the mirror stage, when the 'misrecognition' of oneself as whole takes on a variety of guises which return throughout life: fragmentation, splitting and substitution. For Freud, the impulse to duplication can always be traced back to the primary narcissism of the child and of primitive people. 'Unbounded self-love' forces the ego to produce replicas of itself as a hedge against extinction. But, he writes, 'when this stage has been surmounted, the "double"' reverses its aspect. From having been an assurance of immortality, it becomes the uncanny harbinger of death.' (PF 14: 357)

The double, as Mladen Dolar observes, is always the figure of *jouissance*. On the one hand, it enjoys at our expense, committing acts we would not otherwise (or rather would only ever) dream of. On the other, it does not simply enjoy but rather *commands* enjoyment, forcing us into a position of servitude to our appetites (Dolar, 'I Shall be With You' 13–14). Its uncanniness, therefore, stems from the same compulsion to repeat which the subject is powerless to resist, as many literary examples demonstrate.

Coleridge's unfinished poem 'Christabel' is not an obvious choice for a study of the double, which usually appears in fictional form. But it provides an interesting illustration of the phenomenon in many respects. First, it took the unusual step of treating the duplication of a female figure, with scandalous innuendoes from which the poem was to suffer a chequered publishing history.[6] Secondly, coming as it does out of the heart of the Romantic movement, it combines features of Romantic ideology and Gothic convention which can be said to give it representative status. Coleridge was an avid reader of Gothic novels and works on magic and witchcraft, as well as of the esoteric German philosophy on which much Romantic ideology was founded. These preoccupations combine with characteristic tension in 'Christabel'.

The concept of the Romantic was of course crucially shaped by Coleridge himself, outlined in works like *Biographia Literaria* (1817). Here we find a series of definitions of mental processes touching at times remarkably closely on ideas that were to preoccupy Freud a hundred years later. Chapter 5, for example, is concerned with 'the law of association', traced from Aristotle to David Hartley, whereby 'Ideas by having been together acquire a power of recalling each other' (Coleridge, *Biographia Literaria* 59). This question is part of a larger one which preoccupied Coleridge, what he called 'the absence or presence of the Will' (54) in mental functioning, the extent to which ideas emerge as the result of mechanical association or through creative reconstruction.[7] From this he was led to his famous distinction between the fancy and the imagination. Fancy, he writes in Chapter 13, 'must receive all its materials ready made from the law of association' (167). It

is indeed no other than a mode of memory emancipated from the order of time and space; and blended with, and modified by that empirical phenomenon of the will which we express by the word *choice*. (167)

Imagination, on the other hand, works according to laws which have more to do with what we now call unconscious processes. It is an essentially 'vital' agency, which 'dissolves, diffuses, dissipates, in order to re-create' the elements available to it (167). It moulds images into a new organic whole, not from without, but according to a form dictated from within, 'modified by a predominant passion' (177), producing not μόρφωσις (fashioning) but ποίησις (creation, making) (218).

What makes Coleridge a poet of clear psychological interest is, as Thomas Weiskel puts it, his constant awareness of his mind's projections (Weiskel 59). He described his aim in *Lyrical Ballads* as the attempt to project phantasies 'from our inward nature' out onto 'persons and characters supernatural, or at least romantic' (*Biographia Literaria* 168). His terms at times closely resemble those laid out by Freud in his essay on the 'Uncanny', especially when describing the effects of defamiliarization. Nature, he wrote, can be unexpectedly transformed by a combination of the 'modifying colours of [the] imagination' of the poet and certain effects of nature. A 'known and familiar landscape' has the capacity to change without warning into something different, through 'accidents of light and shade, moonlight or sunset' (168). Suddenly, the familiar becomes unfamiliar, and out of this uncanniness poetry is made. (Shelley, a few years later [in 1821], was to echo this view of Coleridge's in his celebrated 'Defense of Poetry': 'Poetry lifts the veil from the hidden beauty of the world, and makes familiar objects be as if they were not familiar' ['Defense' 424].)

'Christabel' is dominated by an eerie atmosphere of defamiliarization and involution. As with the Ancient Mariner, who has a hypnotic effect on the Wedding Guest, Geraldine, the notorious vampire woman at the centre of the poem, loosens people's control over their own actions, compelling them to 'sin' in ways the text cannot bring itself to name or explain. Pure and undefended, Christabel is a recognizable Gothic heroine. But through contact with Geraldine she is brought to take on the very qualities of licentiousness and guile against which she is defined. Geraldine is a double in a very real sense, in that rather than being an other held separate and distinct, she can be seen to take over her original as the poem progresses, making the two at times interchangeable.

Both Hoffmann's 'The Sandman' and Coleridge's 'Christabel' were published in the famous Gothic year of 1816,[8] when Byron, John Polidori and Mary and Percy Bysshe Shelley met at Lake Geneva and made up the set of ghost stories that was to result in Polidori's 'The

Vampyre' and Mary Shelley's *Frankenstein*. Both, too, share the preoccupation with the demonic and the psychological which had developed from German Romanticism; Coleridge's familiarity with German literature and philosophy meant that he was writing out of a context very close to Hoffmann's. (He did in fact spend the three years which elapsed between the writing of Parts I and II of the poem, from 1797–1800, in Germany.) One of the many features the two works have in common is their presentation of the double as a product of over-excited sexual imaginings, or sexual conflict. Coppola appears with his capacious pockets full of optical instruments at the very time when Nathaniel, installed in his room opposite Olympia's, is attempting to resist the lure of her automatic gaze:

> He was . . . obliged to admit that he had never seen a lovelier figure. Nevertheless, with Clara in his heart he remained wholly indifferent to the stiff, rigid Olympia: only now and then did he glance fleetingly over his book across to the beautiful statue – that was all. (Hoffmann 109)

Christabel, similarly, has stolen out at midnight in response to troubling dreams of her absent lover:

> And she in the midnight wood will pray
> For the weal of her lover that's far away. (ll. 29–30)

In appearing at this very moment to disturb Christabel's prayers, Geraldine, like Coppola, represents an uncanny repetition of her own most reviled impulses. It is as if, by an effect of moonlight and shadow, to use Coleridge's terms from *Biographia Literaria* again, the *Heimliche* turns into the *Unheimliche*. Hearing a moan, Christabel steals behind the old oak tree where she has been praying, and

> There she sees a damsel bright,
> Drest in a silken robe of white,
> That shadowy in the moonlight shone. (ll. 58–60)

Geraldine's 'brightness' in shadow, carried through the poem by the emphasis on her bewitching eyes, recalls again Coppola's proliferating eyes which 'gazed and blinked and stared up at Nathaniel . . . flaming glances leaped more and more wildly together and directed their blood-red beams into Nathaniel's breast' (Hoffmann 109–10). It is thus significant that at the gathering at Lake Geneva, it is a pair of searing, castrating eyes, displaced onto a woman's breasts, which provoked an hysterical reaction in Percy Shelley on hearing Byron recite from 'Christabel'. The incident is recorded by Polidori, the physician, in his diary:

> Twelve o'clock really began to talk ghostly. L[ord] B[yron] repeated some verses of Coleridge's Christabel, of the witch's breast; when silence ensued, and Shelley, suddenly shrieking and putting his hands to his head, ran out of the room with a candle. Threw water on his face, and after gave him ether. He was looking at Mrs Shelley, and suddenly thought of a woman he had heard of who had eyes instead of nipples, which, taking hold of his mind, horrified him. (qtd in Ford 99)

As is well known, Byron was one of the few in his day to admire 'Christabel'. Urging Coleridge to publish the poem in 1815, he spoke in characteristic Romantic terms of being held in thrall by it: the poem's details, he wrote, 'took a hold on my imagination which I never shall wish to shake off' (qtd in Karen Swann 80). Most readers, like Hazlitt, expressed 'disgust'. Something about the poem was uncannily close and appalling, a sentiment expressed also by modern readers, who share their Romantic predecessors' reluctance to name what it is that disgusts them. The dominant image of the poem, which lingers on long after the details of the medieval chivalric narrative are forgotten, is of Geraldine led trustingly by Christabel to her chamber and unrobing before her:

> Beneath the lamp the lady bowed,
> And slowly rolled her eyes around;
> Then drawing in her breath aloud,
> Like one that shuddered, she unbound
> The cincture from beneath her breast:
> Her silken robe, and inner vest,
> Dropt to her feet, and full in view,
> Behold! her bosom and half her side –
> A sight to dream of, not to tell!
> O shield her! shield sweet Christabel!

> Yet Geraldine nor speaks nor stirs;
> Ah! what a stricken look was hers!
> Deep from within she seems half-way
> To lift some weight with sick assay,
> And eyes the maid and seeks delay;
> Then suddenly, as one defied,
> Collects herself in scorn and pride,
> And lay down by the Maiden's side! –
> And in her arms the maid she took,
>   Ah wel-a-day!
> And with low voice and doleful look
> These words did say:
> 'In the touch of this bosom there worketh a spell,
> Which is lord of thy utterance, Christabel!' (ll. 245–69)

What is noticeable here is the series of expressions of resistance on *Geraldine's* part – the rolling eyes, the drawn breath, the shudder, the stricken look, the lifting of the weight 'with sick essay', the sought delay – as if it is she rather than Christabel who is being seduced. The narrator voices shock and horror ('O shield her! shield sweet Christabel . . . Ah wel-a-day!'), but Christabel's own reactions pass unrecorded.

As if the suggested lesbian act were not enough, Coleridge brings the scene yet closer to the most uncanny of all sites, the mother's body, which symbolizes here the source of all desire.[9] Freud, we remember, would write that the place of origin of all human life, woman's body (especially the genital organs), arouses universally a sense of extreme uncanniness because of its ultimate familiarity: 'This *heimlich* place . . . is the entrance to the former *Heim* [home] of all human beings' (PF 14: 368). Geraldine's most appalling feature is her repeated symbolization as the maternal figure, who holds the infant (Christabel) in her arms:

> And lo! the worker of these harms,
> That holds the maiden in her arms,
> Seems to slumber still and mild,
> As a mother with her child. (ll. 298–301)

The battle has been fought and won against Christabel's own mother, now dead but still present as her 'guardian spirit' (l. 212). Significantly, it is the seat of her maternal function, her bosom, which acts as the source of seduction/corruption. On waking, Christabel weeps and smiles like an infant: 'and tears she sheds . . . And oft the while she seems to smile/As infants at a sudden light!' (ll. 315–18) The 'sudden light' which enchants the baby is replaced here, by implication, by the sudden 'shadow' cast by Geraldine, resulting in unnamable horror, the defamiliarization of the most deeply familiar (and desired) of all human memories.

Like much Gothic, the poem exploits the unease caused by the dream-like readiness of forms to shift or metamorphose into something closely related. The most obvious use comes with the association of the two women, first by bard Bracy, to a serpent and dove. In a dream, narrated by the bard to Christabel's father Sir Leoline, he has seen a dove, fluttering on the ground, with 'a bright green snake/ Coiled around its wings and neck' (ll. 549–50):

> And with the dove it heaves and stirs,
> Swelling its neck as she swells hers! (ll.553–54)

Interpreting his dream as a prophetic warning about a threat to Christabel's innocence, Bracy pleads with Sir Leoline to be exempted from his mission to inform Geraldine's father, Sir Leoline's former friend, of her safety, to stay one day and exorcise this evil spirit from the wood. To dream, for the Romantic imagination, is to reveal motives inaccessible to daylight consciousness, which are ignored at our peril.

Sir Leoline, however, has his own narrative to complete. The breach with Geraldine's father, Lord Roland de Vaux of Tryermaine ('his heart's best brother' [l. 417]), back in his youth, has left open wounds. Here again, images of doubling and division predominate. The bond between the two men has been not simply broken but 'rent asunder' as if by some mighty volcano:

> Like cliffs which had been rent asunder;
> A dreary sea now flows between; –
> But neither heat nor frost nor thunder,
> Shall wholly do away, I ween,
> The marks of that which once hath been. (ll. 422–26)

In addition to these two pairs of bonding/doubling (Christabel–Geraldine, Leoline–Roland), the very poem itself is 'cleft' by its

division into two discordant sections, written three years apart and
under very different circumstances.[10]

With his own double to be found and re-joined, Sir Leoline takes
little heed of the change in Christabel, in spite of the fact that even
before Bracy reports his dove–serpent dream, she has begun to take on
qualities of the serpent herself. She draws her breath 'with a hissing
sound' (l. 459) as she remembers Geraldine's powers and watches her
father enfold her in his arms. Through yet another metamorphosis, it
is now Geraldine who becomes, in Leoline's eyes, 'Lord Roland's
beauteous dove' (l. 569). But shortly after it is Geraldine who is again
the dull-eyed serpent rather than the bright-eyed lady, in a description
characteristically focused on the exchange of eyes and glances:

> A snake's small eye blinks dull and shy;
> And the lady's eyes they shrunk in her head,
> Each shrunk up to a serpent's eye,
> And with somewhat of malice, and more of dread,
> At Christabel she looked askance! (ll. 583–87)

To which sight Christabel replies again with a shudder and a 'hissing
sound' (l. 591). Christabel, now in a trance, is depicted as first
'drinking in' then 'imitating' Geraldine; the scene, in psychological
terms, can be described as a complex representation of the processes of
introjection and projection:

> So deeply had she drunken in
> That look, those shrunken serpent eyes,
> That all her features were resigned
> To this sole image in her mind:
> And passively did imitate
> That look of dull and treacherous hate!
> And thus she stood in a dizzy trance,
> Still picturing that look askance
> With forced unconscious sympathy
> Full before her father's view –
> As far as such a look could be
> In eyes so innocent and blue! (ll. 601–12)

In a characteristically Coleridgean image of involuntary osmosis
('forced unconscious sympathy'), characters take each other in

through visual exchanges, producing a slippage of forms and identities which leaves them all both 'cleft' (l. 640) and blended. And this in spite of the narrator's repeated attempts to maintain the old stabilities ('eyes so innocent and blue'). The atmosphere is one of 'jaggéd shadows' (l. 282), the dream and the trance, where characters split and re-form in endless inconclusiveness. Even the supposed abductors of Geraldine partake by metonymic association of her serpentine qualities in the unwitting words of Sir Leoline, whose courtly valour towards her calls him to demand 'that there and then/I may dislodge their reptile souls/ From the bodies and forms of men!' (ll. 441–43) In this way, with evil and innocence, conscious and unconscious action so flagrantly indistinguishable, Gothic conventions are explicitly psychologized. Christabel is racked, simultaneously, by 'sins unknown' (l. 390) and by the consciousness that ' "Sure I have sinn'd!" ' (l. 381). The poem shifts back and forth in specifying the agency of the crime (the other or the self), as in these lines restating Christabel's 'seduction' at the beginning of Part II:

> And Christabel awoke and spied
> The same who lay down by her side –
> O rather say, the same whom she
> Raised up beneath the old oak tree!
> Nay, fairer yet! and yet more fair! (ll. 370–74)

Geraldine, like all doubles, exerts the power of her ever-increasing attraction ('fairer yet! and yet more fair') in inverse ratio to Christabel's will or ability to retain a sense of an undivided personality. Within this context, the 'O rather say . . .' here, representing the poem's acceptance of Christabel's own responsibility for Geraldine's influence over her, is the literature of the double's way of figuring the irreconcilable contradictions of self-division.

Romantic attempts at figuring psychic division found in the device of the double a formula that was to prove increasingly popular throughout the nineteenth century, particularly in fiction. Charlotte Brontë's image in the 1840s of the 'madwoman in the attic' as a projection of the Victorian woman's inexpressible passion has been famously detailed by Sandra Gilbert and Susan Gubar in their book with that title. Dickens was to use it, most conspicuously in his last, unfinished novel, *The Mystery of Edwin Drood* (1870), but also in his repeated depictions of 'brothering' from *The Old Curiosity Shop*

(1840–41) and *Bleak House* (1852–53) to *Little Dorritt* (1855–57) and *Our Mutual Friend* (1864–65). Dostoevsky's depictions of doubling in novels from *The Double* (1846) to *The Brothers Karamazov* (1880) are regarded by many as the century's most profound and powerful. And then at the end of the century, in the Romantic revival that produced Stevenson's *Strange Case of Dr Jekyll and Mr Hyde* (1886) and Wilde's *Picture of Dorian Gray* (1891), the double assumed its most self-conscious form, with psychic schism dissected as a phenomenon of moral and cultural decadence.[11]

HAUNTOLOGIES: DERRIDA, ABRAHAM AND TOROK, AND GASKELL'S 'OLD NURSE'S STORY'

Although we will never know what Coleridge would have done with Christabel had he finished the poem, we know as readers of narratives of doubling that things can only end badly for her. To be split beyond repair is to die, even if, as at the end of Mary Shelley's *Frankenstein*, both self and other engage in combat so close that it becomes impossible to distinguish persecutor from persecuted. With Franken-stein and his monster, desperately pursuing each other over the frozen wastes of the North Pole, the only certainty is that their accelerating indistinguishability will result in the disintegration of both. Instead of each half seeking the completion of union with its other, as in Plato's myth of gender division, with doubles the initial split can never heal. As 'harbinger of death', to use Rank's phrase again, the doubled subject must follow a relentless destiny towards self-extinction.

Death, as Elizabeth Wright observes, as 'the uncanniest thing of all, can only return in fiction' (*Psychoanalytic Criticism* 149). Literature, particularly in the Gothic genre, has since its beginning attempted to represent death's unrepresentability. The ghost could be said to be the form taken by the double which both refuses and enforces death's finality. It is, as Cixous puts it, 'the fiction of our relation to death' made concrete ('Fiction and its Phantoms' 542), literature's favourite device for figuring the human challenge to the inevitable.

Ghosts, and spectrality in a wider sense, have become popular in recent post-structuralist theory.[12] Derrida's *Spectres de Marx* (1993) is characteristic in its use of spectrality to represent deconstruction's challenge to metaphysical distinctions – between presence and absence, past and present, life and death. A Derridean 'hantologie' (hauntology), in playful challenge to a Marxist 'ontology' of presence, is a conception of the world whereby 'everything [by which he means, among other things, truth, law, the Holy Spirit, the 'good cause'] comes back to haunt everything, everything is in everything, that is, "in the class of specters"' (*Specters of Marx* 146).

It is their disruption of temporal and spatial boundaries which makes ghosts such effective figures of psychic and semantic disturbance. In terms of time, spectres have to do with what Derrida calls the 'pre-originary and properly spectral anteriority' of every action, crime or tragedy (*Specters of Marx* 21), the way every human motive is haunted by anterior ones. Hamlet's father, a vivid spectre in Derrida's book, works to suggest but never solve the riddle of Hamlet's indecision; like the repetition compulsion, he returns over and over to disturb the concept of an original origin or cause. As Derrida puts it, 'a specter is always a *revenant*. One cannot control its comings and goings because it begins by coming back' (11). Going back in time, over and over, we 'return'; Marx's definition of 're-volution' meaning return or recurrence, as Jeffrey Mehlman suggests, contains within it the seeds of Freud's definition of the repetition compulsion in terms of the uncanny and the death drive (Mehlman 2–4). One of the many paradoxes of the ghost is that it represents both the first originating 'time' (maybe the 'first paternal character', Derrida speculates, echoing Freud on the primal father [13]), as well as its endless repetition. In *Writing and Difference*, published around twenty-five years earlier, Derrida paid tribute to Freud for his recognition of *différance* (difference/deferral) at the origin, his challenge to the concept of primariness: 'To say that *différance* is originary is simultaneously to erase the myth of a present origin . . . The irreducibility of the "effect of deferral"' – such, no doubt, is Freud's discovery' (203). Repetition is not posterior to the origin, but rather simultaneous with it, 'a trace which replaces a presence which has never been present, an origin by means of which nothing has begun' (295). It is thus within these terms that we need to understand what Derrida calls the 'radical untimeliness or . . . anachrony' of the ghost (*Specters of Marx* 25), with the Greek prefix 'ana-' carrying the idea of repetition.

In spatial terms, the phantom effects similar disturbances. For Derrida, its challenge to identity and presence makes it a crucial concept for modern philosophy. Here he is heavily dependent on the work of French psychoanalysts Nicolas Abraham and Maria Torok, who have argued that what psychoanalysis needs is not Laplanche and

Pontalis' *Language of Psychoanalysis*, a dictionary of equivalences, but rather an 'anasemic' discourse capable of registering 'the untouched nucleus [kernel] of non-presence' (Derrida, 'Me – Psychoanalysis' 10). The spectre, then, for Derrida, functions importantly as

> an an-identity that . . . invisibly occupies places belonging finally neither to us nor to it . . . *this* that comes with so much difficulty to language, *this* that seems not to mean anything, *this* that puts to rout our meaning-to-say. . . (*Specters of Marx* 172)

Roland Barthes used the word 'atopia' to illustrate a similar point, that the language that constitutes the writer is 'always outside-of-place . . . by the simple effect of polysemy' (*The Pleasure of the Text* 34–35).

Much of the attraction of Gothic writing in the late twentieth century has had to do with the way it foregrounds the impossibility of representation, drawing attention, at every step, to what Derrida calls this 'putting to rout our meaning-to-say'. Freud's essay on the uncanny can be said to foreshadow a great deal of this debate. We remember his insistence on the mutual dependence and inter-change-ability of the terms *heimlich* and *unheimlich*. One of the meanings of *heimlich*, of course, is 'belonging to the house' (' "Uncanny" ', PF 14: 342), and it is no accident that Freud was interested in haunted houses as the site of inextricable origins and returns. Indeed, he wonders whether he should have *begun* his investigation of the uncanny by examining the significance of the haunted house (364). Derrida, glossing Freud, calls haunted houses 'a kind of prototype', 'the Thing itself' (*Specters of Marx* 195n37 and 173).

Gothic fiction would certainly agree. If the genre can be said to have any modern 'beginning' at all (for its roots reach way back to classical literature and ancient mythology), it must be in a particular house: Horace Walpole's pseudo-Gothic castle, Strawberry Hill, which formed the basis of his writing of *The Castle of Otranto* (1764).[13] This structure Walpole made the site of repeated visitations from the past (anachronies, to use Derrida's term) in the form of a wide array of psychoanalytic material: incest (Manfred and Frederic's swapping of daughters as love objects), parricide (the illicit murder by Manfred's ancestors of the original 'father', Alfonso), castration and fragmented body parts (the gigantic helmet, hand, leg, sabre, etc., of the suit of armour belonging to Alfonso, which gradually reassemble within the castle walls).

The castle and its ghostly occupant are equated in Walpole's novel in a way that was to be repeated in Gothic fiction in the century that followed, from Ann Radcliffe to Sheridan LeFanu. Norman Holland and Leona Sherman have written a well-known article on Gothic castles in which although warning against the 'easy isomorphism' of castle and body (Holland and Sherman 281), they outline the 'possibilities' of the equation, especially in terms of the way the castle acts, like the maternal body, as a point of ultimate return, the source of birth and sexuality (286). Equally important, it seems to me, is the way the castle serves as an emblem of material status (ownership), undoubtedly one of the reasons for the genre's prominence in a rising capitalist economy. Most ghost stories centre on the family dynasty, that index of temporal continuity of which the castle is its spatial embodiment. The ghost is invariably the agent, either as protector or claimant, of property under threat. In early Gothic, up until the Victorian novel with its increasing emphasis on realism, the house was always a castle. As Holland and Sherman point out, 'Inherited riches mean [that Gothic] characters never work, never, that is, construct distinctive identities for themselves apart from parental inheritance' (286). The genre thus began by offering exclusive insight into inheritance as concurrently economic *and* psychic determinant. As the nineteenth century went on, however, the genre was faced with the challenge of demands for realistic settings, and had to invent alternative sites for haunting.

The first two stories in the 1991 Oxford anthology of *Victorian Ghost Stories*, by Elizabeth Gaskell and Sheridan LeFanu, demonstrate this shift. Gaskell's 'The Old Nurse's Story' (1852) appears to be a cross between old-world feudalism and modern homeliness, and at first sight does not appear to have much to do with inheritance, material or psychic. Much of the tale is taken up by the foregrounded and very *heimlich* presence of the nurse-narrator Hester, whose role, like that of Nellie in *Wuthering Heights* of five years earlier, is to register the Gothic tremors and restore the common light of day. Her story concerns the Furnivall family of Northumberland and the spectral return of the former lord and his outcast daughter and grand-daughter, the latter, as the 'Phantom-Child' wailing at the window, like Cathy Earnshaw, luring the living out to their death in the storm. Furnivall Manor House is at the centre of the story, not explicitly, as in *Otranto*, as the emblem of inheritance, but nonetheless very present in terms of the features of its grounds and architecture:

from its overall mass (compared to a 'wilderness' [Gaskell 4]) to the great oak, the gnarled holly tree, the portrait gallery, the organ, the chandelier, and above all the safe, familiar west wing as opposed to the unfamiliar east one.

And yet the opening words of the tale hint at a different, buried preoccupation: 'You know, my dears, that your mother was an orphan and an only child' (1). Dynastic concerns are the absent presence; the family tree looms invisibly, eliciting anxiety over the safety of its branches and fruit. The orphan and only child of the opening sentence, Rosamond, does manage to make it through the hauntings to bear children. The line is secured. But this is only after the story has worked to show its fragility by two means: first by elaborating on the non-issue of the various other family members, and secondly by focusing on the threat, by the phantom (a rival claimant, for all her garb of childhood innocence) to the one remaining heir (Rosamond) to Furnivall Manor.

The recipients of Hester's narrative are Rosamond's children, the last of five generations of Furnivalls to appear in the story. Like all Gothic readers, at least on the surface, they 'don't care so much' for an elaboration of the past (1). Their interest is in 'what [they] think is to come' (1) (the phantoms), illustrating what Peter Brooks calls 'the contradictory desire of narrative, driving toward the end which would be both its destruction and its meaning' (*Reading for the Plot* 58). But in defiance of her listeners' conscious wishes, Hester's narrative loops and turns back to beginnings repeatedly in its drive to the end, rotating upon an anachronic axis of repetition *and* first time. For the long-awaited ghosts, in the end, lead the narrative as much to the origin of its mystery as to its deferral. The line of descent will remain threatened. 'At bottom', Derrida says, 'the specter is the future, it is always to come' (*Specters of Marx* 39). The Phantom-Child, it is assumed, will return to Furnivall Manor, in spite of its avoidance by the present generation. Rosamond narrowly escapes its clutches through the homely attentions of her nurse. But there will always be the agent of defamiliarization, in this case the 'dark foreigner' (14) who comes to seduce the heiress and release the phantoms. The narrator says that this foreigner 'could easily . . . hide himself in foreign countries' (14). He is the living embodiment of that which 'ought to have remained hidden but has come to light' (PF 14: 225); his concealment, like that of the phantom itself, can only be temporary.

Continuity, the life force, is the contested site of Gothic. From Walpole to today, its enemy, illegitimacy, plots to threaten (or threatens the plot of) this deeply patriarchal genre. In *The Castle of Otranto* the plot is centred on the threat of the possible mixing of the blood of the true heir (Theodore) with that of the usurper (Matilda, Manfred's daughter). The form taken by the threat to continuity/ legitimacy has varied at different historical moments, as we might expect. In *Otranto*, as I have said, it was incest, suggested in the subtle swapping of daughters by Manfred and Frederic, which is prevented only at the last moment. Much the same is true for the Gothic romances published in the following decades. Ann Radcliffe's villains, who only just miss raping the heroine, invariably turn out to be blood relations. With the approach of the Victorian period, as the revisions to *Frankenstein* show, this possibility had to be suppressed. In the first (1818) edition of Mary Shelley's text, as is often noted, Elizabeth is Frankenstein's cousin; the third edition of 1831 changes her to an adopted (foundling) sister.

If it wasn't incest, what was it that threatened legitimacy in Victorian Gothic? In Gaskell's story, even illegitimacy itself is veiled: the foreign musician and Maud Furnivall are said to have married, though in secrecy and defiance of paternal authority, so that their daughter's 'illegitimacy' is moral rather than legal. The uncanny repetition of the family name (and Manor House), seems to suggest that the ultimate crime is the 'evil' of 'fornication' (the Latin *fornix-icis* means both a vault or arch and a brothel, aptly conflating the architectural and the erotic). Or, equally possible, is it the presence of the spinster-companion Miss Stark, whose devotion to the other Furnivall daughter/ heiress, Grace, prevents *her* from marrying and bearing children? Miss Stark is a familiar type in Victorian fiction but a long way from Geraldine as lesbian seducer in Coleridge's poem. It is only the reader conscious of the conventions of veiling in Gaskell's story who would be responsive to her disruptive rather than her nurturing status, and hence her threat to the continuity of the family line.

THE PHANTOM WITHIN: LEFANU'S 'STRANGE DISTURBANCES'

The second tale in the Oxford anthology, Sheridan LeFanu's 'Account of Some Strange Disturbances in Aungier Street', was published only a year later (in 1853) but has a much more modern feel to it. First, like many later Victorian ghost tales, it draws frequent attention to the problem of authentication in the perception of ghosts. 'Was this singular apparition . . . the creature of my fancy, or the invention of my poor stomach? Was it, in short, *subjective* (to borrow the technical slang of the day) . . .?' (LeFanu 22), the narrator wonders. Secondly, it sets the hauntings not in a feudal manor or castle but in the bourgeois Dublin óf 'Aungier Street',[14] in a once semi-fashionable but now rather dissolute part of town inhabited by students and drunkards. In this modern setting, property naturally no longer remains in the same family for generations, keeping its mysteries intact and ingrowing, but instead changes hands at the whim of market forces, as the opening paragraphs detail. The family romance, then, must be split, its traumas dispersed among a wider community.

It is the community, the street (Aungier Street) which carries the burden of the secrets. Without the portrait gallery, which served in Gaskell's tale and earlier Gothic to keep past generations in the consciousness of the living, the modern house rarely ventures back further than one generation of the same family. The house remains at the centre, however. As the narrator Dick puts it: 'what the flesh, blood, and bone hero of romance proper is to the regular compounder of fiction, this old house of brick, wood, and mortar is to the humble recorder of this true tale' (36). Like Furnivall Manor with its west and east wings, it incorporates both the homely (the 'cosy' front bedroom [20]) and the unhomely which disrupts it: the back bedroom with its 'latent discord – a certain mysterious and indescribable relation, which jarred indistinctly upon some secret sense of the fitting and the safe' (21). Here Tom and Dick, the types of modern democratic ordinariness, as their names suggest, are subjected to the violence and vengeance of their luridly-named patrician predecessors in the house, Sir Thomas Hacket, Lord Mayor of Dublin in James II's time, and Judge Horrocks, 'who ha[d] earned the reputation of a particularly "hanging judge"' (20).

The word 'Aungier' itself suggests haunting, revenge and hanging. The crime, it seems, is not so much Judge Horrocks' professional sadism as his final turning of this sadism upon himself. In hanging himself from the banisters with the skipping rope of his unacknow-ledged illegitimate daughter, born of his housekeeper, he projects onto future occupants of the house the burden of his concealment.

According to Nicolas Abraham in 'Notes on the Phantom', the phantom which returns to haunt not just Gothic fiction but all human subjects is 'not the content of repression Freud called a *familiar stranger*', but rather a '*bizarre foreign body*' within us (Abraham and Torok, *The Shell and the Kernel* 175). This alien within results from 'the gap produced in us by the concealment of some part of a love object's life' (171), 'not the dead, but the gaps left within us by the secrets of others' (171), invariably those of parents or grandparents. The illegitimate or taboo past of ancestors, whether direct ancestors as in Gaskell's tale or merely those who shared the same house/topos (anatopia) and history (anachrony) and are responsible for their violence, as in LeFanu's, figure in Gothic as this foreign body which cannot be expelled.

Derrida's 'Foreword' to Abraham and Torok's *Wolf Man's Magic Word*, published some seventeen years before his *Specters of Marx*, elaborates on this theory of the phantom as a figuring of the relation between self and other in a way that throws light on Gothic's concern with gaps and concealments. With Freud's 'Mourning and Melancholia' as a base,[15] Abraham and Torok analyse certain cases of 'possession' of the ego by the object, observing that the Freudian return of the repressed, in clinical experience, does *not* occur in transference in numerous cases of neurosis, including those of the Wolf Man, Little Hans and indeed of Hamlet.[16] Their addition to Freud's theory depends on a distinction between the concepts of introjection and incorporation. Refusing the healthy option of mourning or introjection whereby we 'reclaim . . . as our own the part of ourselves that we placed in what we lost' (Abraham and Torok, 'Mourning *or* Melancholia', *Shell and Kernel* 127), the subject often resorts to incorporation, the process whereby 'the prohibited object is *settled in the ego* in order to compensate for the lost pleasure and the failed introjection (Torok, 'The Illness of Mourning', *Shell and Kernel* 113, emphasis added). Incorporation involves keeping the object alive *as other*, in a crypt, 'a sealed-off psychic space . . . in the ego' (141). It is not until the crypt's contents have been revealed to the subject that the healing process of introjection and transference can begin.

What does it mean to keep the object alive *as other* in the ego? Here, I think, we have the question underlying Derrida's – and to some extent Gothic fiction's – preoccupation with the phantom. Freud's model of the uncanny as the return of the repressed, helpful as it is for a recognition of symbols and symptoms, proves inadequate in face of encrypted objects.[17] The idea of a phantom kept alive as other within us was an attractive one for Derrida for the way it entails a redefinition of the self, 'the paradox of a foreign body preserved as foreign but by the same token excluded from a self that henceforth deals not with the other, but only with itself' ('Foreword' xvii). Whence, with all its enigmatic suggestiveness, his (via Abraham and Torok's) image of the Self as 'cemetery guard':

> The crypt is enclosed within the self, but as a foreign place, prohibited, excluded. The self is not the proprietor of what he is guarding. He makes the rounds like a proprietor, but only the rounds . . . and in particular he uses all his knowledge of the grounds to turn visitors away. ('Foreword' xxxv)[18]

We too, as visitors to the cemeteries of Gothic texts, are no doubt repeatedly 'turned away' from their real secrets, the secrets of their incorporated objects. It is only in the interstices of these texts (these 'mutilated texts') that we may glimpse evidence of their 'riddles with no key' (Abraham and Torok, *Shell and Kernel* 139). I am not suggesting, for it would hardly be possible or even interesting, that we set about writing 'Sixth Acts' to all Gothic tales, like Abraham's to *Hamlet,* to reveal the specific contents of their crypts. What is interesting, however, is to re-think Gothic's figuration of the other in relation to its obsession with ancestral phantoms and with the 'living dead'. Rosemary Jackson, in her influential book on fantasy writing, argues that fictional ghosts ultimately represent a unifying impulse – the drive to 'aid human affairs by restoring justice and moral order' or the drive 'to be unified with th[e] "other"'' (Jackson 97 and 100). In opposition to this I would argue that the ghost embodies the disruption and alienation of that other which resists assimilation (introjection), the other of which the self as cemetery guard is not the proprietor. Its non-present presence makes it inaccessible to symbolization. Its haunting 'untimeliness'/anachrony, to use Derrida's words again, puts to rout our meaning-to-say.

Gothic is rarely about exorcism; ghosts, as I have said, are not laid to rest to enable the restorative process of mourning – as the unresolved endings of most of the tales in the Oxford anthology of *Victorian Ghost Stories* show. Embedded like a small *mis en abyme* in LeFanu's tale is a scene with Dick lying in bed in the unhomely back bedroom waiting for another ghostly visitation. From here, far off in the street, he hears a drunkard singing of 'Murphy Delany', another drunkard who, as the song goes, falls into a river and is pronounced 'dead as a door-nail, so there was an end', only to return to life and prove his 'endlessness' by engaging in pitched battle with the coroner

(LeFanu 30–31). The paradox of phantoms is that they are the dead kept alive in us like a permanent embodiment of the repetition compulsion – or, as the story has it, '*da capo*' (31), from the beginning and all over again, like the song of Murphy Delany repeated in Dick's head. Is the suicide of Judge Horrocks or of the many other suicide ghosts in the anthology (or indeed the pseudo-suicide of the unfortunate Delany) an attempt, however futile, to put an end, once and for all ('dead as a door-nail'),[19] to the line of descent, the line which must go on being haunted? If Gothic is preoccupied with continuity and legitimacy, it is more insistently drawn to their negation.

Recent commentators on Derrida's *Specters of Marx* have agreed that not only has the spectre of Marx *not* been laid to rest in the French philosopher's text; it has also not been completely persuasively called up.[20] It is as if Derrida, as guard but not proprietor of Marx's cemetery, has released his ghost merely to observe its disruptive presence/non-presence, to parade its non-assimilation into late-capitalist society. In this respect, a comment by Fredric Jameson on Derrida's book is relevant. Talking about class, another conspicuous non-presence in *Specters of Marx*, Jameson writes:

> each of the opposing classes [and he has written, earlier, that 'there are only two fundamental classes in every mode of production'] necessarily carries the other around in its head and is internally torn and conflicted by a foreign body it cannot exorcise. ('Marx's Purloined Letter' 94–95)

The messianic, eschatological promise that Derrida holds out for late capitalism is thus little more than this 'tearing', conflictual body incapable of expulsion. The most that can be said for spectrality, as Jameson puts it, is very little:

> Spectrality does not involve the conviction that ghosts exist or that the past (and maybe even the future they offer to prophesy) is still very much alive and at work, within the living present: all it says, if it can be thought to speak, is that that living present is scarcely as self-sufficient as it claims to be; that we would do well not to count on its density and solidity, which might under exceptional circumstances betray us. (86)

Spectrality, he writes, is 'what makes the present waver' (85).

Our investigation of the phantom began by pointing (via Derrida) to the impossibility of origins, and has ended by invoking the interminableness of ends. Between these two (non-) limits, definable (or elusive of definition), the phantom comes to stand for what Abraham calls 'this hiatus . . . this non-presence of the self to itself . . . [which is the] ultimate reason behind all discourse' ('The Shell and the Kernel', qtd in Derrida's 'Foreword' xxxii). Gothic fiction, as an attempt to figure this hiatus, perpetually confronts the problem facing psychoanalysis: 'how to include in a discourse – in any one whatever – the very thing which, being the precondition of discourse, fundamentally escapes it' (*Shell and Kernel* 84).

EXTIMACY

Inevitably, then, phantoms draw us back into the non-presence from which they came – or rather into the impenetrable entanglement of the other within the self. In Lacanian terms, the ghost could be seen as a representation of the *aphanisis* (fading) of the subject through its alienation in the discourse of the Other:

> the subject appears first in the Other, in so far as the first signifier, the unary signifier, emerges in the field of the Other and represents the subject for another signifier, which other signifier has as its effect the *aphanisis* of the subject. Hence the division of the subject – when the subject appears somewhere as meaning, he is manifested elsewhere as 'fading', as disappearance. There is, then, one might say, a matter of life and death between the unary signifier and the subject, *qua* binary signifier, cause of his disappearance. (*Four Fundamental Concepts* 218)

In trying to find a French equivalent for *das Unheimliche*, Lacan came up with 'extimité' (extimacy, as opposed to intimacy), which he called an 'intimate exteriority' (*Seminar 7*: 139). The term is a useful one for signifying the breakdown of the distinction between self and other, inside and out, familiar and unfamiliar, which the uncanny effect produces. For extimacy, as Jacques-Alain Miller points out, is not in fact the contrary of intimacy but rather its complement or destabilizer, designating, ultimately, the presence of the Real in the Symbolic (Miller 122).

All political systems have attempted to integrate alterity, to 'refamiliarize' the uncanny in order to make it bearable. In *The Future of an Illusion* (1927), Freud traced this back to the primitive anthropomorphism or animism which underlies all human culture, the process whereby we people culture with beings like ourselves in order to 'breathe freely . . . [to] feel at home in the uncanny' (PF 12: 196). Religious or political systems attempt to neutralize or muffle this otherness of the other: love thy neighbour, the melting pot. And yet at bottom, no amount of reasoning can erase this basic condition of human subjectivity whereby to appear here as meaning is to be manifested elsewhere as fading. Racism, Miller writes, is founded on 'what one imagines about the Other's jouissance . . . Racist stories are always about the way in which the Other obtains a "*plus-de-jouir*"' (125). Talking (in the 1970s) about the rise of racism as a pathological projection of hatred onto others, Lacan observed:

> With our *jouissance* going off the track, only the Other is able to mark its position, but only insofar as we are separated from this Other. Whence certain fantasies – unheard of before the melting pot. (*Television* 32)

The 'fantasy' of the melting pot is for Lacan (as it would have been for Freud, who was deeply sceptical about the injunction to 'love thy neighbour') an attempt to incorporate or colonize the other in the name of a spurious equality, harmony, or sameness. As the locus of the deployment of speech in the Symbolic, the Other is by its very nature fated (like the image in the mirror) never to coincide with the one, yet perpetually to lure it to identification, marking the fundamental alienation that constitutes the subject as signifier.

Much of Julia Kristeva's work offers another way of looking at this, one which steers a more humane path between colonization on the one hand and alienation on the other. One of the consistent themes in all her work is what has been called a 'thorough commitment to foreignness', a call to submit to 'the pain of liminality' in order to appreciate ourselves as autonomous subjects (Galvan 182–83). A recent book of Kristeva's, *Strangers to Ourselves*, charts what she calls the experience of psychoanalysis as 'a journey into the strangeness of the other and of ourself', a journey with a goal: 'toward an ethics of respect for the irreconcilable. How could one tolerate a foreigner if one did not know one was a stranger to oneself?' (182)

Using Freud's definition of *das Unheimliche* as a touchstone, *Strangers to Ourselves* traces a history of foreignness/unfamiliarity in Western culture from Io in ancient mythology, who was forced to flee her native Argos to escape the wrath of the jealous Hera; to the Old Testament Ruth the Moabite, amidst the alien corn; through the cosmopolitanism of the Enlightenment – to, finally, Freud, who helped, she says, to remove the pathological aspect of the strangeness natural to the psyche. Freud's own 'foreignness' as a Jew in Vienna, she writes,

> conditions his concern to face the other's discontent as ill-ease in the continuous presence of the 'other scene' within us.[21] My discontent in living with the other – my strangeness, his strangeness – rests on the perturbed logic that governs this strange bundle of drive and language, of nature and symbol, constituted by the unconscious, always already shaped by the other. (181–82)

And she continues:

> It is through unraveling transference – the major dynamics of otherness, of love/hatred for the other, of the foreign component of our psyche – that, on the basis of the other, I become reconciled with my own otherness-foreignness, that I play on it and live by it. (182)

Fear of the outside, in other words, needs to be relocated within, so that the *Heimliche* and the *Unheimliche* perpetually confront each other and attempt to come to terms with the inevitability of their irreconcilability. It is not a comfortable solution. But it is the only one possible, Kristeva deems, in a post-holocaust age which is in a position to analyse the nature of the spectres it carries within itself.

6

The Subject of Hysteria

MISS JULIE (*goes towards the chopping block, as though drawn against her will*). No, I don't want to go yet. I can't – I must see – ssh! There's a carriage outside! (*She listens, but keeps her eyes fixed all the while on the chopping block and the axe.*) Do you think I can't bear the sight of blood? You think I'm so weak – oh, I should like to see your blood, your brains, on a chopping block – I'd like to see all your sex swimming in a lake of blood – I think I could drink from your skull, I'd like to bathe my feet in your guts, I could eat your heart, roasted! . . . You think I'm a coward and want to run away? No, now I shall stay. Let the storm break! . . .

JEAN   Have you ever loved your father, Miss Julie?

MISS JULIE   Yes – enormously – but I've hated him too. I must have done so without realizing it. But it was he who brought me up to despise my own sex, made me half-woman and half-man. Who is to blame for what has happened – my father, my mother, myself? Myself? I have no self. I haven't a thought I didn't get from my father, not an emotion I didn't get from my mother . . . I'm so tired! I can't feel anything, I can't repent, can't run away, can't stay, can't live – can't die. Help me! Order me, and I'll obey you like a dog . . . haven't you ever been to the theatre and seen a hypnotist? (Strindberg 139 and 144–45)

In this tirade that precedes her exit and presumed suicide at the end of *Miss Julie*, Strindberg's protagonist gathers to herself a cluster of qualities that would have made her immediately recognizable as the type of the hysteric, as recognizable to her age as she seems histrionic to ours. A product of *fin-de-siècle* emancipation, as Strindberg saw it and explained in his Preface, she is 'more urgently hysterical' (95) than

131

a woman of the previous generation, driven as she is by forces that were blurring the distinctions between man and woman, master and servant. Strindberg's anxiety about such changes gave his Preface its own hysterical agenda, making it a discordant echo of the play itself. But 1888–89 was a sensitive year,[1] with feminist activity gathering force throughout Western Europe, and Strindberg was clearly on edge.

The above scene shows Miss Julie moving through a range of different subject positions: from shrill insecurity (the popular image of the hysteric, to this day), to man-hater, lusting for vengeance, to witch (drinking from skulls, roasting hearts) to, finally, a pathological passivity, pleading for domination. All these positions, as we shall see, have comprised part of the long catalogue of clinical and lay definitions of hysteria since this time. The important thing, as Strindberg himself recognized, was the shifts. 'I have drawn my people as split and vacillating', he wrote in the Preface (95): this 'multiplicity of motives' and personalities is 'typical of our times' (94). The subject, particularly the female subject, was coming to be regarded as the site or meeting-point of an almost infinite range of confused hereditary and environmental forces. 'To 'have no self', as Miss Julie recognizes, is to acknowledge the over-determination of the constitutive elements of the unconscious, their plural and often contradictory etiology.

Miss Julie was received at the time with shock and dismay, and in spite of George Bernard Shaw's championship of the 'naturalistic' drama of both Ibsen and Strindberg, was not performed in London (and even then to a 'bewildered' audience [Strindberg 89]) until 1912, twenty-three years after its first performance in Copenhagen. This probably had less to do with the play's challenge to class and sexual codes than with the exposure of the confusing and outrageous instability in its central character. Unlike Ibsen's Nora in *The Doll's House*, or Shaw's own New Women like Candida or Miss Warren and her daughter Vivie, Miss Julie slams no doors but rather collapses indecisively under the weight of the 'multiplicity of motives' loaded upon her. Above all, she is portrayed as torn between a masculine and a feminine identification, a father's thoughts and a mother's emotions, as she puts it in the above passage. Earlier in the play, the conflict has been rather differently stated. As Miss Julie tells Jean, she was brought up under her mother's regimen of gender role reversal, when the men and women on the estate were set to perform each other's tasks. Her father's authority, however, finally put an end to this and forced marriage on her reluctant mother, who then proceeded to fall ill –

suffer convulsions, go into hiding (Strindberg 130). Strindberg's play thus becomes far more than the punishment of sexual transgression promised in the Preface. It traces a confusing shift in Oedipal identification and object choice, resulting in Julie in a crippling immobility, a splutter of contradictory negations: 'I can't go. I can't stay. Help me! I'm so tired . . . Order me! . . . I can't think, I can't act . . . And then – memories – . . . Kill me!' (134–39) These words could have been spoken by any one of Freud's women patients in Vienna at this very time. And when Jean cries out, in exasperation, 'For the last time – what do you want?' (133), he was anticipating the very words of masculine perplexity that Freud was to use after half a century of inconclusive research into the complexity and inaccessibility of female desire. In staging the irresolutions and oscillations of the hysteric, in other words, Strindberg was depicting a moment when the age's conceptions of gender, subjectivity and psychic disturbance converged under the label of hysteria in a way that would transform the next century's conceptions of all three.

HYSTERIA: CONSTRUCTION AND DECONSTRUCTION

When we trace the stages of Freud's decade-long exploration into hysteria in the 1880s–90s, what is striking is the way the definition of the disorder, far from consolidating through increasing knowledge, became increasingly open and fluid. Certain characteristics, which I shall be examining, were to become distinctive of the Freudian definition of hysteria: the 'conversion' of psychical conflict into somatic symptoms, the particularly acute manifestation of Oedipal anxiety, the dominance by 'reminiscences', and the coincidence with bisexuality. But these characteristics, instead of fixing the definition of hysteria, rather surfaced at different times to contribute to a changing process, to what became a very protean hypothesis. And this is a tendency that has continued to this day. Historians of hysteria draw attention to the way it has acted throughout its long history as a screen upon which are projected different views contingent upon changing clinical and cultural preconceptions. No doubt one of the reasons why hysteria has attracted so much recent attention is its high postmodern interpretability.[2] One of the many recent books to adopt this view is Elisabeth Bronfen's *The Knotted Subject: Hysteria and its Discontents* (1998), where it is argued that hysteria 'is constructed by the cultural images and medical discourses it imitates' (117). In fact, as she puts it, not only does hysteria exist 'only insofar as it results from a given network of medical, supernatural, religious, and aesthetic discourses', but it also 'does so by marking the blind spot or impossibility of the physician's representational gesture' (102). Her argument thus comes close at times to treating hysteria as a vacuum which medical and cultural ignorance or anxiety rush to fill.

At the same time, it is easy to forget that hysteria *as a psychoanalytic diagnosis* was a construction specific to this *fin-de-siècle* period alone. This is partly due to the well-known fact that the word 'hysteria' reaches back through the medieval period to ancient times, which associated erratic female behaviour with a wandering womb (*hystera* in Greek). And from the twentieth to the present century, although the term is no longer used clinically (having been replaced by related diagnoses such as eating disorders or PTSD, Post-traumatic Stress Disorder), people (mainly women) are still called hysterical at the slightest indication of temper, with the implication that their bodies are somehow to blame. As part of a centuries-long vocabulary, the concept of hysteria seems to have a truth status that neither scientific rationalism nor feminist objection has been able to remove.

Behind Breuer and Freud's radical new theories of hysteria in the 1880s–90s lay a century and a half of confused hypotheses of the link between the psyche and the soma. From early Christian times, hysteria had been seen as a sign of the devil, a 'possession' of the mind and the body which only the most drastic forms of persecution could keep under control. But even after the abolition of witch hunts in the seventeenth century, the idea continued as cultural legend that women's physical (in particular their sexual) make-up was liable to disturb their mental stability. Outlandish displays of emotional behaviour were produced as often as they were predicted, as if women could perform, on demand, the role of being, like the young Jane Eyre, 'a trifle beside myself, or rather *out* of myself, as the French would say' (Brontë 44). The eighteenth century made the first important shift in its view of hysteria as a matter not of moral and physical possession but of the nerves. As Foucault puts it in his analysis of hysteria in the Age of Reason (*Madness and Civilization* 146), 'a dynamics of corporeal space was replaced by a morality of sensibility'. And yet without a theory of the unconscious, this 'sensibility' remained a mystery, the source of a whole range of speculations about 'malign vapors' or 'internal heat' (Foucault 139–40). Towards the end of the century, however, the Austrian physician Friedrich Anton Mesmer began to perform spectacular hypnotizing feats on Viennese and Parisian women. In the century that followed, intensive research was undertaken to investigate what hypnosis was beginning to reveal about unconscious mental processes.

The crucial influence of Jean-Martin Charcot on Freud's developing views of the relation between mind and body is well known.[3] What was ultimately important for Freud about Charcot's work at the Salpêtrière hospital in Paris, where the young Viennese trainee spent several months in 1885–86, was less the spectacular visible effects of hysteria on the human body than the emphasis Charcot gave to the fact that these effects do not necessarily correspond to any known organic cause. It was from these insights that Freud was able to make the radical shift from the long-held view of hysteria as a physical disease causing psychological symptoms to that of a psychological disease producing quasi-physical symptoms (Micale 27). From this new shift, it could be argued, modern psychoanalysis was born.

Although he took the radical step of regarding hysteria as a condition common to both men and women, Charcot is remembered mainly for his demonstrations of the dramatic effects of hysteria on the female body at his Tuesday lectures attended by crowds of avid spectators, from medical students to journalists and actors (Showalter, *Female Malady* 148). Charcot's emphasis was on observation, on mapping out what he called the 'hysterogenic zones' of the body and the production and relief of hysterical symptoms through the use of hypnosis. It was from this research that Freud learned to regard the symptom as a form of symbolization, the expression on the body of repressed psychological experiences. Pain that originates in the psyche is projected, by displacement, onto the body.

But in Freud's collaboration with Josef Breuer that followed his return to Vienna from Paris, it was to be the aural rather than the visual symptoms of hysteria that would take priority. Freud always insisted, to the end, that it was Breuer who had founded psychoanalysis as 'the talking cure'. Breuer, for his part, credited his patient 'Anna O.' (Bertha Pappenheim) with the discovery. Pappenheim had been referred to Breuer in 1880 suffering from a nervous cough after a long period of nursing her sick father. This was followed by a series of symptoms ranging from headaches, muscular paralysis and disturbances of vision to sensations that the walls around her were collapsing, sudden mental 'absences', and above all disturbances of speech.

These lead at times to a loss of grammar or syntax and an inappropriate use of one of the several foreign languages she knew, rather than her own native German, or even, to a complete loss of speech. Breuer's innovation was to make use of speech itself to treat her symptoms; somehow, he narrates, her mind was relieved of its terrifying hallucinations if she could be persuaded to 'give . . . verbal utterance to them' (PF 3: 83). He was to discover, too, his own seminal role as interlocutor in releasing this speech. Astonishingly, Pappenheim lived out (or rather 'talked off' [88]) the traumatic events of the previous year of her life, day by day, in precise and later verified order, simply on the production of an orange before her eyes or at the feel of Breuer's hand.

But the problem was that when one symptom disappeared as a result of this method, another would invariably take its place. Symptoms, as analysed by Freud in the years to come, are a curious displacement of mental pain onto the body, a 'conversion' or symbolization of the original trauma, which acts like a 'foreign body' in the system and seeks expression. To expect a direct correlation between exciting cause and manifest symptom is to ignore the complexity of this process. As Lacan was to put it, a symptom can be regarded as a signifier, that which stands in for the indecipherability of unconscious desire. It is thus, by its very nature, arbitrary and elusive.[4]

For Bertha Pappenheim, Breuer's talking cure was far from the success he seemed to claim. Many years later, Freud revealed the details behind the hurriedly-concluded treatment, which left Pappenheim with an array of neurotic disorders, in and out of sanatoria, for at least a decade afterwards. The relationship of locutor and interlocutor had yielded something else: an unconscious erotic entanglement and a phantasy (on Bertha's part) of pregnancy. Breuer had insisted, at the opening of his case narrative, that 'The element of sexuality was astonishingly undeveloped' in his patient (PF 3: 73). It was this failure to confront the sexual etiology of her neurosis which was the greatest source of disagreement between Breuer and Freud, whose ways soon parted after the publication of their *Studies on Hysteria* in 1895.

Controversial in its time, the Anna O. case still has the capacity to arouse strong feelings. Feminists in the 1970s and '80s argued that the case reveals patriarchal blindness rather than psychological insight. Several recent essays have celebrated Pappenheim (and other hysterical patients) for her expression (in symptoms) of what culture represses – in particular anger and resentment. Dianne Hunter believes that 'Hysteria can be considered as a self-repudiating form of feminine discourse in which the body signifies what social conditions make it impossible to state linguistically' (113–14). Hysteria, in this reading, is a form of feminist reaction in a society which disallows it. At the same time, serious doubt has been cast upon the validity of Breuer's clinical method. Building on research done by Henri Ellenberger, Albrecht Hirschmüller, Peter Swales and others, Mikkel Borch-Jacobsen has recently argued that the case can only be regarded as 'a hoax, or at least a folie à deux, between doctor and patient' (*Remembering Anna O*. 75). Bertha's so-called 'illness', he argues, was a construction after the event, the product of a climate of hysterical self-suggestion resulting from intense interest in hypnotism in certain pseudo-medical circles in Vienna at the time. Stage hypnotists throughout Europe were performing remarkable feats, among them examples of hypermnesia in which Breuer was particularly interested.[5] Borch-Jacobsen summarizes reports that

> Some patients could recite whole passages from books. Others spoke languages forgotten since childhood, vividly recalling past events and even past lives. Still others remembered (as Bertha Pappenheim also did) everything that had taken place during previous somnambulistic states, events of which they retained no memory in their normal waking state. (70)

Hypnotic hypermnesia, he argues, is purely self-referential, a memory not of actual events from the past but of previous somnambulistic states. Bertha's astonishing 'memories' under Breuer's treatment were, like all her symptoms, the product of hypnotic suggestion rather than of genuine psychotic trauma. Hysteria, he concludes, 'is not a real illness' (83); like hypnosis, its revelations are *sur*real, simulation pushed to the limits of that mysterious interchange between mind and body (91).

SUFFERING FROM REMINISCENCES

This scepticism is a far cry from Freud's own assessment of the significance of his early work with Breuer. Looking back in 1914 on the history of the psychoanalytic movement, he reasserted the importance of the role of memory. Psychoanalysis, he wrote, soon learned that it 'could explain nothing belonging to the present without referring back to something past' (PF 15: 67), and 'memory', in its newly evolving definition, was crucial to this link. Freud was often to repeat, in later years, the paradox that though we 'forget' nothing, we 'remember' very little.

He appears in this context to be speaking about the power of conscious recall as opposed to unconscious amnesia. But as the *Dreams* book was to argue in detail, our memories 'are in themselves unconscious'. He explains:

> They can be made conscious; but there can be no doubt that they can produce all their effects while in an unconscious condition. What we describe as our 'character' is based on the memory-traces of our impressions; moreover, the impressions which have had the greatest effect on us – those of our earliest youth – are precisely the ones which scarcely ever become conscious. (PF 4: 689)

If '*Hysterics suffer mainly from reminiscences*', as he and Breuer famously put it at the beginning of the *Studies* (PF 3: 58), it is reminiscences as unconscious traces, what he called 'mnemic symbols' (symbols of the repressed memory). Hysterics differ from others in that the affect attached to traumatic experiences they have had has not been discharged ('abreacted') but remains 'strangulated', and the memory of the experience to which it is attached is cut off from consciousness (PF 3: 37).

The process of 'Remembering, Repeating and Working-Through', a title Freud was to give to one of his later papers (1914; SE 12: 145–56), was to become the corner-stone of the analytic method several decades later. But for all his hesitations and resistances, Breuer had hit upon something crucial in his treatment of Bertha Pappenheim, that the acting out of an earlier experience, even if only of an earlier hypnotic experience, as something real and contemporary, brought about some form of change. Cure was not a matter of simple 'catharsis', as Breuer thought, but of processes that Freud was to pick up and develop: namely association, resistance and transference. Later still, as we shall see, Lacan would focus on the role of language in the 'remembrance' of desire, and would restate the matter in a characteristically paradoxical formula: 'one is not cured because one remembers. One remembers because one is cured' (*Écrits* 260).

But all this lay in the future. In the 1890s, the question that was increasingly preoccupying Freud was: what is it that hysterics remember? The 'trauma', so called, in the Anna O. case was traced by Breuer to the death of her 'adored father' (PF 3: 78). But this occurred *after* the first display of symptoms, so could not be regarded as primarily precipitating. In his own cases, however, Freud probed persistently into the etiology of the neurosis, and it was this instinct, to go increasingly further back into the subject's individual history, which led to sexuality.

A discovery of such magnitude, now taken for granted as the essence of Freud's contribution, was described by him later as having taken him by storm when first indirectly suggested by the two men who exerted the greatest influence over him at this formative time. Retrospection no doubt added the touch of drama to the description. And Freud certainly knew how to tell a good story. This is how he describes Breuer's suggestion:

> One day, when I was a young house-physician, I was walking across the town with Breuer, when a man came up who evidently wanted to speak to him urgently. I fell behind. As soon as Breuer was free, he told me in his friendly, instructive way that this man was the husband of a patient of his and had brought him some news of her. The wife, he added, was behaving in such a peculiar way in society that she had been brought to him for treatment as a nervous case. He concluded: 'These things are always *secrets d'alcôve*!' I asked him in astonishment what he meant, and he answered by explaining the word *alcôve* ('marriage-bed') to me, for he failed to realize how extraordinary the *matter* of his statement seemed to me. (PF 15: 70)

The incident with Charcot, described in the next paragraph of the 'History of the Psychoanalytic Movement', contains the same novelistic elements: preparation of setting, character drawing, build-up to the revelation. The difference is that in casting himself this time as the recipient of a badly overheard mystery, whose message is to leave him 'almost paralysed with amazement', Freud has dramatized the incident to the pitch of a Gothic or detective novel:

Some years later, at one of Charcot's evening receptions, I happened to be standing near the great teacher at a moment when he appeared to be telling Brouardel [Professor of Forensic Medicine in Paris] a very interesting story about something that had happened during his day's work. I hardly heard the beginning, but gradually my attention was seized by what he was talking of: a young married couple from a distant country in the East – the woman a severe sufferer, the man either impotent or exceedingly awkward. '*Tâchez donc*' I heard Charcot repeating, '*je vous assure, vous y arrivez*' ['Go on trying! I promise you, you'll succeed.'] Brouardel, who spoke less loudly, must have expressed his astonishment that symptoms like the wife's could have been produced by such circumstances. For Charcot suddenly broke out with great animation: '*Mais, dans des cas pareils c'est toujours la chose génitale, toujours . . . toujours . . . toujours*' ['But in this sort of case it's always a question of the genitals – always, always, always']; and he crossed his arms over his stomach, hugging himself and jumping up and down on his toes several times in his own characteristically lively way. I know that for a moment I was almost paralysed with amazement and said to myself: 'Well, but if he knows that, why does he never say so?' But the impression was soon forgotten . . . (70–71)

Freud's case studies of the late 1880s and early '90s, those of Emmy von N., Lucy R., Katharina and Elisabeth von R., show him working steadily towards the view, later to be modified, that what hysterics remember is the trauma of a childhood seduction, usually by the father. He also learned that traumas of this kind take effect not with one-off finality but in time layers, over many years. Katharina, described as the 'niece' (but actually the daughter) of an innkeeper in an alpine resort Freud visited, had at age 16 witnessed a scene of sexual intercourse between her uncle and her cousin, which led to attacks of hysterical anxiety – breathlessness, hammering in the head and dizziness. Further questioning revealed that she had herself been the victim of attempted seduction by the uncle, on several occasions, when she was around 14. On these first occasions, she had been ignorant of the meaning of his advances. It was only later, when witnessing the scene with her cousin, that she experienced the 'trauma' of their implications. The 'disgust', causing physical vomiting at the sight of the couple, was caused, then, by *memory*, the memory of her own earlier experiences. Freud writes:

in the former experiences an element of consciousness was created which was excluded from the thought-activity of the ego and remained, as it were, in storage, while in the latter scene a new impression forcibly brought about an associative connection between this separated group and the ego. (PF 3: 199)

Charcot, he notes, 'liked to describe this interval as the "period of psychical working-out" [*élaboration*]' (200–1).

Looking back on his work on hysteria in the 1890s (and so much of its effect, like that of hysteria itself, was dependent on retrospective constructions, what we have already seen he was to call *Nachträglich-keit* [deferred action]), Freud came to believe that its importance lay in the processes that emerge, as a side-effect, from the attempt to trace the symptoms back to their sources in past life. These are the processes of resistance and of transference; so central are they to the psycho-analytic process, Freud argued, that failure to take account of them would preclude any practitioner from the right to call him/herself a psychoanalyst (PF 15: 73–74).

But in some ways these early cases threw up as many false leads as they did genuine revelations, and it was to be at least a decade before Freud had established an acceptable set of working hypotheses for the treatment of hysteria. Hypnosis had to be discarded, partly because Freud was inept at it, but also because he was discovering the efficacy of the method of free linguistic association. So did Breuer's theory of catharsis, which gave the false impression that release/abreaction brought its own cure. More importantly, the tracing of neurosis back to its origins in childhood seduction was proving increasingly difficult to support in face of the implausibility of such large numbers of cases leading back to paternal perversion. Freud's 1897 abandonment of the seduction theory in favour of that of the *phantasy* of seduction has received much critical attention and some censure.[6] Its centrality is undeniable, for it changes the view of psychic reaction from that which emanates from the memory of lived experience to that of phantasmatic construction. Psychical reality, in other words, has taken on a new pre-eminence. As Wendy Cealey Harrison has put it, it forces us to the awareness that 'It is phantasy that attaches desire to sensation, rather than sensation which induces desire' (167). To those who object to this denial of the reality of child abuse, it is fair to point out, as well, that Freud did not rule out its significance in the etiology of some cases – as he puts it in one of the 'Introductory Lectures':

A phantasy of being seduced when no seduction has occurred is usually employed by a child to screen the auto-erotic period of his sexual activity. He spares himself shame about masturbation by retrospectively phantasying a desired object into these earliest times. You must not suppose, however, that sexual abuse of a child by its nearest male relatives belongs entirely to the realm of phantasy. Most analysts will have treated cases in which such events were real and could be unimpeachably established. (PF 1: 417)

The controversial line between reality and phantasy, exemplified in the seduction theory, is one which underpins postmodern literature and ideology in their preoccupation with 'history' as 'fiction'. From Salman Rushdie's 'factional' reconstruction of the history of India as autobiography in *Midnight's Children* to Baudrillard's argument that 'there has been no Gulf War', writers have attempted to examine the process of 'retrospectively phantasying a desired object' as the principle on which reality is reconstructed. I shall be returning at the end of this chapter to examine a recent play, Terry Johnson's *Hysteria*, which uses the historical moment of Freud's 1897 change of heart over the seduction theory to highlight postmodern drama's investment in the obscuring of the reality–phantasy distinction.

It has also been pointed out, with hindsight, that it would be more accurate to speak of a modification rather than an abandonment of the seduction theory. Although Freud discounted the factor of paternal seduction as a universal cause of hysteria, in later years he emphasized that 'it was really the mother who by her activities over the child's bodily hygiene inevitably stimulated and perhaps even roused for the first time, pleasurable sensations in her [the infant girl's] genitals' (PF 2: 154).[7] At the end of 1897, however, the recurrence of 'screen' memories of paternal seduction was an important clue for Freud in his research into infantile sexuality and its orientation towards the parents. The discovery of the Oedipal was to be announced to Fliess only a month after the statement of the abandonment of the seduction theory (*The Origins of Psycho-Analysis* 223).

At this crucial period of 1897–99, then, Freud was not only writing the *Dreams* book but was elaborating on the main tenets of his developing clinical technique: dream analysis as offering access to the unconscious, the role of infantile sexuality, 'resistance' (defence and repression), free association and the transference. When 'Dora'

(Ida Bauer) was referred to him at the end of 1900 presenting a range of hysterical symptoms mainly to do with coughing and speechlessness ('It is a hysteria with *tussis nervosa* and aphonia' [*Origins* 327]), Freud was in a unique position to test out the impact of this new set of theories.

TELLING A CLEAR STORY: THE DORA CASE

Freud's skills as a narrator were to be considerably sharpened by the demands of giving coherent form to the case studies in hysteria. By the time he came to write 'Dora', the most well known and influential of his cases, he had discovered that psychoanalytic writing shaded very easily into engrossing literary narrative. In telling Fliess that it was 'the subtlest thing I have so far written' (*Origins* 326), Freud was undoubtedly referring to more than its scientific achievements. In the history of the proximity between literary and psychoanalytic discourses, it is this work which has acted as the show piece.

A crucial aspect of Freud's theory of hysteria had to do with his view of the nature of narrative, the way we tell the stories of our lives. At the beginning of the Dora case, he reports in a footnote on a session with another patient and makes the following observation:

> In my first hour with the patient I got her to tell me her history herself. When the story came out perfectly clearly and connectedly in spite of the remarkable events it dealt with, I told myself that the case could not be one of hysteria. (PF 8: 46n1)

A coherent narrative, in other words, rules out hysteria. Hysteria is about gaps in texts: repressions, amnesias, paramnesias, even conscious silences, as Dora's appeared to be. Freud's description of how he set about putting together his own narrative of the case shows him struggling to assert control, to emphasize his own immunity to such incoherence. And yet the nature of the material is such, he apologizes, that this has not been entirely possible. His account of the difficulty, with its extended similes, takes on a distinctly literary tone:

> This first account may be compared to an unnavigable river whose stream is at one moment choked by masses of rock and at another divided and lost among shallows and sandbanks.

The connections in the narrative, he continues,

> – even the ostensible ones – are for the most part incoherent, and the sequence of different events is uncertain. Even during the course of their story patients will repeatedly correct a particular or a date, and then perhaps, after wavering for some time, return to their first version. The patients' inability to give an ordered history of their life in so far as it coincides with the history of their illness is not merely characteristic of the neurosis. It also possesses great theoretical significance. (PF 8: 45–46)

With its gaps and fragmentariness, the Dora case has often been referred to as a classic piece of Modernist narrative. Beginning this trend in 1974, Steven Marcus compared it to an Ibsen play, calling its organization 'plastic, involuted, and heterogeneous' and its method one of 'nondirectional free association' (Marcus 64–65). More recently, Peter Brooks has written (in *Psychoanalysis and Storytelling* [1994]) that the Dora case

> reads as a kind of failed Edwardian novel, one that can never reach a satisfactory dénouement, and that can never quite decide what the relations among its cast of characters truly are: as if Freud were one of Henry James's baffled yet inventive narrators (as, for instance, in *The Sacred Fount*). (50)

Freud saw from the start that Dora had much to repress in the telling of her tale. Her father was having an affair with a close family friend, Frau K., whose husband had in compensation been making advances to the teenage Dora, with the unspoken complicity of her father. Freud didn't fall for the father's argument that Dora was behaving unreasonably in her rudeness to Herr K.; he saw immediately that she was being used as the object of a sordid exchange. And yet in the analysis, he concentrated on the Oedipal origins of Dora's symptoms and insisted right to the end of the three months' treatment, and in spite of Dora's protests, on her need to recognize her love for Herr K. as the replacement for her Oedipal attachment to her father.

Freud's text, however, is notoriously divided against itself. As has often been pointed out,[8] there is an alternative diagnosis running counter to this, one that appears tentatively, mainly in the footnotes and Postscript added to the later version of the case.[9] Here Freud wrote:

behind Dora's supervalent train of thought which was concerned
with her father's relations with Frau K. there lay concealed a feeling
of jealousy which had that lady as its *object* – a feeling, that is, which
could only be based upon an affection on Dora's part for one of her
own sex. (PF 8: 95)

Freud's discomfort, in 1901, with this scandalous strand of Dora's
tale resulted in 'silences' of his own in his text. What is more, as
Madelon Sprengnether argues, Freud's overemphasis on phallic
aggression in the case, the imperative of the Oedipal, points to his
anxiety about his own feminine identification (suggested in his letters
to Fliess), and about castration. Sprengnether thus turns the tables
completely when she describes Dora, the patient to be relieved of her
silence, as 'a silent witness to the anxieties and repressions of Freud's
narrative' ('Enforcing Oedipus' 270). Freud had taken care to call the
case a 'Fragment of an Analysis of a Case of Hysteria', and spent time,
especially in the Postscript, explaining the reasons for its gaps, above
all those resulting from its being broken off abruptly by Dora in the
middle. In accounting so meticulously for its fragmentariness, therefore, Freud could be said to be attempting to forestall criticism of its
deeper gaps. The explicit gaps or silences act as a defence, a decoy for
the more unconscious ones.

Much of Freud's strategy with Dora, it could be said, worked
towards not so much encouraging her to talk her way to a cure as
teaching her to be silent. We can trace this in the way he listened
attentively to her narratives, but turned a deaf ear to or actively tried
to suppress her reactions to his interpretations. Freud's account reads
like a set of hypotheses punctuated by Dora's denials. These denials
must not be confused with the phenomenon of negation (which Freud
touches on in the case [92n1] and elaborated in detail in later essays),[10]
whereby the patient presents material from the unconscious, couched
in negative form, as a thin disguise for its affirmation. (As Freud
famously remarked, 'there is no such thing at all as an unconscious
"No".' [92]) But Dora's insistent and *conscious* denials of Freud's
interpretations are another matter.[11] In the early stages of the analysis,
we are told, Dora 'persisted in denying my contentions' (94) or 'flatly
denied' (112) a childhood memory; 'her usual reply' to him was ' "I
don't remember that" ' (91). As the case proceeds, however, Freud
charts a decrease in resistance: 'Dora no longer denied my supposition,
although she still remembered nothing' (115–16); 'Dora . . . listened to

me without any of her usual contradictions' (150); 'she nodded assent'
(148); and finally, 'Dora disputed the fact no longer' (145). What is
noticeable here is the speechlessness of Dora's so-called assent – a nod,
a failure to contradict. An 'assent' on her part was only ever 'tacit'
(81). And taciturnity, the reaction of the silent body, was to mark her
final response to Freud's interpretations when she walked out on the
analysis without explanation.

TRANSFERENCE AND THE DORA CASE

The Dora case taught Freud a great deal about 'resistance', both
Dora's and his own, and although he was not always ready to
acknowledge or make use of these lessons at the time, they were of
crucial importance in years to come. Looking back on the case, Freud
was as aware of its shortcomings as he was of its 'subtleties'. It wasn't
just that he blamed himself for his failure to notice the significance of
Dora's 'gynaecophilic' love for Frau K. (162n1). He was also very
aware, soon afterwards, of the significance of 'not succeed[ing] in
mastering the transference in good time', as he put it in the
Postscript (160).

Although Dora's transferential relation to Freud had an arguably
less dramatic outcome than Anna O.'s to Breuer, it was no less far-
reaching in its implications. Freud's neglect of the homosexual element
in Dora's object choices did not mean that he was mistaken in his
perceptions of her Oedipal heterosexuality. Bisexuality, as we shall see,
was soon to become a well-charted feature of the neurosis. But we can
understand the difficulty for Freud in disentangling the threads of
erotic attachment, in recognizing that Dora was as incensed at her own
replacement by Frau K. in her father's affections ('either her or me'
[90]) as she was anxious to secure the woman's affections for herself.
Freud was almost certainly right that her displacement onto him of her
feelings for her father, and via him for Herr K., was the cause of her
abrupt and revengeful termination of the treatment. Yet there were
other reasons, as we have seen: over-determination, the contribution
of several causes to the same effect, was clearly at work here.

Transference has proved to be one of Freud's most important
legacies, not only to clinical psychoanalysis, but to psychoanalytic
literary theory as well. Literary scholars were quick to detect that
Freud's descriptions of the process of transference were couched in

terms very close to those of their own practice. Freud first discussed transference in his essay on 'The Psychotherapy of Hysteria' in the *Studies on Hysteria*. But it was at the end of the Dora case that he elaborated on its therapeutic significance. Here he writes:

> What are transferences? They are *new editions or facsimiles* of the impulses and phantasies which are aroused and made conscious during the progress of the analysis; but they have this peculiarity . . . that they replace some earlier person by the person of the physician. To put it another way: a whole *series* of psychological experiences are revived, not as belonging to the past, but as applying to the person of the physician at the present moment. Some of these transferences have a content which differs from that of their model in no respect whatever except for the substitution. These then – to keep to the same metaphor – are merely *new impressions or reprints*. Others are more ingeniously constructed; their content has been subjected to a moderating influence . . . These, then, will no longer be new impressions, but *revised editions*. (PF 8: 157–58, emphasis added)

The publishing metaphors were characteristic of the way Freud conflated the processes of psychological recall and literary narrative, a tendency which has proved particularly fruitful to theorists of narrative in recent years. The literary appropriation of the model of analytic transference can be traced back to the late 1970s – from Shoshana Felman's 'Turning the Screw of Interpretation' (1977), through important work in the 1980s by narrative theorists such as Roy Schafer ('Narration in the Psychoanalytic Dialogue'), Neil Hertz ('Dora's Secrets, Freud's Techniques') and Donald Spence (*Narrative Truth and Historical Truth*), to the work of Peter Brooks in the last decade and a half (*Reading for the Plot* [1984] and *Psychoanalysis and Storytelling* [1994] in particular). Brooks's 'transferential' model of reading traces the analogies between narrator–narratee (or author–reader) and analysand–analyst, the way no story can take on meaning without relation to its anticipated reception. Citing the argument of Barthes' *S/ Z* that all storytelling is contractual, a demand for something in return for what it supplies, Brooks sets out to move beyond formalist paradigms of narrative analysis by using a Freudian (and to a certain extent Lacanian) model of psychic life, one which engages the dynamics of memory and desire. Narrative truth, he writes, arises from a dialogue among a number of *fabula* and a number of *sjužet*, stories and their possible organizations, as also between two narrators, analysand and analyst. A centerless and reversible structure, dialogue is an agency of narration that creates as it questions the narrative, and designates the field of force of the necessary fiction. (*Reading for the Plot* 284)

In designating both analyst (narratee) and analysand (narrator) as participants of equal significance in the dialogue, Brooks is moving closer to a Lacanian model, which emphasizes the equal significance of the counter-transference in the therapeutic experience, the psychic investment of the analyst's own desire in the process. For Lacan, as we have seen, the desire of the one is inextricably entangled with the desire of the other, so that no real distinction needs to be drawn between transference and counter-transference. For most commentators on the Dora case, Freud's failure to take cognizance of his counter-transferential relation to her, his identification with the 'still quite young and of prepossessing appearance' Herr K. (PF 8: 60n2) was a serious drawback. For Lacan, however, it was inevitable. The analyst's role, he contended, is primarily to set in motion the dialectical process of transference and counter-transference, not as an end in itself but as a means of breaking analytic deadlock: 'the transference is nothing real in the subject other than the appearance, in a moment of stagnation of the analytic dialectic, of the permanent modes according to which it constitutes its objects' . Interpreting the transference is thus merely a 'ruse to fill in the emptiness of this deadlock' . And 'while it may be deceptive, this ruse serves a purpose by setting off the whole process again' ('Intervention' 71).

What, then, is the purpose of keeping the process going? Lacan's answer is that it is to lead the patient 'to the object of her real interest' (71), in this case, in his opinion, not so much Dora's Oedipal desire for Herr K., or even her desire for Frau K., but rather 'the mystery of her femininity . . . her bodily femininity' (67), whose inaccessibility lies behind the moment of fixation before the painting of the body of the Madonna in the second dream recorded in the case. The Dora case for Lacan is especially relevant in the demonstration of the process of transference because it involves hysteria and in hysteria, as he writes, 'there [is] nowhere else . . . where the threshold is lower between the unconscious and the conscious, or rather, between the analytic discourse and the *word* of the symptom'. (72)[12] This vital play between the word of the analytic discourse and the word of the symptom is described, arrestingly, in another essay, 'The Freudian Thing':

> it is out of the forfeits and vain oaths, lapses in speech and unconsidered words [that is, through the play of and gaps between signifiers in the analytic discourse], that is moulded the stone guest who comes in symptoms, to disturb the banquet of one's desires. (*Écrits*143)

The hysteric represents the quintessence of human subjectivity in that he or (but usually) she speaks from a position of lack.[13] What the limbs speak in hysteria is the *jouissance* that exceeds representation. And yet to 'speak' one's *jouissance*, to mime the presence rather than the absence of the object or the signified, is to succumb to neurosis. In her Lacanian study of hysteria, Monique David-Ménard puts it this way:

> In hysterical symptoms . . . language . . . precipitates on to the body instead of continuing to play in the element of the signifiers . . . words . . . solidify in fixing themselves on to a thing. This thing, by the same token, loses its quality as object . . . as residue of a loss taken into account by language, to become a thing, *The Thing*, too present, not sufficiently lost. (114)

What we witness in hysteria and what constitutes it as neurosis, therefore, is the *presence* of the word of the symptom, 'the lack of the lack that gives rise to desire' (Ragland-Sullivan, 'The Sexual Masquerade' 51).

If Lacan sees the transference as a form of 'ruse', for Kristeva, more recently, it needs to be defined as love, the love that is re-enacted in analysis. Her terms are basically Lacanian, however, first in the conception of subjectivity as inseparable from both the other (the original love object) and the Other (the Symbolic order), and more fundamentally, in her positioning of discourse ('that passion of signs') at the centre of the operation. This is how she explains it in *Tales of Love*:

> Transference love is a dynamic involving three people: the *subject* (the analysand), his imaginary or real *object* of love (the *other* with whom what is being played out is the whole intersubjective drama of

neurosis or, in more severe cases, of the disintegration of identity leading to psychosis), and the *Third Party*, the stand-in for potential Ideal, possible Power. The analyst occupies that place of the *Other*; he is a subject who is supposed to know – and know how to love – and as a consequence he will, in the cure, become the supreme loved one and first-class victim . . . it ['this great Other'] ushers in that passion of signs exemplified by free association, displacement, condensation, and so forth, in short, a literature lacking an audience just as it lacks a social code, but nevertheless as disturbing and intense as the cathartic effects of great art. (13–14)

What both 'art' and the transference have in common, in other words, is the fact that the production of meaning, via signs, is dependent upon a dialectic of a subject 'supposed to know' and a subject who presupposes this knowledge in the other. However much this knowledge may be an illusion, it is the basis of the continuity of the signifying chain, upon which desire is dependent.

To illustrate this point, Lacan makes a comparison between the Dora case and the classic seventeenth-century novel, *La Princesse de Clèves* by Mme de La Fayette. An elegant representation of upper-class Parisian manners, the novel depicts, like 'Dora', a woman trapped and silenced under the weight of impossible erotic conflict. Freud's counter-transferential relation to Dora, Lacan writes,

elevates this text, among the psychopathological monographs which make up a genre of our literature, to the tone of a Princesse de Clèves trapped by a deadly blocking of utterance. ('Intervention' 69–70)

What he means, I think, is that both texts depict a triangulation of interlocking and mutually exclusive desires. In 'Dora', Freud's own unacknowledged desire within the complex of transferential and counter-transferential cross-currents prevents continuation of the dialogue with Dora. In La Fayette's novel, the Princess is situated at the point of irresolution between her insertion in the Symbolic (her 'duty' to her sympathetic husband, M. de Clèves) and her rigidly repressed passion for M. de Nemours. Her reaction (until the long-delayed climax with its famous confession) is a prolonged silence and a final retreat to a convent. The 'deadly blocking of utterance', in both cases, marks the mutual dependence of language and *jouissance*. The sign's the thing, to misquote Hamlet. In the literary as well as the analytic encounter, knowledge can be produced only through the unleashing of a full range of expression. To focus on 'the mute aspects of behaviour in the psychological manoeuvre', as was the case in the treatment of hysteria before Freud, is according to Lacan to treat 'the subject [as] no more than an object' ('Intervention' 63).

LITERATURE AS CASE STUDY: GEORGE ELIOT'S *THE LIFTED VEIL*

In his discovery of the difficulty of distinguishing between 'truth' and 'fiction', Freud was of course merely endorsing, from the scientific perspective, what fiction writers had known for a long time. Freud himself was to become interested in this literary knowledge, and to use it for his own purposes, as we have seen in the previous chapter in connection with his analysis of Hoffmann's 'The Sandman'. Gothic fiction, with its overt preoccupation with dreams and disturbed psychic states, was an obvious genre for him to choose. In the development of the novel, it could be argued, Gothic served a crucial function in its contrivance of conventions (such as the double, or supernatural phenomena) for the fictional representation of the unconscious. Scholars of the genre have examined its continuation throughout the nineteenth century alongside the dominant genre of the realist novel, with many authors trying their hand at both (Gaskell, Henry James) or at least a mixture of both within the one work (Charlotte Brontë, Dickens). Even George Eliot, in whose novels English realism is usually held to have reached its peak, made an attempt at it, though the result has not had a very enthusiastic reception.[14] Through its handling of supernatural phenomena, however, Eliot's version of the Gothic offers insight into what can be read as a case of hysteria (this time in a male) at a time, a generation before Freud, when many different scientific and literary sources were working towards its understanding.

   The Lifted Veil (a novella, published in *Blackwood's Magazine* in 1859) is a strange work, a 'history of a young man . . . growing up in morbid physical conditions', to use a phrase from Henry James' review of it (qtd in Charles Swann 40), which reads less like fiction than a psychoanalytic case history *avant la lettre*. Latimer, the first-person narrator, pays lavish attention to his various symptoms, which include melancholy, *taedium vitae*, and inexplicable, semi-hypnotic powers of prevision, which have given him warning of his own imminent death. As he sits in his room, waiting to die, he recounts his circumstances, the loss of his mother at an early age, the harsh and ambitious father, the well-endowed older step-brother. 'My nature', as he assesses it, 'was of the sensitive, unpractical order, and . . . grew up in an uncongenial medium, which could never foster it into happy, healthy development.' (*The Lifted Veil* 8) Like Frankenstein, he studies in a central-European university, where his father hopes to make a scientist of him. But he shuns all such 'knowledge', particularly that relating to 'electricity and magnetism' (7), the two branches of learning which lie at the centre of Mary Shelley's novel as the respective objects of Frankenstein's and Walton's quests. In spite of this, some of the magnetic fervour seems to have infected him (as it did Marian Evans herself [Gray 79–85]), as the seemingly supernatural 'visions' he has of the future bear a strong resemblance to the somnambulistic states produced during magnetic treatment – knowledge of which, as we have seen, almost certainly influenced Josef Breuer in his treatment of Bertha Pappenheim.

Hypermnesia, followed by postsomnambulistic *a*mnesia, is a well-documented feature of nineteenth-century experiments into hypnotic states. Critics of Eliot's novella have noted the way Latimer's powers of prevision function rather like reversed memory (Jacobus, *Reading Women* 259, 261 and 268; Charles Swann 148), as if foretelling what is to come is a form of projection forward of the consequences of past traumas. Jacobus describes the novella as a depiction of 'hysterical paralysis which freezes the onward movement of narrative.' Eliot's story, she writes,

> in effect, refuses the future tense despite being predicated on foresight. Latimer is locked into the narrative tense of hysteria, a reenactment which turns all futures to the inescapability of the past. (261)

Like the traditional Victorian ghost tale, which opens with a statement of horrors-to-come from a pre-informed narrator sitting around the fireside, *The Lifted Veil* opens with a statement of prescience which precludes suspense but at the same time sets up a preoccupation with time: 'The time of my end approaches' (1). Along with the past, it is the future which interpenetrates the present, like Gothic's self-fulfilling curses. Roy Schafer, in his essay on 'Narration in the Psychoanalytic Dialogue', says that

> Once the analysis is under way, the autobiographical present is found to be no clear point in time at all. One does not even know how properly to conceive that present; more and more it seems to be both a repetitive, crisis-perpetuating misremembering of the past and a way of living defensively with respect to a future which is, in the most disruptive way, imagined fearfully and irrationally on the model of the past.
>
> It soon becomes evident that, interpretively, one is working in a temporal circle. (52)

Within the 'temporal circle' of Latimer's narrative, what he calls 'the idea of future evil' (36) checks his every move in the 'disruptive way' Schafer refers to, projecting, simultaneously, back to a past of unspoken secrets. The burden of his neurotic melancholia (Eliot had called the novella 'not a *jeu d'esprit* but a *jeu de melancolie*' [*sic*] [*Letters* 3: 411]) as well as his self-hatred seems to be, according to the process described by Freud in 'Mourning and Melancholia', 're-proaches against a loved object which have been shifted away from it on to the patient's own ego' (PF 11: 257). The death of his mother has made a retrospective idyll of their brief time together, and also scrambled the normal sequence of past, present and future, giving Latimer a present shot through with past memories and projected future losses. His reminiscences return obsessively to questions of time:

> My childhood perhaps seems happier to me than it really was, by contrast with all the after-years. For then the curtain of the future was as impenetrable to me as to other children: I had all their delight in the present hour, their sweet and indefinite hopes for the morrow. (*The Lifted Veil* 4)

The characteristic confrontation here of past (really was . . . then . . . was), present (seems . . . the present hour) and future (all the after-years . . . curtain of the future . . . the morrow) comes with an equally characteristic cluster of images of veils, curtains and impenetrability which dominate the text. But at this early stage it is the future which is impenetrable, which is as it should be. It is the gradual reversal of this situation which brings about the crisis of melancholia.

Latimer, then, could be described as an hysteric who suffers not only from reminiscences but also, to use Schafer's terms again, from a compulsion to defend himself against the feared future consequences of his traumatic past. This involves both clairvoyance (lifting of the veil) as well as blindness (veiling). The confusion of the processes of veiling/hiding and lifting the veil/revealing can be detected in the original (but quickly deleted) title of the novella, *The* Hidden *Veil* (*Letters* 7: 480), which sounds like a Freudian slip. What is hidden? The veil or what the veil conceals? Is anything revealed after all? The text's confusion over this issue continues in the dominant images of blindness associated with Latimer. We are told that he had been blind for a time in childhood, and that one of the few living beings who does not shun him in adulthood is a blind dog. As blinded/castrated/Oedipal subject, he seems to have failed to negotiate an acceptable entry into the Symbolic order. Oedipal aggression towards the father has reversed into pathological timidity, a passive shrinking before any form of authority or 'knowledge'. Instead, he chooses 'not . . . to know' (8) about anything except 'feminine' subjects such as poetry.

All that he can summon up of Oedipal aggression is displaced onto his older brother, Alfred, whose removal in a riding accident reads like the wish-fulfilment of a dream. Alfred's death leaves Latimer free to possess Bertha, Alfred's fiancée, to unleash upon her the profound misogyny at the base of all Oedipal relationships. She is cast as the traditional Romantic Belle Dame Sans Merci – 'syren' (40), 'serpent' (29), 'Water-Nixie' (16) and 'cruel immortal' (63). Perversely, what attracts Latimer to her, he tells us, is the fact that she represents all he least admires:

> in the abstract, no womanly character could seem to have less affinity for that of a shrinking romantic, passionate youth [like himself] than Bertha's. She was keen, sarcastic, unimaginative, prematurely cynical . . . To this moment I am unable to define my feelings towards her: it was not ordinary boyish admiration, for she was the very opposite, even to the colour of her hair, of the ideal woman who still remained to me the type of loveliness. (21–22)

Anna Freud's most influential work was on the mechanisms of defence employed by the ego in its need to ward off unpleasure and anxiety. Reversal, one of the ten modes of defence she analyses, involves turning an unwelcome affect into its opposite (A. Freud

Chs 4–5). Many narratives, she argues, depict an irascible old man submitting defensively to the charms of a young and vulnerable child (or Beauty taming the Beast) (79).[15] *Silas Marner*, begun the year after *The Lifted Veil*, shows Eliot's adoption of this particular kind of defence through the reversal of paternal aggression into tenderness in the character of Silas the weaver. With Latimer, in the extract just quoted, what is 'unwelcome' (intolerable) is the maternal 'type', tormenting him with its loss: 'her caress as she held me on her knee – her arms round my little body, her cheek pressed on mine' (4). The defensive reversal of this imago, from the 'ideal woman' to the 'serpent', is one of a series of inversions which dominate Eliot's text, both stylistically and thematically. Sometimes this pattern takes on a distinctly hysterical tone. In the following passage, a characteristic expression of Latimer's misanthropy, there is a build-up on one side of words associated with tenderness, followed, with chiastic symmetry, by their reversal, an exorbitance of words associated with death and cruelty, a sadistic satisfaction in the crushing of tenderness.

> While the heart beats, bruise it – it is your only opportunity; while the eye can still turn towards you with moist timid entreaty, freeze it with an icy unanswering gaze; while the ear, that delicate messenger to the inmost sanctuary of the soul, can still take in the tones of kindness, put it off with hard civility, or sneering compliment, or envious affectation of indifference; while the creative brain can still throb with the sense of injustice, with the yearning for brotherly recognition – make haste – oppress it with your ill-considered judgments, your trivial comparisons, your careless misrepresentations. (2–3)

The tender/maternal-cruel/paternal antitheses, prevalent throughout *The Lifted Veil*, set up a series of gender possibilities which Latimer struggles, ultimately unsuccessfully, to negotiate.

In his essay on 'Hysterical Phantasies and their Relation to Bisexuality' (1908), Freud put forward the hypothesis that 'Hysterical symptoms are the expression on the one hand of a masculine unconscious sexual phantasy, and on the other hand of a feminine one', adding that bisexuality 'mark[s] the highest degree of complexity to which the determination of a hysterical symptom can attain', and may therefore be found only 'in a neurosis which has persisted for a long time' (PF 10: 93). Contemporary feminist psychoanalysts, however, insist on bisexuality as an inherent and central feature of hysteria. Following Hélène Cixous' analysis of the Dora case in her and Clément's *La Jeune Née* (*The Newly-Born Woman*) of 1975, Juliet Mitchell argued in an often-cited passage from her *Women: The Longest Revolution* (1984) that

> Hysteria is the woman's simultaneous acceptance and refusal of the organisation of sexuality under patriarchal capitalism. It is simultaneously what a woman can do both to be feminine and to refuse femininity within patriarchal discourse. (289–90)

Freud also came to realize that hysteria is not exclusive to women, as Mitchell shows in her summary of his changing views of sexuality from the 1890s onwards. In early 1896 he wrote in one of the papers he sent to Fliess:

> Hysteria necessarily presupposes a primary unpleasurable experience – that is, one of a passive kind. The natural sexual passivity of women accounts for their being more inclined to hysteria. Where I have found hysteria in men, I have been able to trace a large amount of sexual passivity in their anamnesis . . .
>
> Repression and the formation of defensive symptoms only occur afterwards, in connection with the memory; and thenceforward *defence* and *overwhelming* (that is, the formation of symptoms and the onset of attacks) may be combined to any extent in hysteria. (*Origins* 154)

But later, as Mitchell points out, this simple male-active, female-passive dichotomy dissolves in Freudian theory into something much more complex. In his work in the 1930s, he was to elaborate on the process of 'splitting' (*Spaltung*), which he (like Charcot's disciple Pierre Janet) had initially identified as the characteristic syndrome of hysteria. In splitting, through conflict, the subject has become separated from a segment of his/her ideas; the ego adopts two attitudes towards external reality, one taking it into account and the other 'disavowing' it and replacing it with a product of desire.

The main form of splitting, Freud came to believe, occurs in relation to castration, whereby the subject takes up a position in relation to the division between the sexes. The split subject both disavows female castration, clinging to the phantasy of the female phallus, and simultaneously accepts the reality that females have no penis. For Freud, femininity comes to represent the point where consciousness and meaning vanish, a point experienced by the subject as an intense horror of absence that can be filled only with phantasmagoria. Mitchell writes:

> In splitting, the subjectivity of the subject disappears. The horror is about the loss of oneself into one's own unconscious – into the gap. But because human subjectivity cannot ultimately exist outside a division into one of two sexes, then it is castration that finally comes to symbolise this split. The feminine comes to stand over the point of disappearance, the loss. (*Women* 307)

From Terry Eagleton's description of Latimer as an 'incompletely oedipalised wretch' ('Power and Knowledge' 56) to Mary Jacobus' of his tale as a 'hysterical text whose hysteria, in the last resort, can be read as that of the woman writer trapped in male prevision' (*Reading Women* 255), critics have suspected that Latimer's disorders have something to do with the Oedipal, death and castration, though few share Eagleton's mock-cynical refusal to adopt an identificatory model of reading him. The 'horror' of Latimer's predicament, difficult to understand if read within the framework of the Victorian realist project, takes on meaning within these terms of hysteria, bisexuality, splitting and castration. In another of its many reversals, the text works specifically to show Bertha becoming gradually masculine to Latimer's femininity. As a 'half-womanish, half-ghostly' being (20) (the connection between the female and the uncanny is one long familiar to psychoanalytic theory [Jacobus 201]), Latimer calls up in Bertha his gender antithesis : 'the very opposite . . . of the ideal woman' (20): 'I asked myself how that face of hers could ever have seemed to me the face of a woman born of woman' (63). After the father's death, with which it is specifically associated,[16] Bertha's sadistic aggression (the serpent rather than the siren) increases to the pitch of the final scenes. Bertha's maid Archer becomes her veiled lesbian accomplice, an intimate 'associated with ill-defined images of candle-light scenes in [Bertha's] dressing-room' (54). Archer's accusations to Bertha on her death-bed seem far to exceed the terms of their failed plot to poison Latimer: 'you laughed at me, and told lies about me behind my back, to make me disgusting . . . because you were jealous . . .' (65). Through another of the semantic displacements common to the text, the true 'shudder of repulsion' (50) registered by Latimer's misogyny is caused not so much by Bertha's cruelty as by the gender reversal suggested by her 'masculine' relation to Archer.

Much of the attention in the tale, as I have already suggested, centers on a series of scenes of would-be revelation, liftings of the veil – revelations, however, which turn out to be an addition rather than a solution to the mystery. Mystery becomes Latimer's religion. Indeed, he has been attracted to Bertha for her very impenetrability to his powers of prevision: the one 'oasis of mystery in the dreary desert of knowledge' (26). After Alfred's death and before their marriage, an 'additional screen' is thrown up between Latimer and Bertha. This reserve, he says, 'only brought me more completely under her power: *no matter how empty the adytum, so that the veil be thick enough*' (43). This last phrase, which I have italicized, is a significant moment in Latimer's speech, representing the image of the veil and the innermost sanctum ('adytum') through a syntax which itself repeats this obscurity (the conjunction 'so that' is, to me at least, indecipherable here). Shortly *after* their wedding, as the reserve increases between them, Bertha seems to lower the veil by seeing through Latimer, 'a miserable ghost-seer, surrounded by phantoms in the noon-day' (48). For Latimer it would also seem to be a moment of revelation: 'The terrible moment of complete illumination had come to me, and I saw that the darkness had hidden no landscape from me, but only a blank prosaic wall.' (49) Now, finally, 'Our positions were reversed' (49). Woman as dark, mysterious continent has been 'illuminated' as a blank, or absence. And yet the veils continue to shroud the events of the story.

The very last veil is said to fall in the notorious final scene (which Blackwood pressed Eliot, unsuccessfully, to delete [*Letters* 3: 67] and Terry Eagleton has called 'a piece of tawdry melodrama' [58]), when Latimer and his medical friend Meunier attempt a resuscitation of the body of Archer, by whose death-bed Bertha sits jealously guarding the well-advertised 'secret' of their murder plot. At the sight of Bertha's face, 'we all felt that the dark veil had completely fallen' (63).

The reader hardly shares this conviction that all has been revealed. The murder plot is clearly a smokescreen, an attempted justification of the perpetuation of such layers of concealment. For after the removal of so many veils, there is, finally, no body beneath (the 'empty adytum' or 'blank prosaic wall', woman as castrating/ castrated). Like the Wolf Man in Freud's account, whose 'principal subject of complaint was that for him the world was hidden in a veil, or that he was cut off from the world by a veil' (PF 9: 311), Latimer's secrets cannot be traced ultimately to a desire to return to the womb (Freud's hypothesis in the Wolf Man case) or even, as Mary Jacobus argues, to death (*Reading Women* 259), for all the talk of shrouding. Eve Kosofsky Sedgwick writes in her Lacanian reading of Gothic conventions that 'the suffused veil' very often hides not so much nothing, or death, but 'some cheat that means absence and substitution' (*Coherence* 146). Lack, Lacan wrote, 'is never presented other than as a reflection on a veil' (qtd in Heath 52). It is here, I think, that we have the answer to Latimer's horror.

PERFORMING HYSTERIA: TERRY JOHNSON'S *HYSTERIA*

The comparison of *The Lifted Veil* to a psychoanalytic case study, of course, omits the crucial factor of the transference between analyst and analysand, a factor at the heart of the difference between the way the two disciplines of psychoanalysis and literature function. For all the tone of direct address of Latimer's tale (the use of the first person, the appeal to the 'pity . . . tenderness . . . [and] charity' of the implied reader of the manuscript he will leave behind him [3]), his text has no narratee, no 'subject supposed to know' whose anticipated reactions shape the flow of his discourse – unless, of course, we emphasize the transferential relation between text and interpreting reader. With drama, however, characters are more prominently presented in direct interaction; dialogue as agent of change and understanding is its basic ingredient. It is not surprising, therefore, that the case study as theatre has proved a popular genre in recent decades.

I began this chapter by invoking the 'histrionic' enactments of Strindberg's hysteric Miss Julie which, I argued, reflected the developing definition of hysteria in the *fin de siècle* as a disorder characterized by oscillations – between volubility and aphonia, resistance and submission, frigidity and lasciviousness, object choice and identification, masculine and feminine, heterosexual and homosexual. Hélène Cixous writes: 'It is said that the hysteric . . . Plays, makes up, makes-believe . . . unmakes-believe too . . . plays at desire, plays the father . . . turns herself into him, unmakes him at the same time' ('Castration' 47). Cixous herself made the natural choice of the genre of drama to explore the oscillating role play of the hysteric. In her dramatized case study, *Portrait de Dora* (1976, first performed in London in 1979), she makes full use of the significance of the intersubjective element, the transferential and counter-transferential relationship between Dora and Freud, and the way the analysis proceeds, gaining ground, on the basis of constant shifts in the relationships, with each player adopting a variety of different identifications and defences. At one point in her play, as the identifications and counter-identifications among Freud, Dora's father (Mr B.), Mr K., Mrs K. and Dora herself gather together into a spiralling whirl, the character Freud calls out 'who stands for whom in the story?' (*Portrait* 53). In *The Newly-Born Woman*, Cixous asks, in reference to both the process of reading and the transference in all human relationships:

> What is 'identification'? When I say 'identification', I do not say 'loss of self.' I become, I inhabit, I enter. Inhabiting someone, at that moment I can feel myself traversed by that person's initiatives and actions . . . Almost all those involved in Dora's scene circulate through the others, which results in a sort of hideous merry-go-round, even more so because, through bourgeois pettiness, they are ambivalent. All consciously play a double game, plus the games of the unconscious. Each one acts out the little calculations of classic bourgeois comedy – a comedy of clear conscience on the one hand, a comedy of propriety on the other. (148–49)

'Entering', being 'traversed by' or 'circulating through' others, 'acting out': Cixous' own 'circular' prose, turning back on itself constantly as it moves through autobiography, history and psychoanalytic theory becomes a kind of 'acting out' of the different subject positions available to women in a post-Freudian age. When she writes, somewhat histrionically herself (and we remember, of course, that *histrio* is Latin for an actor or stage-player), that 'The hysterics are my sisters. As Dora, I have been all the characters she played . . . I am what Dora would have been if woman's history had begun' (99), we may feel that she is over-estimating the extent of Dora's potential for rebellion and ignoring the crippling capacity of her hysterical symptoms.[17] But she is at the same time putting theory into practice, rehearsing her own participation in a modernity that defines subjectivity as role-playing.

A recent re-enactment of the Dora case (or, at least, an amalgam of some of the details of several of Freud's case studies on hysteria) in dramatic form is Terry Johnson's *Hysteria*, first staged at the Royal Court Theatre in 1993. Set in 1938 in London, where Freud has recently sought refuge from Nazi-occupied Vienna, it depicts the ailing but 'energetic' octogenarian in dramatic (and often farcical) conflict with a last would-be patient named Jessica, the daughter, as it turns out, of a former hysterical patient of Freud's, who has subsequently committed suicide. A third character is Abraham Yahuda (for all the Swiftian suggestions clearly based on Freud's own physician, Max Schur), who is anxious to suppress the publication of the book Freud is working on, *Moses and Monotheism*, which radically challenges the foundations of Judaism at its most historically sensitive moment. Lastly, and with some hilarious consequences, there is Salvador Dali, who comes to pay homage to the 'Maestro' of surrealism and to coerce the unwilling Freud into a lavish celebration of dream symbols. With each character resolutely bent on his or her own scenario, the play hovers deliberately between serious case study and farce, with Jessica spending much of the time, without her underwear (retrieved from the lawn by an indignant Yahuda) in Freud's closet, where she is joined by a randy Dali on several occasions. While in there, she reads the manuscript of the Freud–Fliess correspondence, which she has stolen from Freud's desk in order to investigate the sources of his clinical treatment of her mother.

The text follows the recent trend of highlighting the failure in outcome of Freud's treatment of his hysterical patients in the 1890s, in spite of the theoretical gains. Jessica brings proof, at the end, of the *reality* of the seduction theory in her mother's case, making her a victim of Freud's misunderstanding after his 1897 renunciation of the seduction theory. Freud's new theory, she argues, came about as a result of his desire to protect the memory of his own father, whom he suspected of perverse practices with his children. The full implications of the counter-transference are thus brought forward, as we watch Freud struggling to protect both his theoretical armour and his personal credentials as impartial analyst. The roles of analyst and analysand are reversed, as Freud fends off, by repeated denials, Jessica's accusations of 'opportunism' (55) – just as Dora had attempted to fend off Freud's diagnosis forty years earlier. Feminism attempts its revenge.

But if, as the play presents it, Freud's renunciation of the seduction theory has been a 'fake', a mere defence to protect his reputation, the other characters are no less subject to the general fictionality that overtakes the play to accord with its central thesis of the problematic line between history and phantasy – as Freud states it in the play, 'In the unconscious there is no actual reality. Truth cannot be distinguished from emotional fiction' (55). Psychoanalytic history and postmodernity thus converge in dramatic form, with 'character' turning out to be first and foremost a matter of performance. Jessica's 'hysteria' is here literally simulated, a 'make-believe' to attract Freud's attention. Rubbing her breast and gagging, she reminds us of the way hysterical symptoms are themselves a form of 'private theatre', to use Anna O.'s phrase (PF 3: 74), directed at a particular 'other': a family member, the analyst, or, in the case of Charcot's actress-patients, a large Parisian audience. They are in fact a timely reminder of the Lacanian point that all representation (whether visual or narrative) is an appeal to the other – an other which, by its refusal to reduce itself to an object of need or demand, is always ultimately 'impossible'. The hysteric, in this sense, can be seen as paradigmatic of the way subjectivity is constituted through phantasized relation.

Freud warns Jessica at the beginning of Johnson's play to 'please remember you are in my study, not some boulevard farce' (8). But as the play progresses, it pointedly defies this distinction between theory and theatre: the action speeds up, with characters entering and exiting through the French windows or into the closet, underwear flying, and moves at the climax into the surreal dream sequence of a Dali-esque painting replete with lobster telephone and melted clock. It is at this point that Freud reaches the limit of his tolerance and, hoist in his own petard (the denial of 'reality'), yells at Jessica, whom he has just called 'nothing more than a neurotic manifestation' of his own imagination, to 'get out of my head! House' (72). Having acted out the skeleton in his psychoanalytic closet, however, she is not so easily evicted.

Just as the hysterical woman would not be erased from psycho-analytic theory. By 1938, the year in which Johnson's play is set, fierce debate had begun over feminine sexuality, based directly on issues raised by Freud's work on hysteria. Femininity as performance – or as Joan Riviere had called it a decade earlier, as a 'masquerade', was perhaps its most important legacy.

7
Femininities and Other Masquerades

In calling his recent play *Hysteria*, Terry Johnson plays up the renewed relevance of the concept in our own *fin de siècle* . On the one hand, it raises the question of the twentieth century's dominance by Freudian psychoanalysis, a dominance which repeatedly demands challenge and reassessment – of the sort which supporters of the 'reality' of child abuse (like Johnson's Jessica) would emphasize. And on the other it evokes the new 'cultural' concept of hysteria which has emerged since the more or less universal elimination of the word from medical terminology. This phenomenon, described by Elaine Showalter in a recent book called *Hystories*, redefines the disorder as '1990s millennial panic' (5), contagious epidemics spread by modern communications networks, focusing on issues such as chronic fatigue syndrome, Gulf War syndrome, 'recovered memory' of sexual abuse, multiple personality disorder, Satanic ritual abuse, and abduction. What these modern hysterias have in common with late Victorian equivalents is the susceptibility to suggestion, what Beret E. Strong has called hysteria's 'rampant communicability' (15), inducing an atmosphere like that at the end of Johnson's play where all four characters are locked into their own mutually induced illogic and paranoia. Although placed in the 1930s, Jessica in particular is a character for our times, one whose initially simulated hysteria ends up taking her over as she slides, with the other three characters, into a scene of mixed farce and panic.

Where this new definition of hysteria as a cultural phenomenon (as opposed to a loosely used accusation) differs from that of a hundred years ago is in its shift away from specific gender associations. Showalter's list of contemporary hysterical symptoms, from Gulf War syndrome to Satanic ritual abuse, bears less overt trace of gender

163

marking. While hysteria up to Freud's time was equated with femininity, the balance is being redressed through recent interest in case studies of male hysteria ignored by historians.[1] One of feminism's (dubious) gains could thus be said to be the entitlement of men to inclusion within the sphere of suggestibility. In literary examples, early cases of the male hysteric were distinguished by a chiastic pairing with a masculinized female double: from George Eliot's Latimer (paired with Bertha) in the 1850s to Virginia Woolf's Septimus Smith (paired with Clarissa Dalloway) in the 1920s. It was as if only a double-sexed composite could represent the condition and muffle anxiety about homosexuality or sexual crossing. Nowadays, we have no such scruples. From Philip Roth's Portnoy and Woody Allen to the protagonist of David Lodge's recent novel *Therapy,* men have taken to proudly laying out their hysterical symptoms for inspection. The political correctness of 'feminine' behaviour in men has been one of the many features of the gender politics of the past decade.

Such a shift in gender conceptions, rightly recognized as one of the most far-reaching of the previous century's changes, has its most immediate origins in the climate mentioned at the beginning of Chapter 6, the climate of the 1880s–90s that produced the suffragette movement, the Wilde trial, and Freud's research into human sexuality. The last of these, which I want to concentrate on for the next few pages, has raised a huge number of different areas of debate, many of them still highly contentious and filling hundreds of books over the past fifty or so years. I must confine myself to a sketch summary and the isolation of a few prominent issues, in particular that first raised during early work on hysteria: the notion of sexual identity as role-playing or performance.

FREUD DEFINES THE TERMS

I have already referred, in Chapter 2, to Freud's discussion of the shifting and multiple choices and identifications the subject makes in its relation to primary erotic objects. The Little Hans case, the study of Leonardo, and other works, explored the way the Oedipal stage for the little boy involves *both* the choice of the mother as object of desire *and* identification with her as object of the *father's* desire. Freud's early work on sexuality, in particular the *Three Essays on the Theory of Sexuality* of 1905, did not focus on the specificity of either the male or the female paradigm, but instead tended to regard the two sexes as symmetrical, following a common pattern dictated by the boy's development. But as the numerous footnotes added to the *Three Essays* over the next ten to twenty years testify, Freud's views on this subject underwent significant modification in the middle and (in particular) late years of his work. The symmetry simply did not stand the test of clinical experience. So that when some of his followers like Jung began to use the term 'Electra complex' to describe the female version of the Oedipal, Freud was quick to distance himself from the term and to stress that 'it is only in the male child that we find the fateful combination of love for the one parent and simultaneous hatred for the other as a rival' (PF 7: 375). What is most striking about Freud's later views on feminine sexuality from the point of view of a contemporary who has lived through the vociferous protests of the feminist movement, when a picture of Freud's face was sometimes used as a dart-board, is the (even by today's standards) radical nature of his inquiry. First, there was his insistence that sexual identity had nothing to do with biology or physiology, that 'what constitutes masculinity and femininity', as he put it in his lecture on 'Femininity' (1933), 'is an unknown characteristic which anatomy cannot lay hold of' (PF 2: 147). And secondly, he was prepared, at least in theory, to relinquish the idea of there being 'two sexes' and to regard masculinity and femininity as constitutive elements of infinitely variable combination. As he put it in another essay of 1925:

> all human individuals, as a result of their bisexual disposition and of cross-inheritance, combine in themselves both masculine and feminine characteristics, so that pure masculinity and femininity remain theoretical constructions of uncertain content. ('Some Psychical Consequences of the Anatomical Distinction Between the Sexes', PF 7: 342)

The bold challenge that these statements represent to centuries-old views of the 'naturalness' both of the distinction between the sexes and of heterosexuality somewhat belies the inconsistency and contradiction found in much of Freud's writing on femininity. Freud had noticed bisexuality in hysterical women, as we have seen, from an early date, drawing attention, for example, to the way one patient held her dress tightly against her body with one hand (performing 'femininity') while with the other she tried to tear the dress off (performing 'masculinity') (PF 10: 94). And although he would insist repeatedly that bisexuality is common equally to men and women, that all sexual identity is unstable, his tendency at the same time was to regard bisexuality as more pronounced and determining in women and as part of the instability which contributes to their 'enigma' (Kofman, *The Enigma of Woman* 207). Feminist analysts have noted the problematic nature of Freud's definitions of bisexuality (Parveen Adams, 'Per Os(cillation'; Juliet Mitchell, 'Introduction I'). As Mitchell puts it, in Freud's later work 'bisexuality' shifted its meaning from the mixture of masculine and feminine characteristics in both sexes 'and came to stand for the very uncertainty of sexual division itself' (12).

And yet the concept of bisexuality, read today as what Parveen Adams has called an 'oscillat[ion] between a masculine and feminine position' ('Per Os(cillaltion' 69), has proved enormously fruitful to contemporary psychoanalysts and theorists of gender alike. Joyce McDougall, whose writing and clinical work on what she calls 'homosexualities' combines features of object-relations and Lacanian psychoanalysis, insists that the range of sexual identities available to men and women is as various as those that possess them. Her call over the past thirty-five years for 'a measure of abnormality' in social conceptions of acceptable sexuality has involved a recognition that bisexuality, especially for women, is an integral part of so-called normal adult femininity.[2] Freud had charted the way the little girl's primary desire to possess her mother, a desire common to both sexes, is replaced by the desire for a penis. For McDougall and others, the development of the primary homosexual Oedipal constellation is far more complex. Her case studies, offering a range of different answers, are an attempt to reply to the following question:

> How are the complementary desires to *have* the mother and to *be* the father transformed and integrated into the life of the woman, whether her orientation be heterosexual or homosexual? (*The Many Faces of Eros* 14)

This question, of how the young girl passes from the 'masculine' phase of erotic attachment to the mother to the assumption of a 'feminine' identification can be said to lie at the heart of contemporary debates about femininity and gender. For it involves not only the question of how femininity comes into being, but also the related one of what brings about the difference between the sexes. If both boys and girls share the maternal attachment, how does their division into 'opposite sexes' come about? Many of the answers to these questions in fact render the concept of 'opposition' itself questionable if not highly dubious. The repetition of the word 'difference' in numerous titles of books and essays on gender over the past ten years[3] is indicative of the difficulty yet centrality of its definition.

How, then, to use Freud's words, does the little girl 'pass from her masculine phase to the feminine one to which she is biologically destined?' ('Femininity', PF 2: 152). Where Freud differs from the majority of other psychoanalytic writers on this question in the 1920s–30s is in his view that the difference occurs *after* birth, and not as if by some ultimately chemical reaction. It comes about neither 'biologically' nor 'socially', but 'psychologically', as it were, in the form of the 'trauma' of castration.

When discussing castration from the Lacanian perspective in Chapter 4, I cited Kristeva's point that 'nothing proves' castration; it is rather an 'article of faith' like the big bang theory in astrophysics, which enables explanation of many otherwise inexplicable phenomena (*Kristeva Reader* 197). Keeping in mind its status as symbolic construction may help those outside psychoanalysis overcome the resistance which everyday logic raises against the concept. Although it never 'occurs', it is a crucial factor in the inauguration of the distinction between the sexes. For boys, the traumatic phantasy is of the *possibility* of loss, whereas for girls, the trauma is of a loss that has already (phantasmatically) occurred. And whereas Karl Abraham, whose work on castration was very influential in the years that followed his death in 1925, argued that *both* sexes fear castration (see his 'Manifestations of the Female Castration Complex', 1922), for Freud it was the girl's envy of the phallus that marked her femininity.

Although the concept of penis envy has acted as a focus of feminist attack on Freud, it still appears as a central tenet in most schools of psychoanalysis. In asking why 'the sense of castration and its corollary "penis envy", constitute the almost universal lot of women', Maria Torok has answered that part of the reason must be that men 'foster' it in the form of 'a reverse envy projected on to woman': 'The guilty and envious woman serves as the unacknowledged "feminine part" men need to master and keep under control at all costs' ('The Meaning of "Penis Envy" in Women' 70 and 72). Joyce McDougall has also emphasized the need for therapeutic attention to be paid to the boy's envy of the mother's body (*The Many Faces of Eros* 5). Juliet Mitchell ('Introduction I' 16–17) has discussed the contradictions in Freud's work on penis envy. At times it seems that Freud believes it is the simple visual perception of her own 'inferior' genitalia that causes the girl's envy. At others, as in a letter of 1935, he admits that 'the sight of the penis and its function of urination cannot be the motive, only the trigger of the child's envy' (qtd in Mitchell 17). The same confusion between the penis as bodily organ and the phallus as its symbolic representation has dogged discussion of the phenomenon to this day, particularly in feminist circles. It was Lacan, as we have seen in Chapter 4, who was to draw attention to the castration complex as embodiment of the law that founds human society, the prohibition of incest. Mitchell explains:

> Before the castration complex was given its full significance [in Freud's work up to 1915], it seems that the Oedipus complex dissolved naturally, a passing developmental stage. Once the castration complex is postulated it is this alone that shatters the Oedipus complex. The castration complex institutes the superego as its representative and as representative thereby of the law. Together with the organising role of the Oedipus complex in relation to desire, the castration complex governs the position of each person in the triangle of father, mother and child; in the way it does this, it embodies the law that founds the human order itself. (14)

WOMEN REPLY

Sarah Kofman argued in *The Enigma of Woman* (1985 [1980]) that Freud's acknowledgment of the influence on him of his female colleagues' views on femininity was to a certain extent defensive, enabling him to cleanse his own theories of their numerous suggestions of phallocentrism (Kofman 18 and 206). It would have been hard, however, for him *not* to have acknowledged indebtedness to the 'great debate' on the subject in the 1920s, or to have denied that his own views, as we have seen, had changed considerably, particularly as the result of new evidence on the significance of the mother and of the pre-Oedipal period in the infant girl's development, which he famously described as comparable to the discovery of the Minoan-Mycenaean civilization beneath that of Greece ('Female Sexuality', PF 7: 372). Today, twenty years after Kofman's book, the charge of phallo-centrism, which could perhaps be levelled against different aspects of the arguments on all sides of the debate, seems less important than a recognition of the radical nature of the debate and the extent to which fundamental concepts of femininity were being questioned and re-shaped. For all their differences, Freud, Karen Horney, Jeanne Lampl-de Groot, Helene Deutsch, Ruth Mack Brunswick and others were all moving gradually towards the reversal of the until then taken-for-granted practice of collapsing 'gender' into 'sex'. It was becoming less and less possible, in other words, to assume that if you were born anatomically female, you would behave in a 'feminine' manner.

While the obvious focus of much of the debate was on penis envy and the castration complex in women, it was this gradual release of the words 'masculinity' and 'femininity' from their mooring to anatomy which was shaping its course. One aspect of the debate which is particularly interesting for our purposes is what Karen Horney called the 'flight from womanhood' common to all women at a certain stage, at least, of their development (her article with that title appeared in *The International Journal of Psycho-Analysis* in 1926). Horney argued that while boys in the Oedipal stage give up their attachment to the primary loved object of the opposite sex and have this renunciation further affirmed through the fear of castration, for girls the process is a great deal more difficult. Girls during the Oedipal may be forced to renounce the father as object cathexis, but this is not usually accom-panied by a peaceful identification with their own sex. Girls, as many writers in the period were beginning to affirm, 'recoil from the feminine role altogether' (Horney 333). Horney refers in her article to Helene Deutsch's view that the masculinity complex in women is stronger than the femininity complex in men. She disagrees, however, arguing that men's envy of women is simply more easily sublimated, more easily channelled into culturally valued activities; hence their 'over-compensation in achievement' (330). Through the absence of outlets for female sublimation, girls are constantly being reminded of the inferiority of their femininity. Horney continues:

> these typical motives for flight into the male rôle – motives whose origin is the OEdipus complex – are reinforced and supported by the actual disadvantage under which women labour in social life . . . a girl is exposed from birth onwards to the suggestion – inevitable whether conveyed brutally or delicately – of her inferiority, an experience which must constantly stimulate her masculinity complex. (337–38)

Deutsch's argument, based as it is on views of woman's 'anatomical destiny' ('The Significance of Masochism' 52) rather than her social constructedness, has proved less appealing today than Horney's. Unlike Horney, who seems to have regarded masculinity and femininity as phantasized roles, Deutsch tied her definitions of the feminine to particular attributes like narcissism or a 'passive-masochistic disposition' (48), so that for her, 'Escape into identification with the father is at the same time a flight from the masochistically determined identification with the mother' (55). Modern feminism has tended to assess the work of these Freudian 'daughters' by repeating Juliet Mitchell's view that both Deutsch's and Horney's appeal in the final analysis to 'biological predisposition' renders their theories untenable ('Introduction I' 19).[4] It is important, however, to recognize the extent to which their view of what Deutsch called the constant 'oscillation of libido' in psychic development ('The Psychology of Women' 406) represented a huge step in the conceptualization of gender, one that has had crucial repercussions to this day.

After the 'great debate' of the 1920s, object-relations theorists, Klein being the most prominent, moved away from the question of what distinguishes the sexes and concentrated on the mother–child relationship. In this shift, the father lost his function in the triadic structure, being envisaged as embodied within the mother. 'Identification' became a process more primary than a strict Freudian theory would accept. For Freud, as Mitchell summarizes it, identification with the parent of the same sex is a *result* of the castration complex, which has already brought about the sexual distinction. For object-relations analysts, on the other hand, identification is its *cause*. Both boy and girl undergo a primary 'feminine' phase through their identification with/non-differentiation from the mother. When the girl ultimately re-identifies with the mother (on the basis of her biological sex), it is only as the result of experiencing the frustration of not being able to satisfy the mother because of her lack of the phallus for her (Mitchell 'Introduction I' 22). Once again, the achievement of femininity is figured as a reaction-formation, difficult and incomplete. Kristeva, who cites Klein and other object-relations theorists frequently, writes: 'One cannot overemphasize the tremendous psychic, intellectual and affective effort a woman must make in order to find the other sex as erotic object' (*Black Sun* 30).

FEMININITY AS MASQUERADE

Joan Riviere's essay on 'Womanliness as a Masquerade' (1929), which has now become something of a cult piece in contemporary gender and cultural theory, needs to be interpreted within the context of the debate outlined above. Riviere makes liberal reference to her colleagues in the field whose work, like hers, was being published in *The International Journal of Psycho-Analysis*. Of the British propagators of the new Viennese science of psychoanalysis in this period, Riviere, along with Ernest Jones, was among the most prominent. Riviere had been in analysis from 1916 to 1921 with Jones, who receives lavish tribute from her for his work on female sexuality. (His 'Early Development of Female Sexuality' appeared along with another article by Riviere in the *Journal* in 1927.) Horney and Deutsch are also mentioned in Riviere's 'Masquerade' article for their work on the sources of the castration complex and the role of the oral-sucking stage in relation to 'heterosexual womanhood' (Riviere 40 and 43). A more important influence was that of Klein, with whom Riviere worked closely after Klein's arrival in London in 1926.[5] Klein's own paper on 'The Early Stages of the Oedipus Conflict' had in fact appeared in the *Journal* the year before Riviere's.

In her investigation into masculinity in women, Riviere in fact constructs a model exploiting aspects of both a Freudian and a Kleinian approach, giving an unusual balance of phallocentric and matricentric arguments. The Kleinian influence is felt in the emphasis on the sense of guilt and need for reparation after the phantasized oral-sadistic attacks on the mother. As we have seen in Chapter 2, primary identification with the mother via the breast, which also involves a relation to the father as the penis which inhabits her body, is fraught with fluctuating responses of aggression (what Klein would in the 1930s call the paranoid–schizoid position) and guilt accompanied by the need for reparation (the depressive position). In her 1928 paper in the *Journal* Klein writes:

> The child [of about one year old] himself desires to destroy the libidinal object by biting, devouring and cutting it, which leads to anxiety, since awakening of the Oedipus tendencies is followed by introjection of the object, which then becomes one from which

punishment is to be expected. The child then dreads a punishment corresponding to the offence: the super-ego becomes something which bites, devours and cuts. (*Selected Melanie Klein* 71)

Riviere details the early stages of infantile development in these same terms, stressing that initially it is both parents who are subjected to attack. But then, especially with girls (and this sexual division seems somehow taken as given),

> the mother is the more hated, and consequently the more feared. She will execute the punishment that fits the crime – destroy the girl's body, her beauty, her children, her capacity for having children, mutilate her, devour her, torture her and kill her. In this appalling predicament the girl's only safety lies in placating the mother and atoning for her crime. She must retire from rivalry with the mother and, if she can, endeavour to restore to her what she has stolen. As we know, she identifies herself with the father; and then she uses the masculinity she thus obtains by *putting it at the service of the mother*. (41)

This matricentric emphasis is often ignored by Lacanian analysts of Riviere's essay, who focus exclusively, as Lacan himself did, on the phallus. Riviere's case study concerns a successful professional woman behind whose façade of exaggerated femininity lurked a masculine identification which caused her intense anxiety. Her 'masculinity', under the influence of social convention, was perceived by her as everything to do with her professional ambition and desire to impress her male colleagues, but was always followed immediately by a 'feminine' bid for reparation in order to avoid the expected retribution. Riviere's analysis is acutely sensitive to the oscillations and conflicts in gender identity, with an underlying (but not entirely resolved) suspicion of 'fundamental' (innate) tendencies – as the following passage shows:

> In daily life types of men and women are constantly met with who, while mainly heterosexual in their development, plainly display strong features of the other sex. This has been judged to be an expression of the bisexuality inherent in us all; and analysis has shown that what appears as homosexual or heterosexual character-traits, or sexual manifestations, is the end-result of the interplay of conflicts and not necessarily evidence of a radical or fundamental tendency. (35)

For Klein in her paper of the previous year, the 'impulse to deck and beautify' in women 'has its origin in anxiety and sense of guilt' (*Selected Melanie Klein* 79). For Riviere, a mask of 'womanliness' in the form of an overemphasis on ornamentation can be said to represent femininity itself. In these terms, femininity is thus radically defined as 'a device for avoiding anxiety [rather] than . . . a primary mode of sexual enjoyment' (Riviere 38).

The conflict centres on an Oedipal rivalry with both the mother and the father. Overlying the primary maternal orientation is a dread of paternal retribution for having, by her successful masculine performance, 'exhibit[ed] . . . herself in possession of the father's penis, having castrated him' (37). By displaying herself as 'merely a castrated woman' (38), in her dreams and masquerading practices, however, she could defend herself against the destruction of her own body which she feared she deserved. It was at this point, thirty years later, that Lacan entered Riviere's argument. In 'The Meaning of the Phallus' (1958),[6] which is usually considered one of his most important essays for its exposition of the relation of desire to the signifier, Lacan sets out his argument for the distinction between the sexes in relation to the phallic term. After paying tribute to Deutsch, Horney and Jones, he states his well-known argument in the following steps:

> If the desire of the mother *is* the phallus, then the child wishes to be the phallus so as to satisfy this desire. (Mitchell and Rose 83)

> by keeping to the function of the phallus, we can pinpoint the structures which will govern the relations between the sexes. (83)

> these relations will revolve around a being and a having which . . . refer to a signifier, the phallus. (83)

> [for the woman, what intervenes is] an 'appearing' which gets substituted for the 'having' so as to protect it on one side and to mask its lack on the other. (84)

> it is in order to be the phallus, that is to say, the signifier of the desire of the Other, that the woman will reject an essential part of her femininity, notably all its attributes through masquerade.[7] It is for what she is not that she expects to be desired as well as loved. (84)

Sexuality, in other words, is inseparable from its representation – or, as Lacan was to put it in a 1973 seminar (*Seminar 20*: 39): 'Man and a woman . . . are nothing but signifiers' (a 'culturalist' dictum difficult to live by, if ever there was one!). 'Being the phallus' is the very type of signification as lack. Constructed as it is by reference to the male signifier, femininity can never be anything other than an appearance or mask, an arbitrary sign which, like masculinity, cannot be referred back to anatomy. In 'appearing' to be the phallus, putting on or making up/believe in relation to it, woman is rehearsing the very act of representation itself. It is for this reason, as Stephen Heath points out (57–59), that cinema is the medium *par excellence* of the enactment of the feminine masquerade. Cinema can present womanliness as image, adornment or pose, allowing women to be represented *as representation,* a mere sign in a Symbolic order.

REPRESENTATION AND THE 'OTHER SIDE': CAN ALICE GO THROUGH THE LOOKING GLASS?

In moving now to the question of gender and representation, or gender *as* representation, we are approaching perhaps the most frequently rehearsed of all contemporary cultural debates. I do not need to repeat it here. What I want to do is to look at the specific question, which we have inherited from Lacan and the feminist movement, of the different ways in which received discourse presupposes, constructs or precludes the representation of different genders or sexualities. Underlying Riviere's essay is a complex set of often unresolved contradictions concerning what exactly is meant by 'masculinity' or 'femininity'. Riviere's initial statement that in daily life we can detect men and women who 'plainly display strong features of the other sex' (35) raises the question of whether this 'display' is just that, a performance or masquerade, or whether it is an indicator of a naturalized, innate sexuality. Falling back on 'observation' clearly leads to conformity with culturally specific stereotypes. For Riviere, 'masculinity' stemming from an initial desire to replace the father as the object of the mother's desire, takes the form of the appropriation of the father's discourse, the language of public speaking that Riviere's patient was so anxiously successful with. We are clearly here confronted by what Judith Butler has called 'the slippery distinction between "appearing" and "being"' (*Gender Trouble* 47), where issues of observation, identification, orientation (desire) and representation are confusingly elided. The question of the sexual *object* of Riviere's patient, for example, is left vague in her essay. We are told confidently at the beginning of the case history that she had 'full and frequent sexual enjoyment' with her husband. Her homosexuality apparently took no object, but rather produced a 'sometimes very severe' anxiety (36). As we shall see shortly, one of the distinguishing characteristics of contemporary writing is an increasing freedom from normative or fixed positions of sex, gender and desire, allowing for what Butler calls 'an open coalition' (16) of multiple and shifting identities.

The struggle for the freedom from binarism (masculinity *versus* femininity), from monosexuality (as opposed to bisexuality) and from heterosexism, took many routes after the 'great debate' of the 1920s. Most of them were to lead through Simone de Beauvoir's *The Second Sex* (1949), which still makes arresting reading on the subject of the cultural implications of Riviere's view of femininity as 'made up'. Beauvoir writes:

> as against the dispersed, contingent, and multiple existences of actual women, mythical thought opposes the Eternal Feminine, unique and changeless. If the definition provided for this concept is contradicted by the behaviour of flesh-and-blood women, it is the latter who are wrong: we are told not that Femininity is a false entity, but that the women concerned are not feminine. (286)

But whereas for Beauvoir, received (patriarchal) discourse provides a set place for women as 'other', for Luce Irigaray writing nearly three decades later, 'woman' is by definition excluded from discourse, a 'sex' which is 'not one' (*Ce Sexe qui n'en est pas un*, 1977). Woman cannot be 'other', Irigaray argues, in an economy of the one (le un) where the object can never be autonomous but only an effect of the dominant subject.

From the time of her important first work *Speculum of the Other Woman* (1985 [1974]), for which she was famously expelled from Lacan's *'école freudienne*, Irigaray was concerned with concepts of otherness in relation to what she called 'the *specular make-up* of discourse, that is, the self-reflecting (stratifiable) organization of the subject in that discourse' (*This Sex* 80). Within this, females from the time of the Oedipus complex have no desire, are 'exiled from themselves' (133). Women can only 'find themselves' in masquerade, which represents an attempt to recuperate an element of desire, to participate in man's desire – but at the price of their own. Irigaray writes:

> What do I mean by masquerade? In particular, what Freud calls 'femininity.' The belief, for example, that it is necessary to *become* a woman, a 'normal' one at that, whereas a man is a man from the outset. He has only to effect his being-a-man, whereas a woman has to become a normal woman, that is, has to enter into the *masquerade of femininity*. In the last analysis, the female Oedipus complex is woman's entry into a system of values that is not hers, and in which she can 'appear' and circulate only when enveloped in the needs/desires/fantasies of others, namely, men. (*This Sex* 134)

This definition of masquerade, half a century later, is close to Riviere's, with the same concepts both of femininity as a construct and of the enormous difficulty of this construction. Irigaray, however, goes on to look at the implications of this expropriation and to ask questions about the possibility of 'what a feminine syntax might be' (134). That question, she continues,

> is not simple nor easy to state, because in that 'syntax' there would no longer be either subject or object, 'oneness' would no longer be privileged, there would no longer be proper meanings, proper names, 'proper' attributes . . . Instead, that 'syntax' would involve nearness, proximity, but in such an extreme form that it would preclude any distinction of identities, any establishment of ownership, thus any form of appropriation. (134)

As the above passage shows, this hypothesis about a feminine discourse has a long list of what needs to be challenged (the distinction of identity, of subject versus object, oneness, 'proper' meanings/ names, ownership, appropriation) and a short and hazily defined statement of what would replace it (nearness, proximity). In an interesting experiment, Irigaray attempted to test out this project in the first essay of this same volume, *This Sex Which is Not One*, an essay entitled 'The Looking Glass, from the Other Side'. Here, using the characters from a film called *Les Arpenteurs* (*The Surveyors*) directed by Michel Souter (Irigaray puns on 'sous-terre', underground), Irigaray attempts a representation of the 'elsewhere' of feminine pleasure, like Lewis Carroll using a crossing over to the other side as a radical form of disruption ('déconcertation' [*Speculum de l'autre femme*] 178]) of this side (the 'one').

Carroll's interest, as his full title suggests, had been on going *Through the Looking-Glass And* [examining] *What Alice Found There.*, the emphasis being on the 'finding'. For his Alice in Looking-Glass House, things are 'just the same as our drawing-room, only . . . the other way [round]' (Carroll 146): what are hills for Alice are valleys for the Red Queen. Like Tweedledum and Tweedledee, each side of the opposition depends on the stability of its contrary, what Irigaray calls the 'distinction of identities' of patriarchal discourse. Irigaray's Alice is most like her Victorian counterpart when the latter enters the wood where things lose their names. Once there, she is forced to ask 'who am I?' (Irigaray cites this passage as an epigraph to her text). The gendering of the question, with its psychoanalytic implications echoing back to Freud, leads Irigaray to set up 'characters' who refuse 'identity', who slide between one pronoun, name or identity and another. Alice becomes Ann becomes 'he' becomes 'Lucien' becomes 'Leon', and so on. This makes for extremely confusing reading, as Irigaray intends to show. It forces us into her Alice's dilemma: given that 'I' cannot be distinguished from 'her' in patriarchal discourse, that 'on this side of the screen of their projections . . . I can't live . . . stuck, paralyzed' (*This Sex* 17), all the feminine can do is masquerade and break apart the distinctions, 'jamming the theoretical machinery itself' (78). Irigaray's is not, in other words, an attempt to investigate how the other side (femininity) could be represented, as has sometimes been argued, but rather an exposure of its unrepresentability within the terms available; the *'blur of deformation'* (10) of her 'Looking Glass' text is what results from the impossible attempt to adopt a feminine subject position.

If, as Irigaray argues, there is only ever one, undifferentiated (*indifférent*) discourse, binarism being merely a two-sided oneness, can women ever be anything but 'indifférentes' to it? Is subversive mimicry or masquerade all that is possible? And then, is 'speaking as a woman' (*parler-femme*), the much-publicized project of French feminist theory in the 1970s, something determined by anatomy, culture or neither? As Shoshana Felman has put it recently, 'Is it enough to *be* a woman in order to *speak as* a woman?' (*What Does a Woman Want?* 24) Or do 'masculine' and 'feminine' function merely as markers of a shifting identity, equivalent, perhaps, to a set of clothes that can be changed at will? These are all questions raised by Irigaray's essay in

her adaptation of Riviere's concept of the masquerade to post-
structuralist views of discourse. But they were also questions raised
in a text exactly contemporaneous with Riviere's essay, Virginia
Woolf's *Orlando*, and it is to this that I want to turn next.

ORLANDO[8]

That *Orlando* was published in 1928, at the height of the 'great debate'
and only a year before Riviere's essay on the masquerade, is a point
needing emphasis. Woolf herself, for one, would probably have
discouraged the connection. She certainly made often-quoted remarks
of a derogatory nature about psychoanalysis as it was rapidly developing in the 1920s in Britain,[9] and which impinged directly on her life
in many ways. Aside from her own mental breakdowns, for which she
had psychiatric rather than psychoanalytic treatment (and her vulner-
ability here may have raised her defences against the new science),
there were a great many points of contact. Leonard Woolf had
reviewed Freud's *Psychopathology of Everyday Life* in 1914; Virginia's
brother Adrian and sister-in-law Karin trained as analysts; the Hogarth Press established by herself and Leonard Woolf published many
of Freud's works from the mid '20s onwards, translated by their close
friends James and Alix Strachey (as well as by Joan Riviere herself),
and so on. What is less well documented is the extent to which Woolf
would have been familiar with at least the general terms of the
psychoanalytic debate on femininity, if not many of its specificities.[10]
As J. H. Willis records in his history of the Hogarth Press (297–324),
Leonard Woolf decided in early 1924 to publish translations of
psychoanalytic works from Vienna under the title of the International
Psycho-Analytic Library Series founded by Ernest Jones, yet another
venture of Freud's tireless British disciple, one that ran parallel to his
work on the *International Journal of Psycho-Analysis* in which, as we
have seen, the papers of the 'great debate' were being published at this
time. The Library Series began with the four volumes of Freud's
Collected Papers (1924–25), translated by James Strachey (Lytton's
youngest brother) and his wife Alix, who had studied with Freud and
become professional analysts themselves. Joan Riviere's contribution
to these projects was central; as translator and supervisor of the
venture as a whole, she was responsible for the choice of 'The Ego
and the Id' for Freud's phrase 'Das Ich und Das Es' – not without

debate with Leonard Woolf. As Woolf's biographer Hermione Lee records, Freud 'now became one of the dominant topics of Blooms-bury' (Lee 472). And given her long interest in sexual identity,[11] femininity and women's cultural repression, all of which would culminate in *Orlando* in 1928 and *A Room of One's Own* in 1929, it is hard to believe that Woolf would not have noticed that psycho-analysis was turning its attention to these very same questions right at her door-step.

Bloomsbury, of course, represented a practical experiment in the testing out of sexual identities, and Lee's biography documents the many relationships Woolf had with homosexual men and women where these issues were discussed. In the middle of the decade, Woolf introduced her new friend Vita Sackville-West to the group, and was soon to be involved in an affair with her, with the complicity of both their husbands. Lee's chapter on 'Vita' makes fascinating reading in '20s Bloomsbury sexual ethics, and above all in Woolf's uncensored views on homo- and heterosexual as well as 'other mixed' options for women.

But 1928 was also the year of the notorious obscenity case brought against Jonathan Cape, publisher of Radclyffe Hall's explicitly lesbian novel, *The Well of Loneliness*. Although it appeared on 9 November, a month after *Orlando*, Woolf would have been sensitive to the un-written prohibitions surrounding an open presentation of homosexu-ality in fiction. (Indeed, who could not have been since the Wilde trial two decades earlier? Her close friend E. M. Forster had limited his 'homosexual' novel, *Maurice*, to private circulation, and it would not be published until after his death in 1971.) Whatever openness in personal relations Woolf was inclined to in her immediate circle, she was not prepared to risk public censure. *Orlando*, a fantasy novel about a man who changes into a woman, is an exercise in the art of subterfuge.

Immediately after visiting the Sackville-Wests' vast Kentish man-sion, Knole (granted the family by Elizabeth I) in 1924, Woolf began to 'make Vita up' as Orlando (Lee 485), to construct her as high camp aristocratic gentleman and artist who would live, fantastically, for three-and-a-half centuries. The fabrication of Vita as Orlando could be read as an inverted version of the process described by Riviere. Instead of the woman emphatically parading her 'femininity' in order to distract attention from her 'masculinity', *Orlando* presents a woman masquerading as a man (before, that is, she finally changes into a woman in the nineteenth century), in order to disguise his/her 'feminine' orientation towards other women.[12] The terms may be different, but the process of unstable, mixed or oscillating gender positions is remarkably similar.

According to its subtitle, *Orlando* is 'A Biography'. References to the Sackvilles and Knole are explicit; the first edition even contained photographs of Vita captioned 'Orlando', an aspect which Woolf's arch literary opponent Arnold Bennett called 'the oddest of all the book's oddities' (review in the *Evening Standard* for Nov. 1928, qtd in Majumdar and Mclaurin 232). Bennett was not the only contemporary reviewer to express unease about what it was they were supposed to be reading. The book shows 'too little affection or respect for the reader', complained one; reviewers, complained another, 'have not known quite how to take it' (Majumdar and Mclaurin 229 and 234). *Orlando* also sets itself up as an (admittedly very unusual) 'history' – of aristocratic English culture from the late sixteenth to the early twentieth century, with a great paraphernalia of period detail used to authenticate the descriptions, the sources of which are parodically acknowledged in the Preface with references to various archives. On the face of it, the book is a conventional (indeed a disconcertingly conventional) historical survey in the grand patrician or heraldic manner: the endurance of country estates, royal courts and 'the arts', all interspersed with broad philosophical reflections and moral observations in the armchair style of oldfashioned historical narrative. Here, it would seem, Virginia Woolf is at her most mimetic of the 'master' narratives of history.

As Hermione Lee notes (513), at the time of writing *Orlando* Woolf was reading Michelet's history of France preparatory to a holiday there with Sackville-West. In a letter of January 1928, she wrote to Clive Bell: 'Does it strike you that history is one of the most fantastic concoctions of the human brain? . . . Ought it not all to be re-written instantly?' (qtd in Lee 513) And the following year, in *A Room of One's Own* she was to complain that 'history is too much about wars; biography too much about great men' (103). *Orlando*, I think, can be read as a masquerade of patriarchal biographical and historical narratives. It may not go as far as Irigaray's 'Alice' narrative towards jamming the discursive machinery, but it does, as readers since Bennett have testified, cause a great deal of unease. To refer to *Orlando* in her diary as a 'joke', 'an escapade' and a 'farce' was for Woolf a way of masking protest (Minow-Pinkney 117), a cover for anger about sexual and discursive codes which could only be conveyed via the conciliatory banter that would become the key note of her style in both *Orlando* and *A Room of One's Own*.

The question of representation is central to *Orlando*, which could be described as a text which constantly masquerades its own representational practices. In a passage at the beginning, Woolf draws attention to this preoccupation by focusing with characteristic ambivalence on the question of representation itself, the relationship between an object and the words that could describe it. Orlando has been introduced in the first sentence of the book in this way: 'He – for there could be no doubt about his sex, though the fashion of the time [1588] did something to disguise it – was in the act of slicing at the head of a Moor which swung from the rafters' (9). We have been prepared, therefore, for the deceptiveness of appearances: the phrase 'there could be no doubt' characteristically unsettles certainty, and clothes, from the beginning, are a 'disguise' for ambiguously sexed bodies beneath them. The literal and metaphoric thrust at the Moor's head hanging as a gruesome trophy of imperialist savagery simultaneously sets in motion the mimicry of patriarchal history. After this parodic rehearsal of his ancestors' behaviour, the 16-year-old Orlando then sits down to continue work on his 'Tragedy in Five Acts' whose plot echoes his forefathers' deeds: 'Kings and Queens', 'Vice, Crime, Misery' all 'suffused' with 'noble sentiments' (11). As for the style of his Tragedy, 'there was never a word said as he [Orlando, the author] himself would have said it'. In this context of pure artifice, Orlando then attempts a piece of mimetic realism:

> He was describing, as all young poets are for ever describing, nature, and in order to match the shade of green precisely he looked (and here he showed more audacity than most) at the thing itself, which happened to be a laurel bush growing beneath the window. After that, of course, he could write no more. Green in nature is one thing, green in literature another. Nature and letters seem to have a natural antipathy; bring them together and they tear each other to pieces. The shade of green Orlando now saw spoilt his rhyme and split his metre. (11–12)

The various elements of this passage seem to be pulling in two quite different directions, involving both identification with and ironic distance from the discursive modes it inhabits. First there is the slightly playful condescension of the narrator, who uses phrases such as 'young poets', an attitude always lurking behind even the most seemingly sympathetic description of Orlando. Then there is the confusing mention of the 'audacity' of the artist in looking at the object to be described. Surely this is a joke at the expense of writers who ignore 'nature'? Woolf did, after all, accuse Charlotte Brontë's portrait of Rochester of being 'drawn in the dark' the following year (*A Room* 70). Or does it rather suggest the absurdity of the attempt to 'match' nature 'precisely' with words, as at least one critic has suggested (Roe 94). The rest of the passage certainly seems to endorse this interpretation, and this second reading can be reinforced by reference to Woolf's other famous challenge to the 'materialist' school of literature, which dedicated itself to the project of accurate observation and description.[13] And yet given the narrator's gentle condescension, are Orlando's musings to be taken seriously? Woolf wrote in her *Diary* that one of her intentions in *Orlando* was that '[her] own lyric vein is to be satirised' (qtd in Roe 92). Such literary or philosophical inquiries as this one are surely characteristic of Woolf's 'lyric vein'? This reading would certainly seem to be endorsed by the end of the paragraph in which this passage occurs where Orlando, in despair at his attempt, 'drops the pen, takes one's cloak, strides out of the room, and catches one's foot on a painted chest as one does so. For Orlando was a trifle clumsy' (12). Are the passions and preoccupations of this clumsy youth part of a serious discursive investigation?

The problem has again to do with the narrator who hovers over Orlando's mental processes and who is indicated in the passage just quoted by the pronoun shift from 'he' to 'one'. 'One', that class arrogant word that Woolf often used to evade the personal emphasis, here substituted suddenly for 'he', suggests the narrator's move to identification with Orlando's thoughts. But to sustain this identification over the 230 pages of the book, particularly when the narrative verges on self-mockery throughout, proves something of a strain (to the narrator as well as to the reader).[14] The effect is one of profound ambivalence, as if the narrative cannot decide between complicity with the patriarchal modes it mimes or an ironic send-up of them.

This playful ambivalence is at its most centrally problematic when it comes to the direct discussions of gender in *Orlando*. As a woman in the nineteenth century, Orlando finds herself, of all the centuries she has lived in, least in sympathy with 'the spirit of the age', above all for what the narrator calls its 'evasions and concealments' (161). These are at their most imperative in relation to sex and sexual identity. At first sight, the book would seem to be (and indeed has often been read as) a straightforward argument for androgyny (Marder 110). Orlando's story, after all, is about the interchangeability of his/her experience as woman and man. "Different though the sexes are', the novel's Freudian (or more accurately 'great debate') thesis goes, 'they intermix. In every human being a vacillation from one sex to the other takes place' (133). Gender distinctions are only held up in order to be knocked down. An example here is the following passage, that works towards an ironic climax:

> But Orlando was a woman – Lord Palmerston had just proved it. And when we are writing the life of a woman, we may, it is agreed, waive our demand for action, and substitute love instead. Love, the poet has said, is woman's whole existence. (189)

Except, as we are soon told, Orlando the woman does not fit the formula. Such moments give Woolf the opportunity to indulge in the ironic play that is so characteristic of *A Room of One's Own*: 'love – as the male novelists define it – and who, after all, speak with greater authority? – has nothing whatever to do with kindness, fidelity, generosity, or poetry' (*Orlando* 190) – and so, the reader is encouraged to retort, nothing to do with Orlando as a woman. And yet, in the last resort, Orlando as a woman *does* stake all her hopes in love for a man (Shelmerdine), along with the traditional feminine concerns of motherhood (we see her at the end buying boys' boots in a department store). This leads to the other dominant argument in the text, one which seems to conflict with the androgyny thesis, and which is summed up in this statement: 'when we write of a woman . . . the accent never falls where it does with a man' (220). The cause of this difference seems to be social, or rather, as the narrator suggests, sartorial. 'There is much to support the view that it is clothes that wear us and not we them' (132). As Orlando discovers, dressed as a woman she is constituted in quite different ways than she had been as a man – both by others, and as if by some more fundamental psychic drive. Orlando's 'beauty' as both a man and a woman is associated in the text with femininity, in the way it is in a traditional Freudian view, which treats femininity as a veil to cloak the narcissistic wound of castration. In 'Femininity' (1933), Freud wrote:

Thus, we attribute a larger amount of narcissism to femininity, which also affects women's choice of object, so that to be loved is a stronger need for them than to love. The effect of penis-envy has a share, further, in the physical vanity of women, since they are bound to value their charms more highly as a late compensation for their original sexual inferiority. (PF 2: 166)

The view that 'we incline to', as the narrator puts it in *Orlando*, with a characteristically evasive plural, is that 'the difference between the sexes is, happily, one of great profundity. Clothes are but a symbol of something hid deep beneath' (133). This apparent gesture towards the old guard that would fall back on an essential feminine mystique may in fact mask a more radical view: that 'femininity', figured here as sartorial display, is a quality which needs to be kept quite separate from 'men' or 'women', as well as from the question of women's repression in history.

The next passage I want to look at directly raises the question of the sex of the narrator. This is a key issue, as it is through 'his' mediation (and a very opaque medium he is too) that the text's ambivalences arise. The book opened with unequivocal assertions of the masculinity of Orlando's 'biographer',[15] and any doubt as to whether this may merely be a generic 'he' is quickly dispelled by the assuredly masculine tone of his universalizing pronouncements. The passage I want to investigate comes about two-thirds of the way through the book, after Orlando, as a woman, has been enjoying the company of the women prostitutes. At this point the narrator quotes the 'proof' of various men ('Mr. S. W., Mr. T. R.') that women 'hold each other in the greatest aversion'. He then continues with the following one-sentence paragraph:

As that is not a question that can engage the attention of sensible man, let us, who enjoy the immunity of all biographers and historians from any sex whatever, pass over, and merely state that Orlando professed great enjoyment in the society of her own sex, and leave it to the gentlemen to prove, as they are very fond of doing, that this is impossible. (155)

Here again, several different discourses seem to be in competition. The sentence begins with the patriarchal, with the 'sensible man' and the boundaries of his attention (which of course exclude all female matters). Moving on, it seems that the relation between the 'sensible man' and 'us', the biographer/historian/narrator is direct and one-to-one, except that as the sentence progresses at this point, a second strand of orientation takes over, that of the necessary androgyny of any writer ('let us, who enjoy the immunity of all biographers and historians from any sex whatever, pass it over'), with which position the narrator ('us') is again directly linked. The rest of the sentence (from 'and merely state . . .' onwards) is clearly an alignment with a feminist position, that of the narrator of *A Room of One's Own* again, the narrator who can capitalize so playfully on the exposure of male arrogance, doing so here by the blunt confrontation of 'facts' (Orlando *does* enjoy the company of women) with masculinist opinion (it is 'impossible' that she should).

If we look for clues as to the dominant emphasis of this confusing sentence-paragraph in its grammatical structure, we find that the main clause, 'let us . . . pass it over', is of little help. Or is it? Perhaps this is the point, that to read *Orlando* is to 'pass over' not only the patriarchal discourse (which must be exposed), but also the feminist as well as the 'mixed' (androgynous) discourse as mere reversals or reconstructions of 'the one'. This, the 'passing over', is the feminine masquerade as conceived by Irigaray.

In *A Room of One's Own* the following year, Woolf called for 'a rewrit[ing of] history', pronouncing it, however, a project 'ambitious beyond my daring' (44–45). Inserting women into history cannot be a matter of a mirror reversal in the Lewis Carroll manner. As Irigaray puts it,

> It is not a matter of toppling that [phallocratic] order so as to replace it – that amounts to the same thing in the end – but of disrupting and modifying it, starting from an 'outside' that is exempt, in part, from phallocratic law. (*This Sex* 68)

The genre of fantasy chosen by Woolf for *Orlando* goes some way towards providing the atmosphere of otherness (an 'outside' which admits the disruption and modification of phallocentrism).

In the end, Woolf's text is perhaps best described in relation to the one Orlando is writing throughout his/her life for over three centuries. 'The Oak Tree: A Poem' never actually gets written, because as he scratched out as many lines as he wrote in, the sum of them was often, at the end of the year, rather less than at the beginning, and it looked as if in the process of writing the poem would be completely unwritten. (79)

The poem survives the most hazardous of Orlando's experiences – the sacking of his Embassy in Constantinople, the time with the gipsies – and becomes not only a record of but synonymous with her/his life. By the end, after

> the straits she had been in for writing-paper when with the gipsies [which] had forced her to over-score the margins and cross the lines . . . the manuscript looked like a piece of darning most conscientiously carried out. (166)

This darned, over-stitched, 'unwritten' text can, I think, be read as an image of *Orlando* itself. To put it another way, we could say that in attempting to construct a new historical and biographical discourse, all the woman writer can do is self-consciously masquerade the old forms. Incursions into the other side, into alternative histories or biographies, must inevitably be 'immeasurable' or 'indefinable', to use Irigaray's terms again, when she writes: '*How can anyone measure or define*, in truth, *what is kept* behind the plane of projections?' (*This Sex* 18).

PERFORMING SEXUALITIES: ANGELA CARTER'S 'REFLECTIONS'

What Perry Meisel has called Woolf's 'transgeneric expansiveness' (*The Absent Father* 44), her attempt to leaven historical and biographical discourse with the imaginary (which Meisel traces to the influence of Walter Pater),[16] can be seen as part of a larger project extending beyond the fictionalization of history and biography to the conception of all discursive practice as performative rather than mimetic. As Meisel points out, Woolf's serious attempt at the genre of biography, that of Roger Fry, published at the end of her life, tests out definitions of identity resistant to a fixed or essential self. Characteristically, Woolf cites from a mid-twenties dinner-party conversation in which Fry argued against Oliver Strachey and Leonard Woolf, whom he termed 'mystics', in favour of relativity rather than essence:

They could not accept the complete relativity of everything to human nature and the impossibility of talking at all about things in themselves. It's curious how difficult it is to root out that medieval habit of thinking of 'substances' of things existing apart from all relations, and yet really they have no possible meanings. (Woolf, *Roger Fry* 270)

When Woolf argues for the 'difference' between the sexes, it is a difference to be regarded within these same 'relational' terms, which have meaning only as differential. Masculinity and femininity, like a sartorial code, depend on arbitrary, culturally constructed markers, and can be manipulated as far as transgression permits or requires. Clothes are of primary importance in *Orlando*.[17] Orlando's identity as male or female is signified exclusively through what s/he wears. At one significant moment only are the clothes removed, at the moment of the sex change, which is given in this way:

. . . Orlando woke.

He stretched himself. He rose. He stood upright in complete nakedness before us, and while the trumpets pealed Truth! Truth! Truth! we have no choice left but confess – he was a woman.

*

The sound of the trumpets died away and Orlando stood stark naked. No human being, since the world began, has ever looked more ravishing. His form combined in one the strength of a man and a woman's grace . . . Orlando looked himself up and down in a long looking-glass, without showing any signs of discomposure, and went, presumably, to his bath.

We may take advantage of this pause in the narrative to make certain statements. Orlando had become a woman – there is no denying it. But in every other respect, Orlando remained precisely as he had been. The change of sex, though it altered their future, did nothing whatever to alter their identity . . . but in future we must, for convention's sake, say 'her' for 'his'. (97)

The passage demonstrates a characteristic contrast between the parodically inflated public hullabaloo about the distinction between the sexes (the trumpet peals, the 'Truth! Truth! Truth!') and Orlando's own 'composure' about the matter (aided by the text's emphasis on his/her 'ravishing' beauty irrespective of sex). The issue comes down ultimately to a matter of the discursive inscription of gender, of the 'his' or the 'their' (which seems more appropriate to capture the doubleness or multiplicity) or the 'her'. Crucially, it is the looking-glass which performs the indispensable task of confirming and in-scribing the new identity as an image (Meisel 234). It is at this moment, it could be said, that the postmodern conception of identity as image or performance is born.

Performativity lies at the core of contemporary Queer theory's conceptualization of sexual identity. Queerness, in Eve Kosofsky Sedgwick's definition, is constituted by 'a person's undertaking parti-cular, performative acts of experimental self-perception and filiation' (*Tendencies* 9). In her initial ground-breaking formulation of Queer theory, Sedgwick emphasized the way

> many of the major modes of thought and knowledge in twentieth-century Western culture as a whole are structured – indeed, fractured – by a chronic, now endemic crisis of homo/heterosexual definition, indicatively male, dating from the end of the nineteenth century. (*Epistemology* 1)

Like Judith Butler in *Gender Trouble*, which appeared in the same year (1990) as her *Epistemology of the Closet*, Sedgwick argues that 'masculinity' and 'femininity' are not grounding, ontological cate-gories but rather, as Foucault had argued in *The History of Sexuality* (1976), part of a regulatory discourse dedicated to the persecution of 'peripheral sexualities' (Foucault 40). (Foucault dates the 'birth' of homosexuality at 1870, the moment when it was constituted as a psychological category [43].)

Judith Butler calls gender a form of impersonation or mimicry, something that is 'worn' ('Imitation' 21). At one point she even states that all 'gender is drag' (28). So that when Aretha Franklin sings 'you make me feel like a natural woman', Butler stresses (with no smile of concession at the illusion of ages), she is merely 'momentar[ily] participat[ing] in an ontological illusion produced by the mundane operation of heterosexual drag' (28)! Like Lacan, she believes that identity is neither volitional, something put on or taken off at will (so that here the sartorial metaphor loses its efficacy), nor something 'in' the body. Rather, it makes its appearance through the signifying chain (the Symbolic): 'it is always a surface sign, a signification on and with the public body that produces the illusion of an inner depth, necessity or essence' (28).

So to the question 'what is the mime imitating?', Butler's answer, via Derrida, is: 'nothing'. In his investigation of *mimesis* in *Dissemination* (1972), Derrida had argued that mime is not a copy of an original as in the Platonic metaphysic, but rather a reconstituted 'phantasm' of an original, a 'reality-effect' and nothing more. Analysing Mallarmé's occasional piece *Mimique*, he demonstrates that behind the simulacra, the miming and pantomime, 'there is no simple reference':

> We are faced then with mimicry imitating nothing; faced, so to speak, with a double that doubles no simple, a double that nothing anticipates, nothing at least that is not itself already double . . . In this speculum with no reality, in this mirror of a mirror, a difference or dyad does exist, since there are mimes and phantoms. But it is a difference without reference, or rather a reference without a referent, without any first or last unit, a ghost that is the phantom of no flesh. (206)

For Butler, the performance of gender must be viewed in this same way, as a challenge to concepts of 'the origin, the inner, the true' (29), as a retrospectively produced fabrication.

I would like, finally, to give a short reading of one of Angela Carter's stories, 'Reflections' (from *Fireworks* [1974]), within the context of contemporary theories of gender as performative. Carter's story foregrounds the mimed, ventriloquized aspect of the performance of gender in a manner that has been deeply unsettling to contemporary feminism. To many readers, her writing has at times edged uncomfortably close to a form of male impersonation in which a raw misogyny is often evident. Although some parts of her writing, notably the feminist revisions of fairy tales in *The Bloody Chamber* (1979) or the triumphantly phallic heroine Fevvers in *Nights at the Circus* (1984), have been embraced as programmatically feminist, there is in her work an elusive, shifting relationship to gender and to patriarchal discourse which has proved hard to classify.

Through the central use of mirrors in many of her works, Carter evokes an atmosphere of Derrida's 'speculum with no reality', 'mirror of a mirror', where reflections proliferate to such an extent that the notion of any 'original' reflected object fades from possibility. 'Reflections' epitomizes this tendency in a stark and unsettling specularization of gender. Like Irigaray's 'The Looking Glass, from the Other Side' (published contemporaneously, in the mid 1970s), Carter's narrative attempts to penetrate beyond the plane of projections on 'this side' to test out the reversibility of patriarchal discourse.

The story begins with a quiet, slightly eerie description of a rain-washed woodland scene, where seeming 'transparency' lures the first-person narrator into a mood of discovery beyond. The voice of a girl singing arouses him (or her, for the narrator's sex is as yet undefined) to an awareness of 'a meaning that had no relation to meaning as I understood it' (Carter, *Fireworks* 82). After coming across a magic shell, whose whorls go the wrong way, the narrator confronts the reality of having entered a mirror world, where previous assumptions can no longer be relied upon. Captured by the girl of the singing voice, who has a markedly macho style, the narrator is taken at gun point before a strange being in an old, dilapidated house. The being, who 'acknowledged no gender' (87), has two profiles, one male and one female, and sports 'soft, pale breasts' as well as the 'savage and barbaric . . . phallic insignia of maleness' (89). Struggling with ambiguous pronouns (the 'defect in our language there [being] no term of reference for these indeterminate and indefinable beings' [87]), the narrator, now identified as 'he', is forced to pass through the huge gilt-framed mirror in the house and to negotiate a yet-further-inverted space where he has become '[his] own reflection' (92). At this point in the attempt to represent inversion, the narrative becomes clogged with theoretical speculation, both in the dialogue of this strange threesome and in the description of the implications of their activities. Uncertainty as to 'which was the primary world and which the secondary' (93) leads to dizzying specul(ariz)ation on either side:

> The world was the same; yet absolutely altered. How can I describe it . . . almost as if this room was the colour negative of the other room. Unless . . . the other room, the other house, the other wood that I saw, transposed yet still peeping through the window in the other mirror – all that had been the colour negative of the room in which I now stood, where the exhalations of my breath were the same as the inhalations of my mirror anti-twin who turned away from me as I turned away from him, into the distorted, or else really real, world of the mirror room, which, since it existed in this mirror in this room beyond the mirror, reflected all of this room's ambiguities and was no longer the room I had left. (93)

The effect of these speculative specularities is often what Irigaray calls a '*blur of deformation*' (*This Sex* 10).

The macho girl Anna can function on both sides, her name a palindrome (readable both ways) and her face absolutely symmetrical. The 'androgyne' is more deeply emblematic:

> One half of its face was always masculine and the other, no matter what, was feminine; yet these had been changed about, so that all the balances of the planes of the face and the lines of the brow were the opposite of what they had been before, although one half of the face was still feminine and the other masculine. Nevertheless, the quality of the difference made it seem that this altered yet similar face was the combination of the reflection of the female side of the face and the masculine side of the face that *did not appear* in the face I had seen beyond the mirror; the effect was as of the reflection of a reflection, like an example of perpetual regression, the perfect, self-sufficient nirvana of the hermaphrodite. (94)

Masculine side reflects feminine, which is a mere reflection of the masculine. Yet the sum total is somehow less than, or out of reach of, the perfect balance subsumed under the ideal of hermaphrodism. For one thing, this uncanny androgynous composite, who sits in a Bath chair, knitting interminably, gives off an air of 'infernal suburban complacency' (94). For another, the ideal of synthesis, the knitting of thesis and antithesis, proves to be a crippling and sterile construct, temporary and fragile.

Carter's specular vision attempts a more rigorous inversion than Lewis Carroll's. Here 'light' is black, 'air' is 'solid as water', sound is 'seen', and gravity is 'not a property of the ground but of the atmosphere' (95). Language is forced to continue, but against the corrosive effects of specularity. Flowers have 'inexpressible colours . . . whose names only exist in an inverted language you could never understand if I were to speak it' (96). With language faltering, the scene is finally set for the ultimate test of gender inversion, which is the rape of the by now feminized male narrator by the masculine Anna. Will a reversal of gender attributes be possible, or, more importantly, will it achieve anything? The rape reproduces, in reverse, the degradation of violation, but just as he is about to be killed, the narrator grabs the gun (phallus) and manages to shoot his rapist and her dog. The power of victor over victim is restored to patriarchy, and the narrator returns by reverse motion to the androgyne, to witness her disintegration as emblem of the possibility of synthesis or cohesion. The tale as allegory of gender as performance or simulacrum reaches a conclusion similar to Irigaray's, that all reversals or negations are merely a version of the one and same hom(m)osexuality: 'the negative freshly states the affirmed proposition', as Carter's narrator puts it (91). Masculinity, or femininity, or androgyny, are mere labels that have 'arbitrarily settled' on individual identities just as the words for colours have settled on the flowers (96).

Though not specifically in the service of a Queer discourse, Carter's writing, like Woolf's in *Orlando*, sets the terms 'masculine', 'feminine', 'male' and 'female' in circulation in order to shift and unsettle their binary fixity. Both their texts play out the tension between a Symbolic discourse that would reassert 'identity' within patriarchal terms and an individual experience that resists this. Carter's story, with its emblematic passage through mirrors and back again, reads like a parable; *Orlando* reads more like a rigidly organized game (discourse) in which the rules are rapidly breaking down. The last two sentences of Carter's story offer a vision of radical change:

> Proud as a man, I once again advanced to meet my image in the mirror. Full of self-confidence, I held out my hands to embrace my self, my anti-self, my self not-self, my assassin, my death, the world's death. (101)

Here we are taken from the initial 'death' of the 'self' ('self not-self') at the mirror stage, the moment when a would-be identity becomes a mere image, through Symbolic 'identity' ('proud as a man'), to their violent dissolution amidst the 'world's death' in the ruins of the androgyne's crumbling house. The tone, as always with Carter, hovers on the brink of the grotesque,[18] an over-inflated balloon about to burst. But if her story finally explodes its own fantastic scenario for change, it has, in the process, caused considerable damage to the existing foundations.

*   *   *   *

To summarize. One of the many ways that we could trace the development of twentieth-century psychoanalysis would be to follow its gradual and systematic erosion of the persistent myth of femininity as essence and its replacement by the concept of femininity as a construct. First, as we have seen, Freud saw femininity as a difficult but necessary achievement out of a primordial masculinity ('the little girl is a little man' [PF 2: 151]). Bisexuality for Freud, as Gayatri Spivak notes, is really just another name for unisex ('Displacement' 172). In a move which emphasized considerably further the construct-edness of femininity, Joan Riviere defined it as a form of impersona-tion, a masquerading defence against masculinity, a compensatory strategy aimed at warding off both phallic envy and retaliation by fathers. By the 1950s and '60s, when a sufficient time had elapsed since the 'Controversial Discussions' between the Freudians and the Klei-nians to make a 'return to Freud' a novelty, Lacan was in a position to single out the structuralist elements in Freud's theory and shape them into a view of femininity as a mere effect of symbolization. Sexual difference, in Lacan's terms, is a discursive division which reproduces the very categories it creates. All identity (including sexual identity) is constituted by an order beyond individual agency, one which is dominated by the phallic term which relegates women to objects of exchange. So when he famously claimed that 'there's no such thing as a sexual relationship', or that 'a woman can but be excluded [il n'y a de femme qu'exclue] by the nature of things' (*Seminar 20*: 71 and 73),[19] he was invoking the phantasmatic nature of all discursive constructs, the phallus included. This does not mean that Lacan refuses difference: 'if there was no difference how could I say there was no sexual relation'. Rather, as Jacqueline Rose puts it, 'for him what is to be questioned is the seeming "consistency" of that difference – of the body or anything else – the division it enjoins, the definitions of the woman it produces' ('Introduction II' 56).

Bisexuality, therefore, needed to be re-conceptualized away from Freud's earlier view of an initially undifferentiated sexual nature prior to Symbolic difference and towards the view of the availability to all subjects of both positions, masculine or feminine (Rose 49n14). In Lacan's view, our relation to discourse necessitates lining ourselves up on one or the other side of the masculine/feminine dyad – as he illustrated in his famous sketch of two identical doors with 'Ladies' written over one and 'Gentlemen' over the other. Nouns can be 'doubled' according to the law (in this case of 'urinary segregation') while still leaving the signified (the identical doors) untouched (*Écrits* 151). (A recent popularity of images of gender transgression, such as the one in the TV advertisement showing a woman grabbing access to power by defying these signs and using the Gents, leaves the distinction as intact as it ever was.)[20] Luce Irigaray, as we have seen, has attempted to 'jam the machinery' of this divide and expose its sameness. In other feminist psychoanalytic responses to Lacan, it is this very question of the 'prior to the Symbolic' which has been at the centre of the challenge.

The Kleinian emphasis on the significance of the pre-Oedipal relationship to the maternal body has led, as we have seen in Chapter 2, to the postulation of what could be called a primordial femininity as a response to a Freudian–Lacanian masculinity. Feminism in the 1970s and '80s was dominated by the work of such writers as Cixous, Irigaray and Kristeva or the American Nancy Chodorow, who all in different ways explored the psychological implications of a reorientation to an early maternal space. Like Irigaray, Kristeva pondered the possibility of articulating the psychic processes repressed by language and the Symbolic. But in spite of suggestions in her early work of the 'feminine' character of the pre-Oedipal 'semiotic' (the chora), she has repeatedly agreed with Lacan that 'woman' cannot be represented; or, as the title of a 1974 interview has it, 'La femme, ce n'est jamais ça' (Marks and de Courtivron 137–41). Her statement in 'Women's Time' (1979) can be seen as the foundation of the 1990s gender theory which I have traced through the work of Butler and Sedgwick:

> the very dichotomy man/woman as an opposition between two rival entities may be understood as belonging to *metaphysics*. What can 'identity', even 'sexual identity', mean in a new theoretical and scientific space where the very notion of identity is challenged? (*Kristeva Reader* 209)

Five years earlier, she had used words like 'traversal' and 'oscillation' which have proved important in recent theory's suggestion of new possibilities for gender roles:

> The word 'traverse' implies that the subject experiences sexual difference, not as a fixed opposition ('man'/'woman'), but as a process of differentiation . . . All speaking subjects have within themselves a certain bisexuality which is precisely the possibility to explore all the sources of signification, that which posits a meaning as well as that which multiplies, pulverizes, and finally revives it. ('Oscillation Between Power and Denial' [1974], Marks and de Courtivron 165)

The attempt to inscribe femininity into an inherently patriarchal discourse must therefore be recognized for what it is, a phantasmatic construction of (maternal) origin, of the possibility of an unmediated relationship to bodies. As Jacqueline Rose puts it:

> The 'semiotic' can never wholly displace the 'symbolic' since it relies on that very order to give to it its, albeit resistant, shape . . . the body can only ever be *signified*, it is never *produced*. (*Sexuality in the Field of Vision* 145).

To pass 'through the looking-glass' is to bump flat against its opaque surface and be thrown back again, into a world of endlessly reflecting images – as we shall now see.

8

The Phantasy of Death

Jean Baudrillard, cartographer of the modern universe of appearances, signs and images, has singled out what he calls 'Three Orders of Simulacra' that have developed since the dissolution of the feudal order and the beginning of the Renaissance. In (pre-modern) societies of caste and rank, he argues, signs referred unequivocally to a particular situation and status; far from arbitrary, signs served to link people in the 'inescapable reciprocity' of hierarchy (*Symbolic Exchange and Death* 50). Arbitrariness began to emerge when signs were used to refer to a 'real' world (a signified) to which nobody felt any longer committed. Competitive democracy, the power of all to participate, resulted in a proliferation of signs and products according to demand. In circulating freely, signs soon ceased to be 'bound' to any symbolic order. Hence the Renaissance (and bourgeois) obsession with the problematic of the 'natural', the metaphysics of appearance and reality.

This was what Baudrillard called the 'first order of simulation'. The second, ushered in with the industrial revolution, resulted from the severance of the mass-produced product from any original to which it might have referred. The phenomenon of 'the series' did away with the notion of the original *versus* the counterfeit, and introduced that of equivalence or 'indifference', of indefinite repetition and reproducibility of the same (55–57). The 'ultimatum' of capitalism thus came to lie in reproduction rather than production, as Walter Benjamin wrote in revision of Marx. From this we are led directly into third-order simulacra, whereby only an affiliation to the model, the 'signifier of reference', has any meaning (56). Hence, after the surreal (an attempt to supplant the real, but within its own terms), comes the hyperreal. Through the endless reproductive mechanisms of the media (photography, television, and so on), reality collapses into hyperrealism, the meticulous reduplication of the real . . . Through reproduction from one medium into another the real becomes volatile, it becomes the allegory of death, but it also draws strength from its own destruction, becoming the real for its own sake, a fetishism of the lost object which is no longer the object of representation, but the ecstasy of denegation and its own ritual extermination: the hyperreal. (71–72)

It is within this nexus of elements which constitute postmodern definitions of the hyperreal – reproductions repeating themselves in a vertiginous flight towards their own extinction, the fetishization of the lost object, reduplication as an allegory of death – that I want, in this last chapter, to turn to the subject of ends.

While Baudrillard's work of the late 1970s and 1980s was concerned with a depthless world of simulacra and reflecting images in the absence of a stabilizing reference, his more recent work has explored the nihilistic implications of these tenets and has preoccupied itself, at the end of the millennium, with endings – or rather, with the impossibility of ends. To Francis Fukuyama's claim for the 'end of history' in a post-communist world, Baudrillard replies that the acceleration of modern technology, of the 'event' as inevitably 'mediated', has propelled us to '[fly] free of the referential sphere of the real and of history' (*The Illusion of the End* 1). Instead of 'occurring', events now 'hollow out before them the void into which they plunge . . . [into] the peripheral void of the media' (19). History has become a dustbin – of defunct ideologies, bygone utopias, nuclear waste, where everything is recyclable and thus 'endless'. The Gulf War 'decredibilized' both war and news, drawing us 'so far into simulation that the question of truth and reality cannot even be posed' (58 and 60).

A new violence has entered the human domain: 'our species is automatically switching over to collective suicide' (83). In seeking to construct our own (virtual or technical) immortality through *in vitro* fertilization, cloning, and genetic manipulation, we are abolishing our (living) mortality in favour of the immortality of the dead, fashioning ourselves into a race of 'undead' comparable to Dracula's Transylvanian ancestors – a link I will be exploring shortly. Or is it that we are exterminating death itself by creating indestructible life? Baudrillard considers this question only to dismiss it in favour of a postmodern nihilism: 'by going down these paths of artifice which were supposed to ensure its indefinite survival, it [the human species] is perhaps hurtling even more quickly to its doom' (84). And yet if we are all doomed through genetic simulation, we are at the same time incapable of coming to an end, assured as we are of 'an indefinite recurrence, a backhanded immortality' (115).

Several decades earlier, Maurice Blanchot had explored, with a similar force of paradox, the 'impossibility of death', in his case in relation to the role of language. Following Hegel, he argued that all forms of symbolization such as language are dependent on the replacement and disappearance of the object named or symbolized. Language means that the thing named can be detached from its existence and 'suddenly plunged into nothingness'; language is thus a form of 'deferred assassination' ('Literature and the Right to Death' [1949] 42 and 43). Writing, for Blanchot, thus becomes the expression of a relation to absence. The material presence of language (its acoustic properties, or its presence as ink and paper) can be seen as an attempt to supplement or disguise this originary lack, the destruction of the thing. Thus its paradox is that it simultaneously evokes its own death without being able to die. Blanchot's post-war writings draw on this view of the 'cruelty' of language, the fact that it searches repeatedly for that moment which precedes it, which would but cannot give presence to the object (46). In seeking to recover that which it had to destroy in order to come into existence, literature, like language, perpetually repeats the paradox of death. The Modernist writer saw the writing process as an attempt to 'shelter something from death', as Gide wrote in his *Journals* in 1922 (Blanchot, *The Space of Literature* 94). The Postmodernist, however, like Kafka as cited by Blanchot, 'writes in order to be able to die' (95). The activity of the artist is thus better compared to suicide than to creation.

DRACULA AND THE DEATH DRIVE

Dying, then, is literature's allegory of its own perpetually frustrated flight to extinction, enacted through the repetition of words that would but cannot capture what they replace. Described in this way, Postmodernism's concept of literary production is a direct descendant of Freud's concepts of repetition, symbolization and the death drive as outlined in his 1920 essay 'Beyond the Pleasure Principle'. In fact, it was Freud rather than Baudrillard who first made the scandalous proposition that death can be thought of as an 'illusion'.[1] Freud's point of view in this essay is an extraordinary mixture of the biological and the mythical,[2] of precise, even pedantic descriptions of the actions of instinctive forces and quasi-mystical philosophy which draws on the conceptions of Empedocles and Schopenhauer. All these speculations are loosely yoked together with frequent apologetic asides as to their 'far-fetched' or 'extreme' nature (PF 11: 295 and 310n2). Indeed, as he puts it at the end, if asked how far he himself is convinced of the truth of these hypotheses,

> My answer would be that I am not convinced myself and that I do not seek to persuade other people to believe in them. Or, more precisely, that I do not know how far I believe in them. There is no reason, as it seems to me, why the emotional factor of conviction should enter into this question at all. It is surely possible to throw oneself into a line of thought and to follow it wherever it leads out of simple scientific curiosity, or, if the reader prefers, as an *advocatus diaboli,* who is not on that account himself sold to the devil. (332)

Disingenuously making light of the question of 'conviction' about a theory of such far-reaching implications, Freud set a tone for its reception which has continued to the present,[3] as do its 'daemonic' implications for literary analysis. During transference, Freud wrote, his patients often had the sense of something daemonic at work in them as they watched the instinctual character of their compulsion to repeat, working systematically against their own pleasure (292 and 307). This evil 'fate', however, had to be relocated *within* the human psyche, traced back to tendencies independent of and 'more primitive, more elementary, more instinctual' than the pleasure principle (294). Although humans may 'arrange their own fate' (292) – that is, develop according to the psychic experiences of early infancy rather than in compliance with any external force, they are at the same time subject to instincts or drives inherent in all organic life, drives to restore an earlier *in*organic state of things: 'the most universal endeavour of all living substance – namely to return to the quiescence of the inorganic world' (336). Mental (and perhaps nervous) life is dominated by the tension of internal stimuli seeking relief through the attempt to reduce or remove this tension to zero point – according to a principle of *Nirvana* (329).

In view of this 'conservative' drive backwards, Freud raises the question of evolution, contrasting the 'undeniable' truth of Darwin's theory that species move in their overall progress towards 'higher development' with the 'unquestionable' fact that individual organisms display an opposite, 'retrograde' tendency (314). And it is here, at the point of collision between a confident drive forward and an insidious drive backwards, that we can insert Bram Stoker's *Dracula*.

Published in 1897, *Dracula* shares with many *fin-de-siècle* texts a post-Darwinian anxiety about the 'bestiality' of human origins. If mankind had so much in common with earlier forms, what was the guarantee that it could continue to maintain its distinction from them, without sliding back again? Past and future battle for supremacy within Dracula's person, both literally and metaphorically. On the one hand, his 'immortality' seems to secure him a terrifying hold on the future – as Jonathan Harker, the solicitor's clerk who goes to Transylvania to arrange the legal details of Dracula's transfer to London, observes on contemplating the vampire lying in his coffin:

> There was a mocking smile on the bloated face which seemed to drive me mad. This was the being I was helping to transfer to London, where, perhaps, for centuries to come he might, amongst its teeming millions, satiate his lust for blood, and create a new and ever-widening circle of semi-demons to batten on the helpless. The very thought drove me mad. (Stoker 71)

(Being 'driven mad' repeatedly by this spectre, Jonathan both re-hearses the predicament of all Gothic victims before him and partici-pates in a new psychiatric investigation of horror characteristic of this period, a point I shall return to shortly.) Time, as the Count himself boasts later, 'is on my side' (394) in the battle of the 'civilized' forces of Jonathan and his band against him. For Dracula reaches back several centuries, as he tells Jonathan at the beginning in his description of his descent from a line of Szekely nobility, speaking of ancestral heroism, especially of battles, 'as if he had been [personally] present at them all' (41) – which he has, of course. Dracula refuses bourgeois individual-ism in favour of 'rank', the 'blood of many brave races' (42) which flows in his veins. The two words (rank and blood) reverberate throughout the text in a variety of punning and ambivalent forms.

For all his nobility, Dracula is clearly associated with 'baser' ancestors such as the wolf or the bat, into which he can metamorphose at will. Like his castle, Dracula is both aristocratic and decayed, superior yet regressive. This doubleness is captured in his famous appearance – the strong 'aquiline' face, which at times appears to be that of an old man and at others, such as when he has surfeited himself during his night-time orgies, defies the laws of nature and grows younger. His hands are characteristic of this regressive streak beneath the trappings of nobility:

> Hitherto I had noticed the backs of his hands as they lay on his knees in the firelight, and they had seemed rather white and fine; but seeing them now close to me, I could not but notice that they were rather coarse – broad, with squat fingers. Strange to say, there were hairs in the centre of the palm. (28)

But it is his 'rank' breath which first alerts Jonathan to his host's link with earlier, more primal forms, which causes the first 'nausea' and 'shudder' of horror (28–29).

As critics have noticed, Stoker's novel is clearly signalling the final, inevitable decay of the aristocracy in Europe and its replacement by the bourgeois band equipped with modern technology (such as Winchester rifles and stenographs). 'Blood' has become a scarce commodity, and must be obtained through personal intervention – rather than, as in earlier times, spilled liberally for his sake by the peasant classes. David Punter writes:

> Dracula can no longer survive on blood of this kind; he needs alternative sources of nourishment to suit his socially attenuated existence. The dominion of the sword is replaced by the more naked yet more subtle dominion of the tooth; as the nobleman's real powers disappear, he becomes invested with semi-supernatural abilities, exercised by night rather than in the broad day of legendary feudal conflict. (*The Literature of Terror* 258)

The 'haemosexuality' (Frayling 388) is a threat in many other ways as well. First of all, fear of 'invasion' of British blood by polluted, syphilis-infected strains from abroad, particularly from the East, is clearly suggested in the many references to the difficulties of securing an uncontaminated blood supply for the transfusions that temporarily restore Lucy, Dracula's first victim in England. (Contemporary film versions of the novel like that of Francis Ford Coppola have similarly made use of this theme of sexually transmitted diseases with subliminal references to AIDS.) Homosexuality itself informs an anxious sub-text, with at times explicit references to the sordid details being exposed at the time from the trial and imprisonment of Stoker's compatriot and acquaintance Oscar Wilde – as Talia Schaffer has pointed out recently. At the racial level, the novel has also been read in terms of various threats from Eastern Europe. Like Svengali in George du Maurier's *Trilby* of three years earlier, Dracula had crawled 'out of the mysterious East! The poisonous East – birthplace and home of an ill-wind that blows nobody good' (qtd in Dijkstra 343). Stephen D. Arata has argued that Stoker chose finally to locate his novel (which he had originally set, like LeFanu's *Carmilla* [1872], in 'Styria', S.E. Austria) in the area of the Carpathian Mountains in order to exploit the image of racial conflict and political upheaval then associated with the area in the Western consciousness – very much as it has been in our own *fin de siècle*. It is from such places, the Dutch Professor Van Helsing warns in the book (just as NATO leaders did during the war in Kosovo), that empires/superpowers are under the greatest threat: 'He have follow the wake of the berserker Icelander, the devil-begotten Hun, the Slav, the Saxon, the Magyar' (Stoker 307). The book thus illustrates what Arata calls 'The late-Victorian nightmare of reverse colonization' (629), whereby declining powers are overtaken by 'retrograde' forces: vampire engulfs empire.

Robert Louis Stevenson's Hyde in *The Strange Case of Dr Jekyll and Mr Hyde* of a decade earlier represents a comparatively innocuous threat beside Dracula. His victims are merely trampled on, destroyed. Dracula, on the other hand, seeks to infiltrate and *replicate* himself, spreading his regressive traits *ad infinitum* throughout the world. A more potent image of the 'compulsion to repeat' (or, in Postmodern terms, endless reproduction as an allegory of death) could hardly be imagined. For all his 'higher' attributes – Jonathan repeats that 'he would have made a wonderful solicitor . . . his knowledge and acumen were wonderful' (45) – Dracula clearly represents a drive 'backwards' to something more primitive, a compulsion which, like the death drive, 'over-rides' drives towards pleasure and civilization (PF 11: 293). The band of men pursuing him are in fact in little doubt as to what constitutes higher or lower forms. For all his solicitor's attributes, Dracula is (in Van Helsing's description) a 'criminal type' at the mercy of his own baser drives: 'This criminal has not full man-brain. He is clever and cunning and resourceful; but he be not of man-stature as to brain. He be of child-brain in much' (439). Stoker reinforces the theme of compulsive regression with Freudian-style references to the inorganic or elemental constitution of Dracula's make-up. He can appear not only as a wolf or bat, but 'on moonlight rays as elemental dust' (308). And the territory which spawned him possesses strange elemental properties that seem to reach back infinitely in space and time:

> With this one, all the forces of nature that are occult and deep and strong must have worked together in some wondrous way. The very place, where he have been alive, Un-dead for all these centuries, is full of strangeness of the geologic and chemical world. There are deep caverns and fissures that reach none know whither. There have been volcanoes, some of whose openings still send out waters of strange properties and gases that kill or make to vivify. Doubtless, there is something magnetic or electric in some of these combinations of occult forces which work for physical life in strange way. (411)

Like the gases 'that kill or make to vivify', Dracula seems to hover on that crucial brink of life from the inorganic that Freud saw as the point of return of the death drive.

Dracula's true threat is that he both repeats and reverses the process of transformation of the organic back into the inorganic, through a force, as Freud put it, 'of whose nature we can form no conception' (PF 11: 311), echoing Van Helsing's 'occult'. Like the 'life of the organism [which] mov[es] with a vacillating rhythm' (PF 11: 313), Dracula perpetually repeats the cycle of animation (through living blood) at night followed by a return to inanimation in his coffin during the day. In his chapter on the vampire in *On the Nightmare* (1931), Ernest Jones compares the vampire with the ghoul, the spirit which preys on corpses in Eastern tales. Whereas with the latter, 'necrophiliac traffic is one way', as Maurice Richardson puts it (Frayling 418), with vampirism, Jones writes, 'the dead first visits the living and then drags him into death, being re-animated himself in the process' (Jones 99). As *Dracula* makes clear, the power of this two-way process comes from its instinctual quality:

> in a difficulty he [Dracula] has to seek resource in habit. His past is a clue, and the one page of it that we know – and that from his own lips – tells that once before, when in what Mr Morris [the American] would call a 'tight place,' he went back to his own country from the land he had tried to invade, and thence, without losing purpose, prepared himself for a new effort. He came again, better equipped

for his work; and won. So he came to London to invade a new land.
He was beaten, and when all hope of success was lost, and his
existence in danger, he fled back over the sea to his home; just as
formerly he had fled back over the Danube from Turkey land.
(Stoker 439–40)

To chase him down, the men follow Dracula as the embodiment of all
instinctual forces back to their origin. The chase has all the attributes
of repetition and ritual; all repetitions, as Ellie Ragland puts it, 'bear
the structure of obsession, pointing to the death in desire' (*Essays* 167).
    Another form taken by this interlocked, repetitive battle between
Dracula and his pursuers relates more explicitly to the erotic rather
than the thanatic component of the drives. Each time Dracula sinks
his fangs into Lucy and drains her blood, the men, using a hypodermic
needle to replace the regressive tooth, reinfuse more blood into her.
The process of paired penetrations is repeated four times, using the
blood of Lord Arthur, Dr Seward, Quincey Morris and Van Helsing,
until Lucy finally succumbs. As critics since Stoker's own day have
recognized, there is something very perverse about the book's sexuality, a peculiarly Victorian mixture of prudery and pornography. Its
sadistic elements are immediately obvious in the elaborate array of
phallic weapons wielded by the men: from the vicious three-foot stake
they hammer through Lucy's heart (275–78) to the 'great kukri knife'
that Jonathan finally uses to slit Dracula's throat and the 'great bowie
knife' that Morris uses to stake him (483–84). As early as 1886,
Richard von Krafft-Ebing, Professor of Psychiatry at the University
of Vienna, had published his enormously popular and influential
Psychopathia Sexualis, in which a clear association was made between
vampirism and sadistic sexuality. In *Dracula*, for all its fixation on
penetration, the erotic is anything but 'normally' genital; like the death
drive, it yearns back to earlier stages.
    Genital sex is replaced in the novel by an array of polymorphously
perverse practices which, for all their displacement onto the supernatural paraphernalia surrounding Dracula's habits, rival those of the
Marquis de Sade himself. Bisexuality (or rather, as with Sade, a refusal
to distinguish between the male and female body) is suggested in
Dracula's famous command to his vampire daughters to leave Jonathan to him (55) – in spite of the fact that actual blood-exchange
takes place only between members of the opposite sex. More crucially,
the text reverses Freud's schema of the 'normal' progress in the child's

sexuality from the oral to the anal to the genital. *Dracula*'s most subversive feature is its lurid celebration of orality and anality.

The dominant organ of the book, the mouth is compellingly 'wicked' (276), the source of both the ultimate in eroticism and the utmost horror (as *vagina dentata*). One of the central scenes is when Lucy, now a vampire herself, grovels and snarls over a young child whom she clutches to her breast in ghastly mimicry of the maternal function. After drinking its blood she tosses it to the ground then stands in the moonlight, displaying to the band of men her dripping, blood-smeared mouth, which had now grown 'to an open square, as in the passion masks of the Greeks and Japanese' (272). For Arthur, her fiancé, 'There can be no horror like this ever any more!' (273). The scene derives its force from the subversion of a range of cherished images. Lucy, like her at times inseparable counterpart Mina, has throughout been lavished with a haze of associations with the Madonna. For both women, Stoker draws deeply on the Victorian storehouse of images of angels in the house, so much so that the tedious repetition of their sweetness and purity drags the convention towards its final decadence. In addition to the blasphemous flinging of the child from her breast, Lucy reverses the nurturing process by being the one herself to extract fluid (just as Mina will later be forced to drink from the opened vein in Dracula's 'bosom' [363]). It is as if she figures, with this vampiric gesture, the phantasized bad breast which would devour, engulf and destroy the child. Here we recall Melanie Klein's vocabulary of sadistic 'biting, devouring and cutting' (*The Selected Melanie Klein* 71) to describe the child as it projects its innate aggression out on to the maternal breast in the oral-sadistic stage of libidinal organization. The anxiety experienced in the pre-genital stages arises, according to Klein, 'from the operation of the death instinct . . . felt as fear of annihilation' (179):

> The destructive impulse projected outwards is first experienced as oral aggression. I believe that oral-sadistic impulses towards the mother's breast are active from the beginning of life, though with the onset of teething the cannibalistic impulses increase in strength – a factor stressed by [Karl] Abraham. (180)

In the sadistic stages of development, the subject's dominant aim is to possess the contents of the mother's body, 'to destroy her by means of every weapon sadism can command' (96). In similar manner, the brave band of Christian gentlemen gather their battery of weapons together to take violent revenge on the new 'diabolical' Lucy. The splitting here enacted in Lucy into good and bad objects is a fundamental mechanism of defence against anxiety. Idealization (Lucy's excessive purity), Klein notes, is the corollary of persecuting fear.

> In hallucinatory gratification, therefore, two interrelated processes take place: the omnipotent conjuring up of the ideal object and situation, and the equally omnipotent annihilation of the bad persecutory object and the painful situation. These processes are based on splitting both the object and the ego. (182)[4]

Idealization and splitting had been a fundamental strategy of Gothic characterization of women since the genre's inauguration with Walpole's *Castle of Otranto* (1764) with its cluster of 'spotless' heroines who are either stabbed (Matilda) or retained (Isabella). In *Dracula*, the device reaches its apotheosis with the splitting within the same character (Lucy), who achieves the transformation from nurturing Madonna to violent whore within the space of a few pages.[5]

Milk, semen and blood: the body's fluids, like its erotogenic organs, are exchanged and conflated with orgiastic abandon in what Maurice Richardson has called 'a kind of incestuous, necrophilous, oral-anal-sadistic all-in wrestling match' (Frayling 418–19). Over its long-drawn-out 500 pages, *Dracula* makes only a perfunctory effort to explore the scientific or philosophical implications of its revelations – in comparison, say, with *Frankenstein*. A few psychological references do occur, however. Van Helsing calls himself a 'student of the brain', referring on one occasion to 'the great Charcot' (247) (whom Stoker himself, it seems, had met).[6] Direct exposure to Gothic horror 'unhinges' minds, and Jonathan, as the initial and most extended recipient of Dracula's practices, with his temporary break-down ('violent brain fever' [131]) and whitened hair, is channelled into that well-worn convention – before, that is, he is required to represent the brave Christian brotherhood of Dracula's opponents, which restores his vigour. If there is a scientific base in the novel it is Dr Seward's 'lunatic asylum' in Carfax, next to the deserted house used by Dracula for his invasion of London. Here, Seward, who harbours scientific aspirations comparable to Frankenstein's,[7] keeps detailed notes on his oddest psychiatric case, R. M. Renfield, a 'homicidal maniac' (95) of, however, 'sanguine temperament' (83) – as indeed he might be, given his dietary propensities:

I shall have to invent a new classification for him, and call him a zoophagous (life-eating) maniac; what he desires is to absorb as many lives as he can, and he has laid himself out to achieve it in a cumulative way. (95)

Renfield's 'incorporation' of a chain of raw insects and animals (flies, then spiders, then birds – he is refused a cat) serves as a cannibalistic parallel to the orality of Dracula, his 'Master'. Renfield's non-human prey, suggesting totem sacrifices, is an explicit reminder of the regressive implications of Dracula's erotic practices.

In *Dracula*, orality is treated with the same celebratory profusion as the anal is in Beckett's writing. The anal in Stoker's novel, by contrast, is a dark and smelly secret, which seeps out from the crevices of his Transylvanian castle, his Carfax estate and his Piccadilly house, an 'earthy smell' but also – 'how shall I describe it?', Jonathan hesitates –

It was not alone that it was composed of all the ills of mortality and with the pungent, acrid smell of blood, but it seemed as though corruption had become itself corrupt. Faugh! it sickens me to think of it. (323)

Excrement is the body's product which most conspicuously links it to decomposition, to the inanimate. Dracula returns, literally and with mechanical repetition every morning, to his foul-smelling earth. Talia Schaffer records (406–7) that one of the most damning pieces of evidence against Wilde in his trial was the discovery of faecal stains on his sheets, evidence of anal sex, unleashing a flood of homophobic reaction expressed in terms similar to Jonathan's words here. Such 'retrograde' behaviour had to be purified, exorcised by every means possible before it engulfed the whole of the civilized world.

CIVILIZATION AND ITS SACRIFICES

If the latent drive of *Dracula* is backwards, towards anal and oral fixations, its narrative is manifestly propelled forward in a resolute thrust towards the expulsion of these drives by the triumphantly phallic band of men. Although still narrated in fragments (from journals, letters and memoranda), like the rest of the book, the last eighty pages take on a new and tighter momentum, that of the chase, in which pursuers and pursued are embroiled in lustful anticipation of violence and death. The novel can be read as a masculine quest romance which harks back to the Crusades as an era of heroic conquest. Van Helsing's florid English is at once exhortatory and nostalgic:

> Thus are we ministers of God's own wish: that the world, and men for whom His Son die, will not be given over to monsters, whose very existence would defame Him. He have allowed us to redeem one soul [Lucy's] already, and we go out as the old knights of the Cross to redeem more. Like them we shall travel towards the sunrise; and like them, if we fall, we fall in good cause. (412)

And yet the exaggerated terms of fellowship and union can be read as an anxious defence; the most effective way of detecting desire is to look into the defences against it. In this case, what is being defended against is a murderous rivalry over the women.

I have referred in Chapter 4 to Freud's theory of the origins of civilization in the setting up by the primal horde of taboos against incest and parricide, and the phylogenetic transmission of these events. Van Helsing's Christian brotherhood is an explicit example of men bonding together to prevent antagonism over the impossibility of them all enjoying physical access to the same woman. Lucy has had three of them as suitors, and 'repetition by three', as Peter Brooks notes, glossing Freud, 'constitutes the minimal repetition to the perception of series' (*Reading for the Plot* 99). For her part, Lucy wonders 'Why can't they let a girl marry three men, or as many as want her . . .?' (Stoker 81). But Arthur Holmwood, Jack Seward and Quincey Morris, like the sons of the primal horde, decide in favour of 'civilization' and self-denial: to repress their rivalry, face up to the necessity of laws against incest, and join with the others (Harker and Van Helsing) to eliminate the 'father' Dracula, who would have all the women for himself. 'Your girls that you all love are mine already' (394), the Count snarls in the scene that precipitates the long pursuit back to Transylvania.

Dracula is both totem animal and primal father, embodying all the ambivalence inherent in the two related symbolic forms. The totem can be characterized, according to Freud, as a symptom of the ambivalence towards the father – the desire to murder him and the accompanying guilt it produces, the emblem of a compromise between these two conflicting impulses. The totem animal is both killed and mourned, the mourning allowing the sons to disclaim responsibility for their deed. Then, by a system of 'deferred obedience' (PF 13: 205) characteristic of the 'conscience' inherent in all 'civilized' behaviour, the father/god begins to assert an even stronger sway over them after his death than he had done before it. As un-dead father, therefore, Dracula gathers to himself all the power of the ages, carrying with him 'the sense of guilt for an action [which] has persisted for many thousands of years and has remained operative in generations which can have had no knowledge of that action' (PF 13: 220). It is in this mythopoeic sense that I would agree with Nina Auerbach that vampires 'embody not fear of death, but fear of life: their power and their curse is their undying vitality' (5); as Van Helsing puts it, 'In him some vital principle have in strange way found their utmost' (411).

It is in this sense, also, that we must read the intricate set of totemic rituals repeated so frequently in the book – the use of garlic, the Host and crucifix, the ritualized weapons for staking the vampire and removing its head. Like the Christian communion, which they parallel, these rituals are required as 'a fresh elimination of the father, a repetition of the guilty deed' (PF 13: 217). It is significant that the fraternal clan in *Dracula* celebrates its victory over the totem/father by a ritual return 'over the old ground' of their sacrifice seven years after the event (Stoker 485), at the end of the novel. The sons' guilt at their rebelliousness never becomes extinct, as it is 'the great event in human prehistory', the 'root of every form of religion' (PF 13: 214 and 210). Exogamy has been instituted in the only way possible. 'Woman' has been renounced, either by demonization and murder (Lucy), or by being set up as an impossible ideal (hence the lavish terms of worship in defence of the threatened purity of Mina).

The men eventually find wives elsewhere, thus 'rescu[ing] the organization which . . . make[s] them strong' (PF 13: 205) – and which may, Freud adds in a hugely suggestive aside, 'have been based on homosexual feelings and acts' amongst them (206). Mina and Jonathan's son becomes an emblem of this homoerotic union – with his 'bundle of [all their] names' (485). It has been (with both Mina and Lucy) through and in the women that their union is sealed, in the case of Lucy in a literal sense, as their transfused blood mingles in her veins – before, however, it is finally extracted and infused into his own by Dracula, the feared father on to whom the sons have projected all their own aggression. In this strange reversal of the Sacrament (he drinks *their* communal blood), the injection and extraction of 'the life', as blood is called, reads like a ceaseless cycle of incorporation and evacuation described by object-relations theorists in the processes of introjection and projection. The men's proclaimed victory at the end, the so-called 'blott[ing] out' of Dracula's traces (486), is pure illusion: it is the paternal imago which survives, in domination – as in the Dracula myth – of the Name, and of the Law.

As the above terms suggest, it was Lacan who was to develop the full implications of Freud's theory of the death drive as manifested in social organization and to give it its linguistic framework. Lacan's appropriation of Freud's theory was characteristic. For him, the action of the death drive was manifest first and foremost in the signifying chain.

SYMBOLIC MURDER: LACAN AND THE DEATH DRIVE

Dracula himself would seem to have taken on the function of a mirror in the sense that he has spawned an endless sequence of haemophilic simulacra, repeating himself wherever he bites. And yet the paradox is that he is the only one who has no mirror image. It is as if he has bypassed the mirror stage, and taken on the role of pure symbolization. As such, he represents perpetual 'discordance with his own reality' (Lacan, *Écrits* 2), the alienation of the divided human psyche and the gap between the signifier and the signified. The un-dead is thus a potent metaphor for symbolization as conceived by Lacan. The dead return not so much because, as Slavoj Žižek contends, they have some unpaid symbolic debt to collect, but rather because their role as pure symbolization keeps them within the endless circuit of the signifying chain. Symbolization is perpetual murder (*Écrits* 104), and the place to which Dracula returns, the coffin/grave, as we saw in connection with Antigone in Chapter 4, is *the* paradigmatic symbol in that it represents the way the dead continue to 'live' at a symbolic level in spite of their absence in reality (Žižek, *Looking Awry* 23). Like the signifier, Dracula is both death-bearing (a representative of the perpetual murder of the thing) and immortal, endlessly replicating but never coinciding with himself. At the very end of his seminars for 1954–55, Lacan returned to the idea of the death drive as 'the mask of the symbolic order': 'The symbolic order is simultaneously non-being and insisting to be, that is what Freud has in mind when he talks about the death instinct as being what is most fundamental' (*Seminar 2*: 326).

Lacan was both wary of and drawn to the 'biologism' of Freud's theory of the death drive. On the one hand, he repeats that it is 'not a question of biology' (*Écrits* 102), that the drive cannot be reduced to a matter of energy (*Seminar 7*: 209). And yet in order to explicate its workings, he uses the metaphor of the machine, giving it, as John Forrester notes, 'a novel interpretation of nineteenth- and twentieth-century energetics and its progeny, information theory' (134). It is important, however, to remember Lacan's insistence that 'To take this analogy literally, to translate it into the precise terms used in physics, is a misinterpretation as absurd as the work of Borel's monkey typists' (*Seminar 2*: 115).

The machine serves Lacan's 'anti-organicist' (*Seminar 2*: 81), anti-humanist approach to humanity. Concepts of the 'individual' as autonomous and rationalistic ego need to be countered by the aspects of Freud's theory, especially as in *The Future of an Illusion* (1927) and *Civilization and its Discontents* (1930), which revolve around the formidable question of 'what, in terms of energy, is the psyche?' (*Seminar 2*: 75). The nervous system, like a machine, has a 'restitutive' tendency to return to a state of equilibrium (79). Coincident with the tendency to repeat, this tendency, to which Lacan, borrowing from the field of energetics, gives the label 'entropy', is an integral part of the mode of operation of language, the communication as he examined it in the analytic relation (the transference). Just as when a job is done, some of the energy is expended or lost (entropy), similarly in communication there is a tendency to cease communicating: what in psychology is called 'the jam' (*Seminar 2*: 83). In the transference, the subject is caught up in the repetitive games of language, the games 'in which subjectivity brings together mastery of its dereliction and the birth of the symbol' (*Écrits* 103). What is at issue here is this loss as a 'beyond' of language:

> as soon as we have to deal with anything in the world appearing in the form of the signifying chain, there is somewhere – though certainly outside of the natural world – which is the beyond of that chain, the *ex nihilo* on which it is founded and is articulated as such. (*Seminar 7*: 212)

The drive expresses in its 'historical' dimension (that is, the compulsion to return to the past in analytic speech) the 'limit' of that same act of memorization. At the heart of being is a void, the site of 'the impassable' (*Seminar 7*: 213) or Real (the *object a*) that seeks to fill the gap of loss. This Real constantly invades the Symbolic, reminding us that language is merely a differential system of meaningless elements. As Lacan puts it in the 'Rome Discourse': 'this mortal meaning reveals in speech a centre exterior to language' (*Écrits* 105). Death pulls always to the 'beyond' in language, shooting it through with its own mortality.

MORTAL MEANINGS: KYD'S *THE SPANISH TRAGEDY*

Thomas Kyd's *The Spanish Tragedy* (1592) is widely read as an example of early Elizabethan tragedy, a source for *Hamlet*, with an exemplary range of Senecan features: the Ghost, the revenge plot, the 'unpleasantly sanguinary' bloodshed and horror (T. S. Eliot, 'Seneca' 80). If ever a literary work were about death, it is this one. The first lines introduce the Ghost of Andrea, whose reflections on mortality frame the entire play. Murder, suicide and revenge produce a spectacular pile-up of bodies (nine out of the twelve main characters), to each of which Andrea assigns various forms of mechanical torment: Ixion's wheel, Sisyphus' stone, boiling Acheron. The references are chiefly literary (from Virgil's *Aeneid* Book VI), but the terms are remarkably vivid: physical and elemental. Life has here a tenuous hold over the human body, which is dramatized as being on the brink of the 'passage' to death: when killed in battle, Andrea felt 'life to death ma[king] passage through my wounds' (Kyd 5). Physical death involves passing to a mineral or elemental state, via the 'unquenched fires' of the river of Phlegethon in Hell, or the boiling lake of Acheron, which reduces everything to a state of dissolution (50). Hieronimo, Knight Marshal of Spain whose son Horatio has been treacherously murdered, raves in vengeful despair against Lorenzo, one of the murderers, in a declamatory blank verse that vacillates back and forth along this 'path' to physical extinction. In the following extract from Act III, two innocent 'Portingale' messengers seeking direction to Lorenzo's father's house are packed off by a raging Hieronimo along a macabre metaphorical route to Hades, until finally,

> There, in a brazen cauldron, fixed by Jove
> In his fell wrath upon a sulphur flame,
> Yourselves shall find Lorenzo bathing him
> In boiling lead and blood of innocents. (80)

Hieronimo himself is constantly equipping himself (with poniards and ropes) for the journey:

> Hieronimo, 'tis time for thee to trudge:
> Down by the dale that flows with purple gore
> Standeth a fiery tower; there sits a judge
> Upon a seat of steel and molten brass,
> And 'twixt his teeth he holds a fire-brand,
> That leads unto the lake where hell doth stand.
> Away, Hieronimo, to him be gone:
> He'll do thee justice for Horatio's death.
> Turn down this path, thou shalt be with him straight;
> Or this, and then thou need'st not take thy breath.
> This way or that way? (81)

The two 'ways' here are either murder (of the perpetrators of his son's murder, and thus revenge), or suicide. Death, life's importunate alternative, exerts an inexorable gravitational pull downwards – to 'sulphur', 'lead', 'steel' and 'brass'. Hieronimo's struggle is to resist this elemental or metallic pull until death can wreck its greatest havoc – as it does at the end in the merciless playlet.

The Senecan convention of revenge-crazed hallucinations takes the form in Hieronimo of a projection on to things and other people of the death drive that rules him. When a petitioner presents the Knight Marshal with a lease from a holding from which he is being unjustly evicted, Hieronimo tears it with his teeth, all the while denying his action:

> That cannot be, I gave it never a wound;
> Show me one drop of blood fall from the same:
> How is it possible I should slay it then? (91)

Another petitioner, an old man seeking justice for his own murdered son, is mistaken by Hieronimo for 'my Horatio', 'changed in death's black shade' (92). His 'brainsick lunacy' (118) has given him over to the slips and puns of language that reveal his unconscious. In recognition of their shared grief, he says to the old man:

> . . . I thee, thou me shalt stay,
> And thou, and I and she [his wife], will sing a song,
> Three parts in one, but all of discords framed –
> Talk not of cords, but let us now be gone,
> For with a cord Horatio was slain. (93)

In classic Renaissance manner, the play abounds in references to reflections, appearance and illusion. The old man is 'the lively image of my grief:/Within thy face my sorrows I may see' (93).[8] And just as the death drive within him reflects off the objects and people around him and the words he uses, so the play itself proliferates versions of itself with repetitive compulsion, in a series of *mises en abyme*. First of all the main action is presented as a tragedy witnessed by the Ghost of Andrea and Revenge, who serve as its 'Chorus' (9). Then within this we are given first a Dumb Show, in which a scene of newly-wed love is 'quencheth' with blood (102). And finally, there is the murderous play-within-a-play, the tragedy of Solimon and Perseda, devised by Hieronimo to effect his multiple revenge.

It is within this final inset piece that language is strained to its limits. For reasons that soon become apparent, Hieronimo demands that the actors play their parts in 'sundry', 'unknown' languages (117 and 109) – in Latin, Greek, Italian and French, each character speaking a different language. To Balthazar (an actor in the play but also the other murderer of Horatio, who will soon fall victim to Hieronimo's 'plot' in both senses of the word),

> . . . this will be a mere confusion,
> And hardly shall we all be understood.

Hieronimo agrees, but insists that

> It must be so, for the conclusion
> Shall prove the invention and all was good. (110)

The machinery of his 'invention' leads them all, via the Babel of tongues, to death. It is in and through this linguistic confusion, as Hieronimo himself pronounces in a short soliloquy, that 'the fall of

Babylon' will take place (110–11).[9] The tongue has throughout been for Hieronimo a metaphor for missed meaning ('mine unfruitful words' [72]), plagued as he is by 'thoughts no tongue can tell' (55). It is as if, driven to death, he is taken to that 'limit' of meaning, the 'impassable' point described by Lacan:

> How can man, that is to say a living being, have access to knowledge of the death instinct, to his own relationship to death?
>
> The answer is by virtue of the signifier in its most radical form. It is in the signifier and insofar as the subject articulates a signifying chain that he comes up against the fact that he may disappear from the chain of what he is. (*Seminar 7: 295*)

Behind what is named is the quintessential unnamable, death (*Seminar 2*: 211), so it is fitting that Hieronimo should act as agent of death amidst the confusion of tongues of the playlet.[10] It is fitting, too, that Hieronimo's last act before stabbing himself is to bite out his tongue, having demonstrated to his audience (and to us as audience three fictional levels removed) that the seeming 'fabulously counterfeit' (Kyd 117) deaths they have just witnessed are both real and a timely reminder of the process of death in which all are implicated. It is, finally, the fictional image/theatrical role/signifier that 'kills' in a variety of senses, not least that described by Blanchot, which was analysed earlier in this chapter. As Michael Neill points out in his study of the 'invention' of death in English Renaissance tragedy, the genre was frequently played out against a conflation of death and dramatic closure 'figured as an act of writerly violence' (45). The over-determined (that is, multiple in source) elaboration of Hieronimo's role as playwright, the self-reflexive aspect of the play (211), is characteristic of the revenge motif which harks always backwards towards a narrative in need of revision. The death drive, in its perpetually regressive trajectory, drags the signifier in its wake.

THE FETISH: FROM PERSONS TO THINGS (SYLVIA PLATH)

No discussion of the death drive would be complete without mention of fetishism, in which a libidinal investment is transferred from humans to (usually inorganic) objects. This now very fashionable cultural phenomenon, which has attracted many writers over the past decade, particularly in relation to film theory,[11] derives much of its interest from the fact that its psychological terms translate very effectively into many other fields of analysis – such as anthropology, Marxism and gender studies. According to Laura Mulvey, fetishism provides the 'alchemical link' between Marx and Freud, whose work has more relevance today than ever before for an analysis of social and psychic formations (1–2).

Fetishism is predicated upon a peculiarly intriguing form of ambivalence, a holding together of two mutually exclusive ideas: that women have no penis (are 'castrated') and that they have one all the same. The fetish object, in the classic Freudian formulation, acts as a 'token of triumph over the threat of castration' ('Fetishism' [1927], PF 7: 353), allowing the fetishist to accept the appalling reality of female castration while at the same time still clinging to the ideal of the phallic woman by displacing the maternal penis on to some other part of the body or on to an object. Gilles Deleuze calls fetishism a 'protective and idealizing neutralization' ('Coldness and Cruelty' 32). Typically, it is something like a shoe, or a piece of fur (suggestive of the pubic hair), which in Freud's explanation was probably the last thing seen by the young child before its eyes alighted on the mother's genitals (PF 7: 354). This 'splitting' between conscious acceptance and unconscious repudiation ('disavowal') of castration has come to stand, for commentators since Freud, as an emblem of the radical split in all human beings between the social ego and its inadmissible psycho-sexual drives.[12]

Freud also argued that fetishism is a significant phenomenon for the understanding of male homoerotism and homophobia, as it allows the fetishist to disavow his homosexuality by endowing women with the sexual organ which makes them tolerable. Other more recent psychoanalysts have challenged this and other aspects of Freud's theory. Janine Chasseguet-Smirgel has analysed the post-Freudian emphasis on the pre-Oedipal conflicts that fetishism seeks to resolve in addition to castration anxiety. Arguing that 'it is due to archaic pregenital distortions that the castration complex is insurmountable without the help of the fetish', Chasseguet-Smirgel puts forward the thesis that 'the fetish represents the *anal* phallus in so far as it comes to occupy the place of the genital penis, and excludes it from the sexual scene, and from the psyche in general. It is therefore not only the mother's missing phallus.' (*Creativity and Perversion* 83 and 82, emphasis added) Others like Weissmann, Glover, Sperling and Winnicott have drawn attention to the over-determined nature of fetishism, citing pre-genital factors such as separation anxiety, the trauma of the primal scene, and the loss of the breast or other parts of the mother's body. All seem to agree that fetishism involves a complex set of identifications and displacements (Chasseguet-Smirgel 82–85).

For Lacan and his followers, however, fetishism represents phallic monism in its clearest demonstration. In his paper on fetishism (written with Wladimir Granoff), he underscored Freud's emphasis on the importance of fetishism for an understanding of the Oedipal crisis. Passage through the Oedipal involves, as he sees it, a movement from a two-sided (Imaginary) relationship (child–mother) to a three-sided one which includes the father, 'something which the patient cannot face without vertigo' , which represents 'the realm and the nature of anxiety' (Lacan and Granoff 273). The 'third person' (the father) introduces the law (the Symbolic), and guilt. The fetishist 'vacillates' between anxiety and guilt, the pre-Oedipal and the Oedipal. An exclusively male perversion, as Freud sees it, fetishism entails a refusal of the difference between the sexes (as both have the penis), putting the fetishist in the position of having constantly to invent sexual difference (Parveen Adams, *The Emptiness of the Image* 34). The fetish acts like a veil or screen which conceals the Other's lack, making the fetishist in a very special sense an inhabitant of the Real, the only (and impossible) place where nothing is lacking, where knowledge is certain (Copjec 109).

Deleuze writes in his study of Masoch and masochism that the fetish object allows the fetishist to validate the existence of the penis with obsessive repetition.

> The fetish is therefore not a symbol at all, but as it were a frozen, arrested, two-dimensional image, a photograph to which one returns repeatedly to exorcise the dangerous consequences of movement, the harmful discoveries that result from explorations; it represents the last point at which it was still possible to believe . . . ('Coldness and Cruelty' 31)

This ritualistic aspect of fetishism is important, linking it with the repetition compulsion and the death drive. Deleuze's powerful description of the fetish object as a 'frozen, arrested, two-dimensional image' is clearly informed by Marx's analysis of commodity fetishism, which famously draws a distinction between use value and exchange value, emphasizing the way the original meaning and use of objects was replaced under capitalism by what could be called their two-dimensional commercial value alone. For Walter Benjamin, who examined the aesthetic object within commodity culture, the nineteenth century saw the transformation of the female body into a commodity. Fashion, he writes,

> prescribed the ritual by which the fetish Commodity wished to be worshipped . . . It stands in opposition to the organic. It prostitutes the living body to the inorganic world. In relation to the living it represents the rights of the corpse. Fetishism, which succumbs to the sex-appeal of the inorganic, is its vital nerve; and the cult of the commodity recruits this to its service. (*Charles Baudelaire* 166)

Feminist commentators have drawn parallels between Freud and Marx in their view of fetishism as an act of originary erasure – for Freud of the mother's body, for Marx of the worker's labour (Britzolakis 49).[13] Much post-war literature and cinema has drawn on these convergences, in particular in relation to the female body as *objet d'art*, a manufactured amalgam of dead parts which parades its own disjunction from any concept of a whole or living body.

In Muriel Spark's *The Public Image* (1968), the actress Annabel becomes a cinematic icon through media manipulation, which 'freezes' her in a series of high-life and religious stills (as seductive tiger woman, Madonna, and so on). In Angela Carter's *Love* (1971), the protagonist (also called Annabel) flirts with her own and others' deaths before finally staging her own death-bed scene by decking herself out with dyes and paints to become 'inflexible material', like a baroque figure on the wall of an artificial cave (Carter, *Love* 104).[14] In Fay Weldon's *The Life and Loves of a She-Devil* (1983), the heroine, Ruth, sets about transforming her ugly body and face into a look-alike of her husband's classy mistress, through operation after operation of plastic surgery. In all three novels, the construction of femininity can be described in Christina Britzolakis' words – as an 'aesthetic process which *exchanges* the organic for the inorganic . . . both an addition of value and a subtraction of life' (46).

Woman as commodity fetish, the 'sex-appeal of the inorganic', to use Benjamin's phrase again, are the stuff of Sylvia Plath's most famous poems 'Daddy' and 'Lady Lazarus', written in October 1962, shortly before her suicide. Both poems draw on the holocaust, exploring a lexicon of violence, vengeance and victimization; both move with a 'remorseless, razing onrush' of passion (Marsack 46), hurtling the words and the female body towards death with a jeering triumphalism. Here the female victim participates deliriously in her own fetishization, hovering on the border between organic body and an assemblage of dead parts, raging against her reduction to man's 'pure gold baby' but at the same time utterly complicitous with her own self-destruction.

Descriptions of previous suicide attempts in both poems provide an opportunity for linking death and the fetish in the image of the female body as re-made, 'stuck . . . together with glue' (Plath, 'Daddy' 224) after the event. In 'Lady Lazarus' the commodity is a Hollywood product, the 'smiling woman' (244),[15] 'your opus . . . your valuable', whose heart, like a doll's, 'really goes' (246). In an appalling conflation of the processes of strip-tease and flaying, Lady Lazarus presents her body as an assemblage of parts, on display, the ultimate spectacle:

> The peanut-crunching crowd
> Shoves in to see
>
> Them unwrap me hand and foot –
> The big strip tease.
> Gentlemen, ladies
>
> These are my hands
> My knees.
> I may be skin and bone,
>
> Nevertheless, I am the same, identical woman. (245)

For all this 'There is a charge', a phrase repeated four times with increasingly hysterical intensity. Body parts 'melt to a shriek' and become the ultimate in exchange currency, the Nazi commodity:

> A sort of walking miracle, my skin
> Bright as a Nazi lampshade,[16]
> My right foot
>
> A paperweight,
> My face a featureless, fine
> Jew linen.

> Peel off the napkin
> O my enemy. Do I terrify? – (244)
> . . . .
> Ash, ash –
> You poke and stir.
> Flesh, bone, there is nothing there –
>
> A cake of soap,
> A wedding ring,
> A gold filling. (246)

'Daddy' locates the source of the torment in an ambivalent father figure, inflated by childish worship but loathed as the devil. A ('bag full of') God, however, this figure is responsible for her being: we could say he has constructed or contrived her in the sense of the Portuguese *feitio* (from the Latin f*acticius*) from which the word 'fetish' derives.[17] As Nazi sadist, on the other hand, he delights as much in her decomposition as in her composition. Sade's writing, Lacan argues, 'pursue[s] nature to the very principle of its creative power, which regulates the alternation of corruption and generation' (*Seminar 7*: 260). This alternation is suggested in 'Daddy', where the ambivalently sadistic and erotic focus is on the heavy black boot which would seem to trample her underfoot as Daddy towers, statue-like, over her (and over the American and European continents), blacking out the light:

> . . . O You –
>
> Not God but a swastika
> So black no sky could squeak through.
> Every woman adores a Fascist,
> The boot in the face, the brute
> Brute heart of a brute like you. (223)

Freud explains the significance of the shoe or boot as fetish object in terms of the fact that 'the inquisitive boy peered at the woman's genitals *from below, from her legs up*' (PF 7: 354, emphasis added). Plath's subject, the prostrate little girl or brutalized Jewish woman, reverses or blurs the gendered specificity of Freud's formulation. In 'Daddy' the speaker's own foot is conflated with the father's, making her both fetish object and fetish objectifier at the same time. Primarily, the 'shoe' belongs by acoustic association to 'you' or 'du'; this is a fine example of what Seamus Heaney has called the 'assonantal' drive of Plath's poetry (Heaney 143). But the 'boot in the face' is also an extension of the 'black shoe/In which *I have lived* like a foot/For thirty years, poor and white' (Plath 222, emphasis added). In a note for the BBC, Plath wrote that this is a poem spoken by a girl with an Electra complex (293n183), but this Jungian term to describe rivalry with the mother over the father seems barely adequate to cover the poem's complex identifications. The desire to kill *herself* in order to 'get back, back, back' to the father (in the grave) crosses with the need to 'kill you' for her own survival, effecting an I–you, ich–du confusion which renders the poem a torment of self-division. Or, we could say, this is an enactment of projective identification, whereby the subject projects on to the other her unacceptable aggressivity, only to find it thrown back at her with deadly force.

Identification with the father figure is conceived in 'Daddy' as getting 'through' to him via speech, as well as being 'through' (finished) with his annihilating hold on her. The voice comes to replace the boot as phallic fetish object, as in these lines:

> So daddy, I'm finally through.
> The black telephone's off at the root,
> The voices just can't worm through.
>
> If I've killed one man, I've killed two –
> The vampire who said he was you
> And drank my blood for a year,
> Seven years, if you want to know.
> Daddy, you can lie back now.
>
> There's a stake in your fat black heart
> And the villagers never liked you.
> They are dancing and stamping on you.
> They always *knew* it was you.
> Daddy, daddy, you bastard, I'm through. (224)

The conflations continue in reckless refusal of the separateness of I and you. Now it is the father who must 'lie back' to be trampled on, like a whore. And now the black boot has become the black telephone (voice, language), whose torn-out cord suggests the castrated statue with 'one grey toe' of the second stanza. Similarly the phone/voice, 'off at the root', is associated in stanza 5 with 'your foot, your root'. As with Hieronimo in *The Spanish Tragedy*, the tongue, here 'stuck in a barb wire snare' (223) is mutilated to signal the loss of the Symbolic function.

In 'Daddy', the personal father converges with Freud's father of our 'own personal prehistory' (PF 11: 370), who must be killed over and over for 'civilization' and survival. His loss as Symbolic father, who represents language and the law, is thus a double loss. As Jacqueline Rose writes:

> the poem seems to be outlining the conditions under which that celebrated loss of the symbolic function takes place. Identity and language lose themselves in the place of the father whose absence gives him unlimited powers. (*The Haunting of Sylvia Plath* 227)

The crisis in representation, like that associated with the totem father, Dracula (appropriately invoked in 'Daddy' as the staked vampire who nevertheless remains un-dead), is also reflected in the replacement of language by Nazi emblems – the 'neat moustache', the 'Aryan eye' and the swastika. These circulate and proliferate, just as the speaker makes simulacra ('model[s]', 224) of her phantasized Nazi father in the person of the man with the Meinkampf look to whom she said 'I do'. The point is clearly not whether Otto Plath or Ted Hughes are accurately or fairly represented in these images. If all's lawful in love, which is lawless, the same must certainly be true of death – or is, at least, in phantasy.

The question underlying this chapter has been: how is death to be represented, given Freud's insistence that there is no concept or representation of death in the unconscious? The answer provided by Plath's two poems seems to be that it is the signifier or sign alone which allows the subject a relationship to death. Like the fetish object, the word symbolizes the absence of a theorized presence – Daddy/God/Herr Doktor, meaning, the maternal phallus. Like it, too, it derives its power from its toleration of contradiction, its postulation of presence as a veil over loss. Both provide access to a phantasized utopia, allowing Plath's speakers to perform a triumphant dance over the grave of all that is lost, renounced and mourned.

Notes

PREFACE

1. All references to Freud's work, unless otherwise stated, are to the Penguin Freud Library, abbreviated as PF.
2. For an excellent summary of different modes of psychoanalytic reader theory see Elizabeth Wright, 'The Reader in Analysis'. See also Peter Brooks, *Psychoanalysis and Storytelling* 20–45; Robert Young, 'Psychoanalytic Criticism'; and Shoshana Felman, *Literature and Psychoanalysis* 5–10.

CHAPTER 1

1. For Lacan's reading in the 1930s, as well as his study preparation for the certificate in logic and general philosophy from the Sorbonne, see Roudinesco 32, 61 and 88–89.
2. Roudinesco argues that Lacan first came across Saussure's theory of language in Henri Delacroix's *Langage et pensée* [Language and Thought] (Paris, 1930) (Roudinesco 27).
3. For a description of the debates and the 1927 conference on the topic, see Peter Gay 494 ff.
4. Lacan's 'Mirror Stage' paper was first delivered at a psychoanalytic congress in Marienbad in July 1936. It was later revised and delivered at another congress in Zurich in 1949, and published in the *Revue française de Psychanalyse* in the same year. The text used in this chapter is a translation of the slightly revised version incorporated into the *Écrits* in 1966.
5. For a discussion of the role of the Collège de Sociologie in the intellectual life of Paris in the late 1930s, see Roudinesco 101–2, 135–36 *et passim*.
6. David Macey discusses the influence of Kojève's seminars on the generation of the 1930s in Paris, and argues for the inescapability of Hegel's influence on Lacan (Macey 72–86).
7. My reading of *Paradise Lost* owes a great deal to Jina Politi's enormously suggestive article, '"Is This the Love", or, The Origins of *Logomachia*'.
8. In his essay 'Aggressivity in Psychoanalysis'. Lacan further elaborates on this 'dialectic of the child's behaviour in the presence of his similars' in the mirror stage:

During the whole of this period, one will record the emotional reactions and the articulated evidences of a normal transitivism. The child who strikes another says that he has been struck; the child who sees another fall, cries. Similarly, it is by means of an identification with the other tha[t] he sees the whole gamut of reactions of bearing and display, whose structural ambivalence is clearly revealed in his behaviour, the slave being identified with the despot, the actor with the spectator, the seduced with the seducer. (*Écrits* 18)

9. See IX, 319 and 376.
10. Satan is often referred to in literature and mythology in terms of his per- or in-version of the unfallen state. T. S. Eliot's poem 'Gerontion', for example, refers to 'the backward devils' (*Complete Poems and Plays* 38). (Many thanks to Angelika Gounelas for this point.)
11. At times implicitly Lacanian, Politi's reading of the tropes of vision in *Paradise Lost* makes explicit use of Sartre's *Being and Nothingness* (1943), whose association of self-consciousness with negativity Lacan attacked in his 'Mirror Stage' essay (6). For a brief discussion of the confrontation between Sartre and Lacan on these themes, see Nobus 118 and 135.
12. As Freud pointed out in his essay on 'Instincts and their Vicissitudes' (1915) (PF 11: 105–38), the voyeur and the exhibitionist are mutually implicated in a play of being and having the object of vision, a play which precludes the possibility of stable positions of viewer and viewed.
13. See also IX, 606–11:

> But all that fair and good in thy Divine
> Semblance, and in thy Beauty's heav'nly Ray
> United I beheld; no Fair to thine
> Equivalent or second, which compell'd
> Mee thus, though importune perhaps, to come
> And gaze.

14. And indeed, her fear is justified, as we see at the beginning of Book X, where the rhetorical question is asked: 'what can scape the Eye/Of God All-seeing' (5–6).
15. Adam is now significantly 'estrang'd in look' (IX, 1132).
16. Freud in fact had several different ways of describing what the unconscious 'is' at different stages of his career. One was the 'economic', which describes the amount of excitation or instinctual energy in psychical processes. Another was the 'dynamic', which described what causes us to act in terms of a conflict of instinctual forces. Yet another was the 'topographical' structure, which divided the psychical apparatus into a number of subsystems – such as the early system of the Unconscious, Preconscious and Conscious, and the later one of the id, ego and super-ego.

17. SE refers, from here on, to *The Standard Edition of the Complete Psychological Works of Sigmund Freud.*
18. Freudian commentators, however, have drawn attention to the fact that Freud was repeatedly culpable of the error of symbol reading in dream interpretation. As Sara Flanders points out, Freud's later work on dreams includes recognition that some dream imagery is recurrent and constant in its meaning and yields little in the way of associations (Flanders 4).
19. For a clear assessment of the significance of metonymy and metaphor as part of the twofold character and operation of language in the work of Roman Jakobson, which had an important impact on Lacan's work, see David Lodge 57n. Lacan acknowledges his debt to Jakobson in *Écrits* 177n20.
20. Breton's exact wording here is:

> Nobody expressing himself does more than take advantage of a very obscure possibility of conciliation between what he knew he had to say and what on the same subject he didn't know he had to say and yet has said. (133)

Compare this with Lacan's phrasing in 'The Agency of the Letter in the Unconscious', cited earlier in this chapter:

> It is not a question of knowing whether I speak of myself in a way that conforms to what I am, but rather of knowing whether I am the same as that of which I speak. (*Écrits* 165)

21. This conjunction of human and natural forms in an urban environment was a common trope in surrealist poetry. Compare with the opening lines of Roger Roughton's 1936 poem, 'Lady Windermere's Fan Dance': 'Figures and trees in the street/Are stretching and waving their arms' (qtd in Hynes 225).

CHAPTER 2

1. The word is Freud's own, at least in the adjectival form. See PF 14: 223.
2. Unlike Klein, Freud considers that the infant is first auto-erotic (that is, concerned with sensations without an object), then narcissistic (taking itself as object), and finally object-oriented. See Hanna Segal 104.
3. The term was first used by Sandor Ferenczi, a close colleague of Freud's, in his 1909 paper on 'Introjection and Transference'.
4. See for example 'The Oedipus Complex in the Light of Early Anxieties', where Klein writes:

> Since under the dominance of the oral libido the infant from the beginning introjects his objects, the primary imagos have a counter-part in his inner world. The imagos of his mother's breast and of his

father's penis are established within the ego and form the nucleus of his super-ego. To the introjection of the good and bad breast and mother corresponds the introjection of the good and bad penis and father. They become the first representatives on the one hand of protective and helpful internal figures, on the other hand of retaliating and persecuting internal figures, and are the first identifications which the ego develops. (*Love, Guilt and Reparation* 409)

5. Hanna Segal puts it this way in distinguishing Klein's phantasy from Freud's id: 'Phantasy is not considered by Klein and [Susan] Isaacs as a pure id phenomenon, but as an elaboration by the ego of impulses, defences, and object relationships.' (*Klein* 101)

6. As Adam Phillips puts it, the British School of object relations, as reformulated by Winnicott, 'translate[d] psychoanalysis from a theory of sexual desire into a theory of emotional nurture' (*Winnicott* 10).

7. See Klein's essay on 'Mourning and its Relation to Manic-Depressive States', where she writes that

    Idealization is an essential part of the manic [depressive] position and is bound up with another important element of that position, namely denial. Without partial and temporary denial of psychic reality the ego cannot bear the disaster by which it feels itself threatened when the depressive position is at its height. Omnipotence, denial and idealization, closely bound up with ambivalence, enable the early ego to assert itself to a certain degree against its internal persecutors and against a slavish and perilous dependence upon its loved objects (*Love, Guilt and Reparation* 340).

8. This is the case in *The Ego and the Id*. In the *New Introductory Lectures*, Freud draws a distinction between the two terms. See Laplanche and Pontalis 144–45.

9. However, as Juliet Mitchell points out, Freud was ambivalent about how the castration complex arises. She quotes from a 1935 letter of Freud's to Carl Müller-Braunschweig in which he writes: 'the sight of the penis and its function of urination cannot be the motive, only the trigger of the [girl] child's envy. However, no one has stated this' (Mitchell and Rose 17).

10. Discussing Freud's list of dream symbols, Antony Easthope refers to

    flame – the male genital: and the fireplace 'its female counterpart', confirmed in the English male vulgarism that you don't look at the mantelpiece when you are stoking the fire. (12)

11. Alan Bass, translator of Derrida's *La Carte Postale* (*The Post Card*) in which the essay was later (1980) reprinted, leaves the French title untranslated in order to leave the ambiguity of 'le facteur' undisturbed. I cite from Bass's translation in *The Post Card* rather than its abridged

version in Muller and Richardson's *Purloined Poe*, which translates the title as 'The Purveyor of Truth'.

12. Elsewhere, Derrida confirms that in *Dissemination* 'the concept of castration is indissociable from that of dissemination.' (*Positions* 84)

13. Lacan gives his own list of 'the object[s] described by analytic theory: the mamilla, faeces, the phallus (imaginary object), the urinary flow. (An unthinkable list, if one adds, as I do, the phoneme, the gaze, the voice – the nothing.)' (*Écrits* 315)

14. See the definition in *The Four Fundamental Concepts* 103:

> the *objet a* is something from which the subject, in order to constitute itself, has separated itself off as organ. This serves as a symbol of the lack, that is to say, of the phallus, not as such, but in so far as it is lacking. It must, therefore, be an object that is, firstly, separable and, secondly, that has some relation to the lack.

CHAPTER 3

1. This phrase occurs in Kristeva's essay 'On the Melancholic Imaginary', where she writes:

> if loss, mourning, absence set the imaginary act in motion and permanently fuel it as much as they menace and undermine it, it is also undeniable that the fetish of the work of art is erected in disavowal of this mobilizing affliction. (105)

2. Beckett's most recent biographer, however, attributes more importance to the psychoanalytic influence on Beckett than previous biographers. James Knowlson cites from notes found after Beckett's death which reveal the depth of his interest and reading in psychoanalytic literature (Knowlson 178).

3. When the well-known analyst Didier Anzieu, author of the 1989 essay 'Beckett and Bion', put his interpretations to Beckett in 1984, Beckett dismissed them as 'a psychoanalyst's phantasms!' (Baker 9).

4. The specific phrase, one of the most frequently quoted in all Beckett criticism, appeared in one of Beckett's dialogues with Georges Duthuit, where he spoke of 'The expression that there is nothing to express, nothing with which to express, nothing from which to express, no power to express, no desire to express, together with the obligation to express' (*Proust [and] Three Dialogues* 103).

5. In his monograph on Proust in 1931, Beckett famously defined plot as 'the vulgarity of a plausible concatenation' (*Proust* 81–82).

6. See *Powers* 70: 'Is this a survival of a matrilineal society or the specific particularity of a structure (without the incidence of diachrony)? The question of the origins of such a handling of sexual difference remains moot.'

7. In 'Mourning and Melancholia', for example, Freud writes that

    > If the love for the object – a love which cannot be given up though the object itself is given up – takes refuge in narcissistic identification, then the hate comes into operation on this substitutive object, abusing it, debasing it, making it suffer and deriving sadistic satisfaction from its suffering. (PF 11: 260)

8. Apart from the play of that title, there are numerous uses of the phrase 'Not I' in the trilogy alone. See *Trilogy* 126, 140, 166, 389, 403, 406, 408, 414.
9. The original French, here, does not reproduce the ambivalence and complexity of this final phrase. It reads: 'Mais au fait, s'agit-il de moi en ce moment?' (*L'innommable* 46)
10. Compare this with *Play* (1964), where the heads *protrude* from the neck of each of the three urns: '*the neck held fast in the urn's mouth*' (*Complete Dramatic Works* 307).
11. There are two articles on Beckett's relationship with Bion (see Anzieu and Simon), but neither, in my view, succeeds in drawing anything more than superficial connections between Bion's theory and Beckett's writing.
12. Bion chose to indicate this relationship by the use of the symbols ♀♂, because he thought that symbols have fewer imaged accretions than words. The relation between the container and the contained is for him far from static. As he puts it, 'A word contains a meaning; conversely, a meaning can contain a word'. At any one moment the analyst is ♀ and analysand ♂, and at the next . . . the roles [are reversed]'. (*Attention and Interpretation* 106 and 108)
13. Deirdre Bair traces this view back to Bion himself (Bair 208, 211, 214 and 226–27). Knowlson describes Beckett's 'almost umbilical dependence on and a desire for independence from his mother' (178); Beckett, he writes, was 'almost obsessively preoccupied with the progress and nature of their relationship' (179).
14. Beckett's interest in uterine expulsion, or part expulsion, was said to have been stimulated when he attended, with Bion, a lecture given by Jung on 'Psychopathology and Creativity' at the Tavistock clinic in October 1935. There, Jung described the mythologically significant dreams of a ten-year-old patient of his which, he contended, showed 'She had never been born entirely'. Bair comments:

    > Beckett seized upon this remark as the keystone of his entire analysis . . . He was able to furnish detailed examples of his own womb fixation, arguing forcefully that all his behaviour, from the simple inclination to stay in bed to his deep-seated need to pay frequent visits to his mother, were all aspects of an improper birth. (221–22)

    Knowlson cites a significant extract from a November 1989 interview in which Beckett described the impact on him of the analysis with Bion:

I think it helped me perhaps to control the panic. I certainly came up with some extraordinary memories of being in the womb. Intrauterine memories. I remember feeling trapped, of being imprisoned and unable to escape, of crying to be let out but no one could hear, no one was listening. I remember being in pain but being unable to do anything about it. (Knowlson 177)

15. Of British object-relations theorists after Klein, the names of Winnicott, Bion and Herbert Rosenfeld appear frequently in Kristeva's work.

16. Baker gives a footnote reference to an earlier version of *From An Abandoned Work* which read: 'Her death, I don't remember much about her death, all I remember is the frying pan coming down on her head and the bacon and eggs leaping out like pancakes and going to waste' (179n22). The equation of killing and eating suggested here is characteristic.

17. The four most notorious are 'The Lady's Dressing Room' (1730), 'A Beautiful Young Nymph going to Bed', 'Strephon and Chloe', and 'Cassinus and Peter' (all 1731).

18. Bakhtin's definition of the grotesque body is highly relevant here:

Next to the bowels and the genital organs is the mouth, through which enters the world to be swallowed up. And next is the anus. All these convexities and orifices have a common characteristic; it is within them that the confines between bodies and between the body and the world are overcome: there is an interchange and an interorientation. This is why the main events in the life of the grotesque body, the acts of the bodily drama, take place in this sphere. Eating, drinking, defecation and other elimination (sweating, blowing of the nose, sneezing), as well as copulation, pregnancy, dismemberment, swallowing up by another body – all these acts are performed on the confines of the body and the outer world, or on the confines of the old and new body. In all these events the beginning and end of life are closely linked and interwoven. *(Rabelais* 317)

19. Krapp, who is chronically constipated, asks 'What's a year now? The sour cud and the iron stool' *(Complete Dramatic Works* 222).

20. I have mentioned Malone, Macmann and Mahood from the trilogy alone. In *The Unnamable*, the woman who tends the narrator in his jar is called, variously, Marguerite and Madeleine. (Note, too, the convergence of masculine and feminine names in pairings such as Molloy–Moll.) The ending of Beckett's names is sometimes equally significant in terms of the enunciation of the maternal syllable. As the narrator of *How it Is* puts it, contemplating whether he should give himself the name Bom rather than Pim: 'm at the end and one syllable the rest indifferent' (67).

21. As Toril Moi points out, 'If "femininity" has a definition at all in Kristevan terms, it is simply . . . as "that which is marginalized by the patriarchal symbolic order". This relational "definition" is as shifting as the various forms of patriarchy itself' (Moi 166). Moi rightly stresses that

it is an error to equate the Kristevan definition of the semiotic with femininity. Kristeva's view of gender will be briefly analysed at the end of Chapter 7 here.

22. See Cohn 101. Cohn also makes this point about the relation between the concept of 'limbo' and Beckett's own life choices.

CHAPTER 4

1. *Seminar* 2: 234: 'Desire always becomes manifest at the joint of speech, where it makes its appearance, its sudden emergence, its surge forwards. Desire emerges just as it becomes embodied, in speech, it emerges with symbolism.'

2. According to Lacan, *Trieb* is 'a word that is improperly translated as "instincts", but that one should translate strictly as "drives" (*pulsions*) – or as "drifts" (*dérives*), so as to mark the fact that the *Trieb* is deflected from what he [Freud] calls its *Ziel*, its aim.' (*Seminar* 7:110) For a recent discussion of the arguments for and against Strachey's translation (in the Standard Edition of Freud, which is reprinted for the Penguin Freud) of the word as 'instinct', see Robyn Ferrell, *Passion in Theory* 16–18.

3. See 'The Unconscious', PF 11: 184: 'we have gradually been led into adopting a third point of view in our account of psychical phenomena. Besides the dynamic and the topographical points of view . . . we have adopted the *economic* one. This endeavors to follow out the vicissitudes of amounts of excitation and to arrive at least at some *relative* estimate of their magnitude.'

4. Both Evans (1–13) and Ragland (*Essays* 158) emphasize the shifts of meaning in Lacan's definitions of *jouissance* from the 1950s to the 1970s.

5. This phrase is used by Cynthia Chase as the title of her 1986 article reprinted in Maud Ellmann's *Psychoanalytic Literary Criticism*.

6. A notable exception is the work of Gilles Deleuze and Félix Guattari, especially their *Anti-Oedipus: Capitalism and Schizophrenia* (1977). Deleuze and Guattari insist that libido has no need of the Oedipal as mediator, and that its enforcement by psychoanalysis represents a form of imperialism.

7. Ernest Jones, *Hamlet and Oedipus*, 78n2. Jones is here summarizing the thesis of E. P. Vining in *The Mystery of Hamlet* (Philadelphia, 1881). The 'femininity' of 'Gentle Will' is often referred to in extrapolations from Shakespeare's plays to his life. See for example Frank Harris, *The Man Shakespeare and his Tragic Life-Story*, 1909, 273: 'Whenever we get under the skin, it is Shakespeare's femininity which startles us' (cited in Jones 78n2).

8. The phrase occurs in Lacan's seminars of May 1955 when he said: 'If the tragedy *Oedipus Rex* is an exemplary work, analysts should also be acquainted with this beyond of the drama realized in the tragedy *Oedipus at Colonus*' (*Seminar* 2: 210). Shoshana Felman's article, 'Beyond Oedipus: The Specimen Story of Psychoanalysis' explores the implications of Lacan's statement.

9. The major feminist challenges to phallocentrism will be examined in later chapters. Wendy Cealey Harrison has argued recently that

> It does not much matter whether phallocentrism turns out to have been mistaken or to be a transitory clinical phenomenon in the history of analysis. But what it *represents* in terms of the possibility of the libido, the libido's initially auto-erotic character, its 'bisexuality' in the sense of its *indifference* to the gender of its object, the essentially phantasmatic place of the body (within which sensations and impulses find a place), represents all that is radical in psychoanalysis. (168)

Janine Chasseguet-Smirgel, summarized by Harrison, argues that

> Phallic monism represents a defensive phantasy which offers the child, boy or girl, the means of coping with the narcissistic wound entailed by the difference in the generations and the child's insufficiencies in respect of the adult it desires. (Harrison 168)

10. This was one of several seminars in a series of 1959–60 entitled *The Ethics of Psychoanalysis*, which make up Volume 7 of Lacan's seminars.
11. The French phrase 'la chose Freudienne' suggests 'the whole Freudian business', which in Lacan's opinion had to do with Freud's insight into the inextricability of these three concepts. Freud, like Kant, had used the phrase 'das Ding'. See his essay on 'The Unconscious' in which he discusses the relationship between the 'word-presentation' and the 'thing-presentation' (PF 11: 206–7).
12. See '*Écrits* 122: 'I wander about in . . . the dream, in the way the most far-fetched conceits, the most grotesque nonsense of the joke defies sense'.
13. The traditional critical view, of course, is that, as C. M. Bowra puts it, 'Antigone acts for the gods, and in resisting her Creon resists them and pays for it' (Bowra 366).
14. Julia Kristeva, who discusses *Oedipus at Colonus* as illustration of the way Oedipus is a 'being of abjection', doesn't refer to Lacan's seminar, but follows his reading to the extent that she emphasizes the function of the Symbolic ('nominal') in the play. Oedipus, she writes, 'recognizes himself as mortal (so much so that he leaves no male issue) and subject to the symbolic (one will note the purely nominal handing down of his mortal jouissance to the foreigner, Theseus)' (Kristeva *Powers* 88). As the statement shows, she ignores the role of Antigone as carrier of her father's desire.
15. The well-known phrase is Ben Jonson's, in his prefatory verse to the *First Folio*. I am indebted on several points here to the essay by Joel Fineman, 'The Sound of *O* in *Othello*'.
16. This passage is also cited by Mary Jacobus (*First Things* 19), whose chapter on 'Freud's Mnemonic: Screen Memories and Feminist Nostalgia' gives an excellent assessment of feminist myths of origin.

CHAPTER 5

1. This phrase is taken from Cixous ('Fiction and its Phantoms' 526).
2. Although Freud spoke of writing the paper in the spring of 1919 (it was published in the autumn), it was almost certainly based on an earlier piece dating back to as early as 1912–13. See Editor's note, PF 14: 336.
3. Freud's repeated negatives in his refutation of Jentsch suggest this anxiety: 'Jentsch's point of an intellectual uncertainty has nothing to do with the effect' (351); 'There is no question, therefore, of any intellectual uncertainty' (352); 'The theory of intellectual uncertainty is thus incapable of explaining that impression' (352).
4. For a list of recent essays on Freud's reading of 'The Sandman', see Ellmann, *Psychoanalytic Literary Criticism* 29n13.
5. Elizabeth Wright says that an 'adequate psychoanalytic reading' of 'The Sandman' would have, unlike Freud's,

> to account not only for the return of the repressed in the form of the Sandman as Oedipal Father, but also in the form of Clara (and Olympia) as objects of desire which fail the hero, both in their own right (Clara refuses Nathanael's suffering, his 'text' – his poem; Olympia turns out to be an automaton), and by dint of his own blinded narcissism. (*Psychoanalytic Criticism* 148)

6. Wordsworth refused to allow 'Christabel' to be published in the second edition of the *Lyrical Ballads* in 1805. It was eventually published eleven years later.
7. For an analysis of Coleridge's 'complex and equivocal' conception of the will, see Douka-Kabitoglou 203 ff.
8. Coleridge's poem, however, was written much earlier, in 1797 (Part I) and 1800 (Part II), as Coleridge explains in the Preface.
9. All forms that evolve 'organically' within the mind, through the work- ings of the imagination, according to Coleridge, will result in symbols. (Fancy, on the other hand, produces allegory.) The symbol, he wrote, is characterized by 'the translucence of the Eternal through and in the Temporal. It always partakes of the Reality which it renders intelligible, and while it enunciates the whole, abides itself as a living part in that Unity.' (qtd in Albert Cook 76).
10. Humphrey House writes that 'the two parts differ so much from each other, that they scarcely seem to belong to the same poem', and explains:

> One of the most obvious differences between the two parts is caused by the physical move from Somerset to the Lake District. In Part I there is the castle in the woodland, with oak and moss and mistletoe, a landscape which has its function only in relation to the persons and the atmosphere. There are no proper names but those of the three main persons. In Part II we plunge straight into the detailed

geography of the region; Wyndermere, Langdale Pike, Dungeon-ghyll, Brodale and the rest, organize the reader's attention as if this were matter of history rather than of imagery. (House 122–23)

11. For a detailed historical study of what was known as 'the duality of man' in nineteenth- and twentieth-century Anglo-American literature, see Karl Miller, *Doubles: Studies in Literary History*.

12. See for example Peter Buse and Andrew Stott (eds), *Ghosts: Deconstruction, Psychoanalysis, History* (1998). What follows in the next few pages is a revised version of my own essay in that volume, 'Anachrony and Anatopia: Specters of Marx, Derrida and Gothic Fiction'.

13. See the famous letter Walpole wrote in March 1766 describing the origin of his 'Gothic story', an extract from which is cited by Mario Praz ('Introductory Essay' 17).

14. David Punter has discussed 'LeFanu's insistence on not Irish but anglicised Gothic settings', relating them both to those of Collins and the Brontës, and to LeFanu's own obsessional dreams about 'vast and direly foreboding old mansions . . . in a state of ruin and threatening imminently to fall upon and crush the dreamer rooted to the spot' (*The Literature of Terror* 236).

15. For Abraham's summary of the aspects of Freud's article which provided the starting point of their theory, see *Shell and Kernel*, especially p. 93.

16. The Wolf Man is of course Abraham and Torok's most famous subject. (See their *The Wolf Man's Magic Word: A Cryptonymy* [1976, transl. 1986]). For their discussion of Little Hans, see Torok's 'Story of Fear', *Shell and Kernel* 177–86; for Hamlet, see Abraham's 'The Phantom of Hamlet *or* The Sixth Act *preceded by* The Intermission of "Truth"', *Shell and Kernel* 187–205.

17. For Abraham and Torok's distinction between '*constitutive* [i.e. dynamic] *repression*' apparent in hysterics, and the '*preservative repression*' specific to cryptophores, see 'The Topography of Reality: Sketching a Metapsychology of Secrets', *Shell and Kernel* 159.

18. In this section of (and indeed throughout) the Foreword, Derrida is heavily indebted to Abraham and Torok's 'The Topography of Reality' (*Shell and Kernel* 157–61). For Abraham and Torok's discussion of the 'cemetery guard', see p. 159.

19. Later in the story, one of the many other victims of Judge Horrocks's visitations is pronounced 'dead as a mackerel' (LeFanu 35).

20. Simon Critchley asks: 'What force does Marxism retain if [like Derrida] we set to one side its materialist account of life, production, praxis and history?' (5) Aijaz Ahmad complains that '[Derrida's] gesture of affiliation with Marx includes the acceptance neither of the principal categories of political Marxism nor of the slightest responsibility for any part of its history' (106).

21. This phrase is Freud's. Writing to Fliess in Feb. 1898, he said that he was 'deep in the dream book' and that on reading other literature in the field,

'The only sensible thing on the subject was said by old [Gustav] Fechner in his sublime simplicity: that the psychical territory on which the dream process is played out is a different one. It has been left to me to draw the first crude map of it.' (Freud, *The Origins of Psycho-Analysis* 244–45) Fechner's phrase for the scene of the unconscious, *ein anderer Schauplatz*, is cited in the Dream book (PF 4: 112). Lacan refers to the term in *Écrits* 264: 'by opening up the dialectic of the transference, we must establish the notion of the Other with a capital O as being the locus of the deployment of speech (the other scene, *ein andere Schauplatz*, of which Freud speaks in "The Interpretation of Dreams").'

CHAPTER 6

1. *Miss Julie* was written in July–August 1888 and first performed (to a small university audience in Copenhagen) in March 1889.
2. See for example Janet Beizer; Monique David-Ménard; Evelyn Ender; Claire Kahane; and Elaine Showalter (*Hystories*). Like these studies, much recent material on hysteria is a direct descendant of Cixous and Clément's feminist study of hysteria, *The Newly-Born Woman* (1986 [1975]). (See also Bernheimer and Kahane, *In Dora's Case*.) This feminist argument still has the capacity to arouse unease in other critics – see, for example, Mark Micale (especially 82–86) and Paul Verhaeghe.
3. While in Paris, Freud wrote (in November 1885) to his fiancée Martha Bernays that Charcot,

    > who is one of the greatest physicians, a genius and a sober man, simply uproots my views and intentions . . . Whether the seed will one day bring forth fruit, I do not know; but that no other human being has ever acted on me in this way I know for certain. (qtd in Gay 49)

4. In the famous 'Rome Discourse' Lacan writes:

    > the hysterical symptom reveals the structure of a language, and is deciphered like an inscription which, once recovered, can without serious loss be destroyed . . . compulsion perpetuates in the symbol [symptom] the very mirage in which the subject found himself trapped. (*Écrits* 50 and 52)

5. Breuer's colleague and friend Meriz Benedikt had followed closely the performances of stage hypnotist Carl Hansen, and presented a lecture on 'Catalepsy and Mesmerism' to the Viennese Society of Physicians on 3 March 1880, only months before Breuer began treatment with Pappenheim (Borch-Jacobsen, *Remembering Anna O.* 69–70).
6. For Freud's full statement of the abandonment of the seduction theory, giving four major reasons, see his letter to Fliess of 21 Sept 1897 (*The Origins of Psycho-Analysis* 215–18). Several attacks on Freud's later position were made in the 1980s – see Jeffrey M. Masson, *The Assault on*

Truth: Freud's Suppression of the Seduction Theory (New York: Harper Perennial, 1984).

7. For an excellent brief assessment of Freud's changing views of seduction, see Tomiche 51–57.

8. The most comprehensive study of the various divisions within Freud's text is the collection of essays entitled *In Dora's Case: Freud – Hysteria – Feminism*, ed. Charles Bernheimer and Claire Kahane.

9. The case was first written up in January 1901, just after the treatment finished; it was ultimately published in 1905, after a few significant revisions, especially to the last section of the Postscript, some passages in the Prefatory Remarks, and some of the footnotes. Further footnotes and minor changes were made to the 1923 edition (PF 8: 31–34).

10. See in particular 'Negation' (PF 11: 435–42).

11. To insist as Dora did on a conscious 'no' within the analytic situation is to challenge what has been criticized as its solipsistic formations. Noreen O'Connor outlines the difficulty of this debate:

> A common argument proposed against psychoanalysis is the self-justification of its theoretical stand; disagreements are interpreted in terms of repression and defence. Can the analysand say 'no' to the analyst's interpretation without this being interpreted as a defence? It depends on the specific situation whether the 'no' is in fact operating as a defence or whether it is an assertion of separateness. Can one assert this and remain in analysis? Is every exchange within the analytic situation a matter of transference and counter-transference interpretable, at least in principle, by the analyst? If this 'no' is not transferential yet acknowledged, what then is the status of the interlocutors – do they remain analyst and analysand. . .? (48)

12. Lacan refers on many occasions to the fact that it was through hysteria that Freud hit upon the homologous relation of discourse and desire and through this, the mechanisms of the unconscious. See for example, *The Four Fundamental Concepts* 12:

> Now, the differential feature of the hysteric is precisely this – it is in the very movement of speaking that the hysteric constitutes her desire. So it is hardly surprising that it should be through this door that Freud entered what was, in reality, the relations of desire to language and discovered the mechanisms of the unconscious.

13. Needless to say, the constellation hysteria–feminism–lack remains problematic, if unavoidable here, whether we share Lacan's view or that of post-Freudian feminism, which treats penis envy and castration as what Maria Torok calls 'a reverse envy projected on to woman' ('The Meaning of "Penis Envy" in Women' 72). I shall return to these issues in the next chapter.

14. Beryl Gray writes that from the start, *The Lifted Veil* has been regarded by critics as an 'aberration'. 'On the whole', she concludes (in 1984), 'the

critical (and editorial) tendency has been tactfully to overlook its existence.' (Gray 69–70)

15. See also S. Freud on 'wishful reversal' in 'The Theme of the Three Caskets' (PF 12: 299).

16. Cf. p. 52: 'Some years after my father's death. . . Bertha appeared at the door [of the library] . . . her cruel contemptuous eyes fixed on me, and the glittering serpent, like a familiar demon, on her breast' to fulfil his vision at Vienna and announce the employment of Archer.

17. Catherine Clément, in dialogue with Cixous over the meaning of hysteria for women today, also challenges Cixous' argument for the efficacy of the hysteric's rebellion. To Cixous' claim that 'The hysteric is, to my eyes, the typical woman in all her force . . . that force that works to dismantle structures', Clément replies that hysterics, like deviants and 'crazies', 'all occupy challenging positions foreseen by the social bodies . . . That doesn't change the structures, however. On the contrary, it makes them comfortable.' (*The Newly-Born Woman* 154–56)

CHAPTER 7

1. In her chapter on 'Hysterical Men', Showalter notes the way that in the nineteenth century male hysteria was either denied, given another name, or associated with homosexuality. Charcot, however, published 61 case histories of hysterical men, and left notes on over 30 more. The fact that none of these (or of Freud's) case studies of male hysteria have entered the mythology of the disorder is symptomatic of gender anxieties about the permeability of the masculine–feminine distinction, a subject I shall be looking at later in this chapter.

2. See her *Plea for a Measure of Abnormality* (1990 [1978]).

3. See for example Shoshana Felman's *What Does a Woman Want?* and *Reading and Sexual Difference* (1993), Luce Irigaray's *An Ethics of Sexual Difference* (1993) or Barbara Johnson's *The Feminist Difference* (1998). 'Difference', of course, is also the touchstone of signification for both structuralism and deconstruction. See for example Barbara Johnson's other books, *The Critical Difference* and *A World of Difference*.

4. Kristeva, although pointing out weaknesses in Deutsch's theories of the psychology of women, argues that when reading her work 'one does not sense a hymn to feminine surrender, as has often been suggested' (*New Maladies of the Soul* 194).

5. Riviere championed Kleinian views in the 'Controversial Discussions' of the 1940s, and in 1936 published with Klein a volume on hate and aggression (see Athol Hughes).

6. This essay is translated by Alan Sheridan as 'The Signification of the Phallus' in *Écrits: A Selection* 281–91.

7. Alan Sheridan's translation of this phrase is less ambiguous than Rose's. It reads: ' it is in order to be the phallus . . . that *a woman will reject an essential part of femininity, namely, all her attributes in the masquerade.*' (*Écrits* 289–90, emphasis added). While Sheridan's translation empha-

sizes woman's rejection of her masquerading practices, Rose's emphasis is on the way the woman uses the masquerade as part of the process of her broader rejection of her femininity in general. Lacan's original phrase reads: 'c'est pour être le phallus . . . que la femme va rejeter une part essentielle de la féminité, nommément tous ses attributs dans la mascarade' (*Écrits* [French] 694).

8. An earlier and rather different version of this analysis of *Orlando* appeared in *Gramma/Γράμμα: Journal of Theory and Criticism* 1 (1993): 137–53.

9. See for example Woolf's 'Freudian Fiction'; also Goldstein ('The Woolfs' Response to Freud'), Kushen ('Virginia Woolf and "Dr Freud"') and Abel (*Virginia Woolf and the Fictions of Psychoanalysis*). The first chapter of Abel's book gives an excellent summary of the relationship between Woolf and other Bloomsbury members and the psychoanalytic movement in London in the 1920s–30s.

10. Abel has argued for Woolf's identification in the 1920s with a 'matri-centric', Kleinian view of human development rather than a 'patri-centric' Freudian one (xvii). This dichotomy, I think, is more a construction of 1980s feminism than of the period itself, when women psychoanalysts advocating an investigation of pre-Oedipal, maternal object relations considered themselves as working within a Freudian tradition. As I shall be arguing, it is not the matri- versus the patricentric debate which is relevant to Woolf's work so much as the terms being used to attempt new definitions of femininity.

11. Her friend Lytton Strachey, with whom she first learned to discuss homosexuality openly, was a member of the British Society for the Study of Sex Psychology, founded in 1914. In a diary entry for January 1918, Woolf recounted Strachey's description of a meeting where incest between parents and children had been discussed, and added: 'I think of becoming a member' (Abel 139n79).

12. See for example the following passage in Ch. 4: 'as all [the male] Orlando's loves had been women, now [as a woman], through the culpable laggardry of the human frame to adapt itself to convention, though she herself was a woman, it was still a woman she loved' (*Orlando* 113).

13. The most well known example is her essay 'Mr. Bennett and Mrs. Brown', which was read as a paper in Cambridge in 1924. Here it could also be speculated that Woolf was reacting against not only Arnold Bennett and other male Edwardian novelists, but also against her father Leslie Stephen as critic in his defence of Balzac, French realism and the privileging of 'accuracy' as a fictional criterion. For Leslie Stephen's interest in realism, see Parkin-Gounelas 167–68n35.

14. Woolf wrote in her *Diary* that though *Orlando* was begun 'as a joke', it became 'rather too long for my liking. It may fall between stools, be too long for a joke, and too frivolous for a serious book' (qtd in Minow-Pinkney 118).

15. See the early description of Orlando: 'Happy the mother who bears, happier still the biographer who records the life of such a one! Never need she vex herself, nor he invoke the help of novelist or poet' (10). The

distinction between maternal and literary creation is here a matter of 'she' versus 'he'.

16. In a passing reference, Meisel calls *Orlando* 'the consummate Paterian portrait' (45) in the genre of 'new biography' experimented with by Lytton Strachey and Woolf.

17. Vita Sackville-West's reaction to reading the book was to protest to Woolf, rather coyly, that she had 'hung so splendid a garment on so poor a peg' (qtd in Knopp 33).

18. Elaine Jordan has written of the 'disparate effects' of Carter's style: 'the banal and the extraordinary, the prim and the offensive, the baroque and the offhand' (123). Carter herself described the style of the Gothic tale, which influenced her *Fireworks* stories, in this way: 'Its style will tend to be ornate, unnatural – and thus operate against the perennial human desire to believe the world as fact . . . It retains a singular moral function – that of provoking unease' ('Afterword' 122).

19. Jacqueline Rose translates this phrase as 'There is woman only as excluded' (Mitchell and Rose 144).

20. Another typical example of the recent popularity of the reversal of the adjectives 'masculine' and 'feminine' to refer to men and women has appeared in a Sunday newspaper as I write this chapter. It describes the actress Cher as 'masculine' ('logical, quick and precise') in her shopping habits, while the boxer Chris Eubank shows a 'feminine' lack of decision at the till. The accompanying photographs, however, reinforce the traditional distinctions: Cher stretches languidly in a scanty bathing suit, while Eubank glowers sweatily, nostrils flaring (*Sunday Express*. 7 March 1999, 13). As in the TV advertisement mentioned above, the *frisson* of transgression is dependent upon a clearly marked, untouched association between masculinity and power, femininity and the lack of it.

CHAPTER 8

1. In 'Beyond the Pleasure Principle' Freud discusses the assumption that 'all living substance is bound to die from internal causes', and wonders whether it may be 'only another of those illusions which we have created' in order to avoid the uncomfortable responsibility for its avoidance. (PF 11: 317)

2. In his New Introductory Lecture on 'Anxiety and Instinctual Life', Freud writes: 'Instincts are mythical entities, magnificent in their indefiniteness. In our work we cannot for a moment disregard them, yet we are never sure that we are seeing them clearly.' (PF 2: 127)

3. Many, like Harold Bloom, read Freud's drives (such as the death drive) as 'tropes' or 'fictions' with no stable referent, and argue that the dialectic of the life and death drives should be characterized not as scientific *praxis* but rather as 'a great writer's Sublime interplay between figurative and literal meanings' ('Freud and the Poetic Sublime' 222, 229 and 223).

4. In her study of the ego ideal as heir to primary narcissism, Janine Chasseguet-Smirgel argues that 'The ceremony surrounding religion is

easily superimposed on the ceremonial of the pervert, not only because in both cases an element of ritual is involved . . . but also because both involve idealization' (*The Ego Ideal* 20).

5. The classic virgin/whore splitting figured in much literature echoes another kind of splitting played out in Lucy in the defence against colonial anxiety, the West's anxiety about penetration by the East. Lucy's surname, Westenra, which is repeated twice, emphatically, in the passage describing her transformation (Stoker 271), seems to rehearse the break-up of Western integrity by some added force, the clumsy -ra suffix removed from Dracula's name. This orientalizing process centres in this passage on Lucy's mouth, which takes on qualities of the Eastern (Greek and Japanese) passion mask.

6. In his Introduction to the Penguin edition of *Dracula* (xxiv), Maurice Hindle records how in the 1880s Charcot visited the Lycaeum Theatre to hear Henry Irving perform in a Shakespeare play. Stoker was Irving's manager at the Lycaeum from 1878 to 1898.

7. See, for example, p. 96:

> Why not advance science in its most difficult and vital aspect – the knowledge of the brain? Had I even the secret of one such mind – did I hold the key to the fancy of even one lunatic – I might advance my own branch of science to a pitch compared with which Burdon-Sanderson's physiology or Ferrier's brain-knowledge would be as nothing. If only there were a sufficient cause! I must not think too much of this, or I may be tempted; a good cause might turn the scale with me, for may not I too be of an exceptional brain, congenitally?

8. See also p. 89: 'I in thy mishaps may see/The lively portrait of my dying self'.

9. The Editor of this edition of *The Spanish Tragedy* makes the following Note at this point:

> the Geneva Bible (in use at Kyd's date of writing) uses 'Babel' both for the Tower of Babel and for the wicked city of Babylon: the two would be closely associated in the audience's mind. For the destruction of Babylon see Isaiah xii, Jeremiah, and Revelation xviii (110n195).

10. In 'The Spanish Tragedy, as Babylon Revisited', S. F. Johnson argues against M. C. Bradbrook and others that although the extant version of *The Spanish Tragedy* gives us the playlet in English rather than in the 'sundry tongues', explaining in a note that this has been done for the 'easier understanding' of the reader, this part of the play itself would almost certainly have been originally acted in the four different languages. Johnson also gives an extended analysis of the significance of the concepts of Babel and Babylon in Elizabethan England.

11. See for example Apter and Pietz; Mulvey; and Žižek, *The Plague of Fantasies*, Ch. 3 ('Fetishism and its Vicissitudes').

12. Freud's last important statements on fetishism occur in his 1938 essay, 'Splitting of the Ego in the Process of Defence' (PF 11: 457–64).

13. Christina Britzolakis, who cites this same passage from Benjamin, gives an impressive Bejaminian reading of Angela Carter's work. Žižek's summary of the analogy between Marx's and Freud's use of the notion of fetishism is useful:

> in both cases, fetishism stands for a displacement (relations between men are displaced on to relations between things; the subject's sexual interest is displaced from the 'normal' sexual object to its substitute); this displacement is in both cases a 'regressive' shift of focus towards a 'lower' and partial element which conceals (and at the same time designates) the true point of reference. The analogy further consists in the fact that for Marx and Freud, the fetish is not simply a 'lower stage' of development (of society, of genital Oedipal sexuality), but a symptom of the inherent contradiction within the 'higher' stage itself: commodity fetishism, for example, reveals the crack in spiritual Christianity and in the 'mature' free individual of 'developed' society itself. (*Plague of Fantasies* 124n16)

Žižek argues persuasively that there is a 'strong temptation today to renounce the notion of fetishism' within a postmodern culture. Its basic mechanism, 'the obfuscation of the process of production in its result' is, he writes, 'no longer operative in our era of a new kind of "false transparency"' (101–2).

14. In these same terms, Janine Chasseguet-Smirgel discusses the Egyptian practice of embalming as the production of a fetish object: 'Make-up is applied to the putrefying body, which is then decorated with jewels, dressed up with a golden mask, and made into a god' (*Creativity and Perversion* 88).

15. In his descriptions of Plath and of their relationship in his volume of poetry, *Birthday Letters* (1998), Ted Hughes returns frequently to the image of her celluloid smile: 'And your grin./Your exaggerated American/Grin for the cameras, the judges, the strangers, the frighteners' (3); 'your face/A rubbery ball of joy/Round the African-lipped, laughing, thickly/Crimson-painted mouth' (15).

16. As Robyn Marsack notes, this is undoubtedly a reference to the wife of a Nazi commandant who had lampshades made of human skin (75).

17. See Charles Bernheimer, 'Fetishism and Decadence':

> The word [fetish] comes from the Portuguese *feitio* 'artificial, skilfully contrived,' which in turn derives from the Latin *facticius*, 'made by art.' The sense of human fabrication as opposed to biological origin, of cultural signs replacing natural substance, is at the basis of other words in the Romance languages deriving from the same Latin root: Spanish *afeitar*, 'to make up, adorn, embellish,' and *afeite*, 'dress, ornament, cosmetics'; French *feint*, 'feigned, simulated.' (63)

Works Cited

Abel, E., *Virginia Woolf and the Fictions of Psychoanalysis* (Chicago: University of Chicago Press, 1989).

Abraham, K., 'Manifestations of the Female Castration Complex', *The International Journal of Psycho-Analysis*, 3.1 (March 1922), 1–29.

Abraham, N., 'The Shell and the Kernel: The Scope and Originality of Freudian Psychoanalysis', in N. Abraham and M. Torok, *The Shell and the Kernel: Renewals of Psychoanalysis*, (trans.) N. T. Rand (Chicago: University of Chicago Press, 1994), pp. 79–98.

Abraham, N. and Torok, M., *The Shell and the Kernel: Renewals of Psychoanalysis*, (trans.) N. T. Rand (Chicago: University of Chicago Press, 1994).

Adams, P., *The Emptiness of the Image: Psychoanalysis and Sexual Difference* (London: Routledge, 1996).

——, 'Per Os(cillation)', in *Psychoanalysis and Cultural Theory: Thresholds*, (ed.) J. Donald (Houndmills, Basingstoke: Macmillan, 1991), pp. 68–88.

Ahmad, Ajaz, 'Reconciling Derrida: "Spectres of Marx" and Deconstructive Politics', *New Left Review*, 208 (Nov./Dec. 1994), 88–106.

Anzieu, D., 'Beckett and Bion', *The International Review of Psycho-Analysis*, 16.2 (1989), 63–69.

Apter, E. and Pietz, W. (eds), *Fetishism as Cultural Discourse* (Ithaca: Cornell University Press, 1993).

Arata, S. D., 'The Occidental Tourist: *Dracula* and the Anxiety of Reverse Colonization', *Victorian Studies*, 33.4 (Summer 1990), 621–45.

Auden, W. H., *Collected Poems* (London: Faber & Faber, 1976).

——, 'Psychology and Art To-Day', in *Freud: A Collection of Critical Essays*, (ed.) P. Meisel (Englewood Cliffs, N.J.: Prentice-Hall, 1981), pp. 61–72.

Auerbach, N., *Our Vampires, Ourselves* (Chicago: University of Chicago Press, 1995).

Bair, D., *Samuel Beckett: A Biography* (London: Vintage, 1990).

Baker, P., *Beckett and the Mythology of Psychoanalysis* (Houndmills, Basingstoke: Macmillan, 1997).

Bakhtin, M., *Rabelais and His World*, (trans.) H. Iswolsky (Bloomington: Indiana University Press, 1984).

Barthes, R., 'The Death of the Author', *Image Music Text*, (trans.) S. Heath (London: Fontana, 1977), pp. 142–48.

——, *The Pleasure of the Text*, (trans.) R. Miller (Oxford: Blackwell, 1994).

——, *Roland Barthes by Roland Barthes*, (trans.) R. Howard (New York: Hill & Wang, 1977).

Baudrillard, J., *The Illusion of the End*, (trans.) C. Turner (Cambridge: Polity Press, 1994).

——, *Symbolic Exchange and Death*, (trans.) I. Hamilton Grant (London: Sage, 1993).

Beauvoir, S. de, *The Second Sex*, (trans.) H. M. Parshley (New York: Vintage, 1974).

Beckett, S., *Collected Shorter Prose 1945–1980* (London: John Calder, 1986).

——, *The Complete Dramatic Works* (London: Faber & Faber, 1986).

——, *How it Is* (London: John Calder, 1996).

——, *L'innomable* (Paris: Minuit, 1953).

——, *Murphy* (London: Pan Books, 1973).

——, *Proust [and] Three Dialogues* (London: John Calder, 1965).

——, *[Trilogy] Molloy Malone Dies The Unnamable* (London: Calder, 1994).

Beizer, J., *Ventriloquized Bodies: Narratives of Hysteria in Nineteenth-Century France* (Ithaca: Cornell University Press, 1994).

Benjamin, W., *Charles Baudelaire: A Lyric Poet in the Era of High Capitalism*, (trans.) H. Zohn (London: NLB, 1973).

Bernheimer, C., 'Fetishism and Decadence: Salome's Severed Heads', in *Fetishism as Cultural Discourse*, (ed.) E. Apter and W. Pietz (Ithaca: Cornell University Press, 1993), pp. 62–83.

Bernheimer, C. and Kahane, C. (eds), *In Dora's Case: Freud – Hysteria – Feminism* (London: Virago, 1985).

Bettelheim, B., *The Uses of Enchantment: The Meaning and Importance of Fairy Tales* (London: Penguin, 1991).

Bhabha, H. K., 'A Question of Survival: Nations and Psychic States', in *Psychoanalysis and Cultural Theory: Thresholds*, (ed.) J. Donald (Basingstoke: Macmillan, 1991), pp. 89–103.

Bion, W. R., *Attention and Interpretation: A Scientific Approach to Insight in Psycho-Analysis and Groups* (London: Tavistock, 1970).

——, *Second Thoughts: Selected Papers on Psycho-Analysis* (New York: Jason Aronson, 1967).

Blanchot, M., 'Literature and the Right to Death', *The Gaze of Orpheus and Other Literary Essays*, (trans.) L. Davis (New York: Station Hill, 1981), pp. 21–62.

——, *The Space of Literature*, (trans.) A. Smock (Lincoln: University of Nebraska Press, 1989).

Bloom, H., 'Freud and the Poetic Sublime: A Catastrophe Theory of Creativity', in *Freud: A Collection of Critical Essays*, (ed.) P. Meisel (Englewood Cliffs, N.J.: Prentice-Hall, 1981), pp. 211–31.

Borch-Jacobsen, M., 'The Freudian Subject, from Politics to Ethics', in *Who Comes After the Subject?* (ed.) E. Cadava *et al.* (New York: Routledge, 1991), pp. 61–78.

——, *Remembering Anna O.: A Century of Mystification* (New York: Routledge, 1996).

Bowie, M., *Lacan* (London: Fontana, 1991).

Bowra, C. M., *Sophoclean Tragedy* (Oxford: Clarendon Press, 1944).

Breton, A., *What is Surrealism?: Selected Writings*, (ed.) F. Rosemont (London: Pluto Press, 1978).

Britzolakis, C., 'Angela Carter's Fetishism', in *The Infernal Desires of Angela Carter: Fiction, Femininity, Feminism*, (ed.) J. Bristow and T. L. Broughton (London: Longman, 1997), pp. 43–58.

Bronfen, E., *The Knotted Subject: Hysteria and its Discontents* (Princeton, N.J.: Princeton University Press, 1998).

Brontë, C., *Jane Eyre* (Harmondsworth, Middlesex: Penguin, 1972).

Brooks, P., *Psychoanalysis and Storytelling* (Oxford: Basil Blackwell, 1994).

——, *Reading for the Plot: Design and Intention in Narrative* (Oxford: Clarendon Press, 1984).

Bryden, M., *Women in Samuel Beckett's Prose and Drama: Her Own Other* (Houndmills, Basingstoke: Macmillan, 1993).

Buse, P. and Stott, A. (eds), *Ghosts: Deconstruction, Psychoanalysis, History* (Houndmills, Basingstoke: Macmillan, 1998).

Butler, J., *Gender Trouble: Feminism and the Subversion of Identity* (New York: Routledge, 1990).

——, 'Imitation and Gender Insubordination', in *Inside/Out: Lesbian Theories, Gay Theories*, (ed.) D. Fuss (New York: Routledge), pp. 13–31.

Caldwell, L., 'Interview with André Green', *Psychoanalysis and Culture*, 26 (Autumn 1995), 15–35.

Carroll, L., *Alice's Adventures in Wonderland and Through the Looking-Glass* (London: Macmillan, 1975).

Carter, A., 'Afterword', *Fireworks: Nine Profane Pieces* (London: Quartet Books, 1974), pp. 121–22.

——, *Fireworks* (London: Virago, 1987).

——, *Love: A Novel* (London: Picador, 1988).

Castoriadis, C., 'Logic, Imagination, Reflection', in *Psychoanalysis in Contexts: Paths between Theory and Modern Culture*, (ed.) A. Elliott and S. Frosh (London: Routledge, 1995), pp. 15–35.

Chase, C., 'Oedipal Textuality: Reading Freud's Reading of *Oedipus*', in *Psychoanalytic Literary Criticism*, (ed.) M. Ellmann (London: Longman, 1994), pp. 56–75.

Chasseguet-Smirgel, J., *Creativity and Perversion* (London: Free Association Books, 1992).

——, *The Ego Ideal: A Psychoanalytic Essay on the Malady of the Ideal*, (trans.) P. Barrows (London: Free Association Books, 1985).

Cixous, H., 'Castration or Decapitation?', *Signs*, 7.1 (Autumn 1981), 41–55.

——, 'Fiction and its Phantoms: A Reading of Freud's Das *Unheimliche* ("The Uncanny")', *New Literary History*, 7.3 (Spring 1976), 526–48.

——, *Portrait of Dora*, (trans.) A. Barrows (London: John Calder, 1978), pp. 27–67.

Cixous, H. and Clément, C., *The Newly-Born Woman*, (trans.) B. Wing (Minneapolis: University of Minnesota Press, 1986).

Cohn, R., *Back to Beckett* (Princeton, N.J.: Princeton University Press, 1973).

Coleridge, S. T., *Biographia Literaria* (London: J.M. Dent, 1967).

——, *Poetical Works*, (ed.) E. Hartley Coleridge (London: Oxford University Press, 1969).

Cook, A., *Thresholds: Studies in the Romantic Experience* (Madison: University of Wisconsin Press, 1985).

Copjec, J., *Read My Desire: Lacan Against the Historicists* (Cambridge, Mass.: MIT Press, 1995).

Critchley, S., 'On Derrida's *Spectres of Marx*', *Philosophy and Social Criticism*, 21.3 (May 1995), 1–30.

David-Ménard, M., *Hysteria From Freud to Lacan: Body and Language in Psychoanalysis*, (trans.) C. Porter (Ithaca: Cornell University Press, 1989).

Deleuze, G., 'Coldness and Cruelty', *Masochism*, (trans.) J. McNeil (New York: Zone Books, 1989), pp. 7–138.

Deleuze, G. and Guattari. F., *Anti-Oedipus: Capitalism and Schizophrenia*, (trans.) R. Hurley *et al.* (New York: Viking, 1982).

Derrida, J., 'Coming into One's Own', *Psychoanalysis and the Question of the Text*, (ed.) G. H. Hartman, (trans.) J. Hulbert (Baltimore: Johns Hopkins University Press, 1985), pp. 114–48.

——, *Dissemination*, (trans.) B. Johnson (London: Athlone, 1993).

——, 'Foreword: *Fors*: The Anglish Words of Nicolas Abraham and Maria Torok', (trans.) B. Johnson. *The Wolf Man's Magic Word*: A Cryptonymy, (trans.) N. Rand (Minneapolis: University of Minnesota Press, 1986), pp. xi–xlviii.

——, 'Me – Psychoanalysis: An Introduction to the Translation of "The Shell and the Kernel" by Nicolas Abraham', *Diacritics*, 9.1 (March 1979), 4–12.

——, *Positions*, (trans.) A. Bass (London: Athlone, 1987).

——, *The Post Card: From Socrates to Freud and Beyond*, (trans.) A. Bass (Chicago: University of Chicago Press, 1987).

——, *Specters of Marx: The State of the Debt, the Work of Mourning, and the New International*, (trans.) P. Kamuf (New York: Routledge, 1994).

——, *Writing and Difference*, (trans.) A. Bass (London: Routledge, 1995).

Deutsch, H., 'The Psychology of Women in Relation to the Functions of Reproduction', *The International Journal of Psycho-Analysis*, 6.4 (Oct. 1925), 405–18.

——, 'The Significance of Masochism in the Mental Life of Women', *The International Journal of Psycho-Analysis*, 11.1 (Jan. 1930), 48–60.

Dijkstra, B., *Idols of Perversity: Fantasies of Feminine Evil in Fin-de-Siècle Culture* (New York: Oxford University Press, 1986).

Dolar, M., 'At First Sight', in *Gaze and Voice as Love Objects*, (ed.) R. Salecl and S. Žižek (Durham: Duke University Press, 1996), pp. 129–53.

——, 'I Shall be With You on your Wedding Night', *October*, 58 (Fall 1991), 5–23.

Douka-Kabitoglou, E., 'Phantom or Fact: Coleridge's "Scientific" Account of the Imagination', *Real [Yearbook of Research in English and American Literature]*, 8 (1992), 195–230.

Eagleton, T., 'Power and Knowledge in "The Lifted Veil" ', *Literature and History*, 9.1 (Spring 1983), 52–61.

Easthope, A., *The Unconscious* (London: Routledge, 1999).

[Eliot, G]. *The George Eliot Letters*, (ed.) G. S. Haight (London: Oxford University Press, 1954–78).

Eliot, G., *The Lifted Veil* (London: Virago, 1985).

Eliot, T. S., *The Complete Poems and Plays of T.S. Eliot* (London: Faber & Faber, 1970).

——, 'Hamlet', *Selected Essays* (London: Faber & Faber, 1976), pp. 141–46.

——, 'Seneca in Elizabethan Translation', *Selected Essays* (London: Faber & Faber, 1976), pp. 65–105.

Elliott, A. and Frosh, S. (eds), *Psychoanalysis in Contexts: Paths Between Theory and Modern Culture* (London: Routledge. 1995).

Ellmann, M., 'Eliot's Abjection', in *Abjection, Melancholia, and Love: The Work of Julia Kristeva*, (ed.) J. Fletcher and A. Benjamin (London: Routledge, 1990), pp. 178–200.

——, (ed.), *Psychoanalytic Literary Criticism* (London: Longman, 1994).

Ender, E. *Sexing the Mind: Nineteenth-Century Fictions of Hysteria* (Ithaca: Cornell University Press, 1995).

Evans, D., 'From Kantian Ethics to Mystical Experience: An Exploration of Jouissance', *Key Concepts of Lacanian Psychoanalysis*, (ed.) D. Nobus (London: Rebus Press, 1998), pp. 1–28.

Feldstein, R. and Sussmann, H. (eds), *Psychoanalysis and . . .* (New York: Routledge, 1990).

Felman, S., 'Beyond Oedipus: The Specimen Story of Psychoanalysis', *Lacan and Narration: The Psychoanalytic Difference in Narrative Theory*, (ed.) R. Con Davis (Baltimore: Johns Hopkins University Press, 1983), pp. 1021–53.

——, (ed.), *Literature and Psychoanalysis: The Question of Reading Otherwise*. Baltimore: Johns Hopkins University Press, 1982).

——, 'Turning the Screw of Interpretation', in *Literature and Psychoanalysis: The Question of Reading Otherwise*, (ed.) S. Felman (Baltimore: Johns Hopkins University Press, 1982), pp. 94–207.

——, *What Does a Woman Want?: Reading and Sexual Difference* (Baltimore: Johns Hopkins University Press, 1993).

Ferrell, R., *Passion in Theory: Conceptions of Freud and Lacan* (London: Routledge, 1996).

Fineman, J., 'The Sound of *O* in *Othello*: The Real of the Tragedy of Desire', in *Psychoanalysis and . . .*, (ed.) R. Feldstein and H. Sussman (New York: Routledge, 1990), pp. 33–46.

Fink, B., *The Lacanian Subject: Between Language and Jouissance* (Princeton, N.J.: Princeton University Press, 1995).

Flanders, S., 'Introduction', *The Dream Discourse Today*, (ed.) S. Flanders (London: Routledge, 1993), pp. 1–25.

Ford, J., *Coleridge on Dreaming: Romanticism, Dreams and the Medical Imagination* (Cambridge: Cambridge University Press, 1998).

Forrester, J., *The Seductions of Psychoanalysis: Freud, Lacan and Derrida* (Cambridge: Cambridge University Press, 1992).

Foucault, M., *The History of Sexuality: An Introduction*, (trans.) R. Hurley (Harmondsworth, Middlesex: Penguin, 1987).

——, *Madness and Civilization: A History of Insanity in the Age of Reason*, (trans.) R. Howard (London: Routledge, 1993).

Frayling, C., *Vampyres: Lord Byron to Count Dracula* (London: Faber, 1991).

Freud, A., *The Ego and the Mechanisms of Defence* (London: Hogarth Press, 1968).

Freud, S., *The Origins of Psycho-Analysis: Letters to Wilhelm Fliess, Drafts and Notes: 1887–1902*, (ed.) M. Bonaparte, A. Freud and E. Kris, (trans.) E. Mosbacher and J. Strachey (London: Imago, 1954).

——, *The Penguin Freud Library*, vols 1–15, (trans.) J. Strachey *et al.* (London: Penguin, 1990–93) [Abbreviated as PF]).

——, *The Standard Edition of the Complete Psychological Works of Sigmund Freud*, (trans.) J. Strachey *et al.* vols. 1– 23 (London: Hogarth Press, 1953–74 [Abbreviated as SE]).

Gallop, J., *Reading Lacan* (Ithaca: Cornell University Press, 1985).

Galvan, J., Review of *Julia Kristeva Interviews*, *Journal for the Psychoanalysis of Culture and Society*, 2.2 (Fall 1997), 181–83.

Gaskell, E., 'The Old Nurse's Story', in *Victorian Ghost Stories: An Oxford Anthology*, (ed.) M. Cox and R. A. Gilbert (Oxford: Oxford University Press, 1992), pp. 1–18.

Gay, P., *Freud: A Life for Our Time* (London: Papermac, 1989).

Goldstein, J. E., 'The Woolfs' Response to Freud: Water Spiders, Singing Canaries and the Second Apple', in *Literature and Psychoanalysis*, (ed.) E. Kurzweil and W. Phillips (New York: Columbia University Press, 1983), pp. 232–55.

Goux, J.-J., *Oedipus, Philosopher*, (trans.) C. Porter (Stanford, Calif.: Stanford University Press, 1993).

Gray, B., 'Afterword', in G. Eliot, *The Lifted Veil*. (London: Virago, 1985), pp. 69–91.

Green, A., 'Prologue: The Psycho-Analytic Reading of Tragedy', in *Psychoanalytic Literary Criticism*, (ed.) M. Ellmann (London: Longman, 1994), pp. 39–55.

——, *The Tragic Effect: The Oedipus Complex in Tragedy*, (trans.) A. Sheridan (Cambridge: Cambridge University Press, 1979).

Harrison, W. C., 'The Socialization of the Body's Pleasures', *New Formations*, 26 (Autumn 1995), 163–71.

Heaney, S., 'The Indefatigable Hoof-Taps', *TLS* (5–11 Feb.1988), 134 and 143–44.

Heath, S., 'Joan Riviere and the Masquerade', in *Formations of Fantasy*, (ed.) V. Burgin, J. Donald and C. Kaplan (London: Routledge, 1986), pp. 45–61.

Hertz, N., 'Dora's Secrets, Freud's Techniques', in *In Dora's Case: Freud – Hysteria – Feminism*, (ed.) C. Bernheimer and C. Kahane (London: Virago, 1985), pp. 221–42.

Hoffmann, E. T. A. *Tales of Hoffmann*, (trans.) R. J. Hollingdale (Harmondsworth, Middlesex: Penguin, 1982).

Holland, N. and Sherman., L. F., 'Gothic Possibilities', *New Literary History*, 8.2 (Winter 1977), 279–94.

Homer, *The Odyssey*, (trans.) E. V. Rieu (Harmondsworth, Middlesex: Penguin, 1954).

Horney, K., 'The Flight from Womanhood: The Masculinity Complex in Women, as Viewed by Men and by Women', *The International Journal of Psycho-Analysis*, 7.3 (July–Oct. 1926), 324–39.

House, H. *Coleridge* (London: Rupert Hart-Davis, 1967).

Hughes, A., 'Joan Riviere: Her Life and Work', in *The Inner World and Joan Riviere: Collected Papers: 1920–58*, (ed.) A. Hughes (London: Karnac Books, 1991), pp. 1–43.

Hughes, T., *Birthday Letters* (London: Faber, 1998).

Hunter, D., 'Hysteria, Psychoanalysis, and Feminism: The Case of Anna O.', in *The (M)other Tongue: Essays in Feminist Psychoanalytic Interpretation*, (ed.) S. N. Garner *et al.* (Ithaca: Cornell University Press, 1985), pp. 89–115.

Hynes, S., *The Auden Generation: Literature and Politics in England in the 1930s* (London: Pimlico, 1992).

Irigaray, L. *Speculum de l'autre femme* (Paris: Minuit, 1974).

——, *Speculum of the Other Woman*, (trans.) G. C. Gill (Ithaca: Cornell University Press, 1985).

——, *This Sex Which is Not One*, (trans.) C. Porter with C. Burke (Ithaca: Cornell University Press, 1985).

Ishiguro, K., *The Remains of the Day* (London: Faber & Faber, 1990).

Jackson, R., *Fantasy: The Literature of Subversion* (London: Methuen, 1981).

Jacobus, M., *First Things: The Maternal Imaginary in Literature, Art and Psychoanalysis* (New York: Routledge, 1995).

——, *Reading Women: Essays in Feminist Criticism* (New York: Columbia University Press, 1986).

Jameson, F., 'Marx's Purloined Letter', *New Left Review*, 209 (Jan./Feb. 1995), 75–109.

Johnson, B., *The Feminist Difference: Literature, Psychoanalysis, Race, and Gender* (Cambridge, Mass.: Harvard University Press, 1998).

Johnson, S. F., '*The Spanish Tragedy*, or Babylon Revisited', in *Essays on Shakespeare and Elizabethan Drama*, (ed.) R. Hosley (London: Routledge & Kegan Paul, 1963), pp. 23–36.

Johnson, T., *Hysteria: or Fragments of an Analysis of an Obsessional Neurosis* (London: Methuen Drama, 1995).

Jones, E., *Hamlet and Oedipus* (London: Victor Gollancz, 1949).

——, *On the Nightmare* (London: Hogarth Press, 1931).

Jordan, E., 'The Dangers of Angela Carter', in *New Feminist Discourses: Critical Essays on Theories and Texts*, (ed.) I. Armstrong (London: Routledge, 1992), pp. 119–31.

Kahane, C., *Passions of the Voice: Hysteria, Narrative, and the Figure of the Speaking Woman, 1850–1915* (Baltimore: Johns Hopkins University Press, 1995).

Klein, M., *Love, Guilt and Reparation and Other Works 1921–1945* (London: Virago, 1994).

[——], *The Selected Melanie Klein*, (ed.) J. Mitchell (London: Penguin, 1991).

Knowlson, J,. *Damned to Fame: The Life of Samuel Beckett* (London: Bloomsbury, 1997).

Kofman, S., *The Enigma of Woman: Woman in Freud's Writings*, (trans.) C. Porter (Ithaca: Cornell University Press, 1985).

Kowsar, M., 'Lacan's *Antigone*: A Case Study in Psychoanalytical Ethics', *Theatre Journal* (March 1990), 94–106.

Kristeva, J., *Black Sun: Depression and Melancholia*, (trans.) L. S. Roudiez (New York: Columbia University Press, 1989).

——, *Desire in Language: A Semiotic Approach to Literature and Art*, (trans.) T. Gora, A. Jardine and L. Roudiez (Oxford: Basil Blackwell, 1987).

[——], *The Kristeva Reader*, (ed.) T. Moi (Oxford: Basil Blackwell, 1986).

——, *New Maladies of the Soul*, (trans.) R. Guberman (New York: Columbia University Press, 1995).

——, 'On the Melancholic Imaginary', in *Discourse in Psychoanalysis and Literature*, (ed.) S. Rimmon-Kenan (London: Methuen, 1987), pp. 104–23.

——, 'Oscillation between Power and Denial', in *New French Feminisms*, (ed.) E. Marks and I. de Courtivron (Brighton, Sussex: Harvester, 1981), pp. 165–67.

——, *Powers of Horror: An Essay on Abjection*, (trans.) L. S. Roudiez (New York: Columbia University Press, 1982).

——, *Revolution in Poetic Language*, (trans.) M. Waller (New York: Columbia University Press, 1984).

——, *Strangers to Ourselves*, (trans.) L. S. Roudiez (New York: Columbia University Press, 1991).

——, *Tales of Love*, (trans.) L. S. Roudiez (New York: Columbia University Press, 1987).

——, 'Word, Dialogue and Novel', *The Kristeva Reader*, (ed.) T. Moi (Oxford: Blackwell, 1986), pp. 34–61.

Kurzweil, E. and Phillips, W. (eds), *Literature and Psychoanalysis* (New York: Columbia University Press, 1983).

Kusher, B., 'Virginia Woolf and "Dr Freud" ', *Literature and Psychology*, 35.1 and 2 (1989) 35–45.

Kyd, T., *The Spanish Tragedy*, (ed.) J. R. Mulryne (London: Ernest Benn, 1970).

Lacan, J., 'Desire and the Interpretation of Desire in *Hamlet'*, in *Literature and Psychoanalysis: The Question of Reading Otherwise*, (ed.) S. Felman (Baltimore: Johns Hopkins University Press, 1982), pp. 11–52.

——, *Écrits* (Paris: Éditions du Seuil, 1966). (Cited as *Écrits* [French].)

——, *Écrits: A Selection*, (trans.) A. Sheridan (London: Tavistock, 1985).

——, *The Four Fundamental Concepts of Psycho-Analysis* [Seminar 11], (ed.) J.-A. Miller, (trans.) A. Sheridan (Harmondsworth, Middlesex: Penguin, 1991).

——, 'Intervention on Transference', *Feminine Sexuality: Jacques Lacan and the* école freudienne, (ed.) J. Mitchell and J. Rose, (trans.) J. Rose (Houndmills, Basingstoke: Macmillan, 1982), pp. 61–73.

——, *The Seminar of Jacques Lacan*, Book 1, (ed.) J.-A. Miller, (trans.) J. Forrester (New York: W.W. Norton, 1991).

——, *The Seminar of Jacques Lacan*, Book 2, (ed.) J.-A. Miller, (trans.) S. Tomaselli (Cambridge: Cambridge University Press, 1988).

——, *The Seminar of Jacques Lacan*, Book 7, (ed.) J.-A. Miller, (trans.) D. Porter (London: Routledge, 1992).

——, *The Seminar of Jacques Lacan*, Book 20, (ed.) J.-A. Miller, (trans.) B. Fink (New York: W.W. Norton, 1998).

——, 'Seminar on "The Purloined Letter" ', (ed.) J. P. Muller and W. J. Richardson, *The Purloined Poe: Lacan, Derrida & Psychoanalytic Reading* (Baltimore: Johns Hopkins University Press, 1988), pp. 28–54.

——, *Television: A Challenge to the Psychoanalytic Establishment*, (ed.) J. Copjec, (trans.) D. Hollier, R. Kraus and A. Michelson (New York: Norton, 1990).

Lacan, J. and Granoff, V., 'Fetishism: The Symbolic, the Imaginary and the Real', in *Perversions: Psychoanalysis and Therapy*, (ed.) S. Lorand (London: Ortolan Press, 1965), pp. 265–76.

Laplanche, J. and Leclaire, S., 'The Unconscious: A Psychoanalytic Study', *Yale French Studies*, 48 (1972), 118–75.

Laplanche, J. and Pontalis, J.-B., *The Language of Psycho-Analysis*, (trans.) D. Nicholson-Smith (New York: W.W. Norton, [1973]).

Lee, H., *Virginia Woolf* (London: Chatto & Windus, 1996).

LeFanu, J.S., 'An Account of Some Strange Disturbances in Aungier Street', in *Victorian Ghost Stories: An Oxford Anthology*, (ed.) M. Cox and R.A. Gilbert (Oxford: Oxford University Press, 1992), pp. 19–36.

Lodge, D. (ed.), *Modern Criticism and Theory: A Reader* (London: Longman, 1988).

Macey, D., 'On the Subject of Lacan', in *Psychoanalysis in Contexts: Paths Between Theory and Modern Culture*, (ed.) A. Elliott and S. Frosh (London: Routledge, 1995), pp. 72–86.

Majumdar, R. and Mclaurin, A. (eds), *Virginia Woolf: The Critical Heritage* (London: Routledge & Kegan Paul, 1975).

Marcus, S., 'Freud and Dora: Story, History, Case History', in *In Dora's Case: Freud – Hysteria – Feminism*, (ed.) C. Bernheimer and C. Kahane (London: Virago, 1985), pp. 56–91.

Marder, H., *Feminism & Art: A Study of Virginia Woolf* (Chicago: University of Chicago Press, 1968).

Marks, E. and Courtivron, I. de (eds), *New French Feminisms: An Anthology* (Brighton, Sussex: Harvester, 1981).

Marsack, R., *Sylvia Plath* (Buckingham: Open University Press, 1992).

McCall, T., 'Oedipus Contemporaneous', *Diacritics*, 25. 4 (Winter 1995), 3–19.

McDougall, J., *The Many Faces of Eros: A Psychoanalytic Exploration of Human Sexuality* (London: Free Association Books, 1995).

——, *Plea for a Measure of Abnormality* (London: Free Association Books, 1992).

Mehlman, J., *Revolution and Repetition: Marx/Hugo/Balzac* (Berkeley: University of California Press, 1977).

Meisel, P., *The Absent Father: Virginia Woolf and Walter Pater* (New Haven: Yale University Press, 1980).

——, (ed.), *Freud: A Collection of Critical Essays* (Englewood Cliffs, N.J.: Prentice-Hall, 1981).

Meisel, P. and Kendrick, W. (eds), *Bloomsbury/Freud: The Letters of James and Alix Strachey 1924–25* (London: Chatto & Windus, 1986).

Micale, M.S. *Approaching Hysteria: Disease and its Interpretations* (Princeton, N.J.: Princeton University Press, 1995).

Miller, K., *Doubles: Studies in Literary History* (Oxford: Oxford University Press, 1985).

Milton, J., *Paradise Lost: A Poem in Twelve Books* (New York: Odyssey Press, 1962).

Minnow-Pinkney, M., *Virginia Woolf and the Problem of the Subject* (Brighton, Sussex: Harvester, 1987).

Mitchell, J., 'Introduction', *The Selected Melanie Klein*, (ed.) J. Mitchell (London: Penguin, 1991), pp. 9–32.

——, 'Introduction I', *Feminine Sexuality: Jacques Lacan and the* école freudienne, (ed.) J. Mitchell and J. Rose, (trans.) J. Rose (Houndmills, Basingstoke: Macmillan, 1982), pp. 1–26.

——, *Women: The Longest Revolution: Essays on Feminism, Literature and Psychoanalysis* (London: Virago, 1984).

Mitchell, J. and J. Rose (eds), *Feminine Sexuality: Jacques Lacan and the* école freudienne, (trans.) J. Rose (Houndmills, Basingstoke: Macmillan, 1982).

Moi, T., *Sexual/Textual Politics: Feminist Literary Theory* (London: Methuen, 1985).

Muller, J. P. and Richardson, W. J. (eds), *The Purloined Poe: Lacan, Derrida & Psychoanalytic Reading* (Baltimore: Johns Hopkins University Press, 1988).

Mulvey, L., *Fetishism and Curiosity* (Bloomington: Indiana University Press, 1996).

Neill, M., *Issues of Death: Mortality and Identity in English Renaissance Tragedy* (Oxford: Clarendon Press, 1997).

Nobus, D., 'Life and Death in the Glass: A New Look at the Mirror Stage', in *Key Concepts of Lacanian Psychoanalysis*, (ed.) D. Nobus (London: Rebus, 1998), pp. 101–38.

Nokes, D., *Jonathan Swift: A Hypocrite Reversed: A Critical Biography* (Oxford: Oxford University Press, 1987).

O'Connor, N., 'The An-Arche of Psychotherapy', in *Abjection, Melancholia, and Love: The Work of Julia Kristeva*, (ed.) J. Fletcher and A. Benjamin (London: Routledge, 1990), pp. 42–52.

Ovid, *The Metamorphoses*, (trans.) M. M. Innes (Harmondsworth, Middlesex: Penguin, 1986).

Parkin-Gounelas, R., *Fictions of the Female Self: Charlotte Brontë, Olive Schreiner, Katherine Mansfield* (London: Macmillan, 1991).

Phillips, A., *Winnicott* (London: Fontana, 1988).

Plath, S., *Collected Poems*, (ed.) T. Hughes (London: Faber, 1981).

Poe, E. A., 'The Purloined Letter', *The Purloined Poe: Lacan, Derrida & Psychoanalytic Reading*, (ed.) J. P. Muller and W. J. Richardson (Baltimore: Johns Hopkins University Press, 1988), pp. 6–27.

Politi, J., '"Is This the Love", or, The Origins of *Logomachia*', *Literature and Theology*, 9.2 (June 1995), 135–52.

——, 'The Lover of his M(other)land', Trans. J. Politi, Σημείο, 1 (1992), 161–71.

Praz, M., 'Introductory Essay', *Three Gothic Novels*, (ed.) P. Fairclough (Harmondsworth, Middlesex: Penguin, 1987), pp. 7–34.

Punter, D., *The Literature of Terror: A History of Gothic Fictions from 1765 to the Present Day* (London: Longman, 1980).

Ragland, E., *Essays on the Pleasures of Death: From Freud to Lacan* (New York: Routledge, 1995).

Ragland-Sullivan, E., 'The Sexual Masquerade: A Lacanian Theory of Sexual Difference', in *Lacan and the Subject of Language*, (ed.) E. Ragland-Sullivan and M. Bracher (New York: Routledge, 1991), pp. 49–80.

Rank, O., *The Double: A Psychoanalytic Study*, (trans.) H. Tucker, Jr (New York: New American Library, 1979).

Read, H. (ed.). *Surrealism* (London: Faber & Faber, 1936).

Rimmon-Kenan, S. (ed.), *Discourse in Psychoanalysis and Literature* (London: Methuen, 1987).

Riviere, J., 'Womanliness as a Masquerade', in *Formations of Fantasy*, (ed.) V. Burgin, J. Donald and C. Kaplan (London: Routledge, 1986), pp. 35–44.

Roe, S., *Writing and Gender: Virginia Woolf's Writing Practice* (Hemel Hempstead, Hertfordshire: Harvester Wheatsheaf, 1990).

Rose, J., *The Haunting of Sylvia Plath* (London: Virago, 1996).

——, 'Introduction II', *Feminine Sexuality: Jacques Lacan and the école freudienne* (ed.) J. Mitchell and J. Rose, (trans.) J. Rose (Houndmills, Basingstoke: Macmillan, 1982), pp. 27–57.

——, *Sexuality in the Field of Vision* (London: Verso, 1986).

Roudinesco, E., *Jacques Lacan: An Outline of a Life and a History of a System of Thought*, (trans.) B. Bray (Cambridge: Polity Press, 1999).

Schafer, R., 'Narration in the Psychoanalytic Dialogue', *Critical Inquiry*, 7.1 (Autimn 1980), 29–53.

Schaffer, T., '"A Wilde Desire Took Me": The Homoerotic History of *Dracula*', *English Literary History*, 61.2 (Summer 1994), 381–425.

Schwartz, R., 'Through the Optic Glass: Voyeurism and *Paradise Lost*', in *Desire in the Renaissance: Psychoanalysis and Literature*, (ed.) V. Finucci and R. Schwartz (Princeton, N.J.: Princeton University Press, 1994), pp. 146–66.

Sedgwick, E. K., *The Coherence of Gothic Conventions* (New York: Methuen, 1986).

——, *Epistemology of the Closet* (New York: Harvester, 1991).

——, *Tendencies* (London: Routedge, 1994).

Segal, H., *Klein* (London: Karnac, 1991).

Segal, J., *Melanie Klein* (London: Sage, 1992).

Shakespeare, W., *The Tragedy of Hamlet, Prince of Denmark*, (ed.) E. Hubler (New York: New American Library, 1963).

——, *The Tragedy of Othello: The Moor of Venice*, (ed.) A. Kernan (New York: New American Library, 1963).

Shelley, P. B., 'A Defense of Poetry', *Selected Poetry*, (ed.) H. Bloom (New York: New American Library, 1966), pp. 415–48.

Showalter, E., *The Female Malady: Women, Madness, and English Culture, 1830–1980* (London: Virago, 1987).

——, *Hystories: Hysterical Epidemics and Modern Culture* (London: Picador, 1997).

——, 'Representing Ophelia: Women, Madness, and the Responsibilities of Feminist Criticism', in *Shakespeare and the Question of Theory*, (ed.) P. Parker and G. Hartman (New York: Methuen, 1985), pp. 77–94.

Simon, B., 'The Imaginary Twins: The Case of Beckett and Bion', *The International Review of Psycho-Analysis*, 15.3 (1988) 331–52.

Sophocles. *The Theban Plays*, (trans.) E. E. Watling (Harmondsworth, Middlesex: Penguin, 1979).

Spence, D. P. *Narrative Truth and Historical Truth: Meaning and Interpretation in Psychoanalysis* (New York: Norton, 1982).

Spivak, G. C., 'Displacement and the Discourse of Woman', in *Displacement: Derrida and After*, (ed.) M. Krupnick (Bloomington: Indiana University Press, 1983), pp. 169–95.

Sprengnether, M., 'Enforcing Oedipus: Freud and Dora', in *In Dora's Case: Freud – Hysteria – Feminism*, (ed.) C. Bernheimer and C. Kahane (London: Virago, 1985), pp. 254–75.

——, 'Mourning Freud', in *Psychoanalysis in Contexts: Paths between Theory and Modern Culture*, (ed.) A. Elliott and S. Frosh (London: Routledge, 1995), pp. 142–65.

Stoker, B., *Dracula* (Harmondsworth, Middlesex: Penguin, 1993).

Strindberg, A., *The Father, Miss Julie and the Ghost Sonata*, (trans.) M. Meyer (London: Methuen, 1976).

Strong, B. E., 'Foucault, Freud, and French Feminism: Theorizing Hysteria as Theorizing the Feminine', *Literature and Psychology*, 35.4 (1989), 10–26.

Sussman, H., 'Psychoanalysis Modern and Post-Modern', in *Psychoanalysis and . . .*, (ed.) R. Feldstein and H. Sussman (New York: Routledge, 1990), pp. 129–50.

Swann, C., 'Déjà Vu: Déjà Lu: ' "The Lifted Veil" as an Experiment in Art', *Literature and History*, 5.1 (Spring 1979), 40–57.

Swann, K., 'Literary Gentlemen and Lovely Ladies: The Debate on the Character of *Christabel*', in *Coleridge, Keats and Shelley*, (ed.) P. J. Kitson (Houndmills, Basingstoke: Macmillan, 1996), pp. 74–91.

Swift, J., *Gulliver's Travels* (London: Dent, 1965).

Symington, J. and N., *The Clinical Thinking of Wilfred Bion* (London: Routledge, 1996).

Todorov, T., *The Fantastic: A Structural Approach to a Literary Genre*, (trans.) R. Howard (Ithaca: Cornell University Press, 1975).

Tomiche, A., 'Rephrasing the Freudian Unconscious: Lyotard's Affect-Phrase', *Diacritics*, 24.1 (Spring 1994), 43–62.

Torok, M., 'The Meaning of "Penis Envy" in Women', in *The Shell and the Kernel: Renewals of Psychoanalysis*, N. Abraham and M. Torok, (trans.) N. T. Rand (Chicago: University of Chicago Press, 1994), pp. 41–73.

Verhaeghe, P., *Does the Woman Exist?: From Freud's Hysteric to Lacan's Feminine*, (trans.) M. du Ry (London: Rebus, 1997).

Walcott, D., *Omeros* (London: Faber & Faber, 1990).

Weiskel, T., *The Romantic Sublime: Studies in the Structure and Psychology of Transcendence* (Baltimore: Johns Hopkins University Press, 1976).

Willis, J. H. *Leonard and Virginia Woolf as Publishers: The Hogarth Press, 1917–41* (Charlottesville: University Press of Virginia, 1992).

Woolf, V., 'Freudian Fiction', *Contemporary Writers* (London: Hogarth Press, 1965), pp. 152–54.

——, 'Mr. Bennett and Mrs Brown', *The Captain's Death Bed and Other Essays* (London: Hogarth Press, 1950), pp. 90–111.

——, *Orlando: A Biography* (Harmondsworth, Middlesex: Penguin, 1974).

——, *Roger Fry: A Biography* (London: Hogarth Press, 1940).

——, *A Room of One's Own* (London: Granada, 1977).

Wright, E., *Psychoanalytic Criticism: Theory in Practice* (London: Methuen, 1984).

——, 'The Reader in Analysis', in *Psychoanalysis and Cultural Theory: Thresholds*, (ed.) J. Donald (Houndmills, Basingstoke: Macmillan, 1991), pp. 158–68.

——, 'The Uncanny and Surrealism', in *Modernism and the European Unconscious*, (ed.) P. Collier and J. Davies (Cambridge: Polity Press, 1990), pp. 265–82.

Young, R., 'Psychoanalytic Criticism: Has it Got Beyond a Joke?', *Paragraph*, 4 (Oct. 1984), 87–114.

Žižek, S., *Looking Awry: An Introduction to Jacques Lacan through Popular Culture* (Cambridge, Mass.: MIT Press, 1995).

——, *The Plague of Fantasies* (London: Verso, 1997).

Index

Abel, Elizabeth   237n9, 237n10
abjection   xi, xiii, 53–81, 103,
   231n14
Abraham, Karl   62, 71, 167, 205
   'Manifestations of the Female
      Castration Complex'   167
Abraham, Nicolas   xi, xii, 124–6,
   128, 233n15, 233n16, 233n17,
   233n18
   anasemia   xi, 119–20, 127–8
   cryptonymy   233n16, 233n17
   and Derrida   119–20, 122, 125–8,
      189, 233n18
   'Notes on the Phantom'   124–8
Adams, Parveen   166
Adorno, Theodor   27
Ahmad, Aijaz   233n20
Alexander the Great   21
Allen, Woody   164
anal   70, 73–80, 204–5, 207, 229n18
anasemia   xi, 119–20, 127–8
Anna O. (Bertha Pappenheim)   135–9,
   146, 152, 162
anti-Oedipus   84, 230n6
Anzieu, Didier   227n3
aphanisis   10, 51, 128
Arata, Stephen D.   202
Aristotle   91, 95, 100, 110
Até   92–3
Auden, W. H.   xiii, 24–8
   'As I Walked Out One
      Evening'   25–8
   'Psychology and Art
      Today'   24–5
Auerbach, Nina   209
automatic writing   23–5

Bair, Deirdre   70, 228n13, 228n14
Baker, Phil   73, 229n16
Bakhtin, Mikhail   5, 75, 229n18

Balzac, Honoré de   237n13
Barthes, Roland   xiii, 7–10, 66–7,
   83–4
   atopia   120
   death of the author   66–7, 84
   doxa (and para-dox)   9–10
   image   7–10
   textual pleasure   xi, 9–10, 83
Barthes, Roland: **Works**
   'The Death of the Author'   84
   The Pleasure of the Text   83
   *Roland Barthes by Roland
      Barthes*   7–10, 19
   S/Z   147
Bataille, Georges   57, 63
Baudrillard, Jean   142, 196–8
Bauer, Ida, *see* Dora
Beauvoir, Simone de, *The Second
   Sex*   175
Beckett, Samuel   xiii, 1, 9, 25,
   57–61, 69, 70, 81, 227n2, 227n3,
   228n13, 228n14
   and abjection   57–80
   anal   70, 73–80
   art   70, 80
   and Bion   57–8, 69–70, 227n3,
      228n11
   characters   65–70, 74–5, 76, 81,
      228n9, 229n20
   desire (*jouissance*)   60, 79
   fictional narrator   65–6
   food   75–7, 229n16
   and Freud   1, 57–8
   language (representation,
      speech)   58, 65–70, 78, 227n4
   limbo   79–81, 230n22
   mother (maternal
      function)   61–81, 228n13,
      229n16, 229n20
   novelistic conventions   65, 227n5

oral   68, 70, 72–7
psychoanalysis   57–8, 227n2,
    227n3
pun   1, 73–4
the sacred   59–60
subject   65–8, 228n9
womb fixation   70, 77, 80–1,
    228n14
Beckett, Samuel: **Works**
'The End'   81
Endgame   70
Footfalls   81
From an Abandoned Work   73,
    229n16
How it Is   79, 229n20
Krapp's Last Tape   80, 229n19
Murphy   1
Not-I   64, 68, 72, 81, 228n8
Play   70, 228n10
Rockaby   81
Trilogy (*Molloy, Malone Dies, The
    Unnamable*)   xiii, 58–80
Waiting for Godot   60
Bell, Clive   180
Benedikt, Meriz   234n5
Benjamin, Walter   196, 218, 240n13
Bennett, Arnold   180, 237n13
Bergson, Henri   2
Bernays, Martha   234n2
Bernheimer, Charles   240n17
Bettelheim, Bruno   35–6
Bhabha, Homi   45
Bion, Wilfred   xii, 57–8, 69–70, 71,
    228n12, 228n13, 228n14, 229n15
and Beckett   57–8, 69–70, 227n3,
    228n11
container/contained   69–70,
    228n12
and Kristeva   229n15
language   70, 228n12
Second Thoughts   70
bisexuality   88, 133, 145–6, 155–7,
    165–6, 172, 175, 193–4, 204; *see
    also* homosexuality
Blackwood, John   158
Blanchot, Maurice   198, 215
Bloom, Harold   238n3
Bloomsbury   179, 237n9

Bonaparte, Marie   49
Borch-Jacobsen, Mikkel   5, 30, 137
Bowie, Malcolm   90
Bowra, C.M.   231n13
Bradbrook, M.C.   239n10
breast   5, 31, 33–4, 41, 52, 55, 71,
    171, 205, 225–6n4; *see also*
    Klein, object
Brecht, Bertolt   8
Breton, André   22–4, 28–9,
    225n20
Breuer, Josef   134, 135–8, 139, 141,
    146, 152
British Society for the Study of Sex
    Psychology   237n11
Britzolakis, Christina   218, 240n13
Bronfen, Elisabeth   133
Brontë, Charlotte   36, 117, 151,
    233n14
Brontë, Emily, *Wuthering
    Heights*   121
Brooks, Peter   122, 208
*Psychoanalysis and
    Storytelling*   144, 147, 223n2
Reading for the Plot   147–8
Brunswick, Ruth Mack   169
Bryden, Mary   61, 81
Butler, Judith   174–5, 188–9, 194
Gender Trouble   188
Butler, Samuel, *The Way of All
    Flesh*   38
Byron, George Gordon   111, 113

cannibalism   35, 70–2, 205, 207; *see
    also* oral
Cape, Jonathan   179
Carroll, Lewis   4, 176–7, 191
Through the Looking-Glass   177,
    185, 191
Carter, Angela   240n13
The Bloody Chamber   189
literary style   238n18
Love   218
Nights at the Circus   189
'Reflections'   189–92
case history   2, 135–40, 143–50,
    159–62, 164, 166
Castoriadis, Cornelius   19

castration 7, 24, 47–52, 55, 59, 60, 63, 88, 89, 90, 103, 104–8, 120, 145, 156–9, 167–71, 216, 222, 226n9, 227n12, 235n13; *see also* Freud, Kristeva, Lacan
catharsis 91, 93–4, 138, 141, 150
Céline, Louis-Ferdinand 77, 78
Chaplin, Charlie 74
Charcot, Jean-Martin 135, 139–40, 141, 156, 162, 206, 234n3, 236n1, 239n6
Chase, Cynthia 97, 230n5
Chasseguet-Smirgel, Janine 216, 231n9, 238n4, 240n14
Chodorow, Nancy 30, 194
Cinthio, *Hecatomithi* 101
Cixous, Hélène 104, 194
  castration 104, 108
  'Fiction and its Phantoms' 104, 118, 232n1
  hysteria 159–60, 236n17
  La Jeune Née (*The Newly-Born Woman*) 156, 160, 236n17
  Portrait de Dora 159–60
  uncanny 104
Clément, Catherine 236n17
Cohn, Ruby 230n22
Coleridge, Samuel Taylor 110–11, 232n7
  Biographia Literaria 110, 112
  'Christabel' 110–17, 232n6, 232n8, 232n10
  imagination 232n9
  Lyrical Ballads 111, 232n6
  'The Rime of the Ancient Mariner' 111
  unconscious xi, 20, 110–11
Collége de Sociologie 223n5
Collins, Wilkie 233n14
condensation 22, 26, 89, 150
conscious mind 3–4, 24–8, 32, 138, 216
Controversial Discussions 193, 236n5
Copjec, Joan 18
Coppola, Francis Ford 201
counter-transference, *see* transference

Critchley, Simon 233n20
cryptonymy 233n16, 233n17
cultural theory xi, 2, 19, 20, 41, 54, 104, 163, 171, 194, 215

Dali, Salvador 24, 26, 161, 162
Darwin, Charles, *Origin of Species* 1, 98, 199
David-Ménard, Monique 149, 234n2
death drive xi, 10, 83, 92, 100–1, 103, 105, 119, 157, 196–222, 238n2, 238n3
  and *Dracula* xiii, 197, 200–10
  Freud on 41, 83, 92, 105, 119, 198–203, 222, 238n2, 238n3
  Klein on 34
  Lacan on 92, 101, 105, 210–12, 215
deconstruction x, 20, 51–2, 236n3
defence mechanisms xii, 20, 34–5, 41, 61, 67, 138, 141–2, 145–6, 154–6, 160, 206, 208, 226n5, 226n7, 231n9, 232n3, 235n10, 235n11, 240n12; *see also* denial, repression, reversal, splitting
deferred action (*Nachträlichkeit*) 45, 47, 102, 104–5, 119, 140–2, 209
Defoe, Daniel, *Robinson Crusoe* 45
Delacroix, Henri, *Langage et pensée* 223n2
Deleuze, Gilles 216, 217, 230n6
denial (as defence) xii, 61, 67, 145–6, 226n7, 232n3, 235n10, 235n11
Derrida, Jacques xiii, 233n20
  anachrony 119–20, 122, 125–6
  castration 104–5, 227n12
  deconstruction 51–2, 104–5, 118–20, 127–8
  différance 104, 119
  dissemination 52, 104, 227n12
  and Freud 104, 119
  Hamlet 119
  and Lacan 51–2
  Poe's 'Purloined Letter' 49–52

psychic writing xi
and Abraham and
    Torok 119–20, 122, 125–8,
    189, 233n18
spectre 119–26, 189
Derrida, Jacques: **Works**
Dissemination 52, 189, 227n12
'Le facteur de la Vérité' 51–2,
    226n11
'Foreword: *Fors*: The Anglish
    Words of Nicolas Abraham
    and Maria Torok' 125–8,
    233n18
Specters of Marx 118–28
Writing and Difference 119
Descartes, René 3–4
desire xi, xii, 5, 6, 9–19, 14, 18, 30,
    32, 45, 47–52, 59, 60, 62–3, 79,
    82–102, 103, 136, 138, 141,
    147–51, 156, 159, 162, 168,
    173–6, 227n14, 230n1, 231n14,
    235n12; *see also* Freud, Lacan
impossible object of 14, 48, 62–3,
    82–3, 90–1, 100, 156, 162
as lack/loss xii, 6, 18, 30, 45,
    47–52, 83–4, 89–91, 97,
    99–101, 148–50, 159, 173–4,
    227n14
of/for the o/Other xii, 5, 6, 14,
    32, 83–4, 90–1, 148, 162
and signifier xii, 5, 9–10, 49–52,
    82, 90–1, 94, 97, 99–100,
    230n1
Deutsch, Helene 99, 169–71, 173,
    236n4
dialectic 6, 14–16, 25–6, 148,
    223–4n8, 234n21
Dickens, Charles 117–18, 151
Dombey and Son 38
disavowal 156–7, 216
discourse analysis 7
displacement 22, 51, 89, 136, 146,
    150, 217, 240n13
Dolar, Mladen 16, 110
Dora (Ida Bauer) x, 3, 142–8; *see
    also* Freud **Works**, 'Fragment of
    an Analysis of a Case of
    Hysteria'

Dostoevsky, Fyodor
    Mikhailovich 118
double 12, 106–7, 109–18, 151,
    233n11
Douka-Kabitoglou, E. 232n7
dreams 19–22, 25–6, 28, 45, 85,
    105, 106, 115, 142, 225n18,
    226n10, 231n12, 233n21
dream-work 19–22, 26
drive (instinct) xi, 34, 41, 82, 85,
    103, 105, 130, 199, 216, 230n2,
    238n2, 238n3; *see also* death
    drive
Driver, Tom 70
Duras, Marguerite 57
Duthuit, Georges 227n4

Eagleton, Terry 157
Easthope, Antony 226n10
eating disorders 134
ego psychology 7, 10
Electra complex 165, 221
Eliot, George (Marian Evans) 151,
    152
The Lifted Veil 151–9, 164,
    235n14, 236n16
The Mill on the Floss 38
Silas Marner 155
Eliot, T. S.
'Gerontion' 224n10
'Hamlet' 87
The Waste Land 79
Ellenberger, Henri 137
Ellmann, Maud 79
Empedocles 199
Evans, Dylan 230n4
exhibitionism 224n12
existentialism 67

fairy tales 35–6
father (paternal function) 7, 24, 31,
    33, 36, 37–41, 43, 45–7, 49, 55,
    59, 63, 64, 90, 96–9, 107–8, 119,
    140–2, 164–6, 168, 170, 171, 193,
    208–10, 217, 221–2, 225–6n4,
    229n21, 237n10; *see also* Freud,
    Klein, Kristeva and Lacan
Fechner, Gustav 233n21

Felman, Shoshana xiii, 49, 177,
223n2, 236n3
'Beyond Oedipus' 230n8
'Turning the Screw of
Interpretation' 147
femininity 31–2, 40–1, 86–9, 131–2,
137, 155–6, 162–95, 236n7,
238n20
feminism 33, 40, 47–8, 87–8, 89, 99,
102, 131–2, 136–7, 155, 161, 164,
165–8, 170, 174, 185, 189, 194,
218, 231n16
Ferenczi, Sandor, 'Introjection and
Transference' 225n3
Ferrell, Robyn 230n2
fetishism 83, 197, 215–22, 227n1,
239n11, 240n12, 240n13,
240n14, 240n17
Fineman, Joel 101, 231n15
Flanders, Sara 225n18
Fliess, Wilhelm 84, 142, 143, 145,
156, 161, 233n21, 234n6
Forrester, John 211
Forster, E. M. 179
Maurice 179
fort-da game 41, 52, 57, 100
Foucault, Michel 134, 188
The History of Sexuality 188
free association xii, 20–1, 23, 24,
43, 138, 141, 142, 144, 150,
225n18
Freud, Anna 154–5
Freud, Sigmund xiii, 1, 2, 31–3, 83,
84, 101–2, 105, 130, 133, 137–8,
139, 142, 145, 161, 165, 178, 216,
234n3, 237n10
case histories 135–40, 143–50,
160, 236n1
castration 47–8, 88, 89, 105–8,
145, 156–7, 167–71, 216,
226n9
and Charcot 135, 139–40, 141,
156, 234n3
creative writing 19
day-dreams 19, 28
death drive 41, 83, 92, 105, 119,
198–203, 222, 238n2, 238n3
desire 82–3

double 106–7
dreams 19–24, 26, 28, 85, 105,
106, 142, 225n18, 226n10,
233n21
dream-work 19–22, 26
drive (instinct) 41, 82, 85, 199,
238n2, 238n3
ego xi, 19, 37, 40–2, 47, 62, 83,
109, 156, 224n16, 226n5
father 31, 37–41, 98–9, 107–8,
119, 140–2, 164, 208–10
fetishism 83, 216–8, 220, 240n12,
240n13
fort-da game 41, 52, 57, 100
free association 20–1, 23, 24, 138,
141, 142, 225n18
group psychology 40
hysteria 2, 3, 132–48, 155–7,
159–62, 164, 235n8, 235n12,
236n1
id xi, 37, 41, 224n16, 226n5
jokes 21
language x, 2, 3
as literary critic x, xiii, 30, 84–5,
238n3
literary style of x, 139–40, 143–4
and literary theory xii
melancholia 42, 45, 62, 153
mother (maternal function) 5,
31–2, 41–3, 87, 107, 114, 142,
164, 166, 168–70, 218
mourning 42–7, 56, 62, 98, 102,
209
object 30–2, 41, 47, 59, 82, 103,
164–5, 225n2, 228n7
Oedipus complex 59, 84–6, 90,
91, 95, 98, 101–2, 107, 142,
164–5
'other scene' 130, 233n21
penis envy 47–8, 166–8, 226n9
phallic 86, 88–9, 105, 145, 156
pleasure principle 83, 199, 202
reality 83
religion 37, 98, 129, 209–10
repetition compulsion 45, 100,
105–6, 119, 198–9, 202–4, 208,
209, 214, 217
secondary revision 20, 23

seduction theory 140–2, 161–2, 234n6, 235n7
self-analysis 84
sexuality 31–2, 47, 87–9, 140–2, 164–70
subject 5, 83
super-ego 37–41, 168, 224n16, 226n8
taboo 98, 208
thing-presentation vs. word-presentation 19, 231n11
totem 98, 208–10, 222
transference 106, 138, 141, 142, 146–50, 159, 161, 199
uncanny xi, 103–9, 114, 119, 120, 125, 129–30
unconscious xi, 3, 19–21, 28, 37, 42, 86, 142, 222, 224n16, 230n3
woman 133, 156, 164–70, 176, 177, 183–4, 209; *see also* mother
Freud, Sigmund: **Works**
'Analysis of a Phobia in a Five-Year-Old Boy "Little Hans"' 107, 125, 164, 233n16
'Anxiety and Instinctual Life' 238n2
'Beyond the Pleasure Principle' 41, 42, 83, 105, 106, 198–9, 238n1
Civilization and its Discontents 37, 211
'The Dissolution of the Oedipus Complex' 86
The Ego and the Id 37, 87, 178, 226n8
'Femininity' 165, 183–4
'Fragment of an Analysis of a Case of Hysteria ("Dora")' 143–8, 235n8, 235n9, 235n11
'From the History of an Infantile Neurosis (The "Wolf Man")' x, 88, 125, 158, 233n16
The Future of an Illusion 129, 211

'Hysterical Phantasies and their Relation to Bisexuality' 155
'Identification' 31
'The Infantile Genital Organization' 88–9
'Instincts and their Vicissitudes' 82, 224n12
The Interpretation of Dreams 20, 85, 105, 138, 142, 233n21
Introductory Lectures 141–2
'Leonardo da Vinci and a Memory of his Childhood' 32, 164
Moses and Monotheism 31, 161
'Mourning and Melancholia' 41–2, 125, 153, 228n7
New Introductory Lectures on Psychoanalysis 39, 226n8
'On the History of the Psychoanalytic Movement' 139–40
Psychopathology of Everyday Life 178
'The Question of Lay Analysis' 3
'Remembering, Repeating and Working Through' 138
'Splitting of the Ego in the Process of Defence' 240n12
(and Josef Breuer), *Studies on Hysteria* 135–7, 147
'The Theme of the Three Caskets' 236n15
Three Essays on the Theory of Sexuality 164–5
Totem and Taboo xiv, 31, 86, 98
'The "Uncanny"' 47, 52, 103, 120, 232n2, 233n3
'The Unconscious' 230n2, 231n11
Fry, Roger 186–7
Fukuyama, Francis 197

Gallop, Jane 7, 47–8
Gascoyne, David 25
Gaskell, Elizabeth 151
'The Old Nurse's Story' 121–3, 124, 125
Gay, Peter 223n3

gaze 8, 11–18, 224n12, 227n13
gender 47–8, 81, 87–9, 131–3,
  156–7, 160, 163–95
  and object relations 31, 33, 80–1,
    87–8, 110, 132–3, 163–75, 216,
    220
Gestalt 14
ghost (phantom) 90, 111–13,
  118–28, 130, 212
Gide, André, *Journals* 198
Gilbert, Sandra 117
Glover, Edward 34, 216–17
Gosse, Edmund, *Father and Son* 38
Gothic (fantasy) writing 105,
  106–28, 151–3, 159, 185, 192,
  200, 206, 233n13, 233n14,
  238n18
Goux, Jean-Jacques 87
Granoff, Vladimir 217
Gray, Beryl 235n14
'great debate' (on female sexuality)
  168–70, 175, 178, 183
Green, André xii, 91, 93
Guattari, Félix 230n6
Gubar, Susan 117

Hall, Radclyffe, *The Well of
  Loneliness* 179
hamartia 91–2, 95–6
Hansen, Carl 234n5
Hardy, Thomas, *Tess of the
  d'Urbervilles* 38
Harris, Frank 230n7
Harrison, Wendy Cealey 141,
  230–1n9
Hartley, David 110
haunting (spectrality) 103, 118–28
Hazlitt, William 113
Heaney, Seamus 221
Heath, Stephen 174
Hegel, Georg W. F. 2, 6, 22, 83, 93,
  198, 223n6
Heidegger, Martin 2, 94
Hertz, Neil 106, 107–8
  'Dora's Secrets, Freud's
    Techniques' 147
Hindle, Maurice 239n6
Hirschmüller, Albrecht 137

Hitchcock, Alfred 17
Hitler, Adolf 40, 90
Hoffmann, E. T. A., 'The
  Sandman' xi, xiii, 106–9,
  111–13, 151, 232n4, 232n5
Hogarth Press 178
Holland, Norman 121
Homer 42–7
homoerotic 209–10, 216
homosexuality 32, 114, 157, 164,
  166, 172, 175, 179, 188, 201–2,
  209–10, 216, 236n1, 237n11; *see
  also* bisexuality
Horney, Karen 99, 169–71, 173
  'The Flight from
    Womanhood' 169
House, Humphrey 232n10
hubris 95
Hughes, Ted 222, 240n15
  Birthday Letters 240n15
Hunter, Dianne 137
Husserl, Edmund 2
hypermnesia 137
hypnosis (mesmerism) 131, 135,
  137–8, 141, 152, 234n5
hysteria 85, 103, 131–64, 233n17;
  see also Freud
  and bisexuality 145–6, 155–6,
    165–6
  and feminism 132, 145, 159–64,
    234n2, 235n13, 236n17
  and gender 131–4, 145–6, 155–6,
    163–4, 236n1
  interpretability of 132–4, 163–4
  and narrative 143–7
  Oedipal origin of 133, 144
  oscillation 131–3, 159
  psyche and soma
    (conversion) 132–6, 149–51,
    234n4
  and reminiscence/
    memory 137–43, 147, 153–4,
    156

Ibsen, Henrik 132, 144
  The Doll's House 132
id xi, 37, 41, 224n16, 226n5
idealization 41, 206, 226n7, 238n4

identification 6–8, 10, 12, 14, 30–2, 37, 40, 42, 47, 62, 69, 81, 94, 160, 164, 169–70, 175, 217, 221, 224n8, 225–6n4, 228n7
image 6–18, 20, 22–8, 33, 36, 45, 48, 109, 174, 188, 192, 195, 196–7, 205, 214, 217
image repertoire 7–10
Imaginary 7, 10–18, 30, 45, 46, 55, 90, 91, 94–9, 217, 227n13; *see also* mirror stage
incest 37, 49, 59, 85–6, 88, 93, 95, 120, 208, 237n11
incorporation 125–6, 129
International Journal of Psycho-Analysis 169, 171, 178
International Psycho-Analytic Library Series 178
intertextuality xiv, 58
introjection 5, 32–4, 37, 39, 62, 71, 103, 116, 125, 171, 210, 225n3, 225–6n4
Irigaray, Luce 99, 108, 175–8, 185–6, 191–2, 194
  An Ethics of Sexual Difference 236n3
  'The Looking Glass, from the Other Side' 176–7, 180, 190–2
  Speculum of the Other Woman 175
  This Sex Which is Not One 175–7, 185–6
Irving, Henry 239n6
Isaacs, Susan 226n5
Ishiguro, Kazuo xiii, 39
  The Remains of the Day 38–41

Jackson, Rosemary 126
Jacobus, Mary 48, 152, 157, 158–9, 231n16
Jakobson, Roman 225n19
James, Henry 151
  The Sacred Fount 144
Jameson, Fredric 127
Janet, Pierre 156
Jaspers, Karl 2
Jentsch, Ernst 107, 232n3

Johnson, Barbara 49, 51–2, 236n3
Johnson, S.F. 239n10
Johnson, Terry, *Hysteria* 142, 160–3
Jones, Ernest 171, 173
  aphanisis 10
  'Early Development of Female Sexuality' 171
  Hamlet and Oedipus xii, 86, 230n7
  On the Nightmare 203
Jonson, Ben 231n15
Jordan, Elaine 238n18
jouissance 59, 62–3, 72, 77, 79, 83–4, 110, 129, 149, 150, 230n4, 231n14; *see also* desire
Joyce, James 25, 57, 65, 73–4
  Finnegans Wake 26
  Ulysses 43, 73–4
Jung, Carl Gustav 19–20, 30, 165, 221
  Collective Unconscious xi
  'Psychopathology and Creativity' 228n14

Kafka, Franz 198
Kant, Immanuel 92, 94, 231n11
Klein, Melanie xii, xiii, 5, 30, 32–3, 70, 171, 237n10
  aggression (sadism) 33–6, 56, 69, 71, 171–2, 205
  and Bion 69
  breast (good and bad) 33–4, 41, 71, 171, 205, 225–6n4
  creativity 56
  death drive 34
  depressive position 34–5, 69, 171, 226n7
  ego 32–5, 226n7
  father 33, 36, 171, 225–6n4
  and Freud 71, 225n2
  idealization 41, 206, 226n7
  mother (maternal function) 5, 29, 31–6, 71, 87, 99, 170–1, 194, 205, 237n10
  mourning 62
  object 5, 32–53, 59, 206, 225n2, 225–6n4, 226n5, 226n7

Klein, Melanie (*cont.*)
  oral 71, 171, 205, 225–6n4
  paranoid–schizoid position 34–5,
    69, 171
  (pre-)Oedipal 33, 36, 87, 171, 194
  projective identification 69
  and Riviere 171
  unconscious xi
Klein, Melanie: **Works**
  'The Early Stages of the Oedipus
    Conflict' 171
  'Mourning and its Relation to
    Manic-Depressive
    States' 226n7
  'Notes on Some Schizoid
    Mechanisms' 34
  'The Oedipus Complex in the
    Light of Early
    Anxieties' 225–6n4
Knole 179–80
Knowlson, James 227n2, 228n13,
    228n14
Kofman, Pariah 168
Kojéve, Alexandre 6, 223n6
Kowsar, M. 92
Krafft-Ebing, Richard von,
    Psychopathia Sexualis 204
Kristeva, Julia xii, xiii, 54–81, 194
  abjection 53, 62–81, 231n14
  avant-garde writing 57
  and Beckett 57–81
  castration 48, 55, 59, 60, 63, 167
  chora 56, 194
  the cultural and the psychic xiv,
    227n6
  dialogic 5
  father (paternal function) 55, 59,
    64, 229n21
  and Freud xiv, 48, 53, 54, 56, 130
  Helene Deutsch 236n4
  intertextuality xiv
  jouissance (desire) 59, 62–3, 83,
    231n14
  and Klein 53, 54–5, 70, 170,
    229n15
  and Lacan 53, 54, 55, 81, 194,
    231n14

language (discourse, signifier,
    speech) 55–6, 58, 64, 72, 78,
    130, 149–50, 194, 195
love 149–50
melancholia 60, 62
mother (maternal function) 53,
    55–6, 59–81, 99, 194–5, 227n6
mourning 55–7, 62, 227n1
object (relations) 53–81, 170,
    229n15
Oedipus at Colonus 231n14
Oedipus complex 55
oral 63–4, 70–3, 75
other/Other 55, 59, 62, 75, 83,
    129–30, 149–50
the sacred 59–60, 63–4
semiotic 56, 194, 195
subject 54, 68
Symbolic order xiv, 55, 68, 149,
    195, 229n21, 231n14
theory of writing 55–7, 227n1
transference 130, 149–50
unconscious 55
unnamable 56–8, 61
woman 81, 99, 170, 194, 227n6,
    229n21, 236n4; *see also*
    mother
Kristeva, Julia: **Works**
  Black Sun 54, 56, 57
  Desire in Language 57
  'On the Melancholic
    Imaginary' 227n1
  Powers of Horror xiv, 54–68,
    70–80
  *Revolution in Poetic
    Language* 56, 57
  Strangers to Ourselves 129–30
  Tales of Love 53, 54, 149–50
  'Woman's Time' 48, 194
Kyd, Thomas. *The Spanish
    Tragedy* 212–15, 222, 239n8,
    239n9, 239n10

Lacan, Jacques xii, xiii, 6, 15, 22–4,
    28, 30, 147, 175, 193, 223n1,
    225n19
  Antigone 91–7, 231n14

castration 7, 24, 47–52, 90, 104–5, 168
and cultural theory 2
death drive 92, 101, 105, 210–12, 215
desire 5, 14, 18, 30, 32, 48–52, 82–102, 136, 138, 147–51, 159, 168, 173, 235n12
dialectic 6, 15–16, 25–6, 148, 223–4n8, 234n21
Dora case 148–51
dream-representation 21–2, 231n12
ego vs subject 17, 10–11, 14–15, 18, 94
entropy 211–12
extimacy 128
Father (law) 7, 24, 46, 49, 90, 168, 217
fetishism 217
Freudian Thing 93–4, 96, 99, 231n11
gaze 15–18, 227n13
Hamlet 89–90
Imaginary 7, 10–18, 30, 90, 91, 94–9, 217, 227n13; *see also* mirror stage
jouissance 83, 110, 149, 150, 230n4
and Klein 89
language (discourse, signification, speech) 2–7, 10–11, 21–4, 49–52, 82, 94, 99, 128, 138, 148–51, 174, 210–12, 225n19, 225n20, 234n21, 234n4, 235n12
Shakespeare's Lear 96
as literary critic 49–52, 89–90, 102
literary style of 4, 30, 94, 231n12
méconnaissance
(misrecognition) 3, 6, 8, 19, 45, 96, 99, 109
mirror stage 6–18, 30, 94, 109, 210, 223–4n8; *see also* **Works**. 'The Mirror Stage'
mother (as phallus) xii, 10, 50–2, 89–90, 94, 99, 168, 173–4

mourning 89–90, 96
Name-of-the Father 46, 90, 98, 210
object 82–3, 90, 94, 151, 227n13, 227n14
objet a 16–18, 52, 83, 99, 101, 212, 227n14
Oedipus at Colonus 91, 97, 230n8
Oedipus complex 7, 84, 88–94, 101, 102, 168, 217, 230n8
Other 5–7, 9, 12, 84, 96, 128, 148, 162, 173, 234n21
paranoia 2, 6, 18, 24–5
phallus 48–52, 88–90, 99, 172–3, 193, 227n13, 227n14, 236n7
psychoanalysis (role of) 7, 9, 89, 94, 96
Real 4, 57, 90, 91, 99–101, 105, 128, 212, 217
return to Freud 2, 20, 52, 82, 91, 95, 102, 193, 210, 211, 230n2, 231n11, 235n12
Sade 220
sexual difference 47–52, 173–4, 193; *see also* woman, mother
signifier and signified xii, 4, 9, 10, 23–4, 46–7, 49–52, 89–90, 99, 101, 128, 136, 173–4, 210–12, 215; *see also* language
sociology 5, 223n5
splitting 18, 91, 99, 100, 109
subject 2–5, 10–11, 18, 28, 30, 48–52, 89–90, 93, 99, 101, 128, 149, 211–12, 215, 227n14
super-ego 37–8
and surrealism 22–4, 28, 225n20
Symbolic xii, 6–7, 10–18, 48–52, 90, 91, 94–9, 128, 188, 193, 210–12, 217
tragedy 91–101
transference (and counter-transference) 148–51, 211, 234n21
unconscious xi, 3, 10, 21–2, 55, 93–4, 136, 148, 235n12
woman 50–1, 81, 148, 173–4, 193, 236n7, 238n19; *see also* mother

Lacan, Jacques: **Works**
  'The Agency of the Letter in the
    Unconscious or Reason Since
    Freud' 21–2, 225n20
  'Aggressivity in
    Psychoanalysis' 223–4n8
  'The Freudian Thing' 148–9
  'The Function and Field of
    Speech and Language in
    Psychoanalysis' ('The Rome
    Discourse') 212, 234n4
  'The Meaning [Signification] of the
    Phallus' 51, 89, 91, 173,
    236n6
  'The Mirror Stage' 3, 5, 6–10, 94,
    223n4, 224n11
  'Of the Gaze as *Objet Petit a*'
    15–18
  Seminars 49–52, 91, 94, 174,
    210–11, 230n8, 231n10
  'The Subversion of the
    Subject' 101
  La Princesse de Clèves 150–1
Lampl-de Groot, Jeanne 169
language (discourse, speech) *see*
  Freud, Kristeva, Lacan
Laplanche, J. 37, 119–20
Lautréamont, comte de 57
Lawrence, D. H. 65
lay analysis 3, 223n3
Lee, Hermione 179
LeFanu, Sheridan 121, 233n14
  'An Account of Some Strange
    Disturbances in Aungier
    Street' 121, 123–8, 233n19
  Carmilla 202
Lévi-Strauss, Claude 59
Leviticus 63–4
life drives xi; *see also* drives
Little Hans, *see* Freud, **Works**,
  'Analysis of a Phobia in a Five-
  Year-Old Boy'
Lodge, David 225n19
  Therapy 164

Macey, David 223n6
Mallarmé, Stéphane 57, 189

Marcus, Steven 144
Marsack, Robyn 219, 240n16
Marx, Karl 22, 119, 196, 216,
  217–18, 233n20, 240n13
masculinity 31–2, 40–1, 80, 87–9,
  108, 163–95, 208, 238n20
Masoch, *see* Sacher-Masoch,
  Leopold von
masochism 103, 170, 217
masquerade 103, 162–95, 236n7
maternal phallus 50–2, 71, 89–90,
  94, 99, 168, 173–4, 216, 222
matriarchy, *see* mother
matricide 73, 87
Maurier, George de, *Trilby* 202
McDougall, Joyce 166, 167
méconnaissance (misrecognition) 3,
  6, 8, 19, 45, 96, 99, 109
Mehlman, Jeffrey 119
Meisel, Perry 238n16
melancholia 42, 45, 60, 62, 153; *see*
  also Freud, Kristeva
memory 101–2, 137–43, 147, 152–4,
  156
Mesmer, Friedrich Anton 134–5
metamorphosis 115–16
metaphor 22–3, 28, 225n19
metonymy 22, 117, 225n19
Michelet, Jules 180
Miller, Jacques-Alain 128–9
Milton, John, *Paradise Lost* xiii,
  10–19, 223n7, 224n9, 224n10,
  224n13, 224n14, 224n15
mirror stage 6–18, 30, 94, 109, 192,
  210, 223–4n8; *see also* Lacan,
  Imaginary, **Works**, 'Mirror
  Stage'
Mitchell, Juliet 5, 33, 156, 157, 166,
  167–8, 170, 226n9
  The Longest Revolution 156
Modernism 65, 67, 80, 144, 198
Moi, Toril 229n21
mother (maternal function) xii, 5,
  10, 29, 30–6, 41–3, 45–7, 50–3,
  55–6, 59–81, 87, 89–90, 94, 99,
  107, 114, 121, 142, 164, 166,
  168–74, 194–5, 205, 218, 221,
  227n6, 237n10

mourning   42–7, 55–7, 62, 89–90,
96, 98, 102, 103, 125, 209, 222,
227n1; *see also* Freud, Klein,
Kristeva, Lacan
Müller-Braunschweig, Carl   226n9
Mulvey, Laura   216, 239n11
myth   3, 11, 26, 35, 44, 84, 98,
101–2, 120, 199, 224n10,
231n16, 238n2

narcissism   30, 32, 68, 103, 105, 108,
109, 170, 183–4, 225n2, 228n7,
231n9, 232n5, 238n4
Narcissus   6, 12, 30, 109
Nazi   219–20, 222, 240n16
Neill, Michael   215
Nerval, Gérard de   57
neurosis   14, 48, 59, 88, 98, 106, 125,
149
Nietzsche, Friedrich   2
Nobus, Dany   224n11
Nokes, David   74
nostos   45

object, *see* Freud, Klein, Kristeva,
Lacan
object relations   5, 30–53, 54–80, 89,
166, 170–3, 226n5, 226n6,
229n15, 237n10; *see also* breast
O'Connor, Noreen   235n11
Oedipus complex   xii, 7, 31, 33, 36,
37, 55, 59, 62, 84–95, 98, 101–2,
103, 107, 133, 142, 144, 154, 157,
164–5, 166–9, 171, 173, 176, 194,
217, 230n5, 230n8; *see also*
Freud, Klein, Kristeva, Lacan
in *Oedipus Rex*   xi, 85, 230n8
oral   63–4, 68, 70–7, 171, 204–7,
225–6n4, 229n18; *see also*
cannibalism
other/Other   xii, 5–7, 9, 10, 12, 18,
55, 59, 62, 75, 83, 84, 96, 101,
109, 125–6, 128, 129–30, 148,
149–50, 162, 173, 175, 234n21;
see also Kristeva, Lacan
over-determination   146, 215, 217
Ovid   12

Pappenheim, Bertha, *see* Anna O.
parricide   59, 73, 85–6, 93, 95, 120,
208
Pater, Walter   238n16
pathography   32, 225n1
patriarchy, *see* father
penis envy   47–8, 166–8, 184, 193,
226n9, 235n13
performance   4, 186–95
phallus   48–52, 86, 88–90, 99, 105,
145, 168, 170, 193, 207, 221,
227n13, 227n14, 231n9, 236n7;
see also maternal phallus
phantasy   19, 20, 33–5, 48, 55, 56,
71, 77, 79, 85, 99, 105, 141–2,
161–2, 167, 170, 222, 226n5
Phillips, Adam   226n6
Plath, Otto   222
Plath, Sylvia   240n15
'Daddy'   xiii, 218–22
'Lady Lazarus'   218, 222
Plato   118
pleasure principle   41
Poe, Edgar Allan, 'The Purloined
Letter'   49–52
Polidori, John   111–13
The Vampyre   111–12
Politi, Jina   11, 15, 45, 223n7,
224n11
Pontalis, J.-B.   37, 119–20
post-colonial literature   42–7
postmodernism   x, xiv, 66, 67, 133,
142, 161, 188, 196–8, 202, 240n13
Post-traumatic Stress Disorder   134
pre-Oedipal   31, 33, 37, 67, 87–8,
168, 216, 217, 237n10
primal scene   216–17
projection   7, 28, 32–3, 35, 36, 103,
111, 116, 167, 210, 213
projective identification   69, 221
Prophets   75
Proust, Marcel   227n5
psychoanalyst (role of)   7, 9, 10–11,
69, 85, 89, 94, 96, 149–50,
235n11
psychoanalytic literary
criticism   x–xiv, 84–7, 143,
146–7, 223n2

psychosis 14, 34, 69, 71
puns 1, 73–4
Punter, David 201, 233n14
Pynchon, Thomas 10

Queer theory 188–9, 192

Radcliffe, Ann 121, 123
Ragland, Ellie 100, 105, 204,
 230n4
Rank, Otto 109, 118
Read, Herbert 26, 28
reader-response theory xii, 121,
 122, 159
Real 4, 57, 90, 91, 99–101, 105, 128,
 212, 217
'rebus' 21
religion 3, 37, 38, 238n4
repetition compulsion 45, 100,
 105–6, 119, 127, 198–9, 202–4,
 208, 209, 214, 217
repression xii, 27, 32, 36, 41, 84, 85,
 86, 104, 125, 136–7, 142, 143,
 156, 232n5, 233n17; *see also*
 defence mechanisms
reversal (as defence) xii
Rich, Adrienne 48
Richardson, Maurice 203, 206
Riviere, Joan xii, xiii, 171–6, 178,
 179, 193
 and Klein 171, 173, 236n5
 'Womanliness as a
  Masquerade' 171–6
Romantic
 definition of the
  unconscious 19–20
 movement 110–13, 115, 154
Rose, Jacqueline 48–9, 54, 87, 193,
 195, 222, 236n7, 238n19
Rosenfeld, Herbert 229n15
Roth, Philip, *Portnoy's
  Complaint* 164
Roudinesco, Elisabeth 223n1,
 223n2, 223n5
Roughton, Roger 225n21
Rushdie, Salman 10, 142
 Midnight's Children 142

Sacher-Masoch, Leopold von 217
Sackville-West, Vita 179–80,
 238n17
Sade, Marquis de 92, 204, 220
sadism 35, 42, 204, 220
Sartre, Jean-Paul, *Being and
  Nothingness* 224n10
Saussure, Ferdinand de 2, 9, 22,
 223n2
Schaffer, Roy, 'Narration in the
  Psychoanalytic Dialogue' 147,
 153–4
Schaffer, Talia 202, 207
schizophrenia 69
Schopenhauer, Arthur 199
Schur, Max 161
scopic drive 16–18
screen memories 142
Sedgwick, Eve Kosofsky 159, 188,
 194
 Epistemology of the Closet 188
seduction 140–2, 161–2, 164,
 234n6; *see also* Freud
Segal, Hanna 33, 226n5
Segal, Julia 36
semiology 7
Seneca 101, 212–13
sexuality 31–2, 47, 121, 136,
 139–40, 164–74, 182–4
Shakespeare, William xiii, 101,
 230n7
 Hamlet xiii, 85–90, 119, 125, 126,
 212, 233n16
 King Lear 96, 100
 Othello xiii, 100–1
Shaw, George Bernard 132
 New Woman 132
Shelley, Mary,
 Frankenstein 111–13, 118, 123,
 152, 206
Shelley, Percy Bysshe 111–13
 'Defence of Poetry' 111
Sheridan, Alan 236n6, 236n7
Sherman, Leona 121
Showalter, Elaine 89, 234n2, 236n1
 Hystories 163–4
signifier and signified xii, 4, 8–9,
 10, 20, 23–4, 46–7, 49–52, 82,

89–90, 99, 101, 104, 128, 136, 173–4, 196, 210–12, 215, 222; *see also* language
simulacrum 196–8, 210, 222
Sophocles 101
  Antigone 91–7, 210, 231n13, 213n14
  Oedipus at Colonus 91, 97, 230n8
  Oedipus Rex xi, xiii, 85, 87, 91, 96–7, 230n8
Spark, Muriel
  The Prime of Miss Jean Brodie 40
  The Public Image 218
Spence, Donald, *Narrative Truth and Historical Truth* 147
Spinoza, Baruch 2
Spivak, Gayatri Chakravorty 193
splitting xii, 18, 34–5, 91, 99, 100, 109, 156–7, 206, 216, 239n5, 240n12
Sprengnether, Madelon 102, 145
Stephen, Adrian 178
Stephen, Karin 178
Stephen, Leslie 237n13
Stevenson, Robert Louis, *The Strange Case of Dr Jekyll and Mr Hyde* 118, 202
Stoker, Bram xiii, 201–2, 239n6
  Dracula xiii, 197, 200–10, 239n5, 239n7
Strachey, Alix 178
Strachey, James 178, 230n2
Strachey, Lytton 178, 237n11
Strachey, Oliver 186–7
Strindberg, August xiii, 131–2
  Miss Julie 131–3, 159, 234n1
Strong, Beret E. 163
structuralism x, 7, 106, 193, 236n3
subject 2–5, 10–11, 18, 28, 30, 48–52, 54, 68, 83, 89–90, 93, 99, 101, 128, 133, 149, 211–12, 215, 227n14; *see also* Lacan, ego vs subject
  of abjection 62–81
  divided against itself 3, 5, 7, 8
  and image 6–18, 22–8, 30, 94–9, 109, 188, 192, 195, 214

linguistic definition of 2, 7–8, 10–11, 128–9
  and object 30–53, 162
  no referent 8–10, 90
  'supposed to know' 150, 159
sublimation 19, 56, 169
super-ego 37–41, 168, 224n16, 226n8
surrealism 2, 22–9, 161, 162, 196, 225n20, 225n21
Swales, Peter 137
Swift, Jonathan 74, 229n17
  Gulliver's Travels 74
Symbolic order xii, xiv, 6–7, 9, 10–18, 48–52, 55, 68, 90, 91, 94–9, 128, 129, 149, 154, 174, 188, 192–4, 195, 210–12, 222, 229n21, 231n14
symbols xii, 8, 20–1, 25, 49, 50, 97, 105, 125–6, 135, 161, 225n18, 226n10, 228n12, 232n9, 234n4
symptom 105, 125–6, 135–6, 141, 234n4

textual pleasure xi, xii
Todorov, Tzvetan, *The Fantastic* 106–7
Torok, Maria xii, 125–6, 167, 233n16, 233n17, 233n18, 235n13
totem 98, 208–10, 222
tragedy 85–101, 212–15
transference (and counter-transference) xii, 106, 125, 130, 138, 141, 142, 146–51, 159, 161, 199, 211, 234n21, 235n11
trauma
  of birth 34
  of loss 56, 60, 68, 99, 167, 216–17
tyche 91, 100, 101

uncanny xi, 8, 17–18, 27, 103–30
  and castration 104–8, 120
  Cixous on 104, 108, 118, 232n1
  and Coleridge's 'Christabel' 110–17
  and death 105, 118–22, 124

uncanny (*cont.*)
  definition of   103–4, 120
  Derrida on   104–5, 118–20, 122,
    125–8
  and the double   106–7, 109–18
  Freud on   xi, 103–9, 114, 119,
    120, 125, 129–30
  and Gaskell's 'Old Nurse's
    Story'   121–3, 124, 125
  and Gothic castle/house   120–1,
    124–5
  and Hoffmann's 'The
    Sandman'   106–9, 111–13
  and LeFanu's 'Account of Some
    Strange Disturbances in
    Aungier Street'   121, 123–8,
    233n19
  and mother's body   114–15
  other in self   128–30
  and repetition   105–6, 119–20, 127
  spectres/spectrality   118–22, 124–8
unconscious   xi, 42, 55, 130, 132,
    134–5, 216, 233n21; *see also*
    Freud and Lacan
  Coleridge on   xi, 20, 110–11
  and desire   xi, 82–102
  discourse of the other   5–7, 9, 12,
    84, 96, 128, 148, 162, 173,
    234n21
  elusiveness of   xi, 4–5, 10, 20, 23,
    27–8
  Freud on   224n16, 230n3
  Lacan on   xi, 3, 10, 21–2, 55,
    93–4, 136, 148, 235n12
  'memory traces' of   xi
  representation of   xi, 5
  structured like a language   xi, 3,
    21–2, 55, 94, 136, 235n12
uterus   70, 77, 80–1, 228n14

Victorian literature   121, 123, 124,
  151, 157
Vinci, Leonardo da   32, 164
Vining, E. P., *The Mystery of
  Hamlet*   230n7
Virgil, *Aeneid*   212
voyeurism   224n12

Walcott, Derek   xiii
  Omeros   42–7, 49
Walpole, Horace, *The Castle of
  Otranto*   120–1, 123, 206, 233n13
Weiskel, Thomas   111
Weldon, Fay, *The Life and Loves of a
  She-Devil*   218
Wilde, Oscar   xiii, 3–4, 164, 179,
  201–2, 207
  The Picture of Dorian Gray   118
Willis, J. H.   178
Winnicott, Donald   33, 54, 69,
  216–17, 226n6, 229n15
Wolf Man, *see* Freud, **Works**: 'From
  the History of an Infantile
  Neurosis'
woman, *see* femininity, Freud,
  Lacan, mother
Woolf, Leonard   178–9, 186–7
Woolf, Virginia   x, xiii, 65, 178–87,
  237n9, 237n10, 237n11
  and biography   180, 186–7, 238n16
  and history   180, 186
  'materialist' school of
    literature   182, 237n13
  and psychoanalysis   x, 178–9,
    183, 237n9, 237n10
  sexual identity   178–80, 182–4,
    237n10
Woolf, Virginia: **Works**
  Diary   182, 237n11, 237n14
  'Freudian Fiction'   x, 237n9
  'Mr Bennett and Mrs
    Brown'   237n13
  Mrs Dalloway   164
  Orlando   178–87, 237n12, 237n14,
    237n15, 238n16, 238n17
  Roger Fry: A Biography   186–7
  A Room of One's Own   *179*, 180,
    181, 182, 183, 185
Wordsworth, William   232n6
Wright, Elizabeth   27, 118, 223n2,
  232n5

Young, Robert   52, 223n2

Zizek, Slavoj   xiii, xiv, 17, 210,
  239n11, 240n13